Unions, Change and Crisis: French and Italian Union Strategy and the Political Economy, 1945–1980

PETER LANGE, *Duke University*

GEORGE ROSS, *Brandeis University*

MAURIZIO VANNICELLI, *Holy Cross University*
and
Harvard University Center for European Studies

London
GEORGE ALLEN & UNWIN
Boston   Sydney

George Allen & Unwin (Publishers) Ltd,
40 Museum Street, London WC1A 1LU, UK

George Allen & Unwin (Publishers) Ltd,
Park Lane, Hemel Hempstead, Herts HP2 4TE, UK

Allen & Unwin Inc.,
9 Winchester Terrace, Winchester, Mass 01890, USA

George Allen & Unwin Australia Pty Ltd,
8 Napier Street, North Sydney, NSW 2060, Australia

First published in 1982

British Library Cataloguing in Publication Data

Lange, Peter
    Unions, Change and Crisis.—(Harvard Center for
European Studies Project on European Trade Union
Responses to Economic Crisis; v.1)
1. Trade unions—France 2. France—Economic
policy—1945– 3. Trade unions—Italy
4. Italy—Economic policy—1945–
I. Title II. Ross, George III. Vannicelli,
Maurizio IV. Series
330.994   HC276
ISBN 0-04-331088-5

Library of Congress Cataloging in Publication Data

Lange, Peter Michael.
    Unions, change, and crisis.
'Harvard University Center for European Studies.'
Includes bibliographical references and index.
1. Trade-unions—France—History. 2. Trade-unions—
Italy—History. I. Ross, George, 1940–
II. Vannicelli, Maurizio. III. Harvard University Center
for European Studies. IV. Title.
HD6684.L185 1982   331.88'0944   82-11515
ISBN 0-04-331088-5

Set in 10 on 11 point Times by
Rowland Phototypesetting Ltd, Bury St Edmunds, Suffolk
and printed in Great Britain
by Mackays of Chatham

To the Harvard Center for European Studies, with Gratitude

Unions, Change and Crisis: French and Italian Union Strategy and the Political Economy, 1945–1980 is the first volume of the Harvard Center for European Studies Project on European Trade Union Responses to Economic Crisis conducted by Peter Gourevitch, Peter Lange, Andrew Martin, George Ross, Chris Allen, Stephen Bornstein, Andrei Markovits and Maurizio Vannicelli.

Contents

Acknowledgements

Unions, Change and Crisis: French and Italian Union Strategy and the Political Economy, 1945–1980 is the first of two volumes reporting and analyzing European trade union responses to contemporary economic crisis. Volume Two will review the British, West German and Swedish cases. The study on which both volumes are based emerged initially from long talks among colleagues in 1976–7 prodded by Peter Gourevitch, at the Harvard University Center for European Studies. An initial paper drafted by Andrew Martin, George Ross, Peter Gourevitch and Peter Lange was then subjected to the probing and far-sighted criticisms of participants in the Research Planning Group on Comparative Labor Studies, financed by the Council on European Studies. A final research proposal was funded by the Ford Foundation (where Mr. Peter Ruof was of great help), enabling members of the project group – expanded from the original four to include Chris Allen, Stephen Bornstein, Andrei Markovits and Maurizio Vannicelli – to carry out field research in 1978–9. During the periods of research design, field investigation and subsequent analysis of results the group met often at Harvard CES, where most of the final writing was done.

Unions, Change and Crisis is dedicated to the Harvard Center for European Studies. For more than a decade Harvard CES has been a major crossroads for students of European societies, a place where dignity, civility, great rigor and intellectual energy and extraordinary tolerance across disciplinary, political and cultural lines have coexisted. In one way or another all of the researchers in this trade union project have been uniquely helped by their association with the Center. The kind of openness and vitality which they have known at Harvard CES is rare anywhere. The dedication of *Unions, Change and Crisis* is presented in the fervent hope that, at a moment when the value of cross-national research is being doubted in some quarters, the Center's past decade of great success will serve as the foundation stone of an even more brilliant and vital future. Three people in particular have made CES happen. To Stanley Hoffmann, Guido Goldman and Abby Collins we therefore express our special gratitude. To those many scholars for whom Harvard CES has been a stopping place on important intellectual voyages, and whose presence has enriched our work, we also give thanks.

Unions, Change and Crisis benefitted from the specific help of a number of people. Abby Collins, in addition to her general responsibility for providing our project with a wondrous environment, has seen us through thick and thin with intelligence, authority and grace. Bruno Trentin, Cesare Merli-Brandini, Aris Accornero, Bianca Beccalli, Lorenzo Bordogna, Massimo Paci, Gianfranco Pasquino, Gino Giugni, and Ugo Ascoli helped with criticism of different versions of the Italian chapter and conclusions. Readers who know the work of Alessandro Pizzorno will recognize his intellectual presence throughout the entire volume. Marino Regini has been of great importance as well. For the French chapter the help and encouragement of Jean-Louis Moynot was essential, along with that of Hubert Prevôt, René Mouriaux and Jane Jenson. Others whose work 'in the trenches' of French union life continues are thanked, if not named. In Italy the research institutes of the CGIL and CISL, plus the Gramsci Institute, were very welcoming. In France the *Centre Confédéral d'études économiques* of the CGT, the *Service Economique* of the CFDT, the libraries of the CGT, CFDT, FO and the CGC were of great help, as was the library and staff of the *Fondation Nationale des Sciences Politiques* in Paris.

Cambridge

Introduction

This is a study of European trade union response to the economic crisis that engulfed the advanced industrial countries in the mid-1970s. This crisis, the most serious since the interwar Great Depression, confronted unions, along with most other economic actors, with new risks and, perhaps, new opportunities. How the unions understood the crisis and reacted to it was bound to be important, not only for its impact on the unions themselves but also for the structure of relationships existing between unions and other major social groups. That the reactions of governments and business should be important was evidently taken for granted; that union responses mattered as well seemed more easily overlooked. It was precisely our recollection of the significance of union responses to the crisis that began in 1929 that prevented us from overlooking it.

How unions understood the Great Depression and the extent to which the policies they urged to cope with it were implemented had a great deal to do with the subsequent unfolding of events. British unions broke with balanced budget orthodoxy and called for expansionist, proto-Keynesian policies. They failed to convince their Labour Party allies who were then governing the country, however. German unions proposed similar policies but likewise failed to convince their Social Democratic allies. In both cases, the results were setbacks for the unions and their members, severe in Britain and disastrous in Germany. In Britain, the Labour Government's insistence on orthodoxy precipitated the split that brought its fall, and a continuation by its successor of policies imposing the immense burden of unemployment on the workers. Still, British democracy proved sufficiently robust to survive. In Germany, by contrast, economic orthodoxy played a key role in undermining the coalition on which the preservation of Germany's fragile democracy depended, opening the way for Hitler's seizure of power. In France, Popular Front efforts to expand the economy, prompted by unions, were thwarted by a rapid reversion to orthodoxy, although not before uncertainty and confusion about economic policy had strained the French social fabric in ways that contributed to the capitulation of 1940 and the Vichy regime. Only in Sweden did the unions and their Social Democratic allies agree on unorthodox expansionist budget policies, which in turn laid the political basis for the development of Sweden's welfare state under continuous Social Democratic rule.

Of course, the economic crisis beginning in the mid-1970s was not the same as the Great Depression. No complete collapse of economic activity occurred. Yet the postwar pattern of growth was drastically and, perhaps, irreparably disrupted. Inflation reached peak rates even as unemployment rose toward its highest postwar levels. Having been ever more completely integrated into the international economy, national economies found it increasingly difficult to remain competitive in the face of the changed international structure of production. This, together with the collapse of the postwar monetary system, amplified the effects of the oil shock, making equilibrium in many of the countries' foreign transactions an ever more elusive goal. Thus, after an unprecedented period in which nearly every-thing seemed to work, policy makers faced an economic environment in which all options were increasingly bad ones.

With the breakdown of growth, the possibility of meeting the terms for what we shall refer to as the 'postwar settlements' was called into question. While these terms varied from country to country, they provided essentially for the preservation of a predominantly capitalist economy in exchange for continued full employment and expansion of the welfare state. Whether the settlements were the outcome of explicit negotiations as in Britain, or the implicit result of the perceived balance of social power, as in Sweden and France, they were sustainable as long as growth continued. The Great Depression tore asunder one socioeconomic world and, ultimately, led to the establishment of another. In the confusion, conflict, and pain of all this, unions both suffered a great deal and played important roles. Similarly, the crisis of the 1970s challenged and threatened to tear apart the socio-economic world of the postwar settlements. Only this time, the unions, endowed by these settlements with substantially more power and centrality than they had possessed in the 1930s, were less likely to suffer such wide-spread defeat in struggles with other actors over alternative responses to crisis.

Accordingly, our expectation was that unions would develop new analyses and strategies of their own to counterpose to those of the other actors, and that they would be much more influential in shaping national responses to crisis than in the 1930s. It seemed to us that crisis-induced social renegotiations, whatever their final shape might turn out to be, would not be simple linear translations of the schemes of official policy makers and economists. Whatever happened it would be the product of complicated social conflict involving all the major collective actors in advanced industrial societies. In this conflict the specific coalitions which developed between different social and political actors would be central— who allied with whom for what reasons would be a deciding factor. In this process of new coalition-building for social renegotiation precipitated by crisis, unions' analyses of the situation and union strategies to cope with it were likely to be very important. What the unions thought was happening in the economy, what programs they decided to advocate and how they decided to deploy their resources to realize these programs would make certain patterns of collaboration possible between unions and political actors, for example, while excluding others. Economic policy proposals which the unions came to endorse would, by virtue of such endorsement, become more plausible.

Our initial intuition about the importance of unions in the modern crisis situation plus our memory of how they had been important in the past led us, therefore, to want to know more about European union responses to the changing economic circumstances of the 1970s. In the past, union perceptions of the economic world had been essential in the constitution of union actions. How, and for what reasons, did the unions come to perceive and understand the crisis of the 1970s? What kinds of agendas and programs did the unions derive from such theories and maps of the new situations, and why these? What types of general strategies did the unions devise to mobilize their own resources and to influence other actors? What features in the unions' environments most influenced such union analytical, programmatic and strategic reflection? Did economic change directly cause union reevaluations? Or did such change lead to reevaluation through the prisms of politics, union organizational considerations, and ideology?

From the outset, we were firm believers in the comparative method. We knew enough about European unions to be aware of the quite striking differences which existed from one nation's labor movement to the next. We therefore wanted to research a sufficiently broad range of European cases to make possible generalizations about trends of response to crisis which were common across all union movements, while also facilitating the classification of different types of responses which might turn up in one or several of the cases. Our ultimate task, of course, was to arrive at an explanation for such similarities and differences.

Given the complexity of union movements, the wide range of different national situations which we wished to sample, the relatively long period (1970–80) in which we were interested and limitations on our own resources—personal and financial—we obviously had to make a choice between what was possible to research and what lay beyond our scope. Our first decision was to focus on the economic thought, programs and strategies of unions. We were aware of the problematic implications of such a decision—we were looking primarily at what unions *said*, which was not exactly the same thing as what they were doing. We thus assumed that what unions said had something to do with what they did, not necessarily a safe assumption. We did our best to control this problem, however. We chose to study not only formal union economic thought (i.e., unions' 'high theories' about the dynamics of the economic environment), but also unions' desired policy programs and unions' general strategies. Both of the latter were, of course, still in the realm of union thought and declaration, but they were both behaviorally oriented. Thus any major contradictions between union high theory and practical orientations towards behavior would be likely to turn up in our research, even though we were to remain within the realm of thought more generally. Secondly, the period of union response to economic change in which we were interested was quite long. In reviewing such a long period, any major contradictions between union thought and behavior were bound to manifest themselves clearly.

We also decided to focus primarily on the economic thought, programs and strategies of trade union peak associations—the coordinating national confederal organizations in each country (only *one* in countries with unified movements, several in those with pluralistic movements). This choice simplified our task greatly. We could zero in on confederal statements, documents, publications on union economic perspectives, programs and strategies and interview peak-level officials, researchers and experts. At the same time we could de-emphasize what happened at sub-central organizational levels (federations, branches, locals) and thorny questions of measuring actual rank-and-file behavior. This focus, of course, created greater or lesser problems for our national researchers, depending upon the degree to which theoretical and strategic matters were centralized or decentralized in their countries. We tried to build in some control for this problem as well. In each national case we gathered data not only for peak associations, but also for union organizations in certain industrial areas which we thought were likely to be particularly sensitive to the crisis (iron and steel, autos, construction and municipal workers). While this data did not figure greatly in our final papers, it was useful in informing our works in progress where, in a specific national case, confederal level data was not predictive of the concerns of particular unions.

Anyone experienced in social science research will understand why we made such strategic choices. A project which set out to understand European trade union responses to the crisis of the 1970s by documenting union thought at peak and other organizational levels plus developing some effective measures for deciding the influence of such thought on organizational and rank-and-file behavior, not to speak of the behavior of other actors in European political economies, would have called for methodological sophistication of an extraordinarily ingenious kind plus financial resources which were far, far beyond our reach. We had to deal with such problems, as do many researchers—by simplifying. We assumed that union thought and intention had some significant relationship to union behavior, that unions were 'conscious actors.' Moreover, we knew that one could never test the specific behavioral implications of union thought and intention without knowing, first of all, what these thoughts and intentions were. So we proceeded to try to find out what they were, with the confidence that we were looking at an important component of trade union practice and that our work might be of use subsequently to others with the much larger resources needed to look at the broader range of union practices.

In thinking about our general problem—accounting for the whys and wherefores of European trade union choices in response to contemporary economic crisis—we also were motivated by a sense of intellectual malaise. The 'conventional wisdom' about unions and workers, especially in North America—we have labelled it 'liberal optimism' in a more extensive discussion to be found in the third chapter of this volume—was, we believed, profoundly economistic and historicist in its basic orientations. These biases, we felt, rendered 'liberal optimism' quite problematic for understanding and predicting union behavior. 'Liberal optimism' asserted an underlying logic in industrialism which led, over time, to a growing similarity in institutions in different societies. Advancing industrialism brought with it quite precise functional demands which had to be satisfied by all advanced industrial societies in more or less similar ways, regardless of national particularities. While, of course, such a convergence thesis was true in the most general of ways—if one stands far enough away from any social phenomena, they do tend, ultimately, to resemble one another—the 'liberal optimists' were more specific in their projections. Unions, in particular, were likely to move towards increasing 'sub-systemic' autonomy, in which their major focus increasingly fell on issues specific to the 'industrial relations system'—relationships between themselves and employers around a limited number of questions. Moreover, with the development of a 'web of rules' and consensus upon it within this industrial relations system unions would become both more moderate and more 'functionally specific.' In particular, trade union politicization would decline. Behind such predictions lay a huge, almost teleological, assumption. In contrast to Marxian thought, which posited that 'capitalism' was a social order fraught with such contradictions that it would ultimately be transcended, through class conflict, to 'socialism,' 'liberal optimist' theory saw major social conflict around industrialism confined to the long transition period between 'traditional' and 'industrial' societies. This transition might be painful, and it usually created utopian expectations among those most affected by such pain, but, once completed successfully, it would give way to an industrial society in which the division of labor and industrial rationality would be generally acceptable to all.

We were troubled by this conventional wisdom, both for epistemological and empirical reasons. In many of the studies of industrial relations this logic of advancing industrialism, once posited by analysts, seemed to become the *subject* of historical evolution. In contrast, unions (along with all other significant actors) were relegated to the status of *objects* of this subject, whose task it was to register and react to exogenous change. In other words, the intervention of real actors did not make history occur, rather something labelled industrialism marched forward, obliging actors to adapt. Industrialism tended to become the first cause of human behavior in an almost metaphysical way. Our sense, very different, was that major organizational actors—like unions—were 'conscious subjects,' armed with systems of perceptions, values and goals, which attempted, through complex patterns of resource generation and exchanges with other actors, to shape their environments. To the extent that there was any 'logic of industrialism,' it did not exist *a priori*. Rather it emerged from the interaction of such conscious organizational subjects.

Such philosophical reservations were only one part of our malaise. From what we knew, almost from the outset, about the union movements which we were studying, we were certain that most of the specific hypotheses/ predictions of the 'liberal optimists' didn't work. In recent years European unions had not gravitated towards the moderation, depoliticization, 'functional specificity,' and 'sub-systemic autonomy' which the liberal optimists had anticipated. Rather, from the late 1960s onwards at least, there had been a striking increase in union militancy which, far from being confined within earlier established 'limits' on union demands, had focused on a number of radical new issues. In addition, this new militancy was everywhere connected to increased union involvement in politics, both in terms of new union concern about state policies and commitment to partisan political programs and activities. Furthermore, not only did the specific predictions about union behavior not work, the more general assumption of convergence across national boundaries due to a general logic of industrialism did not pan out either. Union movements did change their outlooks, goals and behavior as industrial economies developed, of course. But such change seemed to lead as much towards divergence between different national movements as towards convergence.

If 'liberal optimist' conventional wisdom was not useful as a theoretical guide, then where were we left? Marxist perspectives had attractiveness, to the degree that they were somewhat less sanguine about the automatic propensities of industrial societies to produce moderation and consensus and much more sensitive to the profundity of cleavages between different major groups in capitalist industrial orders. Despite these assets, Marxist accounts also tended to suffer from many of the central conceptual problems which we found in 'liberal optimism.' In Marxian views there also was an historical logic exogenous to central social actors which propelled them forward inexorably as historical objects. This 'logic of capital accumulation,' in its externality to major collective actors, seemed to us quite as metaphysical and economistic as the 'logic of industrialism.' Moreover, the historicism of most Marxist accounts—inevitable movement towards bigger and better class conflict—seemed quite as unreliable a guide to empirical events as did the 'liberal optimists'' belief in the inevitability of consensus. Finally, most such Marxist writing was quite as replete with 'epicyclic' explanations for deviations from expected trajectories as was 'liberal optimist' work.

We were on our own, or so it seemed, with our instincts. These were twofold from the beginning. First, we felt that explanations of trade union behavior rooted in general theories of economic development were unlikely to be effective for explaining European union responses to the crisis of the 1970s. The crisis obliged all of the national union movements we were studying to devise responses, to be sure. But the crisis, in itself, did not necessarily lead to any set of specific union responses which we were likely to find in all national cases. Rather we were strongly inclined to think that the nature of each national union movement's response, even where the indices of crisis were relatively similar to those elsewhere, was more likely to be forged out of the particular structures of the economy, labor market and political system which it faced in its own country. In other words, if circumstances of crisis obliged unions to adapt, the ways in which they chose to do so could not be explained directly by any 'functional demands' derivable from crisis itself. Our second instinct told us that, since we regarded unions as 'conscious actors' in their specific national environments, the nature of their responses to changing environmental circumstances would depend, in important ways, on their 'consciousness.' At any given point in time a union movement had to be seen as possessing an identity (which included distinctive ways of mapping the world, values and goals) which would serve as a prism for integrating stimuli from outside and as a constraint on the range of likely responses to them. In turn, this identity had to be seen as constituted developmentally out of the union's past exchanges with class structure, other actors and economic realities. When placed together, these two instincts led us very far away from conventional wisdoms. While we were far from denying the existence of powerful constraints placed on unions by economic development, if we took the vantage point of a union making choices at any given moment it did seem that how unions as actors responded to such constraints depended quite as much upon their identities as organizations—their 'consciousness'—and upon the national nature of the fields of action which they faced, as upon the nature of these constraints themselves. Furthermore, viewed in the light of process, the very constraints of the economy faced by a union at time T^1 were, to a certain extent, the products of intergroup action and conflict in which the union had participated at time T.

These instincts, plus our concern for tapping the widest possible range of trade union responses to crisis, were the initial premises for the choice of national union movements to research. To begin with, we wanted to find cases where the structures of the unions' political environment varied significantly. Basically this meant seeking out national situations in which the nature of union ties to the state, policy processes and political parties were different. Another politically related variation of whose importance we were well aware was the presence or absence of trade union organizational pluralism. We were also concerned with large variations in the structuring of labor markets, such as the degree of institutionalization (in Kerr's 'web of rules' sense) of the industrial relations system, the strength/weakness of unions themselves (often connected to institutionalization) and the centralization/decentralization of union organization. Finally we were concerned with finding cases where the incidence of economic crisis itself varied.

Since we were interested in European national cases, and since there were only a limited number of such cases available, it was obviously not possible for us to develop a sample sophisticated enough to test national trade union responses to crisis against variations in all of these different environmental factors. Thus we were obliged to proceed in a more rough-and-ready way, choosing national cases both because some or all of these variations existed and because the specific countries were important and/or interesting economically. The United Kingdom, West Germany, and Sweden were all cases in which ties between unions and Social Democratic political parties were of central importance. Even if the exact nature of these ties varied substantially from case to case, their existence meant that the unions in question had all had experience with allied political parties holding governmental power. In consequence, each of the unions had had to develop some perspectives on behaving 'responsibly' in order to help the party ally gain and keep power. In other ways, however, the three 'Social Democratic' cases were very different. While in all three cases there existed a high degree of labor-market institutionalization (although of different kinds in each case), in West Germany and Sweden union movements were highly centralized, while in the UK the TUC, the British peak association, was relatively weak in its control over events. Finally, the incidence on each country of the crisis of the 1970s was very different. The UK was hurt dramatically very early on, while West Germany proved very resilient until very late. Sweden, a very small economy long used to the volatility of international markets, was hurt by crisis, to be sure, but managed to postpone major economic drama by specific national policy choices, again until very late.

The French and Italian cases were very different from these three Northern European ones in which Social Democratic partisan affiliations were central to unions. In both France and Italy the most important union organizations had strong ties with Communist parties. From this a number of other differences flowed. Since Communist parties had been excluded from political power since the immediate postwar years, much of organized labor in France and Italy had little or no experience in situations where trade union support for the economic policies of an allied party in power was called for. Instead the experience of at least CP-affiliated segments of French and Italian labor had been one of exclusion—sometimes brutal exclusion—and opposition in relationship to the state and to state power. Another significant difference came with this CP–union affiliation—trade union pluralism. Strong Communist labor presence in both countries implied the fragmentation of organized labor along lines of partisan political cleavage resulting in an often bitterly divided union movement in which several different confederations existed. There were also specific labor market correlates to such political phenomena. In both countries individual union confederations tended to be strongly centralized, while all unions tended to be weak, especially when compared with the 'Social Democratic' cases, at shopfloor and firm level. In addition, industrial relations systems in both countries were relatively underinstitutionalized. If France and Italy resembled one another more than they resembled our other three chosen cases, they also differed. The Communist parties in each country had different traditions, faced very different coalitional settings and had quite different strategies for achieving their goals, facts which influenced the union movements in important ways. The French and Italian states were structured differently and performed differently—the first highly centralized and effective, the second decentralized and ineffective. Finally, economic crisis hit the two countries in different ways. France was touched severely, but nowhere near as severely as Italy.

It did not take us long, once we had begun our research, to uncover a serious problem. Our major task was to discover, analyze, explain and compare the responses of five different national union movements to the economic crisis of the 1970s. With much of the material in hand, however, we discovered that it was impossible to discuss European trade union responses to the crisis of the 1970s while restricting our purview to the events of the 1970s themselves. In effect, what we found, almost universally, was that our union movements responded to crisis through systems of perceptions, values and goals which had been formulated substantially *before* the crisis occurred, often in the later 1960s. In other words, rather than dramatically changing their frameworks of analysis because of crisis, the unions reacted to crisis on the basis of frameworks which had been developed prior to crisis and in other circumstances. We were forced to recognize, then, that the historical development of our unions *prior to the crisis* was quite as important to their response in crisis as, say, the economic shape of the crisis itself. In each case, then, we found ourselves drawn back from the 1970s towards earlier union behavior in search of full explanations for union action in the 1970s. For this reason, and because we soon realized that the literature in English on the modern history of most of our movements was scanty at best, we expanded our scope.

In all of our national cases there seemed to have been roughly parallel developments. Union response to crisis in the 1970s was formulated from within union ideas and strategies which had been worked out in the later 1960s. These ideas and strategies, in turn, had been devised in response to major changes in the basic parameters of postwar social settlements which had occurred at that time. We were therefore also thrown back to an examination of these settlements, which everywhere had emerged to blunt the thrust of postwar reformism, and the unions' place within them. Our explanatory tasks were therefore considerably enlarged—we had to become historians as much as social scientists interested in the present. And our national case studies were lengthened.

As our work progressed we also realized that we would gain most from undertaking three different, if interrelated, comparative analyses, instead of the one with which we began. Our initial sense, that the nature of union-politics relationships was the most important variable in explaining different union responses to crisis, turned out to be accurate. This gave us two sub-types of union response—the 'Social Democratic' and the 'Communist presence/union pluralist.' Yet it was also true that substantial differences *within* these sub-types were also significant. We decided, therefore, to proceed analytically on three different levels. We would compare the Communist presence/union pluralist cases, France and Italy, with one another. Then we would compare the three Social Democratic cases—the United Kingdom, West Germany and Sweden—together. Finally, in order to discern response trends general to *all* union movements, in order to reconsider the utility of the Social Democrat/Communist presence dichotomy, and in order to isolate and discuss responses which were purely individual to national cases, we had to undertake a full five-case comparison.

It was the logic of these three separate comparisons which structured our study into its present two-volume form. Volume One, which follows, is composed of three main chapters. The first two are separate national case studies of trade union responses to crisis in the Communist presence/union pluralist setting of France and Italy. The third chapter is an essay which attempts to develop an analytical approach to comparative union studies and applies this approach to the specific French and Italian materials exposed in the preceding country chapters. Volume Two will contain the three Social Democratic national case studies (the UK, West Germany, Sweden), comparative analysis of these cases and, in conclusion, a chapter comparing all five union responses to crisis and assessing the implications of these responses for the future of West European political economies.

* * *

It is common for analysts to group France and Italy together as members of a common 'type.' The most prominent reason for this is the presence of powerful Communist parties in the party systems of both countries. Since World War II these parties have played significant roles in creating ideological and coalitional structures which have developed differently, often quite strikingly differently, from those which emerged in Northern Europe. In both France and Italy the exclusion of Communists from access to political power narrowed down the number of possible claimants to power considerably and, because it removed the major Left component from the national game of power, skewed the composition of regimes and the nature of their policies more towards the Center–Right than would have been the case otherwise. This, plus the energetic efforts of the Communists themselves, perpetuated visions and vocabularies of strident class conflict in political and intellectual life in both countries through a period in which these same notions were declining in Northern Europe, where the moderate and mollifying hand of catch-all Social Democratic parties was felt.

In France and Italy power over the trade union movement was perhaps the major vehicle used by the Communist parties to maintain (expand, when possible). mobilize and socialize a mass base. The profound ambiguity of party–union ties which followed this, and which also followed specific party strategies—was the union to function primarily as a union, or was it to be a disguised 'transmission belt' for the party's political goals?—had important effects on the shape of postwar French and Italian labor movements and on labor relations more generally in both countries. On occasion the CP unions did acquire strong political vocations which eclipsed their identities as trade unions. As this occurred their abilities to maintain broad non-partisan bases were impaired. In the context of the agonizing political divisions in both countries caused by the coming of the Cold War, strident CP–union politicization plus anti-Communism led to the creation of pluralistic union movements in both countries where different union Confederations came to represent different working-class political and ideological 'families'. That this division of French and Italian unionism greatly contributed to union labor market weakness goes almost without saying.

The task of detailed enumeration of the general similarities between French and Italian unions will be better left to the individual essays which follow. Here we desire mainly to announce the paradox which our intra-type French–Italian comparison will reveal (and which Chapter 3 of this volume will try to explain). The French and Italian union movements were strikingly similar in composition, strategies, labor market positions and organizational structures from Liberation in 1944 well into the postwar period. Yet the responses which each devised to the economic crisis of the 1970s were dramatically different. The French movement's response we later label 'maximalist.' Major French unions analyzed the crisis as a knot of contradictions from which capital could only escape by undermining social justice, democracy, and the national integrity of France. They saw—in different ways for each organization—the only viable response to crisis as rupture with capitalism and the transcendence of existing social and economic arrangements. And, for the most part, they saw the route towards such rupture passing through politics. French unions, in effect, had very few specific ideas about new policies which might make French capitalism more successful in changing international economic circumstances. Instead, they advocated a radical new economic order to be installed through political change. It was their task, in this scenario, to hasten such political change.

Italian unions, in contrast, proposed an 'interventionist' response. Concerned less with the basic principles of the economic system, they accepted analytically that the source of Italy's grave problems was insufficient and inadequately allocated investment–investment of all kinds, social, public sector and private—given Italy's position in the international division of labor. Thus they criticized the specific policy choices made by the Italian state and private sector capital which had established the 'model of development' which led to the crisis of the 1970s, rather than making abstract criticisms of capitalism as a mode of accumulation. What they proposed were different specific *policies* for moving Italy out of crisis in ways which would shift Italy onto the trajectory of a different model of development, rather than proposing transition to a new mode of accumulation. Finally, they focused primarily on deploying their own trade union forces—shopfloor, collective bargaining at industrial level, pressure on the state—to weigh in the policy-making balance, rather than seeking to use these forces indirectly via partisan politics.

How can we account for the divergent responses to crisis of two union movements whose recent pasts were so similar? This is our ultimate task. First, however, we must turn to national studies of French and Italian unionism which will highlight and analyze the nature and sources of their respective responses to crisis.

1 The Perils of Politics: French Unions and the Crisis of the 1970s

George Ross

Part 1

Introduction

France's two major trade union organizations, the *Confédération Générale du Travail* (CGT) and the *Confédération Française Démocratique du Travail* (CFDT) responded to the arrival of economic crisis in the 1970s from within economic perspectives and strategies which both had evolved in the very different economic surroundings of the 1960s. Moreover, it was not until 1978, prompted by a political event, the French elections of 1978, that both began to reconsider their earlier positions. The circumstances surrounding these belated union reevaluations of their economic world provided a striking summary of the general dilemmas of organized labor in modern France.

French labor has, historically, tended to divide into separate and competing organizations, each with its own specific outlook on desirable goals in the labor market and on the proper mix between labor market and political action to achieve trade union objectives. Partly because of such divisive tendencies, French unions have also been consistently weak, both organizationally and in terms of shopfloor mobilizing capacities. Because of such weakness—which has both been enhanced by, and encouraged the perpetuation of, strong anti-union inclinations in the French employer class—French unions have been unusually 'political,' in several different ways. They have regularly sought state intervention in terms of regulation and legislation as a substitute for labor market victories which they have been unable to win on their own—a search which has contributed powerfully to the politicization of industrial conflict in France. Such politicization, given the power of the French Communist Party over major segments of the union movement plus the desire of other political forces to enlist trade union allies for their own political goals, has usually included a substantial component of partisan mobilization. Past a certain point of partisan intensity, trade union politicization has, in turn, contributed to the union movement's schismatic tendencies and, hence, to labor's weakness.

What happened to the CGT and CFDT in 1978 well illustrated the difficulties which French unions have faced in navigating through this sea of contradictions. From a point of very great weakness in the 1950s, the CGT and CFDT took important new measures in the 1960s to unify their action goals. An increase in union strength and mobilizing power followed in the later 1960s and early 1970s. Economic crisis hit, however, at almost exactly the moment when the French political Left unified, for the first time in twenty-five years, around the 1972 Common Program in order to challenge the Right–Center political majority which ran Fifth Republic France. In this context, the CGT and CFDT, each in its own particular way, chose to use most of their energy to promote the political success of the Left, to the neglect of their labor market activities. When *Union de la Gauche* split apart into partisan conflict and then failed to win the 1978 elections, the CGT and CFDT found themselves at loggerheads politically, newly divided in terms of labor market action, and greatly weakened. Both Confederations then drew back to reassess their positions on France's economic difficulties in the worst conceivable circumstances.

The essay which follows will discuss the origins, nature and implications of CGT and CFDT responses to the contemporary economic crisis. It will attempt to do so by setting such responses in the broader context of the turbulent cycle of contradictions (division → weakness → unity-in-action → growing strength → politicization → division → weakness) which has characterized French trade union life in the modern period. Thus Part 2 of this Chapter will examine the positions of French trade unionism in the 'labor excluded' French postwar settlement. We will then turn in Part 3 to the processes of change in the 1960s which led the CGT and CFDT to develop the positions with which they were later to analyze changing economic circumstances. Part 4 will review the early crisis period itself, stressing union responses to changing economic fortunes before the critically important electoral period of 1977–8. Part 5 will describe the contradictory reevaluations of both Confederations in the aftermath of the 1978 elections.

Part 2

French Unions in the Postwar Settlement

In France, as in most other advanced capitalist countries, major political and social change occurred in the immediate postwar period. Moreover, again as in other societies, this period of major reform came to an end with the arrival of the Cold War. From this point the French version of a welfare state began to be consolidated. It was from within the institutional/political context of this 'postwar settlement' that France's postwar economic boom emerged, lasting for nearly three decades. The specifics of the sociopolitical equilibrium struck in France in its postwar settlement, in particular the relationships between French organized labor and the broader political economy, were substantially different from those of Northern Europe in particular. Since these differences created important preconditions for the later response of French trade unions to the economic crisis of the 1970s, it will be worth our time to review a brief outline of them.

The Period of Reform: 1944–7

Events surrounding the war—the decline of the Popular Front, Munich, the Spanish Civil War—and those of the war period itself—the defeat of 1940, Vichy and the Resistance—created a large bloc of political and social forces committed to reform at Liberation. The size of this bloc could not conceal, however, its internal divisions around the desirable extent and nature of such change. Gaullists wanted primarily to set up new presidentialist political institutions. Christian Democrats and, to a greater degree, Socialists, wanted a number of 'welfare state' type changes. Communists, whose power vastly increased in the Resistance and Liberation period, wanted to forge a new United Front with the Socialists for the dual, ultimately conflicting, purposes of promoting waves of social reform (nationalization, economic planning, income redistribution) to push France towards popular democracy and of keeping France on amicable terms with the Soviet Union. At the war's end the task of governing France fell to governments formed from this heterogeneous, reform-oriented and ultimately unstable national Resistance coalition.

Organized labor in France was an important component of this broad Resistance–Liberation bloc. The CGT, by far the most significant labor organization, had reunified during the war (PCF-oriented and more moderate 'reformist' elements having divided under the pressures of political disagreement in the late 1930s) and a massive influx of new members after 1944 brought CGT membership levels to an historic high point of 6 million in 1946. At the same time as the CGT itself gained in strength, Communist power within the Confederation grew to the point where PCF control over most parts of the organization became unassailable.[1] The CGT had traditionally been a 'class oriented' union movement in which strong efforts to shape labor market and other action to achieve broad 'class'—as opposed to category and particularistic—goals had always been made. New PCF power in the Confederation ensured that this orientation would continue, with, in addition, the PCF using its power to shape the CGT's class goals to conform, in general ways, to PCF political objectives. In time the PCF's shaping power over CGT class goals was bound to pose problems. The CGT had committed itself as early as the Amiens Charter in 1906 to partisan neutrality. The Confederation had always conceived of itself as a component of the French Left, but one whose positions were based on the generalized objectives of a politically pluralistic class rather than those of any specific partisan family within this class. The Catholic CFTC (*Confédération Française des Travailleurs Chrétiens*) held very different orientations, refusing class struggle perspectives in deference to the Church's doctrines of social harmony.[2] The CFTC emerged from the war with reformist intentions and increased membership as well, but it remained a weak trade union sister in terms of mobilizational and organizational power compared to the CGT.[3]

Installed in power at the war's end, the Resistance coalition promoted extensive changes in a very short time. A new social security program was legislated. Several industrial sectors were nationalized, mainly, but not exclusively, public utilities. Works councils for employee representation in the firm were set up in all companies above a certain size. New measures of statutory job security protection in the civil service were enacted. The health care and educational systems were reconstructed. An economic planning apparatus was established. Finally, after painful and difficult national debates, the new political institutions of the Fourth Republic were put into place. The period of energetic postwar reformism proved short-lived, however. Tensions between different components of the Resistance coalition proved impossible to contain once the unifying influence of the war was removed. First the Gaullists left the government, creating a new reduced governing bloc composed of Christian Democrats, Socialists and Communists. Then as a result both of the emerging Cold War and of conflicting domestic objectives in this bloc, the Communists were forced out of power in Spring 1947, leaving government in the hands of the Socialists and Christian Democrats. From this point onwards no further reforms were forthcoming. Government alliances of the Center-Left and Center-Right either had no interest in reform or could not generate the political resources for it.

Union perspectives and action during this tumultuous post-Liberation period are what interest us most. The CGT had firm goals for restructuring France's economic order in these years and used its considerable organizational power to advance them. It desired to see an extended public sector both for reasons of principle and to give governments major new sources of leverage, through economic planning, over the course of capital accumulation. It advocated tripartite administration over newly nationalized firms, with unions, the government and 'consumers' forming boards of directors. It hoped to see works committees assume a degree of decision-making power in all firms, its way of establishing a new union presence on the shop floor (in fact, works committees were established, but rapidly relegated to peripheral tasks, such as recreation and vacation programs, away from any role in administration). And, of course, it backed the creation of new social security and welfare bodies, preferably with strong union representation in their operations. In order to obtain such changes, the CGT acted in two major ways. Whenever and wherever possible, it intervened in the political process, either by direct organizational pressure on government or by indirect mass mobilizational efforts, to see that such changes were legislated and in the ways desired by the Confederation. Moreover, it was also willing to enter into quasi-'corporatist' arrangements with governments as long as reforms were forthcoming.[4] It quite energetically fought what it labelled the 'battle for production,' actively prevented strikes and participated in wage control programs. The CFTC, much weaker and smaller, went along with such trade union productivism and self-control in much the same spirit.

It is important to underline here that the CGT's goals in the immediate postwar period were informed less by any coherent desire to set up a mixed economy along the lines which did ultimately emerge than by a transformative *political* logic. The PCF, which by 1945 had won a dominant position within the Confederation, was attempting to use the postwar months of reconstruction and reform by a national Resistance coalition to lay the political groundwork for a new Popular Front alliance of the Left which would initiate a further period of more thorough-going change. Its goal was to set in motion processes which might again begin transforming the accumulation process, and the social relationships underlying it, away from capitalism altogether. To get to such a point it was necessary for PCF and CGT, first of all, to devote their efforts and energies to postwar reconstruction, for only through successful reconstruction could French society establish the economic independence necessary for further change.

The PCF's general strategy failed in 1946–7 for want of willing United Front political allies—the Socialists chose to ally to their Right rather than to their Left—and the Cold War. Ironically, certain of the postwar reforms enacted, in large part because of PCF and CGT insistence, provided the most important instrumentalities for the later postwar boom in France. And the CGT's momentary corporatism, productivism and devotion to labor discipline helped to reestablish the French capitalism which the Confederation, in theory, desired to transcend.[5] Perhaps more important, the unravelling of general PCF–CGT strategy occurred at great organizational cost to the CGT, and ultimately to French unionism as a whole. Conflict within the Confederation, fueled both by efforts by Communist-oriented trade unionists to consolidate their hold over the bulk of the CGT, and by simultaneous attempts by these same unionists to prod the CGT to pursue pro-PCF policies, finally led, in the early Cold War, to organizational schism. Almost all of the CGT's industrial federations and thus most of the CGT's membership stayed in the CGT, which PCF unionists operated as a classic Leninist 'transmission belt' until the later 1950s. But a minority of members, plus a few federations (mainly in the public service area of the public sector) split to form the Social Democratic *CGT–Force Ouvrière*, while the very large teachers' Federation (FEN) became autonomous.

The Postwar Settlement

The consolidation of postwar change and the turn towards postwar economic expansion in France coincided with a dramatic downturn in the fortunes of French trade unionism. Despite the split of 1948, the CGT remained the most powerful segment of the French labor movement, but its strength and mobilizing power declined significantly. The split ushered in a new era of trade union organizational pluralism in France and created a situation in which agreements for unified action between different union organizations became essential for any trade union success. Despite this, the CGT proved generally unwilling to take the steps necessary on its part to generate unity in action with its counterpart and rival organizations, *Force Ouvrière* and the CFTC. *Force Ouvrière*, although much weaker than the CGT, categorically refused even to contemplate unified action with the CGT. The CFTC hid its own refusal of unity in action behind a public commitment to collaborate with the CGT as long as FO went along. At the core of this destructive pattern of conflict was politics. Following the PCF, the CGT vigorously defended the Soviet side on Cold War issues. *Force Ouvrière* quite as resolutely supported the American side. Such an imposition of basic partisan positions on top of organizational differences drastically reduced the capacity of French unions to act in defense of working-class interests in the labor market. As a result a rapid downturn in union membership and mobilizational power occurred while, simultaneously, unions' organizational apparatuses became progressively more and more isolated from ordinary workers.[6]

The Cold War break of 1947–8 was a critical switchpoint in French postwar economic and labor history. French unions had traditionally been weak organizationally and at shopfloor level. Membership fluctuated wildly over time. In the absence of any institutionally sanctioned dues check-off system, actual card-carrying union members had to be recruited practically on a day-to-day basis, a situation which made union finances precarious and unpredictable and placed membership recruitment at the center of unions' organizational agendas. Moreover, no upturn in union fortunes—membership, mobilizational capacity—had, prior to 1944, been powerful and sustained enough to make major inroads into employer anti-union hostility. Nothing resembling the contractually sanctioned 'web of industrial relations rules' which had come to exist in many other societies had been codified in France. Instead, industrial relations in France were, and were understood by central actors to be, unending warfare. Where factors such as a tightening labor market or a militant 'climate' at the base allowed for union mobilization unions sought concessions from employers whenever, wherever, and on whatever grounds possible. When the situation favored employers, as it tended more often to do, the French *patronat* moved to crush and humiliate the labor movement.[7] Unions had no legal place on the shopfloor while stable contractual arrangements about critical economic matters such as wages, hours, job security and working conditions were rare. When they did exist they were regarded by both employers and unions as brief moments of respite to be disregarded or overthrown when the balance of forces underlying them changed. This comparatively under-institutionalized industrial relations system, of course, was one important reason why both unions and employers consistently chose political activity and pressure on the state as tactics in industrial conflict, a choice which made French industrial relations highly politicized.

The ordinary anti-labor balance of forces in French industrial relations was altered in important ways by the upsurge of political reformism and support for organized labor in the Resistance–Liberation period. The credibility of the *patronat* fell to a low point while the potential power of organized labor to impose new industrial relations arrangements was very high. However, the Cold War break intervened before any substantial change in the French industrial relations system could be worked out. The precipitous decline in union effectiveness which followed the reemergence of conflictual pluralism in organized labor, reinforced by virulent partisan political conflicts between organizations, allowed the French *patronat* to reestablish positions of industrial power and domination which had been severely undermined by the stresses of the 1930s and the war.[8] The traditional refusal of French business elites to consider the possibility that trade unions might become useful 'social partners' was reaffirmed, as was employer resistance to allowing unions any legitimate place in the firm. Any prospect that the postwar situation might lead towards a more fully institutionalized labor market based on regulated collective bargaining was therefore blocked. Employers, who seized upon the Cold War break as a convenient reason to reassert old positions, did not want new arrangements. The CGT, in its Cold War guise as a 'transmission belt' for PCF political purposes, did not want them either. Moreover, no post-1947 Fourth Republic government could hope to generate the political resources needed to impose new arrangements on industrial relations, even had the desire been present. Finally, *Force Ouvrière* and the CFTC, both of which might have been amenable to change, were too weak to play any significant role in bringing it about.

Thus events and power relationships conspired to create a 'labor exclusionary' postwar settlement in France. As France moved towards postwar boom in the 1950s it did so in the absence of two of the more central attributes of postwar arrangements present in most other Western political economies. Potential or actual 'liberal corporatism,' in which organized labor was available as a legitimate participant in aspects of societal economic decision-making, usually in exchange for some limitation on union power to disrupt economic life, became inconceivable in France.[9] Perhaps more important, no 'New Deal–Wagner Act' type of industrial relations system came to exist. The French postwar boom was to be structured around private-sector decisions and a state economic planning apparatus grounded in collusion between technocrats and business interests which *de facto* disregarded organized labor. It was to occur despite more or less continual open warfare between employers and unions in the labor market, warfare in which most of the battles were won by the employers.[10]

Trade union economic perspectives were ultimately altered by the Cold War break. Following the PCF (and the Cominform) the CGT first saw the post-1947 situation through the eyes of a revised and updated version of Lenin's *Imperialism*. The Cold War shift in French politics, in this view, involved the subordination of French economic policy, and the French economy, to US interests. In this process of 'Marshallization' France would ultimately suffer the fate of all imperialized societies. It would lose its economic autonomy and, eventually, the Americans would promote French economic decline altogether. This was an analysis which allowed the CGT, in 1947–8, to generate a series of powerful strike movements in an attempt to block the progress of 'Marshallization' and then, from 1949 into the early 1950s, to subordinate bread-and-butter union actions to peace movement agitation against NATO, German rearmament and the Indochina War. However, in terms of official economic thought, the Confederation persisted in its postwar 'structural reformist' views until 1954–5. In the new Cold War context this mainly involved confederal encouragement to CGT federations to draw up detailed, industry-by-industry 'programs' which attempted to demonstrate the kinds of more equitable and more effective industrial activities which would be possible under a more progressive government which refused American tutelage. The organizational purpose of these programs was to expose the costs which, according to the CGT, were incurred by the French economy by governmental pursuit of Cold War and 'Marshallizing' policies.

These structural reformist and anti-'Marshallization' views were abruptly and dramatically dropped in 1954–5, however, in response to the PCF's reevaluation of the French political situation. In 1954–5, with the appearance on the scene of Pierre Mendès-France and a slight shift to the Left in the electorate which brought the Socialists and Radicals close to power, the PCF leadership decided that militant struggle against 'reformism' was necessary to prevent the 'modernist' appeals of Mendès-France from success amongst the PCF's traditional working-class base of support. The result of such reflection was PCF Secretary-General Maurice Thorez's theory of 'pauperization.' According to this theory, which built on the earlier 'Marshallization' analysis, the imperialization of the French economy had gone so far that French workers were undergoing relative and absolute 'pauperization.' Because the CGT had maintained a 'reformist' program into the 1950s the PCF leadership reached the conclusion that such a program, which might 'mislead' workers about economic reality and lead them to overlook their immiseration, had to be dropped. And so it was, officially, at the 1955 CGT Congress, when the CGT adopted its own version of the pauperization theory.[11]

In almost all theoretical respects, this new pauperization perspective on the dynamics of French capitalism was perfectly absurd, an example of how far out of touch with French reality the PCF and CGT leaderships had fallen. It was, in fact, promoted by the PCF and CGT at almost exactly that moment when the French economy had begun to turn towards the longest period of sustained growth in modern French history. However absurd it was as theory, its adoption by the CGT had certain paradoxical effects. During the deep Cold War the CGT had degenerated in its action objectives to the point of virtually becoming an agency of political agitation for the PCF among workers rather than a trade union. The CGT's adoption of the pauperization theory allowed it to move away from the more overt forms of politicization which had marked its behavior in the Cold War and turn back towards more genuinely trade-unionist labor-market activity. According to the pauperization analysis, the central contradiction of French capitalism was its growing inability to maintain the living standards of the French people. With this in mind, then, militant, economistic, unpoliticized trade-union action to keep wages up was the best way to promote an anti-capitalist resolution of this contradiction. Thus while the CGT abandoned its official commitment to the direct promotion of alternative macroeconomic arrangements at this point (it was to resume this commitment much later), it shifted *de facto* to a strategy of union action to maintain and enhance popular consumption, based on its newly acquired conviction that any degree of union success in the labor market would precipitate crisis and open up prospects for political change, since French capital would not be able to deliver the goods.[12]

The bizarre vicissitudes of PCF–CGT relationships led, then, to a new, and ultimately more promising, situation in the mid-1950s. The CGT, for its own odd reasons, came to believe that militant bread-and-butter unionism in the labor market was the cutting edge of class struggle, after costly years of trying to impose inappropriate political crusades onto its union activities. With its return to more classical trade unionist perspectives it came closer in outlook to its much smaller trade union colleagues, FO and the CFTC, both of which had *de facto* 'working-class Keynesian' economic viewpoints. Although both had more elaborate macroeconomic programs—FO's a social-democratic, welfare-state program, the CFTC's a Church-inspired vision of harmonious class collaboration—they also believed that the central focus of French economic policy should be on expanding popular consumption in the domestic market. All French unions, then, had by the mid-1950s come to believe that the most important immediate issue which they faced was the stimulation of popular consumption through labor market action. Much was to continue to divide them in the labor market and make the generation of union activity difficult —Budapest and Suez in 1956, the Algerian War and the fall of the Fourth Republic in 1958, to name only the most important things. But the worst of the Cold War was behind the French labor movement.

The Cold War break did leave a profound legacy, however. The French postwar boom never came to be promoted within any general Keynesian consensus, in contrast to the courses followed in many other European settings. Significant economic actors, and not only the unions, rejected such consensus. Moreover, as we have already noted, postwar expansion did not proceed using either 'liberal corporatist' deals between unions, employers and the state or a predictable, highly regulated industrial relations system. Instead the trade-union advances of the immediate postwar years were beaten back, union mobilizational power was drastically reduced and unions were, once again, prevented from establishing any legitimate shopfloor presence. In turn, the rhetoric and reality of class conflict persisted in France, indeed perhaps intensified. Unions, the powerful CGT in the first instance, refused to assume any responsibilities for 'managing capitalism.' Nor were they invited to do so. Transformative radical ideologies thus retained their hold over critical segments of the French labor force, despite postwar economic expansion.

Part 3

Redefinitions in the 1960s

The French 'labor exclusionary' postwar settlement inevitably created its own contradictions. Its premises, isolating and minimizing organized labor, rather than innovating new and more cooperative arrangements between labor and other major actors in the political economy, had historical limits. Throughout the twentieth century the capacity of French labor to mobilize has varied cyclically. Because unions were unusually weak at one point in time there existed no guarantee that they would remain so. This was as true for the situation in the late 1940s and 1950s as it had been in the past. At the beginning of the postwar boom French union weakness followed from the divisions and distortions of Cold War politics. As the effects of the Cold War faded these causes would become less and less operative and union strength was likely to be renewed. This, in fact, was what happened, beginning in the mid-1960s. The process was greatly enhanced by the major changes in French domestic politics which followed the change in Republics in 1958. Not only was union strength in the labor market to be regenerated: in addition, new union perspectives on the political economy were to be developed.

The Unraveling of the Postwar Settlement

Internationally, the worst of the Cold War was over by the later 1950s, although it took longer for the effects of international change to penetrate French domestic life. 'Peaceful coexistence' was destined to make French political life less manichaean in itself. As a result the PCF felt less and less obliged to gear its domestic behavior to Soviet foreign policy goals. This, in turn, allowed the CGT to continue depoliticizing its trade union actions and to move away from the extreme 'transmission belt' relationship which had earlier characterized its ties to the PCF.[13] The change of regimes in 1958 was of great importance in altering the structure of French political debate as well. With the consolidation of Gaullist political predominance in the early 1960s, a solid Right–Center parliamentary majority came into being. This meant that the coalition-mongering politics of majority formation between Center-Left and Center-Right which had characterized the Fourth Republic no longer worked. In particular Gaullism in power made it virtually impossible for the Socialists to approach government without some form of alliance arrangement with the PCF. New possibilities were therefore created for an end to the PCF's extreme Cold War isolation, which the PCF began to seize upon eagerly in the 1960s.

On another plane, the new regime was committed to a new economic strategy, of great importance to unions. The Gaullists were well aware that, once the agony of decolonization was terminated, France would be obliged to shift its economic sights away from protected domestic and colonial markets towards the broader, highly competitive, international market then developing apace. A vigorous 'catch-up' economic course was necessary both to ensure that France would survive the chill winds of the international market and to endow France with the economic muscle needed for General de Gaulle's ambitious diplomatic goals. The details of this course are well known.[14] The regime engaged in powerful statist interventions in market processes, through the national economic planning apparatus and other tools at its disposal, to promote the concentration of French capital into larger units and to stimulate very high levels of corporate investment. In certain areas which the regime judged of critical future importance—the 'national champion' sectors—it also directly promoted sectoral change.[15]

Gaullist strategy had two general foci. It aimed first to foster a French industrial sector which could thrive in the international market. Secondly it wanted to open up the French economy to this market, through participation in the EEC in the first instance. General de Gaulle and his advisors perceived early on in their tenure one of the more important dynamics at work in the capitalist world. The postwar competitive advantage of American economic power was rapidly disappearing. In the near future there would be new openings of comparative advantage for a modernized France in an economically advancing Europe. De Gaulle's anti-Americanism and strong appeals to French nationalism were important aspects of Gaullist strategy as well, designed to undercut French economic and political subordination to the US and establish a new French autonomy needed to facilitate French success in the multipolar rivalry which French elites correctly saw on the horizon. Gaullist strategy had a different significance for French workers, however. To the extent that industrial structures and their markets changed, dislocations in the lives of workers were inevitable. Certain backward and inefficient industries might go under, while others prospered. Entire regions were likely to decline or grow in accordance with the effectiveness of their economic base and their position in new market flows. The raw materials of new working class discontent were therefore embedded in Gaullist policies.

A great deal depended, however, on the regime's policies for handling and channelling the tensions which would inevitably arise from its economic ambitions. Here the regime was, of course, handicapped from the start by the absence of preexisting propensities to corporatist arrangements in France and the chaotic unpredictability of the French industrial relations system. It might perhaps have taken urgent steps to overcome such handicaps, as more progressive parts of the Gaullist coalition advocated. Instead, the regime chose to ignore the problem and to leave French workers, together with their unions, to react to the labor market effects of extensive economic change according to their own lights. Gaullism was afflicted with a powerful belief that intermediary social groups such as unions were nuisances to be disregarded and isolated through magisterial claims, delivered by the General himself, that the regime stood above sectoral conflicts and reflected the national interest. Gaullist governments may also have been convinced of the then current economic myth that steady economic growth in itself would be a powerful enough solvent for popular discontents to render them unimportant. But in a situation in which full employment existed and workers desired to win real income gains in order to participate more fully in the emerging consumerist social order such disdain for working-class protest capacities was dangerous.

By the early 1960s the positions of major trade union actors had begun to change in ways which presaged an end to union weakness. The CGT, responding in large part to the PCF's shift back towards a United Frontist political line (1963–4), began a serious search for new trade union allies. In the Cold War period the CGT had played a major role in making trade union unity-in-action impossible—even had other unions been willing—by consistently insisting upon a broad list of preconditions for any unity negotiations which amounted to humiliation and surrender for any potential union partners. After the end of the Algerian War this changed. CGT policy shifted significantly as the Confederation demonstrated new willingness to accept unity-in-action on existing issues of common concern which were shared by different union organizations. The CGT, ever since 1948, had anticipated that its most likely unity partner would be *Force Ouvrière*, which, if anti-Communist, at least shared, on paper, the CGT's commitment to class-struggle perspectives. The CFTC, on the other hand, was always thought of as a 'class collaborationist' tool of the Church and thus an unlikely and unreliable ally. As the CGT became more ecumenical in its approach to labor market unity-in-action, however, *Force Ouvrière* refused to respond, maintaining its hard-line Cold War animosity to the CGT.

What intervened at this point was the complex change which turned the CFTC into the CFDT (the *Confédération Française Démocratique du Travail*). For more than a decade, in fact, the CFTC had been internally divided between old-line Catholic unionists and newer, more class-oriented forces. By the early 1960s these forces had gained the upper hand. Left Catholics from the Resistance had finally penetrated the upper reaches of the CFTC, for example. Ex-*jocistes* (*jeunesse ouvrière chrétienne*) had also acquired power. The Church itself had begun to change its attitudes on class issues both in France (the episode of the 'worker priests' was only one among many attempts by the French Church to build new links with workers) and more generally (Vatican 2 was not far off). Catholic union *militants* had also been radicalized by the struggle against the Algerian War. All of these, and other, processes came together in 1964 as the CFTC 'deconfessionalized' and became the CFDT. Abandoning older Christian doctrines of class harmony and adopting more aggressive class conflictual perspectives was only the beginning of a longer process of change for the CFDT, about which we will say more later. What was important about the change of 1964 was that it prepared the way for CGT–CFDT unity-in-action.[16]

The new leaders of the CFDT were strongly concerned with two connected issues. First, they desired to strengthen the CFDT as an organization, to increase its membership and relative power, particularly in those industrial sectors (essentially those where large numbers of 'new working class' personnel existed, scientific and technical workers who were badly integrated into the labor movement) where the CGT was weak. Secondly, they were aware that only through renewed labor market militancy could new strength be acquired. However, the period did not lend itself easily to this project. The important miners' strike of 1963, perhaps the first sign of French labor's changing fortunes, had led to a rigorous governmental stabilization plan which, by deflating the economy, had made any labor action more difficult. In this context the CFDT set out on an energetic search for new unity-in-action partners. Approaches to *Force Ouvrière* failed, so the CFDT turned to the CGT. The CGT, initially surprised to face unity initiatives from an unexpected source, seized the occasion. The final result was the CGT–CFDT unity-in-action pact in January 1966, the critical turning point towards the greatly increased union militancy of the late 1960s and early 1970s. New collaboration at-the-top between the CGT, France's most powerful union organization, and a CFDT endowed with new determination to make its mark, coincided with new rank-and-file militancy due both to the government's economic policies and to the situation in the labor market. The result was the opening of a new era of labor activity in which the number of strikes, trade union membership and union mobilizing power greatly increased.[17]

The CGT–CFDT accord was simply a priority listing of issues around which the two confederations agreed to struggle together.[18] No agreement could be reached on *how* to approach these issues, for the simple reason that the two confederations disagreed profoundly about labor market strategy and tactics. The CGT desired to mobilize strictly on bread-and-butter issues of wages, hours and working conditions with the goal of shaping any action which resulted towards broad, general movements which might, in turn, lead to spectacular high-level negotiations. Because of the CGT's concern with generalization, it tended to frown on local, hyper-militant actions which might not be understood by unaffected sectors of the labor force. The CFDT, in contrast, favored the promotion of local, hyper-militant actions, focusing often on sectors of the work force and regions where the CGT was weakest. In both cases, there were *arrière pensées* in such preferences. For the CGT, the PCF's political projects were of great importance. The PCF was seeking to construct a United Front of the Left and felt that high level, general, labor-market mobilization would contribute to this end. The CFDT had no desire to aid and abet the PCF's mobilization plans. More positively, the CFDT felt that the CGT's perspective tended to sacrifice union effectiveness for symbolic demonstrations, while it desired concrete results. Moreover, the CFDT was the distant number two of French trade unionism, ambitious to close ground on number one, the CGT. To the degree to which the CGT's strategic biases led it to a certain caution in the labor market, the CFDT could establish the new reputation for militancy which it sought by fostering the strong local struggles which it was best placed organizationally—either by its presence in regions or occupational areas where the CGT was weak—to promote in any case.[19]

With such differences in strategy and tactics, the two confederations joined to promote unity-in-action which, if it did succeed in generating considerable new labor activity, was also very turbulent from 1966 into the early 1970s. When the two could agree upon full united action, the superior organizational power of the CGT tended to shift the balance of union activity in the directions desired by the CGT. As this occurred local actions were turned towards broader, more generalized mobilization campaigns. Great stress was laid, in particular, on periodic 'days of action,' symbolic mass protests which could call out workers in an entire industrial branch, the entire private or public sector, or even the entire labor force. As such shifts in the balance of union action towards the CGT's goals occurred, the CFDT would become progressively more disturbed until it eventually would pull back from full unity. When the cycle ran its full course, as it did, for example, in the period from 1966 to May–June 1968, the rank-and-file would be mobilized, in complex ways, from the strategic perspectives of both confederations.

The May–June 1968 strikes, the largest in modern French history, were the high point of the great increase in French labor action after the mid-1960s, although a high degree of action continued until 1973–4. CGT–CFDT mobilization, meeting a responsive rank-and-file climate, was the background to May–June. Growing militancy after 1966, enhanced by the effects of the 1967 recession, had been created by both *patronal* and state intransigence prior to May, intransigence which, rather than intimidating workers and unions, intensified their determination. The example of students successfully defying the regime was the spark which ignited the great 1968 strike wave which broke out initially in those places, and around those issues, of earlier CGT–CFDT agitation. More generally, the combination of hyper-militant local actions and massive national-level mobilization in May–June reflected the complicated logic of CGT–CFDT unity-in-action. The strikes concluded with the settlement of a huge backlog of outstanding union demands, plus at least the short-term scuttling of many of the Gaullist regime's economic policies.[20]

When the cycle of CGT–CFDT unity ran its course to open disagreement, both confederations resorted to mobilizing in their own separate ways until they realized, once again, that some unity was indispensable. Such was the case after May–June—when political disagreements and trade union problems led to new divisions—until early 1970. From the new CGT–CFDT unity treaty in 1970 until 1974 there existed tentative unity-in-conflict between the two confederations. In this period the CFDT was able to maintain a broader measure of strategic and tactical autonomy in the private sector, leading to what, in retrospect, looks like a *belle époque* of CFDT-coordinated local actions ending with the LIP watch factory occupation in 1973.[21] The CGT grumbled a great deal about the CFDT's wayward course, but in the public sector both confederations, the CGT in the lead, massed together to do battle with the regime's post-1969 attempts to institute a new public sector incomes policy (through Chaban Delmas' *Nouvelle Société* schemes).[22] Union membership continued to expand, despite public controversy between the CGT and CFDT, strikes continued at a high level and working-class living standards continued to rise.[23]

It is important to note, however, that despite a significant upturn in trade union capacities to mobilize and act, the Gaullist regime and the private sector *patronat* managed to maintain the 'labor exclusionary' nature of France's postwar settlement. The great strikes of May–June 1968 did elicit a promise from the government to produce new legislation to reinforce trade union presence on the shop floor. The measure, when it was passed, allowed for the establishment of legal trade union 'sections' in most industrial settings, and, in addition, codified a number of new trade union rights at firm level. With the passage of time, however, it became abundantly clear that the new legislation had not institutionalized any substantial new trade union power on the shop floor. *Patronal* resistance to unions and to union participation in shopfloor life marginalized the new union sections and neutralized the new procedures. The 'French May,' in other words, led to nothing like the accentuated trade union shopfloor power which followed the Italian 'hot autumn.' Similar things could be said about the economic concessions which the May–June strikes forced on the French regime and *patronat*. Subsequent economic policies, in particular a highly successful devaluation of the franc in 1969, prevented any appreciable absolute shift in national income shares towards labor. Trade union strategy itself, in particular the CGT's desire to translate the new union militancy into a political currency which would further the PCF's goals, was also an important factor in deciding the ultimate directions in which renewed union energies were to flow in France. In order to understand this, however, we must turn back to the realm of trade union economic and strategic thought.

New Trade Union Thoughts on the Economy

In France, as in many other European societies, the mid- and later 1960s marked what Crouch and Pizzorno have called a 'resurgence of class conflict.'[24] In each European case, however, renewed union and working-class mobilization pointed in specific national directions towards the changed economic circumstances of the 1970s. In France, as elsewhere, the new mobilization caused organized labor to begin reevaluating its understanding of economic realities. In turn, these new economic frameworks were to provide new sources of union orientation when economic crisis did arrive.

The CGT began to change its economic perspectives in the early 1960s, concurrent with the PCF's shift back towards United Frontism,[25] but the full process of reconceptualization was completed only in the aftermath of the May–June 1968 'events.' The CGT's general theoretical conclusion, reached by 1969–that is, long before the 1973–4 upheavals in the international economy—was that the French economy had entered a *crisis* of new dimensions. Indeed, the first major heading in Secretary-General Georges Séguy's report to the 1969 CGT Congress was 'the general crisis of capitalism.' The reader will forgive a rather lengthy citation from this report, since it imparts rather well both the tone and the content of CGT thought better than any summary:

> International and national events . . . could not underline any better the aggravation of the crisis of capitalism and the impossibility which it faces of finding ways out of a rapidly deteriorating situation.
> In France, the masters of the great banking and industrial feudalities have nonetheless used all means in their power to try and resolve

their difficulties and overcome the contradictions which overwhelm them.

They have taken over the state apparatus and totally submitted it to their needs; they have installed an authoritarian regime in order to impose their class imperatives on the nation; they speculate legally, scorning monetary equilibria; they despoil the public coffers for their profit, crushing the people with taxes while they exempt themselves; they give themselves substantial privileges on the backs of nationalized and public enterprises, they extract enormous subsidies from the state for their own investments, their operations of reconversion, merger and their concentrations which never stop growing. Their power, combined with that of the state, provides them with considerable means to exploit wage earners, to resist the demands of workers and those of other social categories victimized by their policies.

Despite all this, they continue to sink deeper into difficulties and contradictions which are ever more inexorable given the fact that they are not phenomena specific to our country but part of a crisis which affects all European and world capitalist countries.[26]

Séguy's remarks indicate the general theoretical context of the CGT's new crisis analysis. In certain ways, the Confederation was echoing its past views on the French economy, since it had always been *de rigueur* in the CGT to portray French capitalism as in the throes of crisis. But the CGT's views had changed away from the old 'Cold War–pauperization' perspectives. Now the crisis theory was embedded in the PCF's developing 'state monopoly capitalist analysis,' the Party's theoretical adaptation to the Left Unity which was beginning to unfold. One could follow the progress of this analysis on either or both sides of the CGT–PCF ledger, but its general outlines were in place by 1970.

According to the new views, French capitalism had entered a new stage in the 1960s, that of 'state monopoly capitalism.' The central characteristic of this stage was the domination of both the economy and the state by the 'monopoly caste,' that fraction of the bourgeoisie controlling the monopoly sector. Pushed to use state intervention to counteract the general tendency for the rate of profit to decline, the monopoly caste thereby set in motion a whole series of connected contradictions. Its control over the state and its use of state power and general revenues for specifically monopolistic ends tended to undermine the legitimacy of the liberal democratic political system which it needed to pursue such ends. To the extent to which such state intervention succeeded economically in countering the falling rate of profit, it propelled the economy forward towards intensified rationalization in work (more Taylorism) and in the structuring of capital, both processes being accompanied by an accelerated use of science and technology.

In Marxian terms, state monopoly capitalism promoted an ever greater 'socialization of production' which entered into ever greater conflict with the private appropriation of capital. Science and technology were not used to enrich human possibilities, but for profit. The constraint of profit maximization limited possibilities for expanding the supply of collective goods—education, health, leisure, housing, public transport, etc.—which were desperately needed. Whole sectors of production were threatened with extermination because they fell outside the purview of the monopoly sector—smaller capital, for example—or menaced with dramatic re-structuring because of monopoly capital's need to rationalize distribution and financing. Ultimately, the theory predicted, a huge cluster of social opponents would emerge from all of this, workers, of course, but also *couches moyennes* (engineers, technicians, white collar employees, small producers and retailers), intellectuals, even segments of the 'competitive' fraction of capital.[27]

It is important to underline both what this PCF–CGT theory of crisis was, and what it wasn't. It was not a perspective which suggested new forms of economic 'fine-tuning,' new 'industrial policies,' and/or changes in international economic arrangements which would make France more competitive. The changes which the CGT advocated for overcoming crisis were not in the realm of 'economic policy' as ordinarily understood. The Confederation postulated that the problems of French capitalism were innate to capitalism and could not be resolved within a capitalist frame-work. Only a change in the basic structures of accumulation promised a way out of crisis. Working this kind of change was essentially *modifying relationships of economic and social power*, rather than implementing different policies. The 'monopoly caste' had to be dispossessed, in the first instance. Reflection on how to make the existing French economy work better, how it fit within a changing international market, for example, or how to adjust things to control inflation and unemployment, was of little importance. Genuine solutions to such problems would only come from movement towards socialism. And this, at least initially, was a *political*, and not an economic, problem.

Because of the transformative nature of its crisis theory the CGT was obliged to have two different levels of focus on action. In the short run, in the labor market the CGT proposed continuing in much the same way as it had earlier, urging broad-ranging agitation around bread-and-butter issues, eschewing hyper-militant (*gauchiste*, in the CGT's post-May vocabulary) tactics and new demands for workers' control emerging out of May–June. The maintenance and enhancement of popular consumption were, there-fore, the CGT's immediate concerns. Struggle for popular consumption through union militancy was, however, to be connected with longer-term concerns for basic change. Bread-and-butter union action was to be shaped, to the maximum possible extent, to contribute to building the social underpinnings of protest which would help in the PCF's drive towards the formation of a common front of Left political forces. Moreover, because the CGT considered itself to be part of the French Left, it did not hesitate to announce what it desired to see embodied in the program of such a common political front. Its main goal was, therefore, a series of new nationalizations to promote what it, and the PCF, called 'genuine democ-racy.' Here the new 'state monopoly capitalist' theoretical discussion could not obscure the fact that the CGT was returning to the central program-matic questions which had preoccupied the Confederation in the immediate postwar period.

The document entitled 'Nationalizations, a Decisive Means to Realize Economic and Political Democracy,' adopted at the 1969 CGT Congress, clearly expressed the CGT's logic.[28] The purpose of nationalizations was political, to dispossess the 'monopoly caste' and give the people the necessary economic leverage to orient economic life in a 'democratic way.' Only secondarily would they make the French economy more effective, and this not because of any specific policy orientations, but because 'genuine democracy' would bring a more rational and equitable distribution of social power. The list of nationalizations proposed by the CGT reflected this political logic—the credit sector, monopoly groups, technically advanced firms dependent on state subsidies for research and development, plus other firms which might facilitate the implementation of a 'democratic plan.'[29] Newly nationalized enterprises would be controlled by tripartite boards of directors involving extensive personnel participation in management through unions. Moreover they would be tied into a complex national planning operation in which branch and sectoral goals, generated through the calculations of both public and private sector firms, would be harmonized and turned into a coherent whole at the national state level. What the new public sector would *do*, economically, was not discussed. Nor were the almost certain international implications of a huge wave of nationalizations for the French economy.

The CGT was not alone in reevaluating its economic surroundings in the later 1960s. The CFDT did likewise. The CFDT did not use the word 'crisis' in the way the CGT did, nor did it reach back into its past for a new program, even if the CFDT's reflections were very much in the line of another traditional French transformative logic, anarcho-syndicalism. The CFDT's evolution in the 1960s was remarkable. With 'deconfessionalization' the CFDT became strongly reformist in its social views, demanding a greater union voice in 'democratic planning' plus other changes of a quasi-corporatist kind. But this reformist stage proved relatively brief. The CFDT was profoundly marked by May–June 1968, changed more by the 'ideas of May' than perhaps any other major French social force. By its 35th Congress in 1970 the CFDT was ready to commit itself publicly to the quest for socialism. In the words of this Congress' Main document, 'no modification of the system is adequate to respond to the workers' fundamental aspirations for liberty and responsibility.'

Like the CGT, the CFDT couched its views in Marxian vocabulary, although in the CFDT's case its relative lack of familiarity with such vocabulary was evident. But the CFDT's new Marxism was quite unlike that of the CGT. The Confederation consciously avoided what it called the 'economism' of the Third International/Communist tradition. Instead it adopted the tone of rebelliousness of the French student movement of May–June 1968, strongly infused with Left Catholic social humanism. Its intellectual debts were not to Marx and Lenin, but to French writers like Serge Mallet and André Gorz, and to the more progressive sides of Vatican 2.[30] The following citation from an important CFDT position paper of 1971, when contrasted with Séguy's 1969 CGT Congress speech, will make the differences between the confederations clearer:

> Analysis of the situation of men and women workers in today's society shows that capitalism, developing in accordance with the double law of profit and domination . . . creates a model of civilization which alienates people. It tends to turn them into objects, developing in them dependency, submissiveness, passivity in work and in social life . . .

For the CFDT capitalism is, then, a system composed of:
– a certain economic organization (private property and economic liberalism)
– a certain type of social relationships (hierarchy, minority power)
– an ideology whose purpose is . . . to condition individuals to ensure the power of minority social groups.[31]

To the CFDT, then, French problems could not be reduced to the economic level alone. Indeed, in the intense ideological debate which followed May–June 1968 and lasted into the early 1970s, the CFDT repeatedly indicted the CGT for economism.[32] Rather, to the CFDT capitalist *society* and its 'model of development' were in crisis. Not only were the workings of the economy at issue, but also alienation in work and spiritual exploitation in spheres of culture and consumption. The keys to resolving such multifaceted problems were struggles for a 'new type of development.' For trade unionism the cutting edge of this struggle was action to promote workers' control, *autogestion. Autogestion*, democratic planning and social decentralization were the only ways to begin correcting the *three* primary evils of the capitalist model of development: economic exploitation, authoritarian domination and alienation. To the CFDT any scheme for change which did not address all three of these issues simultaneously risked itself being statist, authoritarian and alienating (*viz*. the Soviet Union).

Thus the CFDT, like the CGT, refined a transformative trade union logic in the late 1960s. But the CFDT's logic was very different from that of the CGT. Whereas the CGT sought to shape simple bread-and-butter union action into general mobilization for a Left political alternative, the CFDT believed that the process of change should begin in the labor market itself. Its immediate goal, then, was to shape the labor-market struggle in ways which would lead those involved towards direct demands for *autogestion*. For the CFDT a viable strategy for social change had to be connected *directly* to trade union activity and not seek to use trade union mobilization for a process of political change which might put change in the workplace aside. For the CGT 'genuine democracy' would follow the implementation of major reforms in the political sphere which would make possible change in the basic structures of accumulation. For the CFDT democracy was to be constructed at the workplace itself by tying day-to-day union struggle to *autogestion* demands, such that workers might begin to take control over their own lives even as they fought with employers in the short run, whatever happened in the political sphere. The CFDT thus rejected the dual focus—labor market and political—of CGT strategy. Instead it opted for a neo-syndicalism in which the defense of workers' immediate interests and broader social change both would take place in the workplace.

In important general ways, however, the CFDT's new analysis of its environment was similar to that of the CGT. It was not a blueprint for coping with French economic problems as they existed. It contained few proposals for new economic policies. To the degree to which it addressed the existing economic setting it did so in similar ways to the CGT, advocating the maximum possible growth of popular consumption. Its basic concern, however, was how to *transcend* the fundamental structures

of the economy as it stood, its logic was not ameliorative, but transformative. If anything, in fact, the CFDT's vision was even more abstract
and removed from concern with immediate economic issues than the
CGT's. If the CGT's nationalizations were designed to begin transcending
capitalist property relations and were therefore *political* in essence, they at
least were concrete, tangible proposals. *Autogestion* was also a *political*
goal in this sense. Workers should struggle for new increments of power at
workplace level because the struggle in itself would create in them new
levels of democratic decision-making maturity which would eventuate in a
new ability to shape their own destiny. Such a program, however appealing
one might have found it, was vague in the extreme, in addition to being
quite devoid of economic policy content. How *autogestion* and working-
class labor-market action might connect, how it could cumulate into social
change, what kind of economic structures might result, and how the whole
process would articulate with political and market realities, all remained
open questions.

Focusing on the general theoretical preoccupations of the two most
important French union organizations may seem, to some readers, to place
inordinate weight on what are usually labelled 'ideological' factors. Such a
focus, of course, does illuminate the economic discourses, such as they were,
of the CGT and CFDT, and this *is* one of our concerns. Beyond this,
however, 'ideological' factors had had, and have, considerable weight in
forming the orientations of French unions. As we have seen, there was a
'resurgence of class conflict' in France at this point in time. Unions, as the
major organizational conduits of this resurgence, were well placed to steer
it in one direction or another, in accordance with their general maps of the
situation. Insofar, then, as CGT and CFDT maps pointed towards the
future in certain specific ways, the nature of these maps became a crucially
important variable in shaping trade unions' responses to the changing
economic circumstances which were to emerge in the mid-1970s.

Part 4

Crisis and the Price of Politics: To 1978

Almost everywhere in Europe unions reconsidered their economic setting in the later 1960s. What was at issue for the CGT and CFDT in France was not specific economic policy, but the general structures of capital accumulation. Proper policies could not occur without a profound change in these structures. Both confederations, in different ways, had firmly established chains of reasoning which began with economic problems and moved through dramatic *political* action before concluding with consideration of new economic policy. Thus there was a significant gap in their reflections between what existed, to be subjected to corrosive criticism, and what might exist after political change. Moreover, neither Confederation expressed any willingness to assume managerial responsibility for helping the French economy to work better, as it stood.

Crisis and *Union de la Gauche*

The French economy bounced back brilliantly from the social crisis of May–June 1968. As of the early 1970s, France's economic record seemed enviable. The difficult transition from a closed, colonial economy towards a world-competitive export-oriented economy had, according to all accounts, been dramatically successful. From 1968 to 1973 the economy as a whole grew at a rate averaging about 6 per cent, rarely below 5 per cent and sometimes close to 7 percent.[33] Figures for the growth of industry were equally impressive.[34] Moreover, the postwar boom had fundamentally changed the structure of French industrial production, away from an orientation towards simple consumer goods and towards more sophisticated capital goods and consumer durables.[35] Most important, French exports rose in 20 years from 9 percent to 21 percent of GNP, while simultaneously shifting away from the franc zone (42 percent of exports in 1952, 10 percent in 1970) towards the advanced capitalist world, the EEC in particular (50 percent of exports in 1970).[36] Investment and capital formation figures were also impressively high (23 percent of GNP in 1960, 26 percent in 1970).[37]

Shadows began to appear on this bright picture as the decade turned, however. Inflation rates began to rise steadily—from 4.8 percent per annum in 1970 to 7.3 percent in 1973. Unemployment, which had been virtually non-existent throughout French postwar history, slowly began to edge upwards. No one—except the unions and the Left—seemed particularly alarmed about such trends, however. The usual explanation of inflation was that capital and labor were colluding to maintain a high growth rate and regular wage raises. Because of this the perpetuation of high investment rates led to wage drift and firm indebtedness, both leading, in turn, to inflation. Demography was invoked to explain the rising unemployment rate which, although very low in absolute terms, was high for France. The baby boom was entering the labor market in large annual cohorts with which job creation could not keep pace. Table 1.1 (p. 37), which presents important economic indicators from the late 1960s to the late 1970s for France and the other societies we are examining, shows how superficial such explanations were to prove.

The oil crisis of 1973–4 did not immediately cause any change in French economic policies. Undoubtedly electoral politics was important in this, since a very close presidential election occurred in May 1974 which made any change away from high-growth policies a dangerous risk for the regime. The results of this were not pleasant, however. Inflation doubled, unemployment continued to rise slowly, while the French balance of payments deteriorated catastrophically (from a surplus of $112 million in the first half of 1973 to a deficit of nearly $6 billion in 1974). With this news in hand, the government put on the brakes with an anti-inflationary program which lasted from the last quarter of 1974 until late 1975. These policies reduced inflation somewhat, to slightly over 10 percent, and brought the balance of payments nearly to equilibrium. They also succeeded in stopping growth altogether—GNP went down by 4.3 percent (industrial production −12.7 percent)—during the period. More predictably, unemployment took a huge jump upwards to 4 percent, doubling in absolute numbers.[38]

The government's next step was to restimulate the economy, to 'promote expansion without inflation and balance of payments problems,' from the end of 1975 until the fall of 1976. A 5.6 percent growth rate returned, but inflation stuck at 10 percent and unemployment continued to rise. The balance of payments, alas, registered one of its highest deficits in modern times. These results, plus political disagreements between Prime Minister Chirac and President Giscard d'Estaing, brought on Raymond Barre, the 'leading economist of France,' as the press labelled him. The Barre Plan, introduced in the last quarter of 1976, had many of the same goals as the earlier anti-inflation program, with the addition of a more stringent incomes policy. Inflation stuck at 10 percent, unemployment went up to 4.9 percent while growth dipped to below 3 percent in the year following. The sole bright spot was a balance of payments turnaround. The deficit was halved in 1977 and disappeared—briefly—in the first quarter of 1978.[39]

In policy terms, then, French governments dealt with the new problems of the mid-1970s by what looked like classic 'stop–go' methods. In the new period, however, such methods did not work. Inflation seemed intractable, hovering around 10 percent, no matter what was done to lower it, while flashing dangerously upwards in 'go' moments. Unemployment continued to go up, whether stopping or going was the order of the day, although it did rise rather more when the economic brakes were on. But the most terrifying problems lay elsewhere. In this new setting the French balance of payments could only be equilibrated at a point of very low growth. For every percentage point of positive growth, France's international exchange position deteriorated. Since France could not sustain anything like the kind

Table 1.1 *Important Economic Indicators from the Late 1960s to the Late 1970s.*

	1969	1970	1971	1972	1973	1974	1975	1976	1977	1978
Growth of Real Gross Domestic Product at Market Prices (Percentage Change from Previous Year)										
France	7.0	5.7	5.4	5.9	5.4	3.2	0.2	5.0	2.8	
Germany	7.8	6.0	3.2	3.7	4.9	0.5	−1.8	5.2	2.7	
UK	1.5	2.3	2.8	2.4	8.0	−1.5	−1.0	3.7	1.3	
Italy	5.7	5.0	1.6	3.1	6.9	4.2	−3.6	5.9	2.0	
Sweden	4.8	5.3	−0.2	1.6	3.4	4.2	0.8	1.3	−2.7	
Consumer Prices (Percentage Change from Previous Year)										
France	6.4	4.8	5.5	6.2	7.3	13.7	11.8	9.6	9.4	
Germany	1.9	3.4	5.3	5.5	6.9	7.0	6.0	4.5	3.7	
UK	5.4	6.4	9.4	7.1	9.2	16.0	24.2	16.5	15.8	
Italy	2.6	5.0	4.8	5.7	10.8	19.1	17.0	18.8	17.0	
Sweden	2.7	7.0	7.4	6.0	6.7	9.9	9.8	10.3	11.4	
Current Balances (Millions of Dollars)										
France	1,475	68	525	284	−675	−5,980	−66	−6,097	−3,328	
Germany	1,913	870	830	795	4,604	9,852	3,463	3,433	4,220	
UK	1,221	1,862	2,800	520	−2,289	−7,911	−3,587	−2,158	−341	
Italy	2,340	1,133	1,902	2,043	−2,662	−8,017	−751	−2,816	2,465	
Sweden	−196	−264	210	264	1,221	−950	−1,614	−2,089	−2,782	
Source of the above: *OECD Economic Outlook* (December 1979).										
Unemployment (as Percentage of Total Labor Force)										
France	1.6	1.7	2.1	2.3	2.0	2.3	4.0	4.4	4.9	5.2
Germany	0.7	0.6	0.7	0.9	1.0	2.2	4.1	4.1	4.0	3.8
UK	2.0	2.2	2.9	3.2	2.3	2.1	3.4	5.1	5.5	5.5
Italy	3.4	3.1	3.1	3.6	3.4	2.9	3.3	6.6	7.1	7.2
Sweden	1.9	1.5	2.5	2.7	2.5	2.0	1.6	1.6	1.8	2.2

Sources: OECD *Labour Force Statistics* 1969–72 (May 1975), 1973–5 (May 1976), 1976–8 (November 1979).

of deficit which high growth implied, the growth targets of the postwar boom had therefore become unattainable.[40] The facts seemed obvious. French exports were relatively inelastic to growth. On the other hand, French imports were highly elastic, rising directly with growth levels. The break-even point (that growth level at which exports covered imports) was far below the growth figures which had been achieved in the postwar boom. On the other hand, low—or no—growth, in addition to running up against the expectations of the French people for a steadily rising standard of living, also increased unemployment and did relatively little to control inflation.

In the face of such evidence the French regime and mainstream French economists realized quickly that France faced something more than a cyclical downturn and/or a one-shot situation caused by rising energy costs. While a whole range of conflicting short-term remedies were advocated—monetarism, classic deflationary policies, a 'return to free market capitalism' to allow increased profits, among others—most actors were aware that the issue transcended the simple management of a temporary period of 'stagflation.' General insistence on the need for 'industrial redeployment' followed, which came to be reflected in the rhetoric and reality of longer-term governmental reflection (particularly in the planning process). Discussion in favor of 'industrial redeployment' began with criticism of earlier Gaullist industrial policy. It was generally agreed that French growth in the 1960s, if impressive in percentage terms, had not given France the solid place in international markets which it needed to survive the new circumstances. There were important sectoral exceptions to this, but the general trend seemed clear. Too much French growth had been in inefficient firms sheltered by boom conditions and there had been too much conscious Gaullist protection of lame ducks. In crisis conditions the shape of France's international industrial specialization was increasingly unfavorable. Too many sectors were vulnerable to growing competition from newly industrializing countries. There were too few large firms, and there had been too little research and development, in the sophisticated technological goods market where future international trade was promising. In addition, French firms had not integrated forward into the production of complex producer goods, such that when high rates of growth occurred the importation of such goods became automatic.[41]

The policy formulae derived from such discussion by the Barre government involved a combination of liberalism for the weak and state help for the strong. Gaullist-style protection of lame ducks had to be ended. More generally, various governmental programs of subsidization and market regulation-had to be dismantled to allow prices and costs to settle at their true market levels. Secondly, the state had to structure its fiscal and monetary activities to promote profitability and, by inference, investment, while simultaneously increasing its selective intervention to promote industrial activities which had a clearly promising international future. France needed to develop new niches of comparative advantage (*créneaux*) in the growth areas of international trade. Were such *créneaux* to be created and reinforced, export-led growth would follow, allowing both a favorable international payments position and rising domestic living standards. With successful 'industrial redeployment' the serious risk of relative economic decline might be averted. The models to be emulated were Japan and West Germany.

Despite what became a new orthodoxy of 'industrial redeployment' the degree to which actual government policy was connected to such goals was unclear. The Barre government did begin to knock out some of the props underneath protected weak industries. This led, for the first time in modern French history, to the bankruptcy of some very large firms: Boussac in textiles, Manufrance in metal finishing, the shipyards of La Ciotat, Sacilor, and Usinor in iron and steel, all in 1977–8.[42] The government also began, in the interests of a 'new liberalism,' to dismantle price controls. Simultaneously both Giscard and Barre stumped the country to promote a social consensus on the need for austerity and discipline. Both often announced that full employment was a thing of the past. But the outlines of specific 'industrial redeployment' policies remained obscure. Only in steel, where the industry's virtual collapse occurred, did planning seem to be going on in a serious way. In fact, despite the 'industrial redeployment' rhetoric, the government's goal seemed almost exclusively to be to promote a regeneration of private-sector profitability through austerity and the liberation of prices, in the hope that investment would follow.

Some of the inconsistency and uncertainty of government policy until 1978—grand talk about industrial policy accompanied by action mainly directed towards managing stagflation and increasing profits—may be attributable to politics. The coming of crisis in the French economy was not the only, or perhaps even the most important, focus of government action in this period. Changing economic circumstances also coincided with the most serious political threat which the Gaullist/post-Gaullist majority had ever faced. With the signature of the Common Program in 1972 a United Left was created. As politics began to polarize between this Left and the majority, the regime faced an electoral fight for its life. By the May 1974 presidential elections, the Left had become sufficiently strong that Giscard d'Estaing could manage to defeat François Mitterrand only by a bare 1 percent of the votes cast. The Left made further gains in the 1976 cantonal elections and won an effective majority in local government at the March 1977 municipal elections. Throughout 1977 and early 1978 opinion polls steadily predicted a Left majority at the critical March 1978 legislative elections.[43] In this context the regime had to move with great caution in the realm of economic policy to avoid precipitating its own demise. Given the difficult international setting, it could not heat up the economy for electoral purposes, since balance of payments catastrophes would have followed. Yet at the same time it could not take any dramatic steps towards 'industrial redeployment' in the face of electoral risks in affected regions which might follow.

The Left Common Program, which provided an alternative economic perspective to the regime's, was a decisively important political fact in itself. Its contents were biased strongly towards the general propositions for change which the PCF had formulated in the later 1960s. (In the long negotiations between Communists and Socialists prior to 1972, the PCF had set the framework and limits, with the Socialists mainly acting to soften the PCF's original proposals.)[44] Nationalizations of industry were the heart of the program, along with 'democratic planning' and new structures for industrial democracy. Less comprehensive than the PCF had desired, the list of nationalizations was still extensive, including the entire banking sector and nine industrial groups. The central criterion for choosing industries to be nationalized was 'strategic positions *vis à vis* key sectors of the economy.' This meant

(1) firms fulfilling collective functions of a 'public service' kind;
(2) firms living off public funds (in public markets, benefiting from large subsidies, etc.);
(3) major centers of capitalist accumulation dominating entire productive sectors, i.e. monopolies and oligopolies;
(4) firms controlling branches essential for the development of the national economy (by virtue of technological level, position in international exchange, roles in specific regions).[45]

'Democratic management' of any new public sector firms was to involve tripartite administrative control over operations (representatives of workers, consumers and government on boards), plus extensive new worker-power in firms. Democratic planning would promote the elaboration of economic objectives through coordination between the state and such firms.

The Common Program was remarkably innocent of any picture of the actual day-to-day dynamics of the French economy. The chapter entitled 'industrial policy' noted simply that, as defined by the plan, Left industrial policy would seek

(1) to secure national independence within a context of developing inter-national exchanges and equilibrated international cooperation;
(2) to reorient the expansion of production to national and social needs;
(3) to increase the economic and social return (*rendement*) of the produc-tive apparatus, notably in order to overcome the backwardness and reduce the disequilibria inherited from earlier mismanagement. (In-cluded here were proposals for the restructuring and development of sectors producing 'public' goods [construction, pharmaceuticals, leisure, culture, tourism] and the expansion and modernization of sectors critical to high growth [mechanical goods, electrical construction, chemistry].)[46]

The most noteworthy aspect of the economic proposals of the Common Program was the absence of specific scenarios for future French economic development. Achieving French economic *independence* was perhaps the Program's central goal. France had to be protected from submersion and loss of control in an international division of labor dominated by foreign multinationals. The economic generality of the Program was no accident, however. The logic of the Program was *political* rather than economic. Nationalizations and other economic changes were designed to dispossess 'the monopolies' and install greater democracy (a thrust carried through in other sections of the Program outlining proposed changes in political institutions, major income redistribution, and a new foreign policy). A new economic logic would presumably *follow* political changes, waiting upon the democratic deliberations of the French people working through new institutional arrangements, rather than standing as the *a priori* goal of such changes.

One major reason for the relative lack of attention of the Common Program to specific problems of economic policy was that the Program had been put together during the last years of successful postwar growth, prior to the coming of crisis. Economic optimism may have made questions of immediate economic strategy seem superfluous at that time. Indeed, disagreement between Communists and Socialists about the meaning and implementation of the Program in new crisis circumstances was one of the central issues in the unraveling of *Union de la Gauche* in the fall of 1977.[47] The PCF argued that crisis made the strengthening of the Program more urgent, while Socialists were clearly apprehensive that implementing the Program in the 1972 form might be a recipe for economic disaster.[48] Even taking this dispute into account, however, it is clear that the Common Program exerted a powerful hold over economic thinkers of the French Left up through the 1978 elections. Trade union thinkers were not exceptions to this, as we will see.

Trade Union Thoughts on a Changed Economy

The dramatic turnaround of French economic fortunes inevitably provoked further union reflection on the French economy. The critical issue was whether such reflection would lead to a basic reevaluation of the new positions which the CGT and CFDT had defined in the late 1960s. The fact that economic crisis coincided with a rise in the strength of the French Left was essential. Both confederations officially adhered to a strict division of labor between trade unions and political parties. The job of unions was to advance working-class interests in the labor market, broadly conceived. The job of political parties was to work towards change in the political sphere. Yet, in different ways, both confederations saw themselves as decisively important components in the social movement for progressive change upon which any success of the political Left would have to be based. The CGT conceived of itself as an integral part of Left Union, if a nonpolitical part. The CFDT, while officially critical of the logic of the Common Program and reticent about *Union de la Gauche*, was also quite conscious of the importance of its position in the firmament of French Left forces. Thus neither confederation, each in its own way, could avoid being caught up in the broader dynamics of *Union de la Gauche*.

The coming of crisis refocused CFDT energies on problems of economic analysis. In a series of internal confederal documents beginning in 1974 a crisis analysis was developed culminating in 1976–7 in a special crisis issue of the CFDT weekly (*Syndicalisme-Hebdo*) and in an official book entitled *La Crise*.[49] The CFDT saw the crisis as originating in two interconnected historical processes, changes in the international economic order and increasingly more successful international working-class struggle. The CFDT refused, however, to confine its general reflections on the crisis to the narrow realm of economic problems. In effect, the crisis involved a global repudiation of the advanced capitalist 'model of development.' Workers and others were rejecting not only economic exploitation, but also the degradations of consumerism, the inability of capitalism to put science and technology to socially progressive uses, the ideology of 'productivist' growth, and alienation in the cultural sphere. These words had a familiar ring, of course. The CFDT was trying to fit new economic events within the perspectives on French society which it had developed in the later 1960s.

The CFDT's situation of the origins of crisis in international economic change led it to review postwar economic history, which it divided into three parts. The first period involved complete American domination over international capitalism and was dated from the Marshall Plan of 1947 until the early 1960s. During this period, international stability and the postwar boom were administered by American political and economic power and US management of the international system of payments. The second period was one of 'precrisis,' dating from the early 1960s and lasting into the early 1970s. The major characteristic of this period was the decline of American economic and political power. Hot pursuit of the US in international trade by European and Japanese economies bent on 'catch-up' strategies was perhaps the major reason for this. Economic expansion continued, accompanied by a vast growth in international trade and ever more severe competition in international markets marked by the emergence of multinational corporations as central actors. An international resurgence of rebellion—working-class struggle in Europe, national liberation struggles in the Third World—also marked the period. American response to mounting problems simply aggravated an already volatile situation. The US tried to export to others the costs of the Indo-Chinese adventure, along with the costs of its own relative economic decline (inflation, balance-of-payments problems, declining productivity), by using its political and financial muscle. The transition from precrisis to crisis was marked by the rising inflation and unemployment of the early 1970s plus the collapse of the Bretton Woods system. To the CFDT, then, the arrival of crisis, its third period, predated the OPEC initiatives of 1973–4. Its indices were rising inflation and unemployment, vastly intensified international competition and the breakdown of international financial arrangements. Energy problems simply aggravated these difficulties, albeit in a large way. The central economic process at work in the crisis, the CFDT contended, was a general profits squeeze.[50]

The CFDT was also concerned to analyze the place of the French economy in this general perspective. 'Growth at all costs' had been the Gaullist goal in the 1960s. Gaullist concentration policies had indeed promoted growth, but had also led to a regeneration of class struggle directed against the distorted social effects of this growth. Class struggle in the later 1960s had forced capital towards high growth rates in the early 1970s, financed through massive borrowing, which had been inflationary. With crisis, however, the weakness of France's international position made the 'growth at all costs' line unworkable. Recovery through the stimulation of popular consumption was not feasible, given the elasticity of French import demands to growth and the relatively fixed nature of French exports. The 'go' cycles of 1973–4 and 1975–6 amply demonstrated that consumption-led recovery created huge balance of payments problems.[51] Other governmental strategies, Barre-type attempts to depress the internal market and increase profit levels while simultaneously scrambling around the world to increase French exports, could not work either. If all countries did the same thing, a general depression of domestic markets would close down exports altogether. 'Growth can no longer be built on the development of exports. It is absurd to count on the growth of exports from advanced societies towards one another to reestablish their balance of payments.'[52]

The CFDT had one general conclusion to all this. 'Certainly it is not possible to foresee autarkic economic life inside any country, but it is first of all internal demand which must 'carry' growth. From this it follows that we must develop industry which will reduce imports (machine tools, industrial goods . . .).'[53] While it might have seemed logical for Confederation thinkers to proceed from this assertion towards the proposal of specific industrial policies which would outline the CFDT's preferences for the kinds of industrial structures needed for the task of 'allowing internal demand to carry growth,' no such process was to be found in CFDT documents. Instead, the Confederation chose to reassert its transformative vision. In the words of Michel Rolant, the CFDT's chief economic spokesman, 'we do not believe that there exists a durable solution to this crisis within the confines of a capitalist society.'[54] It was not clear *why* the CFDT felt this to be true, although the reason may have been contained in the CFDT's very broad definition of the crisis itself. Since the crisis was one of the capitalist model of development, " . . . the only true way out of the crisis will be another logic of development, the one proposed by the CFDT, whose purpose is to end exploitation, alienation and domination over workers. This is to say a *development oriented towards self-managed socialism [socialisme autogestionnaire]*.'[55]

There was a great deal in the CFDT's analysis which remained obscure. One thing, however, was clear. The CFDT had not been moved by the crisis to the point where it was willing to consent to sacrifice and austerity in the interests of some abstract 'national interest' to resolve economic problems. Instead it claimed to want to *use* the crisis to begin the transformation of French capitalism in the direction of socialism. Ground-level union action was its chosen means to initiate such change. Presumably this meant union actions at firm, branch, and other levels not only to promote investment decisions which would make the economy work better and more responsively but which would also give workers increments of new power over the investment decision-making process itself, through *autogestion*. But the CFDT offered very few indications about how, precisely, such union actions might take shape. The gap between the Confederation's general analysis of the crisis and its proposals for resolving it through *autogestion* was nearly complete.

Since this gap was so large in the CFDT's analytical literature on the crisis, it will be worth our while to look at specific CFDT action proposals for the period to see if they betray an agenda which could begin to fill in the gap. The CFDT *Plateforme* of 1977, an action program which was the product of long confederal debate, was probably the best source of such proposals.[56] The core of its contents is as follows:

(1) *Wages, Purchasing Power, and the Reduction of Inequality*—proposed, among other things, a major raise in minimum wage levels; real

national collective agreements; a simplification, branch by branch, of job classifications; a compression in the wage hierarchy between different categories of workers, from operatives through *cadres*; equalization of male and female wages (pp. 11–12).

(2) *Employment*—proposed to end unemployment as fast as possible; to establish a right to guaranteed employment; establish a right of veto by works committees over collective firings until a local employment committee has given its opinions; the creation of tripartite (unions, employers, local government) local employment committees which would ultimately become part of future democratic planning; the creation of 200,000 public-sector jobs; regional manpower policies, particularly for declining regions; reduction of the work week initially to 40 hours, ultimately to 35; longer vacations, lower retirement ages; draconian limitations on employers' rights to hire temporary labor (limits on the use of short-term contracts and on 'Manpower Incorporated' types of hiring); then: '. . . with the arrival in power of a Left Government, the immediate establishment of branch industrial committees, made up of union, employer, and governmental representatives, to debate and give advice on investments, after due consultation with concerned local institutions" (pp. 13–15).

(3) *On Working Conditions*—proposed to increase union shopfloor power over working conditions; develop stringent new procedures on industrial health and safety; take measures to limit and control swingshift work (pp. 16–17).

(4) *Social Rights, Health, Cadre de Vie*—here a long list of demands for changed and vastly increased 'social wages.' Most notable is the section on nuclear energy policy, labelled 'a dangerous and out-of-control adventure . . . unacceptable.' The CFDT asks for a three-year suspension of new nuclear spending and a shift towards a more diversified energy policy (pp. 18–20).

(5) *New Rights and Powers in Nationalized Industries*—proposed setting up new decentralized works/service councils to negotiate productive and social goals for the factory/service, with important decision-making powers over working conditions and the organization of work (including the choice of new equipment, technological change, scheduling, on-the-job training). Such councils to be an important part of democratic planning (pp. 28–30).

What was most notable, again, was the lack of connection between the CFDT's general crisis analysis and its day-to-day program. The platform had very little to suggest about specific new industrial policies. It focused rather on higher wages and benefits, a shortened working week, state intervention to create and protect employment and, as its most specific point, rejected the regime's energy policy. How the French economy in crisis might have produced such things was not broached. Raising 'popular consumption' was the CFDT's main proposal. The major change which the platform advocated was vastly enhanced industrial democracy, involving innovations in economic decision-making processes—new powers for existing works committees, the strengthening of trade union powers and prerogatives in general, new tripartite local employment committees, factory/service councils in the public sector and, ultimately, a decentralized system of democratic economic planning. It was also clear that most of these proposals were made not with new economic circumstances in mind, but after consideration of political factors. The CFDT was skeptical of the Left Common Program, which, it feared, might lead to bureaucratic and statist reforms which could not resolve the basic problems of French society. It was thus concerned to disseminate its own *autogestionnaire* notions of change in anticipation of the arrival in power of a *Union de la Gauche* government.

The CGT also refined its economic analyses in the changing situation of the 1970s. And, like the CFDT, it changed its ideas within a broader framework which it had set out in the later 1960s. The core of CGT economic reflection remained the 'state monopoly capitalist' theory which it shared with the PCF.[57] According to this theory the underlying dynamic of crisis was a basic contradiction in the capitalist process of accumulation. In periods of growth and expansion such as the postwar boom, it was inevitable that tendencies towards the overaccumulation of capital would eventually appear. Such tendencies, plus the rising organic composition of capital, would lead to pressure on the rate of profit. Measures designed to counteract the tendency of profit rates to decline (in particular those taken by the state in the state-monopoly capitalist postwar order) might succeed in prolonging expansion for a time. In the longer run, however, the profit rate was bound to begin falling. When this occurred, crisis would follow.

To the CGT what crisis amounted to was the existence of insuperable structural barriers to the continuation of accumulation in habitual ways. Crisis could be overcome by capital, but only at the cost of major changes in the structuring of the accumulation process. What this meant was that a dramatic shakeout of the units of capital accumulation would be necessary —the *dévalorisation* (roughly, disinvestment) of capital was the technical expression used for this by the CGT and PCF. Devalorization might include the actual destruction of segments of capital (business failures) and the 'putting to sleep' of other segments (perhaps by using the state to remove troubled sectors from the profit-making sphere, at public expense). Whatever the strategy chosen to devalorize, the costs in jobs, living standards and general insecurity would be enormous. Other things being equal, however, capital would have no choice but to force workers to bear these costs. The conditions for future profitable accumulation had to be established.[58]

In the most general of terms, then, the crisis of the 1960s and 1970s—the CGT dated its enunciation from 1967–8—resembled earlier capitalist crises. Its specific structural content was different, however. The postwar boom had occurred within the context of state monopoly capitalism, a setting in which the state, which served the interests of national monopolies, had used state power to facilitate monopoly accumulation. The global result of the pursuit of separate national state-monopoly capitalist accumulation strategies had, however, produced a quantum leap forward in the internationalization of capital, such that the field of accumulation had itself become increasingly international (and hence supranational).[59] This internationalization set up a number of new situations. First, strictly national-level state monopoly capitalist strategies for devalorization in crisis had become quite insufficient. In the CGT's words, 'the "classic" means for structural devalorization of capital in SMC and, hence, the regulation of the economy by the state, are in crisis inside each country.'[60] Secondly, no effective *international* mechanisms for regulating the world market existed. This meant that the devalorization process resulting from the crisis of the 1970s would be determined by the relative power of different nationally based 'imperialisms' in the international market, and would inevitably be anarchic. Existing relationships of strength between different imperialisms were what was most decisive for France. Certain imperialisms, represented primarily by multinational corporations, were much stronger than others. In particular, US, West German, and Japanese economic power was much greater than that of other capitalist societies, including France. Ultimately this meant that the crisis-generated shake-out of capital would occur to the advantage of the more powerful imperialisms and to the disadvantage of the weaker, including the French.[61]

Within this broad perspective the CGT's next task was to explain and situate the position of France. To the Confederation's analysts, the foundations of the new French crisis had been laid in the Gaullist development strategy of the 1960s. The goal of this strategy had been industrial concentration to create 'groups of international size' which would be able to survive in a newly open international setting. The strategy had succeeded in creating and reinforcing French monopolies, claimed the CGT, but had left France badly placed in the international division of labor—an 'intermediary country' between the US, West Germany, and Japan and much weaker countries. France's exporting strength had increased, but mainly towards areas of the world and in sectors of industry with an unpromising future.

French trade was divided between selected parts of the Third World and advanced capitalist countries, mainly the EEC. In the Third World French exports were vulnerable to the weak international payments positions of the importing countries, to competition for the same markets from other, better-placed, advanced capitalist exporters, and to goods produced in the Third World itself (the 'newly developing countries' or, as the CGT put it, those parts of the Third World 'inside the orbit' of foreign multinationals, US in particular).[62] The bulk of French exports, however, went to advanced capitalist societies. Here it was France's industrial weakness which presented the problems. France had few secure positions in international high technology areas. French exporting successes had been mainly in consumer durable goods and in simpler consumer products (with small pockets of advantage in engineering and transport goods as well). But in very few of these areas was France well enough placed to confront the superior positions of foreign multinationals in the new circumstances of crisis. As a result, France's market share was likely to decline.[63]

The reasons for France's industrial weaknesses were all connected to the policies of the state and the monopolies which privileged monopoly growth at the expense of the French nation. Insufficient effort had been given to the social expenditures needed to produce scientific and technological advances. More important, Gaullist growth had been based on an inadequately developed domestic market. Instead it had faced outwards, favoring exporting monopolies at the expense of industries focusing on potential domestic demand from popular social strata. As a result Gaullist growth had been dangerously imbalanced. In particular, France had failed to build up a broad range of intermediate industrial links (machine tools was the usual example here) which, had they existed, might have prevented a situation in which economic growth led automatically to higher imports of intermediary goods.[64] Beyond this, the monopoly/export strategy had been undertaken without the necessary creation of international commercial and financial networks adequate to the task.[65]

Governmental and monopoly responses to crisis, thought the CGT, were of two interconnected types. The first was short-term in nature. It consisted of a package composed of austerity for workers and others, attempts to push profit rates back up, and efforts to stimulate exports, largely through diplomacy. The CGT, along with almost everyone else, contended that this 'austerity/profits/exports' strategy was unlikely to work at a moment when other states were pursuing similar policies in ways which caused export markets to shrink internationally. It was the second response to crisis, 'industrial redeployment,' which interested the CGT most, however.

The core of this new 'industrial redeployment' strategy was the urgent promotion of French international specialization to maximize the competitive prospects of French multinationals in the new international division of labor. This, claimed the CGT, was simply a new formulation of French state-monopoly capitalist politics favoring monopoly interests over those of the French people. It was the structure of the international division of labor, and France's relative weakness in this structure, which made 'industrial redeployment' so dangerous. Since French monopolies desperately needed insertion into the international market, and since this market was dominated by American, West German, and Japanese interests, the shape of any such insertion would be dictated, by and large, by these dominant interests. The results of this would be disastrous for France. French monopolies would become ever more dependent on foreign technologies (the collapse of Gaullist 'national champion' plans in nuclear equipment, electronics, and computers into dependence on US technology was cited in illustration of this), further undermining French research and development capabilities. International specialization also would promote greatly increased foreign investment in 'modal' advanced sectors of French industry, another factor increasing dependence. Also likely was increased investment abroad by French monopoly capital which, said the CGT, would amount to disinvestment in France.

More generally, 'industrial redeployment' would eventually make the French economy a disproportionate victim of the internationally dictated 'devalorization of capital' in crisis. A profound division would develop between French monopoly multinationals, favored in 'industrial redeployment' strategies, and a weakened domestically oriented industrial sector, prone both to domestic failure and takeover from outside. Whole sectors of French industry were likely to disappear, creating intolerably high levels of unemployment and popular distress. More important, France would lose her economic autonomy and independence. In the words of the CGT's economists:

This orientation has grave consequences. The monopolies are opposed to the coherent functioning of the national economy. What interests them is using the state as a means to internationalize. Planning should project the future of international markets. Financial markets should be restructured to allow monopoly firms to restructure. State aid is necessary for foreign trade and foreign installations. But this implies that *the coherence of the productive system within national boundaries will no longer be reflected upon and organized*, that [such coherence] has a tendency to fall to pieces.[66] (emphasis in original)

CGT analysts concluded from all this that France in crisis faced a critical choice. On one side was 'industrial redeployment' in favor of the monopolies. This would lead to ever-increasing dependence on the more powerful imperialisms dominating the international capitalist order, with catastrophic implications for the economic and social integrity of France and for the livelihood of the French people. On the other side were dramatic political changes like those contained in the Left Common Program. It was necessary to 'reestablish and reinforce the coherence of the national economy.' To do so it was necessary to 'ensure national mastery over the production of the material basis of industries.' Nationalizations were 'the essential means to put a new industrial policy into practice.'[67] They had to be sufficiently extensive 'so that, from the point of view of the reproduction of the totality of industry, the new public sector will play the predominant role, rather than the . . . private sector controlling the nationalized sector.'[68] Nationalizations, together with democratic planning, would provide the necessary instrumentalities for an independent French economy structured around satisfying the needs of the French people, while massive extensions of democracy generally would allow such needs to be made manifest.

Since the economic logic of the CGT's policy proposals was strongly nationalistic, the Confederation's thoughts on the international position of a post-Common Program French economy were of central importance. Here discussion was vague:

France cannot live in autarky and the possibility of struggling against international aspects of the crisis demands that we build on the balance of power presently being created internationally by those people who are fighting for their economic independence and for a new international economic order, with the support and active solidarity of socialist countries.[69]

The way out of the easily foreseeable problems which Common Program-type changes would inevitably create—the spectre of a siege economy—would therefore lie in the massive reorientation of French international economic activity towards the Third World and socialist countries as part of a concerted international anti-imperialist counteroffensive to promote a new world economic order.[70] The enormous complexity of such a reorientation and the major dislocations which it would clearly involve for the French economy were not seriously acknowledged.

Changed economic circumstances had not, therefore, changed the CGT's commitment to its precrisis transformative goals. If the French economy had *already* entered crisis by the late 1960s, economic events in the 1970s simply made earlier CGT reflections seem more compelling. The CGT's economic theory, like the CFDT's, was 'longer run' in its vision. The economic program derived from this theory depended for its implementation on political circumstances which might be very difficult to obtain. In the case of the CGT, as in that of the CFDT, there existed a substantial gap between the CGT's future plans and day-to-day French economic realities. For this reason, once again, it will be useful to examine the proposals contained in the CGT's 'shorter run' action program. Was it possible to read another economic project out of this program?

The CGT's action program remained substantially the same from its 1975 Congress until 1978.[71] Here we will reproduce the major headings of the 1977 version, together with significant subsections, as we did earlier for the CFDT platform.

(1) *Develop, first of all, the internal market and raise popular consumption to get production going again*—index wages and buying power to the cost of living, raise low wages and social benefits.

(2) *Struggle against inflation, its causes and consequences*—lower VAT tax on essential goods; block industrial prices, rents and the cost of public utilities; control and reduce the profit margins of large firms; selectively reduce inflationary credit facilities granted to large firms; tax capital gains; heavily tax profits gleaned from inflation and speculation; index popular savings to the cost of living.

(3) *Act massively and rapidly to reduce unemployment and to stimulate new job creation*—mainly by satisfying outstanding working-class demands, raise wages, lower retirement age, reduce the length of the working week and set up new protective programs against unemployment; devise new programs to prevent plant closures; create useful public jobs to satisfy popular needs.

(4) *In the face of the development of multinational corporations*—France should declare and apply the principle that every nation has a right to
   (a) oblige MNCs to invest profits where they have been obtained;
   (b) orient foreign investment towards sectors and regions for the goal of national development;
   (c) democratically control capital imports/exports;
   (d) control foreign investment and forbid it when it threatens national sovereignty and control over the economy.

(5) *France's international economic relations*—should be restructured and diversified; economize on imports; expand the technological content of exports; protect and remove France from dependence on the USA and West Germany; more open trade with Third World and socialist countries.

(6) *Stop the abandonment, liquidation, and subordination of entire sectors and innumerable firms to foreign capital*—based on the expansion of the public sector, defend and expand essential sectors of the economy.

(7) *Change France's energy policy*—away from the regime's 'all oil' and 'all American nuclear' policies and its restrictions of investments by *Electricité de France*; nationalize all oil and nuclear activities; new

policies of diversification and coordination using coal, gas turbines near ports and mining areas, hydroelectricity, including tidal; secure imports by diversification; nuclear power is necessary but safety is the first priority; more research on new energy sources.

(8)   *Reorient/coordinate transport policy*—stressing public transport.

(9)   *Budgetary reform*—cut socially unproductive spending and subsidies to big capital; more social investment; create 500,000 new public jobs in three years; use budget against inflation.

(10)   *Stop operations to dismantle the public sector and/or to subordinate it to the interests of the monopolies*—reform the tariff structure of utility rates; more money to public sector, especially for health, education, research and development.

(11)   *Consumption*—strengthen consumer protection laws; block monopoly and other collusion in distribution; provide greater public information; legislate a larger public role in controlling distribution.

(12)   *Promote regional policies*—for regionally equilibrated national development.[72]

In all this, the CGT claimed that there existed a strong connection between its short-term program and its longer term transformative projects. As the introduction to the 1977 program stated, 'These measures directly confront "redeployment," which, in order to assure the position of a few large groups, allows sectors, sometimes decisive ones, either to be destroyed or to be abandoned to foreign multinationals . . .' In fact, if one put aside proposed measures which depended upon political change to be implemented, the core of the program's more strictly 'trade unionist' measures involved action to resist austerity and force the expansion of popular consumption. However, even this simple 'bread and butter' unionism was, in the CGT's eyes, transformative. To cite the Confederation's two major economic writers,

> To struggle against austerity is to struggle against the destruction or the putting to sleep of much productive potential, it is struggle against the principal means by which the rhythm of monopoly capitalist accumulation—the source of crisis—is maintained.[73]

In different ways, then, both the CGT and the CFDT had developed paradoxical positions on the crisis. Each put forward theories which asserted that profound social transformation was the only way to reach a satisfactory resolution of the economic problems of crisis. And both had grandiose visions of the institutional changes necessary to begin such transformation. In the case of the CGT these changes were projected to occur through political modifications at the level of the national state by the election of a United Left government and the implementation of the Common Program. The CFDT deemphasized such national political activity and stressed the need to create decentralized industrial democracy. Yet neither Confederation proposed a strategy which directly connected trade union action in the existing economic setting with the transformed, more equitable and humane economy which they foresaw in the future. For the present, both organizations proposed traditional union action essentially oriented towards the maintenance of popular consumption in the face of crisis-induced austerity. Between such traditional action and the new economy—whether of the Common Program or of *autogestion*—was an intermediary stage of *rupture*. Before rupture unions would behave more or less as they had been behaving. After rupture they would behave very differently, in particular by assuming large new responsibilities in specific economic decision-making processes. Most importantly, before rupture neither the CGT nor the CFDT had very much to say about the policies which the administrators of the existing mixed economy ought to pursue to navigate in the changed circumstances of the mid-1970s.

Theory, Practice, and Politics

What French unions did in response to crisis is the question to which we now must turn.[74] As we have earlier noted, the nature of CGT–CFDT responses to their environment depended, among other things, upon the degree of unity-in-action which prevailed between them. The coming of crisis coincided with a renewal of CGT–CFDT unity. After a period of noncommunicaton (1968–70) and a period of limited and conflictual unity (1970–3) the CGT and CFDT, both sensing the dramatic changes which followed from the crisis, renegotiated their unity-in-action agreement in the spring of 1974. This new formulation was more extensive than earlier agreements, since trade union 'methods of action' (*how* to carry on struggle) were, for the first time, included. Earlier pacts had been simply priority listings of the issues around which the two confederations pledged to move.[75]

Periods of full CGT–CFDT unity-in-action always posed the danger for the CFDT of increased CGT influence over the general course of trade union activity. This time around, unity involved an even more powerful shift in the general balance of unified action towards the CGT's strategic and tactical preferences. In fact, in the quasi-permanent struggle of the CGT to use unity-in-action with the CFDT for those purposes, and only those purposes, desired by the CGT, it would not be an exaggeration to speak of a major CGT victory in the years between 1974–8. As we will see presently, however, it was not a victory without costs.

The first step toward such CGT success came in 1974–5 when the CGT, in an unusually shrewd tactical adaptation, began preempting the CFDT's earlier 'vanguard' role in the promotion of local struggles. What happened was that the CGT decided that the sharp local strikes against layoffs, industrial relocation, shutdowns and regional distress which the CFDT had, in the earlier 1970s, used as a springboard for building its reputation for new militancy, could be turned, in new circumstances, in the general directions desired by the CGT.[76] Thus the CGT began to seek out such local actions, to try and shape them such that they focused on nationally salient 'mass' protest issues ('no to unemployment,' 'no to the dismantling of French industry,' 'no to redeployment,' i.e., generally defensive responses to the symptoms of crisis) and to prosecute them with great vigor. Success was not long in following, as the incidence of CGT-led sharp actions in a number of industries deeply touched by the crisis demonstrated —in shipbuilding, printing, the Post Office, and the railroads. CGT success was helped along by the ways in which the crisis impinged on the labor market. The end of the boom era, inflation and unemployment tended to shift rank-and-file perspectives at least initially towards defensive, bread-and-butter questions of wages and job security. The 'qualitative' rhetoric of the CFDT, premised as it had been on continuing growth, no longer appealed.

However, the development of the crisis rapidly minimized the number of such miltant local actions, whoever took the lead. With unemployment looming as a longer-term trend, workers became less willing to risk their jobs in extensive strikes. These dynamics further favored the CGT's perspectives on trade union tactics. As it became more difficult to promote local action of any extended nature, the thrust of united CGT–CFDT activity shifted towards the promotion of *journées d'action*. 'Days of action' were symbolic strikes, usually 24 hours or less in duration and often accompanied by mass public demonstrations. They were almost always organized around issues of a high level of generality. In terms of demands, the 1975–8 'days' were almost always defensive protest movements against the general symptoms of crisis. They were always designed for the mobilization of large numbers of workers—all workers in an industrial branch, all private sector workers, all public sector workers, or, in the case of general national 'days,' all French workers, period. Their targets, the actors whose behavior they nominally sought to influence, were high level, ranging from peak employers' organizations, the CNPF, to the government itself.

The CGT's tactical claim for *journées* was that they would ultimately pay off in terms of local rank-and-file mobilization. Workers would be educated by participation in 'days' to issues of struggle which they would then feel encouraged to pursue on the level of their firms and branches. In fact, however, the vast bulk of trade union action after 1976 was contained in huge 'days of action' alone. As the CFDT often remarked—despite its participation—days of action didn't seem to lead anywhere except to further days of action. Beginning in 1975, however, days of action grew more spectacularly successful in themselves, attracting ever larger masses of participants, especially after the initiation of the Barre austerity plans in the fall of 1976. Workers were indeed distressed by the incidence of crisis, and 'days' offered them safe ways of demonstrating this distress. The 'days' of 7 October 1976 and 24 May 1977 were, each in its turn, the largest industrial protests to occur in France since May–June 1968. Each featured huge parades from the Bastille to the Republic in Paris. Moreover, each involved unity-in-action of a scope rarely achieved in modern France. Not only the CGT and CFDT, but also the *Fédération de l'Education Nationale* (FEN) joined, while various *Force Ouvrière* organizations also participated.

Thus events, plus the CGT's relative advantage in organizational power, conspired to give the CGT a determining role in shaping the nature of French unions' response to crisis after 1974. What did the CGT choose to do with this new-found power? Here we must return to the first principles of the CGT's position in the 1970s. The CGT's strategic perspective, as we have noted, had two foci, trade unionist and political. The CGT's self-proclaimed first responsibility was to promote action in the labor market in the interests of its supporters and the broader working class. But by design the CGT's practical definition of this responsibility in the 1970s was such that trade union mobilization would serve specific unionist goals and simultaneously advance the political fortunes of the Left. What was all-important, then, in the CGT's strategic calculations—given this dual focus —was the relative weight which the Confederation placed in practice on its trade union and political modes. And here there occurred an important shift in CGT priorities *during* the early crisis years, in response both to the crisis itself, but, more importantly, *to the unfolding political situation.* What happened was at least in part due to the complex relationships existing between the PCF and CGT, a subject which would take another essay to explore properly.[77] What is important to us at the moment, however, is the result. After the signature of the Common Program in 1972, political mobilization became an ever more pressing concern for the CGT and the Confederation began to turn, in consequence, towards union action designed to deepen working-class support for *Union de la Gauche* electorally and increase rank-and-file support for the specific measures of the Common Program. If possible, the CGT also wanted to convince its union partners—the CFDT in particular—to do the same. Before the crisis hit hardest—up into 1975, say—this increased emphasis on politics proved relatively compatible with continuing defensive unionism in the labor market. Even so, the message which the CGT desired to communicate through labor-market action changed somewhat. Workers were to be mobilized to protest and strike, to be sure. But they were also to be led to understand that labor market action could only provide temporary remedies to working-class problems. Real, lasting solutions would come only through the victory of the Left and the implementation of the Common Program.

Beginning in 1975–6, however, political mobilization began to displace trade union action, rather than supplement it. In essence, this meant ever-increasing CGT stress on the 'Left electoral victory is the only solution' line at the expense of more orthodox trade union concerns. Moreover, at the same time, the CGT, in its purely trade union actions, pressed more and more urgently towards general, high level and publicly spectacular trade union actions of the *journée d'action* type, which in their contents, progressively left rank-and-file concerns behind for electoral mobilization. It was during this period that the slogan *union, action, programme commun* became the CGT's marching song.[78]

It would be very wrong to claim that conscious CGT decisions were the only, or even the most important, factors in the growing generalization and politicization of French trade union action after 1975. The highly charged political atmosphere which developed generally in France after the 1973 legislative elections created a setting in which such shifts in union emphasis seemed both natural and reasonable. In effect, France lived for several years (excepting only a twelve-month period of grace after the 1974 presidential elections) in a constant state of preelectoral tension, leading towards the 1978 legislative elections which were to be, everyone knew, the decisive moment for *Union de la Gauche*. To begin with, it had long been traditional for French unions to moderate labor-market activity in preelectoral periods so as not to hurt the chances of progressive candidates. Moreover, the CGT and the CFDT were self-proclaimed participants in the French Left, even if the CFDT never openly supported the Common Program. Whatever their *arrière pensées*, both knew that 1978 represented perhaps the best chance the French Left *had ever had* to begin a process of transformative change in France. And both believed, each in its very different way, that such transformative change was the privileged avenue towards the solution of French working-class problems. In addition, the internal balance of forces in the CFDT, always precarious, shifted towards tactical positions which were closer to those of the CGT. Beyond even this, a crisis-shaped labor market (partly because of which, it should be noted, trade union membership and support was declining somewhat) made rank-and-file union action even of a defensive kind much more difficult. French unions were able to preside over the maintenance of working-class living standards until 1978, but this was at least in part due to the political situation. Problems in generating workplace struggle thus abetted a shift towards symbolic demonstrations as central union tactics. In all, however, CGT *decisions* about how to shape labor action were very important. And rather than resisting tendencies to over-generalize and overpoliticize union action, the CGT pushed such tendencies forward.

What did this all mean in the context of economic crisis? To begin with, what French unions did was to downplay the development of effective defensive labor-market action against the *symptoms* of crisis. Instead, led by the CGT, they shifted resources towards the promotion of mass political suport for *Union de la Gauche*. This process diverted the attention of workers upwards, away from the shop floor towards very general economic concerns, and outwards, towards politics. In essence, such a strategic course had the effect of undermining the capacities of rank-and-file workers, at the 'point of production,' for pursuing union action to promote their day-to-day interests. On quite another plane, to the extent to which this strategy was effective, it tended to produce among workers a mentality which believed that change would come from outside the purview of working-class action, from *politicians*, almost as if miracles, in the form of legislation, would resolve day-to-day difficulties.

It should be obvious that such a trade-union response to crisis was indirect at best. In fact, it was not really designed to be a direct response to crisis. Rather it was a response to the French political calendar. French unions, the CGT in the lead, were following through on their transformative economic logic according to which no progressive response to crisis could occur without major institutional changes. If this view was eminently understand-able, given the paucity of opportunities for access to power which the French Left had had in modern times, it also had its costs. Unfortunately, but not coincidentally, the French Left was granted this opportunity during a period of severe economic difficulty. French unions chose and/or were prodded towards putting their money on political change as a solution to such difficulty. In doing so, these unions diverted union energies towards politics. Such union responses, by their stress on highly general and abstract issues, tended to demobilize workers where they faced the crisis first of all, in the workplace. The ultimate irony in this course of action was, however, that it made little sense *politically*, either. If the Left had come to power in 1978, the prevailing context of economic crisis, plus the inevitable dislocations which serious structural reform would have further created, would have demanded all of the rank-and-file resourcefulness and commitment of which French unions and workers were capable, especially at workplace level. Without any doubt, the situation of the French economy following a Left victory would have forced unions towards bargaining discipline and austerity in exchange for structural reforms in whose definition workers and unions would have played some role. Yet, to the degree that preelectoral union strategy led workers to expect miracles from the Left in power, attempts by unions to persuade workers to delay gratification and behave with the kind of moderation needed to give the Left a chance to implement its program in stability (France, after all, had not had a government genuinely sympathetic to working-class problems for three decades) would have been made immeasurably more difficult. On the other hand, when the Left lost the elections, unions and workers faced a veritable onslaught of austerity and 'redeployment' from a regime and *patronat* finally freed from the restraints which a Left electoral threat had created prior to 1978. Beyond the fact that French trade-union strategy after 1974 virtually guaranteed that workers would be powerfully demoralized were the Left to lose, union neglect of rank-and-file concerns prior to the elections augured badly for any organized working-class response to such an onslaught.

Part 5

Strategic Reevaluations and the New Economic Context

The CGT, and to a lesser extent, the CFDT, had, both by choice and necessity, evolved a political strategy to confront the crisis of the mid-1970s. Rather than reevaluating economic perspectives which both confederations had elaborated *before* the enunciation of crisis, each had chosen to fit new economic evidence into these earlier frameworks of orientation. Rather than devising new labor market-centered approaches to the crisis environment, each had progressively placed more and more hope in the victory of the United Left in the March 1978 elections. As both the CGT and CFDT realized, each in its own way, after the electoral debacle of 1978, the costs of such theoretical and strategic choices had been very high. Because of their relative neglect of labor-market activity in particular, both confederations had to confront a deepening crisis and a reenergized and increasingly antilabor government from a seriously weakened position. Moreover, the ultimately divisive effects of the political bias of union strategy in the preelectoral period made unified union action in the post-electoral setting nearly impossible to promote.

The disappearance of political hopes in 1978 made certain unpleasant realities more apparent to both confederations. The crisis in its various manifestations had begun to have important effects on the structuring of the French labor market. Some aspects of this were already familiar, such as the shift of investment, and jobs, by large firms towards cheaper labor areas of the world. This, plus growing competition from newly industrializing countries in sectors such as iron and steel, shipbuilding, and textiles, had begun to create specific pockets of unemployment and demoralization in regions and amongst categories of workers which had formerly provided important support to organized labor. Accompanying such processes, domestic trends towards job reclassification, the use of temporary and part-time workers, extensive subcontracting by larger firms, the reorganization of work and the emergence of a hidden, but large, 'black' labor market—all visible from the earlier 1970s—were intensifying. The threat of what the CFDT called a *classe ouvrière éclatée* (a disaggregated working class) was a danger to unions beyond existing and potential unemployment.[79] The growing decomposition of the French labor market implied decomposition also of the predictable social base of the union movement. In the shorter run, such changes gave rise to a new particularism among parts of the existing union rank-and-file involving a desire to protect specific existing situations, whatever happened to workers more generally. This tendency in itself, if unions could not devise ways to counteract its effects, could undermine rank-and-file solidarity in ways which capital could easily exploit.

Capital itself seemed to be changing certain of its strategies in crisis in ways which deepened trade-union difficulties. The CNPF, France's most important business association, was beginning to modernize its perspectives on the social relationships of management in more 'American' ways. At the heart of such modernization was an attempt to move away from the authoritarian, class-warfare views of firm operation which had been dominant in the past, towards a more subtle, organic, human relations approach. French unions had rarely had to deal with employers who thought in terms of strategies to create social harmony on the shop floor, if one excepted paternalist approaches, which were usually authoritarian in essence. The general thrust of the new *patronal* line, however, was not to promote harmony through collective bargaining. Rather it was to set up new lines of authority and communication in the firm which *cut out* unions. The most common tactic for doing this was for management itself to take charge of plant grievance procedures through the foreman. French foremen had formerly been simple enforcers of orders from above. In the new strategy the foreman was to become a communicator between ordinary workers and management, in particular on grievance matters, which management was apparently more willing now to take seriously. To the degree to which the new line was implemented it would therefore remove, *de facto*, the grievance task from the elected *délégué du personnel*. Since the *délégué* had long served as the union's main presence on the shop floor, the unions' tenuous place within the firm would be seriously threatened.[80]

On top of all this, the electoral victory of the existing majority gave it new space to implement policies which electoral uncertainty had earlier made unwise. It wasted no time in beginning 'restructuring,' in ways which eliminated tens of thousands of jobs, along with the livelihood of several regions, in steel, shipbuilding, and textiles. Screws went down even more tightly to prevent real wages from rising. 'Reforms' of social security, education, unemployment compensation, and health insurance raised the costs of welfare schemes to individuals, reduced coverage and eliminated more jobs, these in the public sector. The costs of utilities, transportation, and other public services went up dramatically. The elimination of price controls led also to rising food and housing costs. 'Industrial redeployment' still remained obscure in government goals, however. Instead the thrust of policy seemed to be directed towards austerity, cutting 'lame ducks' loose to face the true costs of their inefficiency and, most important, raising profit levels in the hope that higher profits would eventually regenerate investment. Success was mixed into 1980. Inflation declined to just above 10 percent, unemployment continued to rise while growth did jump in 1979, until the dramatic new rise in oil prices intervened.[81] By the end of 1979, nonetheless, profits had indeed risen to the point where firms were at least paying off debts at a rapid rate, if they still seemed rather reluctant to invest in new plant.[82]

The conditions in which this electoral victory had occurred were doubly disastrous for the unions. The 'rupture' of *Union de la Gauche*, consummated in September 1977 and carried through the elections, found the CGT and CFDT on opposite sides of a very high political fence. The CGT, whose own official program was very close to that of the PCF, supported the PCF's side in its dispute with the Socialists, particularly on the critical issue of nationalizations. The CFDT, much more quietly and 'neutrally,' supported the PS. The inevitable consequence of this was that, by early 1978, CGT–CFDT unity-in-action had virtually ceased to exist, to be replaced by mutual recrimination. Beyond this, the general situation of political turmoil fostered demoralization and division *within* both confederations.[83]

The CFDT: 'Recentering' and the Crisis

The CFDT was first to react officially to the new situation.[84] *Recentrage*— 'recentering'—was the slogan summarizing this reaction. Recentering was premised on recognition of many of the profound flaws in union action which we have already discussed. Too much union energy had been deflected towards politics in the hope of a Left victory. General and abstract mobilizational activities of the 'days of action' type had diverted union attention from the growing plight of the rank-and-file facing deepening crisis. In the words of Edmond Maire to the 1979 CFDT Congress: 'Between 1974 and 1978 we 'slipped.' We found ourselves engaged in action policies which were not really in conformity with our basic strategic orientation [which was] to make conscious and massive social struggles the motor of social change. Our practice deviated in reference to our strategy.'[85] Recentering was therefore presented as a *return* to the CFDT strategy which, for various reasons, had been neglected between 1974 and 1978. In its most abstract terms, recentering called for a return to base-level efforts, to mobilization which would be articulated towards massive protest from shopfloor and branch levels upwards. Such mobilization was to be oriented towards negotiations with the *patronat* and government—recentering had a distinctly new 'contractualist' edge to it. Negotiations, in the context of crisis, were not to remain within the framework desired by employers, however. They were to seize upon the restructuring of economic life prompted by crisis to bargain both for union inputs into the shape of such restructuring and for new increments of working-class power. Here the thrust was clearly back towards the CFDT's cherished notions of intervening, through union struggle, in economic decisions both to begin changing the 'model of development' and towards building *autogestion*. Another aspect of *recentrage* was its call for an increased focus on European trade union action, mainly through the European Trade Union Confederation, as one way of coping with the new international division of labor.

As it was publicly presented, then, *recentrage* was a return to pre-1974 CFDT theory and strategy. Edmond Maire was fond of introducing the new posture by comparing May 1968 to March 1978. In May 1968, there had been an explosion of social protest which could find no political outlet in change. In March 1978 political possibilities had existed, but without the profound social mobilization from below which would have ensured their success. *Recentrage*, Maire asserted, was aimed at promoting trade union action which could bring both components together, action which would ensure a profound 'union of popular social forces' upon which sound political change could be based. In this 'reading' of recentering, the economic theory of the CFDT, updated to take account of the crisis, remained essentially the same. Changes were primarily strategic, involving a return to the promotion of base-level union struggle for workers' control, plus steadfast refusal to subordinate such struggle to politics. In particular, the CFDT would henceforth refuse to participate in the kinds of higher-level, abstract and global kinds of union mobilizations of the 'days of action' type of which the CGT was so fond.

The problem was that *recentrage* was open to interpretations other than this 'Left' variant announced by Maire. It was no secret tht *recentrage* was backed inside the Confederation by a coalition of the CFDT's most moderate and politically 'reformist' groups (if it was also backed by militant federations, such as Maire's own chemical workers, who had simply had their fill of politics) whose *autogestionnaire* rhetoric was suspect, so suspect, indeed, that the *recentrage* line barely survived a floor vote at the 1979 CFDT Congress. A 'reformist' reading of recentering, which, in the eyes of many of the policy's critics within the CFDT, conveyed its real meaning, focused on very different questions from those of Maire's 'Left' presentation of the new line. The Confederation's assertion of the need to return to labor-market action leading to new negotiations involved simply that, willingness to lower the CFDT's sights from social change to ordinary contractualism. Put in historical terms, 'reformist' recentering involved an attempt to 'roll back' the radicalizing changes of the late 1960s and early 1970s and to reestablish the *status quo ante* of 1964–5.

Reformist *recentrage*, backed by elements within the CFDT which had never been comfortable with the Confederation's conversion to socialism, was probably motivated by two central concerns. The first was a sense that new labor market-centered contractualism, without the rhetoric of basic social change, was a necessary adaptation to crisis. Given the weakness of French unions and the bleak outlook for the French economy, reformist *recentrage* was the best way to face a bad situation which looked durable. Secondly, reformist *recentrage*, involving a massive turn towards collective bargaining, might give the CFDT a new credibility at the base which the CGT, the CFDT's rival, would be unable to duplicate. This version of recentering had one important, and dubious, premise, however. To work, it needed a new willingness on the part of the French state and *patronat* to engage in serious bargaining. And while the Giscard regime lectured the French constantly about the desirability of new social consensus, and it may well have developed a longer-term grand strategy for opening to the social democratic Left in the aftermath of March 1978, the behavior of the Barre government indicated that the promotion of consensus was not to include the kind of serious bargaining which would provide enough payoffs for the CFDT to take the risk of new moderation. And the *patronat* seemed equally uninterested. Indeed, a simpler governmental and patronal strategy of little bargaining at all, with the goal of drastically minimizing union power altogether, seemed quite as plausible.

In the aftermath of March 1978, then, the CFDT seemed clear about one thing, that what had happened on the trade union front between 1974 and 1978 had been mistaken. Internally, it was anything but clear about what followed from this. In fact, there was good reason to believe that the CFDT had begun a complex, and in all likelihood prolonged, process of renegotiating its identity after the 1978 elections, carried out publicly around the actual meaning which the Confederation should attach to *recentrage*. In this process, the internal opponents of the CFDT's 1960s radicalization were uneasily allied with the proponents of a more 'social democratic' unionism against the partisans of *autogestion*. The *autogestionnaires* had CFDT tradition, and perhaps a majority of the Confederation, behind them, and for this reason the CFDT's debate tended to be cast in *autogestionnaire* vocabulary. But they had to labor against the vagueness of their own position and the fact that it had been the *autogestionnaire* option which had, after all, collapsed into the CGT-dominated overpoliticization of the mid-1970s. Their opponents, to the degree to which they advocated a retreat from the CFDT's commitment to socialist transformation, *de facto* offered major strategic and theoretical change. But, given the nature of the situation in the Confederation, they could not promote such change in any open way. As with all processes of politically negotiated organizational change, however, the main result in the short run was confusion and inconsistent behavior. What the CFDT thought and what it wanted to do were blurred, pending the outcome of internal organizational conflict. As the 1980s turned, the only constant in CFDT behavior was its vehement resistance to unity-in-action with the CGT on the CGT's terms. In terms of French union effectiveness, this resistance was undoubtedly of much greater importance than economic, theoretical, and strategic uncertainty. As we will see, however, the CFDT was not the only contributor to the unity-in-action *impasse*.

The CGT: 'Opposition Force' or 'Proposition Force' Unionism?

The CGT also emerged profoundly divided from the failure of 1978. Despite the PCF's predominant power in the CGT, the Confederation's preelection policies had caused a significant amount of internal dissent and debate at rank-and-file level. After the election the conflict spread, in unprecedented ways, to the highest level of the Confederation, its *Bureau Confédéral*. Wide-ranging strategic disagreement was then magnified in the period of preparation for the CGT's November 1978 Congress. This 40th Congress, which may have been the most open and probing in the CGT's recent history, was preceded by a no-holds-barred discussion in all CGT publications and at all levels of the organization. Thorough debate did not, however, resolve the basic questions of CGT policy which the 1974–8 period had raised. In the aftermath of the Congress internal CGT struggle around two very different perspectives was widespread. The basic issue was whether the CGT should be a trade union "proposition force" or whether it should be an 'opposition force.' Groups within the Confederation advocating a major change in the focus of CGT unionism took the first position, while those following the PCF's post-election shift away from Eurocommunism back to a modified *ouvrièrisme* took the second.

The rise of a 'proposition force' current was potentially one of the more important changes in the CGT's modern history. The premise of this rise was, of course, the inadequacy as response to crisis of the CGT's pre-March dual approach of defensive labor-market action and political mobilization.

The proposition force current believed that, rather than awaiting economic change to be delivered by the political Left, the CGT ought to become a 'proposition force' for industrial solutions in economic life itself, through struggle in the labor market and elsewhere. Rather than simply resisting crisis-induced processes of change in a defensive way, the Confederation should mobilize to propose industrial countersolutions pointing in the direction of social transformation. The inspiration for this new line was clearly the process of strategic innovation undertaken by the Italian CGIL in the earlier 1970s, in which union mobilizing power and collective bargaining were directed beyond simple wages-and-hours issues towards firm and branch investment policies, broader social reform, and state investment plans. 'Proposition force/industrial solution' unionism was meant to lead the CGT towards more direct, if conflictual, involvement in French economic decision-making, away from the Confederation's traditional hands-off policies on such matters. It would also prod the Confederation towards the acquisition of new knowledge of the exact structures and tendencies of the French economy, including its insertion in the international economy. The 'proposition force' current in the CGT primarily advocated *strategic* change for the Confederation, however. Its economic theoretical perspectives remained essentially the same as those developed by the CGT in the pre-1978 years. Independence, economic integrity, and an altered international posture were still the goals.[86]

'Proposition force/industrial solution' unionism did have profound implications for the CGT's relationship to politics, however, and, more specifically, for the CGT's relationship to the Communist Party. Up until 1978 the CGT's understanding of the likely course of social change in France delegated the implementation of such change to the political Left. In the 'proposition force' perspective important aspects of social change could occur, in a step-by-step way, from immediate trade union struggle. The 'proposition force' approach therefore implied a kind of neosyndicalism for the CGT. Indeed its advocates talked both of 'industrial solutions' and of *autogestion*—'industrial solutions' were not simply new industrial policies, but also new increments of working-class power within firms, branches, and sectors. To be sure, even in this new perspective political parties still had their assigned tasks of fighting for power and using the state to work structural reforms. Nonetheless, 'proposition force' unionism, to the extent that the CGT took it seriously, would alter the Confederation's relationships with the PCF. Whereas earlier the CGT's union postures were designed to be congruent with PCF goals in the political sphere such that the PCF was entirely responsible for implementing change, 'proposition force' unionism advocated assumption by the CGT of new responsibility, on its own, for change.

Unionists following the post-electoral line of the PCF simultaneously urged a very different, 'opposition force,' course of action on the CGT. As a result of the election failure, the PCF began to shift towards a new and rather sectarian strategic posture. The premise of this shift was an economic analysis not unlike that held by the CGT prior to 1978. The crisis was *avant tout nationale* ('above all, national') and could be attributed to specific policy choices made by the regime, at the behest of the monopolies, to pursue what the party labelled a 'strategy of decline.' While not denying the international side of the crisis, the PCF stressed what it saw as the eagerness of the regime to pursue international specialization and industrial redeployment at the expense of French workers. The major addition to the analysis as a result of the election was that the Party blamed the French Socialists for collusion in the regime's strategy.[87] What the CGT ought to do in response to the situation described in this analysis was to struggle tooth-and-nail against any and all economic decisions threatening French workers, in particular against shutdowns and cutbacks related to industrial redeployment. In this perspective it was not the CGT's job to counterpose different economic decisions to those made by the government and *patronat*, at least not in any direct way, but to use trade union mobilization to *oppose* such decisions in ways which would make their logic comprehensible to workers (indeed, as conflict between 'proposition' and 'opposition' force advocates in the CGT sharpened in 1979–80, 'proposition forcers' were increasingly labelled 'class collaborationists' and 'reformists' in the corridors of Confederal discussion). The thrust of 'opposition force' unionism was clearly political, but in ways which differed considerably from the politicization of CGT activity prior to 1978. Before 1978 the CGT had been deployed, as we have seen, in the pursuit of bread-and-butter defensive unionism in order to contribute to the success of *Union de la Gauche*. After 1978, to the degree to which the advocates of 'opposition force' unionism prevailed, the CGT was to be deployed in the labor market specifically to increase the PCF's strength and, in particular, to aid the PCF in redressing the political imbalance between it and the Socialist Party. The shift in strategy promoted by the proponents of 'opposition force' unionism was clearly reminiscent of the line of *union à la base* (union from below) urged upon the CGT by the PCF in earlier periods, most notably the Cold War, when the PCF had been either unable or unwilling to pursue a United Front politics of alliance with non-Communist forces. The ultimate purpose of the new line was to demonstrate to workers that only the PCF and CGT were capable of defending their interests. 'Reformists' were the major target. The Socialists were, of course, the major reformists in question. Unfortunately for French trade unionism, there was also strong pressure from 'opposition force' proponents to label the CFDT as 'reformist' as well, in ways which were to make unity-in-action extremely difficult to achieve.

The post-March 1978 dispute in the CGT between 'proposition' and 'opposition' force unionists was primarily a fight over trade union *strategy*. Both sides accepted the general framework of economic analysis set out earlier by the CGT. The question at issue was what to do on the basis of this analysis. 'Opposition forcers' wanted to see the CGT use its power for immediately *political* ends, while 'proposition forcers' wanted to set the CGT on a course of structural reformism through industrial mobilization. Interestingly enough, conflict between the two perspectives, particularly within the CGT *Bureau Confédéral*, involved Communists on both sides. This followed, in part, from the internal crisis in the PCF itself which followed the Party leadership's move towards a more sectarian strategy in the post-March 1978 period, plus the perceived inappropriateness of this strategy when applied to the CGT. In any case, the nature and depth of the conflict clearly belied stereotypic understandings of the CGT as completely controlled by the PCF. However, the immediate results of internal CGT conflict, like those of internal CFDT conflict, were confusion and inconsistency. In the case of the CFDT such confusion and inconsistency led towards very great organizational caution—the CFDT was generally very quiet in action terms after March 1978. In the case of the CGT, in contrast, it was trade union action itself which was confused and inconsistent.

Perhaps the best example of the results of internal CGT conflict occurred in steel. As we have noted earlier, the steel industry in France was a major victim of the crisis. Caught with huge corporate debts when demand for steel declined in the mid-1970s, major French steel firms faced bankruptcy in 1977. The government stepped in, orienting its actions in accordance with its own notions of 'industrial redeployment' and the EEC's Davignon Plan for restructuring the entire European steel sector, and ordered the steel firms to proceed to massive changes. Tens of thousands of jobs in steel were threatened, as were entire regions where steel was the major economic focus of life (the Longwy *bassin* in Lorraine and Denain in the North were the major targets).[88] For a number of internal CGT reasons, the CGT Metalworkers' Federation responded initially to the crisis plan in a 'proposition force' way. Rather than simply saying 'no' to restructuring, the Federation prepared a complex counterproposal for rebuilding the industry on different grounds without substantial employment losses.[89] The initial premise of this counterproposal was that the crisis plan, if enacted, would ultimately deprive France of basic industrial capacity which would be necessary in the future to guarantee French economic autonomy and integrity. The CGT 'memorandum' then proposed governmental action to regenerate domestic consumption of French steel through investment programs in construction, public works, industrial equipment, shipbuilding, and public transportation (in particular the truck industry). Along with this it proposed a series of measures to change work in steel—reducing the length of the work week, eliminating painful labor through technological change, changes in work organization, lowering retirement age, and introducing another shift in steel plants—which would simultaneously make steel a better place to work and preserve jobs. Finally, it demanded serious national and regional planning of diversification for steel, involving forward and backward integration of steel production into metal-finishing and raw materials processing plus stress on producing more marketable steel. Finally, the purpose of all this was to mobilize the steel rank-and-file to press for genuine negotiations with the state and employers over restructuring.

Mobilization around the CGT Metalworkers' proposals was quite successful into the early part of 1979. More important, the CGT initiative caught other actors by surprise. The CFDT, to begin with, was obliged to prepare its own 'counterplan,' which was quite similar to that of the CGT, if less demanding (the CFDT was willling to see jobs lost in steel, as long as job creation in other sectors kept pace with decline in steel).[90] The Ministry of Industry itself was caught short by this unexpected initiative and the skill with which it was executed, to the point where it had to consent to new negotiations with the unions over the government's plan, a step which had not been originally planned. In order to pressure the Ministry and the companies in steel (who were to do the actual firing), the CGT metalworkers decided to promote a 'March on Paris' in March 1979. It was at this point that 'proposition force' initiatives gave way to 'opposition force' tactics.

The steel issue, connected to the EEC via the Davignon Plan, was too good for the PCF to pass up. The party was, by March, in a run-up to the June 1979 elections to the European Assembly and had chosen to make these elections the centerpiece of its highly nationalist, anti-Socialist and anti-'strategy of decline' campaign. What happened was that 'opposition force' leaders in the CGT simply took over the organization of the 23 March demonstration. In the process the issue focus was shifted away from the CGT Metalworkers' counterproposals for the industry towards the nefarious effects of 'German and American' Europe on French workers. In addition, unity-in-action between the CGT and CFDT metalworkers was sabotaged, probably in order to be able to portray the CFDT subsequently as 'reformist' and 'European.' The major result of the CGT's shift in emphasis and the decline of CGT–CFDT unity on steel was that the Minister of Industry was able to deal with steel unions and workers at a much lower cost than might otherwise have been the case. In particular, the Minister consented to no important modifications in his steel restructuring plan. Instead he bought off opposition to the plan by offering substantial severance rewards to workers who offered to leave (about $12,000 in cash). In later contractual negotiations between the Ministry and steel unions the bargaining power of the unions was considerably weakened by the March turn of events.[91]

Strategic Confusion and Economic Perspectives

Living through profound economic crisis is not an easy thing for any trade union movement. Drastic changes in economic conditions are bound to challenge time-honored perceptions and strategies. For the CGT and CFDT, the coming of economic crisis in the mid-1970s coincided with the penultimate stage in a long political process, a process which ended in March 1978 with the defeat of the French Left at the polls. As we have stressed, this coincidence led the two confederations to postpone confronting the new challenges posed by economic crisis in the hope that the French Left would come to political power and restructure the situation through political means. In the aftermath of March 1978, hiding behind politics in the old ways was no longer possible, however. Both confederations were obliged to face the new economic realities. Their earlier detour into political mobilization had made these realities even more formidable, however. The symptoms of crisis—inflation, unemployment, labor-market restructuring—had deepened in ways which had undermined the labor-market mobilizing power of all French unions. The political defeat of the Left had further demoralized the rank-and-file. And, while both confederations were generally aware of the need to reexamine the world after March 1978, the beginnings of such reexamination divided each Confederation internally and each from the other, such that trade union unity-in-action was jeopardized. Thus as a result of important strategic misjudgments made in the mid-1970s the CGT and CFDT both faced the new economic world of the 1980s in seriously debilitated states. Union membership is as good an indicator of this as anything else. Since there is no checkoff system in France, union membership depends directly on rank-and-file enthusiasm for unions. The following figures were given to us confidentially by a source inside one of the confederations and they have to be taken with a degree of skepticism, but they are probably not too far from the truth. The CGT—which in the mid-1970s had approximately two and a half times as many members as the CFDT (2·5 vs 1 million)—lost 20–25 percent of its membership in the 1977–9 period. The CFDT stood up slightly better, losing only 12–15 percent. While the December 1979 *Prud'homme* elections indicated that both confederations maintained their relative shares of allegiance among French workers at large (the CGT declined very slightly, the CFDT increased very slightly), this loss of membership must be regarded as a serious indicator that French unionism has entered a new period of relative decline. Membership decline also represented a net financial loss to both confederations, a fact which in itself had begun to limit action prospects by the beginning of 1980.[92]

Thus if the split and defeat of the French Left in 1978 was catastrophic for the Left in ways which are well known, it was also catastrophic for the French labor movement. With membership low and declining, finances in a parlous state, and existing in an underinstitutionalized labor-market setting in which collective bargaining is precarious and brute strength, more often than not, determines outcomes, the French labor movement currently provides a very tempting target for 'union busting' or, at the very least, 'union disregarding.' New union strategies and perspectives are absolutely necessary. Yet, as we have seen, the circumstances of the post-1978 period made new solutions very hard to come by.

Not that there was a lack of suggestions for new solutions in the *strategic* realm. Two of those which we have discussed were likely only to make things worse strategically, however. 'Reformist' *recentrage* in the CFDT and 'opposition force' unionism in the CGT, as defined according to the logic of the PCF's current 'strategy of decline' analysis, were mutually repellent. Moreover, to the degree to which each Confederation chose these alternatives, as seemed to be the trend in 1980, the prospects for trade union unity-in-action, the *sine qua non* for tendencies to union decline to be reversed, would diminish precipitously as the failure of the CGT and CFDT to renew their unity agreement in the late summer of 1980 indicated. Reformist *recentrage* was, in part, designed to build CFDT strength at the expense of the CGT. 'Opposition force' positions in the CGT were designed to portray the CFDT as 'class collaborationist,' a portrayal which would become more plausible to the degree to which the CFDT actually behaved in a 'reformist' way. Left *recentrage* and 'proposition force/ industrial solution' unionism were, however, potentially complementary. Were each of these options to come out on top in current intraconfederal conflicts, CGT–CFDT unity-in-action might well be restored and new union initiatives could then follow. At the time of writing, however, such an outcome seemed unlikely. Even if it did occur, substantial barriers to union strategic success would remain. 'Proposition force' unionism—of which Left *recentrage* in the CFDT and CGT 'proposition force' groups both partake—would require union labor-market strength which French unions do not presently possess. It would also demand a major reorientation of union attitudes away from traditional 'oppositional' labor-market postures—both in the CGT and CFDT—which would not be easy to promote, especially at critical middle-organizational levels. Ultimately it would demand a drastic change in perspective from the PCF.

It ought not to have been surprising that the core of CGT and CFDT debate after March 1978 was *strategic*, rather than economic and theoretical. It was faulty strategy, after all, which set up the defeats of the mid-1970s. And only a renewal of trade union *action* could have reestablished union fortunes after 1978. There were, however, certain economic theoretical concerns embedded in each position taken in this strategic debate. In the CFDT, reformist *recentrage* implied a CFDT shift away from transformational perspectives on economic life towards a much more limited union role, accepting collective bargaining within a mixed economy. Left *recentrage*, in contrast, implied continuity with earlier CFDT economic perspectives. It sought to promote transformative change through labor-market action involving trade union intervention in economic decisions through conflict and bargaining aimed at transcending the 'capitalist model of development' and promoting *autogestion*. Were this strategic line to be genuinely tested in action, in the context of crisis, its proponents would be obliged to develop both sector-by-sector and global pictures of desirable specific economic decisions. As we have seen, the CFDT had not, of 1981, developed such pictures. 'Proposition force' elements in the CGT, while advocating an action strategy rather similar to the Left 'recenterers' in the CFDT, were strongly informed by preexisting CGT theoretical perceptions. Such perceptions placed the preservation of French economic independence and autonomy at the center of transformational goals. During the period when such views had developed, however, they had been based on the assumption that macroeconomic change, mainly through nationalizations and planning, would follow from political change. It was this assumption which CGT 'proposition forcers' challenged, in the light of March 1978. Whatever happened in the political sphere, 'proposition forcers' believed that unions should use their power to impinge on economic decisions in the shorter run through labor-market and other union mobilizations. This position implied development, on the part of the CGT, of new pictures of desirable sectoral and global changes which might be worked congruent with the Confederation's broader economic theory. In essence, the CGT 'proposition force' advocated a new division of labor between unions and politics in working change, one which implied the creation of new CGT ideas about what kinds of union interventions in economic decision-making might articulate best with desirable political changes and with the CGT's general CGT desiderata about a transformed French economy. 'Opposition force' CGT forces shared these general desiderata, but placed their strategic weight on the continuation of CGT political mobilization. Unlike 'proposition force' groups, they were unwilling to enter relationships of conflict and bargaining with the *patronat* and the state over specific economic decisions to cope with crisis-induced changes. Their goal, rather, was to *oppose* such changes, *tout court*, whatever the shorter-term economic implications of such opposition might be. Intensified nationalism and increased stress on protectionism were obvious theoretical implications of this stance, as was continuing avoidance of any participation in economic decisions short of those made by the Left in power.

Part 6

Conclusions

As the decade of the 1980s turned and economic difficulties for French workers worsened, French unions devoted more energy to attacking one another than to developing the coherent, unified, and innovative trade union responses for which the situation cried out. The CGT, for its part, opted more and more for PCF-oriented 'opposition force' unionism, stressing the promotion of hypermilitant local defensive struggles to promote the PCF's political position *vis à vis* the Socialists and disseminate the PCF's 'strategy of decline' economic analysis. 'Action,' often for its own sake and often condemned to defeat, became the CGT's clarion call. The CGT also turned, guided by the PCF's political strategy, to attacking the CFDT as 'reformist' and 'class collaborationist.' In return, the CFDT maintained a very timid labor-market posture while denouncing, ever more insistently, the CGT as politicized and Communist-dominated. In such a poisonous atmosphere unity-in-action between the two confederations, the *sine qua non* of any effective union response to deepening economic crisis, broke down in the autumn of 1980. Simultaneously, union membership, finances and mobilizing power continued to decline. The 'crisis of unionism' in France became a favorite discussion topic in the press and among many unionists themselves.

What had happened? In the most general of terms, French unions had played out, yet again, the cycle of contradictions which has plagued organized labor in France throughout much of the twentieth century. From a moment of deep division in the Cold War, major French unions had moved towards united action and increasing strength in the changing environment of the 1960s. When presented with the difficult choice of what to do with this growing strength in the 1970s, whether to direct it towards consolidating trade union power in the labor market or to divert it towards mobilization for Left political success, the unions chose the latter—more precisely, the CGT used its superior organizational power to prod the CFDT, despite itself, towards the political course. Alas, the Left political alternative for whose benefit trade union energies had been diverted to politics collapsed into disunity and defeat. This collapse left the union movement stranded. It had structured its actions to obtain political payoffs, to a large extent at the expense of possible labor-market advances. But no such payoffs were forthcoming. In addition, the partisan political squabbling which accompanied the collapse of *Union de la Gauche* worked to divide the labor movement. In itself, the political diversion strategy implied neglect of labor-market activity which, in the context of dramatically changing economic circumstances beginning in the mid-1970s, contributed to declining union strength in the labor market. Events after 1978, leading to the dissolution of CGT–CFDT unity-in-action in 1980, pushed this decline forward. Thus from a position of growing strength and effectiveness in 1970, French unions had, by 1980, moved precipitously towards renewed weakness and divisive pluralism. The cycle of contradictions of which we spoke in the introduction to this essay—division → weakness → unity-in-action → growing strength → politicization → new division—seemed, by 1980, to have run its predictable course, leaving French unions and workers in a precarious position to confront the onslaught of economic change which the 1980s were certain to bring.

Describing such a cycle does not explain it. Many of the explanations lie deep in the history of the French labor movement and industrial relations system. Divisions in French labor about the desirable scope and strategies of unionism long predate the consolidation of the consumer–capitalist order constructed following the Great Depression and World War II. The unionism which emerged from these events, whose evolution we have reviewed, was profoundly marked by such earlier divisions. Most of French organized labor agreed that French unionism should be *class* oriented, as opposed to particularistic, in its general outlook, that union activity should be directed towards the formation of a collective class identity among French workers over and above protecting the interests of specific groups in the labor force. Agreement also existed—Catholic unionism excepted—about the desirability of union action for the transcendence of the capitalist *status quo*, that unions had an important role to play in the specification of general working-class goals in the context of Left political practice to promote social change. Agreement ceased, however, when unions tried to give practical content to their class orientation and social-change goals. Here French unions and workers divided into identifiable families of opinion—families which can be labeled very schematically as 'reformist' and 'revolutionary,' tied, in the modern era, to social democracy on the one hand and communism on the other.

This complex combination of agreement on very general goals and profound disagreement on the practical definition of such goals has been a major problem for French labor in the post-World War II period. In a formal sense, open party political affiliation has been taboo for French unions since the Amiens charter of 1906. Despite this, French unions, with certain exceptions, have been central components of the French Left, broadly considered, throughout the twentieth century. And, more often than not, commitment to partisan neutrality has been ritual, with *de facto* partisanship the rule. The formula of neutrality was devised to prevent divisions between reformists and revolutionaries from undermining trade union effectiveness. In practice, however, French unions could not be abstractly committed to class interests and social change without attaching concrete meanings to such interests and to projects for change. Defining such meanings immediately exposed partisan differences. The disruptive effects on union organizational life—organizational pluralism at the top and conflict at rank-and-file level—of assorted political groups struggling to maximize their relative positions through unions, have, as a result, been a consistent source of French labor weakness.

The milieu within which French organized labor has operated in modern times has been the source of further problems. The French industrial relations system has evolved in significantly different ways from those of its advanced capitalist counterparts. In France, collective bargaining between unions and employers is underinstitutionalized and haphazard. Little in the way of a contractually sanctioned 'web of rules' exists between unions and employers. Rather than regular, predictable and legally sanctioned contract negotiations, agreements on wages and working conditions, at least in the private sector, are ordinarily the products of continuing industrial warfare. Where factors such as a tight labor market or a militant 'climate' at the base allow for trade union mobilization, concessions are forced from employers wherever, whenever, and however they can be attained. When the situation favors employers, few concessions are granted to unions at all. In the public sector there have been periodic attempts to transcend this situation and develop more regular bargaining, but the results have fallen far short of public-sector bargaining arrangements elsewhere. In France, perhaps more than anywhere else, the relative power of industrial actors, measured on a day-to-day basis, has determined the outcome of critical economic decisions about wage levels, hours and the shape of work. Perhaps because of this, French trade unions have never really established a solid operating position within the firm. Up until 1968 unions had *no* legally legitimate place in the firm. As a result they had to do all of their organizing either at great risk on the shop floor or from outside the firm (hence the importance in French unionism of geographical structures). Since then the existence of *sections syndicales*, with certain rights, has been allowed, a change which has somewhat facilitated the maintenance of organizational activities on the shop floor. Nonetheless, after 1968, as before, unions have faced severe handicaps in the firm, with active unionists facing almost certain harassment, sanctions, and intimidation from French employers, whose desire to limit union influence in the prevailing system of continual industrial power struggle has been strong. To this day major French mass production firms—Michelin and Peugeot, for example—which would be fully unionized anywhere else, pursue sophisticated and successful antiunion strategies.

Since class warfare, rather than accommodation, has remained embedded in the French industrial-relations system, it comes as no surprise that class warfare perspectives have thrived in French unionism. Devising strategies and tactics for pursuing such warfare has been a constant problem for French unions, however, given the difficult, even forbidding circumstances within which they have been forced to operate. The simultaneous existence of partisan divisions between union organizations about such strategy and tactics has further limited the capacities of unions to act in the labor market and perpetuated the union weakness which has made the French industrial-relations system a continuous class battlefield. Quite simply put, unions have never been able to force the French *patronat* to accept the legitimate presence of unions on the shop floor. And in the absence of such a legitimate presence, French employers have never been obliged to deal with unions as *interlocuteurs valables*.

Largely because of the French industrial-relations system, French unionism has acquired distinct *structural* characteristics with their own important implications for labor's ability to act.

French unions are organizationally very 'light.' There are few permanent paid officials—and these are generally found at union headquarters (national, industrial federal, or geographical/departmental), rather than at or near rank-and-file level. Grass-roots extensions of union organizations, where contact with ordinary workers is made, are energized and staffed by voluntary *militants*. Since the organizations themselves are poor financially and organizationally, they have had few material rewards to dispense to such militants. Indeed, being a visible trade union militant in France, even today, is likely to be a very costly thing: it is almost certain to close down prospects for advancement on the job and exposes the individual in question to all kinds of sanctions from employers. Thus the real cement of French unions has traditionally been the *ideological commitment* of its militants, a sense of devotion to 'the working class' often connected with political goals. This fact, in turn, has had important implications for the general nature of French unionism and industrial relations, both of which have been dramatically ideological in content compared to other societies.

The meaning of *membership* in French unions is also very different from membership in unions elsewhere. No contractually sanctioned checkoff system exists in France. This has meant that union organizations have had to solicit membership themselves on a year-to-year basis, and, furthermore, collect dues month-by-month. Thus, perhaps *the* major task of the base-level *militant* in France has been membership recruitment and dues collecting, while recruitment and dues collection have been the central occasions for face-to-face contact between rank-and-file workers and unions. These activities have, in turn, often been highly ideological. A further result of this membership structure is the financial weakness of union organizations, a major reason, in turn, for their organizational 'lightness.'

The particularities of French union outlook and structure together with the nature of France's industrial-relations system have led French unionism to a pronounced duality of focus. Since unions have been unable to achieve elementary goals in the labor market, they have understandably sought relief from politics, both through pressure on the state and from quasi-partisan activity. As a result, large numbers of questions which might, elsewhere, have become matters for collective bargaining, have been the object of politics, legislation, and state regulation in France. The length of the work week, vacation time, many aspects of job security (hiring/firing/seniority/job classifications), fringe benefits of many kinds, in addition to more ordinary matters like the minimum wage, have become direct state concerns. If there is a 'web of rules' about industrial relations in France, then it has been predominantly spun by the state. Such tendencies to 'statize' industrial questions have had important implications. One important union strategy to settle shopfloor grievances is resort to the *Inspection du Travail* rather than to contractual obligation. Union wage strategies, particularly when labor-market action has been difficult to mount, have often centered around the level of the minimum wage as a way of jacking up the entire wage bill. More generally, the involvement of the state in industrial relations, given the state's broader responsibilities as economic policy-maker, has greatly contributed to the politicization of industrial questions. The underdeveloped nature of the private sector industrial-relations system has further contributed to this. When labor-market factors have given relative strength to unions, a form of *de facto* collusion between unions and employers to push wages up has occurred, creating wage drift which has often been inflationary. In turn, this has led the state to pressure the *patronat* to limit concessions to control wage drift. This process, to the degree to which governments have appeared to be reinforcing employer resistance to union demands, has also politicized union outlooks.

All modern labor movements, of course, have developed sophisticated strategies encompassing both labor-market and political components. In France, however, political components have assumed unusual importance, and not only because of the partisan preferences of some French union organizations. Given weak organization, low labor-market coverage, weakness in the firm and employer hostility, French unions have been forced to use an unusual amount of energy in cultivating ideological and political mobilization of a systemic-general, as opposed to workplace-specific, kind. To begin with, such mobilization has been a device to pressure the state and government both to temper *patronal* intransigence and to take favorable actions through state policy. General ideological mobilization carries with it a number of possible threats to which governments may be more sensitive than specific employers. The unions' ultimate weapon, ironically, is also the unions' main day-to-day problem, the tenuously organized, unpredictable rank and file. Rank-and-file working-class explosions, of which there have been many even since World War II, can topple carefully constructed government economic policies overnight. They can also play an important role in undercutting the political authority of governments. General ideological mobilization, translated into extensive industrial conflict, has meant that the government itself has been a prime target of rank-and-file movements. The effects of this have often been to set in motion or reinforce shifts in the general political climate and electoral choice, in particular enhancing the chances of the Left while simultaneously providing important incentives for the Left to moderate the internecine conflicts which have been an important barrier to Left political success.

Looked at in comparative perspective, French unions have consistently fallen victim to a particularly complicated and destructive variant of the 'hostage to friendly political forces' dilemma which all labor movements affiliated with political groups seem to face. The usual form of this dilemma, characteristic of postwar union–party affiliations in Northern European settings where social democratic parties exist, has been the 'hostage to a friendly government' problem. In such instances, powerful, well-implanted union movements have consistently been asked by governments led by their Social Democratic allies to moderate their union activity, often to control wage drift and to renounce desired economic policy goals, in order to help the 'friendly government' in power. The 'hostage' dilemma, of course, is contained in the 'lesser evil' choice which union movements must make between moderating their behavior or risking the return of more conservative forces to power.

The 'hostage dilemma' of French unions has been very different. In France very weak unions in an underinstitutionalized industrial-relations system characterized by open class warfare have faced a 'hostage' problem whenever their own labor-market mobilizational capacities have increased beyond a certain point. At this point should the unions push forward to prod employers and the state to create a changed industrial relations system in which unions might become *interlocuteurs valables*? Or should they divert their mobilizational strength towards politics to help the partisan Left to come to power? The first choice has usually been rejected for two reasons. The very hostility of employers and of conservative political forces in power to change in industrial relations has made hope for success in the labor market slim. In addition, connections between parts of the labor movement and specific political parties have militated towards the politicization course. Given the existing labor-market situation in France, it has been plausible for French unions to calculate that scarce mobilizational energy might best be put to use to help the Left to come to power, since the Left, once in power, would almost certainly be willing to legislate change in the unions' interest. The French 'hostage' dilemma has been, therefore, that of 'hostage to a friendly opposition.' Unfortunately for French unions in recent times, this 'friendly opposition' has been unable to come to power. Moreover, given the divisions on the political Left, such a 'friendly opposition' has been prone to foundering in fissiparous ways which have, in their turn, disaggregated united union fronts and undermined union mobilizing capacities.

It would be profoundly wrong to imply, however, that French unions are inevitably condemned to live with the web of contradictions which we have described. If they have been caught in this web in recent times it is, in part, because they have made conscious decisions which led them to be caught. We must ask, therefore, *why* such decisions have been made. There are a large number of reasons, of course. One stands out, however. Throughout the postwar period the CGT has remained the most powerful French union organization. While the CGT has never been able to dictate the course of French unionism, its power has been sufficient to play a major role in shaping the options of French labor as a whole. And the CGT has been controlled since the early postwar years by the PCF. Moreover, it is crystal clear that CGT decisions were central in the political diversion of militancy which led French unions towards the 'hostage' dilemma of the 1970s. And it is quite as clear that such CGT decisions were profoundly influenced by PCF political desires.

The problem of striking an appropriate division of labor between the PCF and CGT has been chronic in the postwar period. The PCF has repeatedly attempted to use the CGT politically in ways which have contributed to general trade union disunity and/or labor-market ineffectiveness. The PCF–CGT 'transmission belt' Cold War relationship, in which the PCF overloaded the CGT with political tasks and, in consequence, undermined the Confederation's ability to defend its own supporters and construct alliances with other unions, is a case in point. After the Cold War declined in importance, it seemed as if the new, post 'transmission belt' PCF–CGT relationship struck in the 1960s—which we have elsewhere labelled 'relative autonomy'—had resolved the political overload problem. The CGT concentrated on promoting defensive, bread-and-butter union struggles in the labor market, when possible in unity with the CFDT, while the PCF worked in the political sphere to create and nurture a new United Front of the Left. As we have seen, however, with the growing prospects of success for *Union de la Gauche* in the mid-1970s, this party–union division of labor, involving struggle on separate fronts, broke down. As the 1978 elections came closer, the CGT shifted gears to emphasize trade union mobilization for political purposes, carrying the reluctant CFDT with it. This shift, urged on the CGT by the PCF, contributed, perhaps more than anything else, to the woefully inadequate responses of French organized labor to the changed economic circumstances which they faced. Worse still, despite the obviously negative results of this for the CGT, the PCF moved to reformulate its ties with the CGT after the failure of the Left in 1978 in ways—redolent of 'transmission beltism'—which seemed destined to lead to an even deeper subordination of the Confederation to PCF political goals.

Detailing the historical facts of PCF–CGT ties does not do sufficient justice to certain *theoretical* issues in question. French communism, since its inception, has maintained a *maximalist* perspective on social change, based originally on Bolshevik practice and on the Soviet turn towards 'socialism in one country.' This perspective had two dimensions. First of all, it posited that social change could only begin with a dramatic 'seizure of state power' in France. The meaning of 'seizure' has changed in PCF strategy over time—from the classic Bolshevik insurrectionary *grand soir* model towards a United Frontist notion which foresaw 'seizure' occurring through waves of radical structural reformism to dispossess capital. But the centrality of 'seizure' has remained. The second dimension has involved the geographical scope of the change following 'seizure.' Here the PCF has consistently posited that socialism could be established in France alone, implying that a socialist French political economy could survive and thrive in relative isolation from its neighbors. The CGT has shared both dimensions of the PCF's transformational vision in modern times, with important consequences for CGT behavior. Since, according to the vision, no significant social change can occur *without* 'seizure of power,' the CGT has tended to see strictly trade-unionist activity primarily as an adjunct, either immediately or in the longer run, to political action aimed towards such 'seizure.' This tendency has had two important, and paradoxical, implications. First of all, and most obviously, the CGT has often judged the political utility of trade union mobilization to be more important than its labor-market uses. Secondly, when the CGT *has* reflected seriously on what to do in the labor market, it has almost always concluded that economistic, bread-and-butter, defensive trade unionism is appropriate. While these reflections have undoubtedly followed, in important ways, the desires of the CGT's rank-and-file, they have also followed from the 'seizure' vision in which social change is the task of *politicians*, to be undertaken in the *political* sphere, and not the business of 'mass organizations' like trade unions. As a result, the CGT has consistently refused to contemplate trade union tactics aimed at achieving major reforms through trade union action. By sharing the 'socialism in one country' view with the PCF the CGT has, in its own theoretical outlooks and policy goals, demonstrated a willingness to contemplate the establishment of a 'siege economy' in France. The persistence of this willingness into recent years, during which the French economy has become ever more integrated into a very complex international division of labor, has led the CGT to hold increasingly unrealistic economic views.

The issue of PCF–CGT ties is not an abstract one. If such ties, and the economic-theoretical and action perspectives which they created, profoundly influenced French unions' strategies in the mid-1970s, leading to the difficulties of the later 1970s, they continue to be of central importance for French unions as they face the 1980s. The conflict between 'proposition force/industrial solutions' unionists and PCF-oriented 'opposition forcers' was about the future shape of such ties. In turn, the outcome of this conflict was destined to be an important factor shaping French unions' decisions about how to face deepening economic crisis in the 1980s. As the decade turned, it looked as if the PCF's 'opposition force' perspective had won. This victory pointed towards a tightening of PCF–CGT ties in the direction of reaffirmed 'transmission beltism.' In this reaffirmation the primacy of political concerns seemed clear. The PCF was seeking to deploy the CGT as a stalking horse in its struggle to reestablish political predominance in the French Left over the Socialists. Within this broader framework of political hegemony—connected to the old 'seizure of power' orthodoxy— the CGT unionism which began to emerge was completely defensive, involving militant resistance to crisis-induced industrial restructuring. Thus whatever its longer-run implications, CGT 'opposition force' unionism tended to place French labor in the position of reacting, rather than acting, in the face of the economic strategies of French capital and the state. Rather than seeking out new and innovative responses to an unprecedented situation, then, the CGT was falling back upon old, shopworn formulae.

The CFDT, for its part, further contributed to the difficulties of French unionism. Faced with a CGT determined to politicize labor action, the CFDT retreated ever more resolutely towards a reformist version of *recentrage*. Perhaps gambling on the prospect that CGT politicization would isolate the CGT among workers, CFDT leaders increasingly turned towards attacking its erstwhile colleague for serving as a PCF front. Such attacks were accompanied by a very timid labor-market stance, resembling the conformist contractualism of France's relatively weak third union confederation, *Force Ouvrière*. In essence, rather than trying to counteract growing CGT sectarianism through more energetic ecumenical tactics to reconstruct trade union unity, the CFDT seemed to perceive the new situation as one in which it might strengthen its own fortunes by exploiting disunity. As a result of the deliberate choices of both major confederations, then, trade union unity-in-action ceased to exist and French trade unionism slipped ever further into labor-market and organizational weakness. Thus despite what was an increasingly desperate objective economic situation, French unions seemed determined to act in ways which would recreate the cyclical *impasse* which had undermined their capacities to act in the 1970s.

Whatever else it may turn out to be, the contemporary economic crisis is clearly not a simple cyclical downturn in an otherwise stable and solid economic setting. Everywhere in the advanced capitalist world the economic orthodoxies which had been used to analyze economic life, and which had provided the policy suggestions for 'fine tuning' at moments of difficulty, are being questioned. Keynesian consumer capitalism has fallen upon hard times. The social treaties negotiated in the immediate postwar period—postwar settlements—which had held solid through the longest period of sustained economic growth in the history of capitalism, have everywhere come under attack. Inflation seems intractable. Vastly higher unemployment figures are coming to be regarded as inevitable. The world system of international trade moves from one trauma to another. Major aspects of the welfare state are under siege. It is, of course, too early to foretell the full extent of the crisis of advanced industrial capitalism. And we have no adequate picture of the nature and causes of this crisis. But it does seem safe to assert that the basic parameters of Western political economies are in a process of profound renegotiation. We have to look back to the upheavals of the Great Depression and World War II to find a comparable period of renegotiation.

Unions are forced to be both actors and reactors in this open-ended process of renegotiation. But they do not approach this new world *de novo*, any more than other central social agents. Everywhere a *specific kind* of unionism, that forged from the experiences of the Great Depression and the War and based essentially in the work force of mass-production industry, is being challenged by crisis. This unionism, long oriented by a customary map of the social world and based on a social movement of predictable dimensions, faces a new environment in which earlier certainties are rapidly disappearing. To take only some obvious examples, certain of the industries which had provided an important backbone to postwar unionism—iron and steel, textiles, shipbuilding, and automobiles—have been profoundly disrupted by economic change. More generally, the sociology of the labor force, upon whose continuity unions' strategies have depended, is rapidly changing. New patterns of employment, important resegmentation of labor markets, new, often internationalized, structures of capital, major new pockets of structural unemployment—all changes which makes unions' strategic calculations problematic—have emerged. Thus unions not only have to act and react in broader processes of social renegotiation due to economic change, they will, in all likelihood, have to reconstruct their own organizational identities at the same time. In short, the unionism of the postwar settlement may well be giving way to a new, post-crisis unionism whose contours are as yet unclear both to unions themselves and to outside observers.

Given the open-ended nature of such renegotiation processes, both prescriptions about, and proscriptions to, unions concerning the courses which they might follow and the problems which they will have to face are out of order. We do know, for example, that a qualitative leap forward in the internationalization of capital has been occurring, that it is one central variable in the crisis, and that it has called into question the capacities of national states to regulate their domestic economies in older, 'postwar settlement' ways. We know also that national states are everywhere turning their concerns towards policies designed to reestablish or strengthen positions of international comparative advantage. What unions should do in response to such changes is not clear, however. Should they themselves internationalize their focus? Few national union movements seem inclined in this direction. Should they accept what look to be the emerging parameters of the new situation and work towards new 'neocorporatist' arrangements to participate in nation-state oriented missions to create world-class competitive national industrial sectors? Some union movements seem to be leaning in these directions, although not yet the French. Should they accept these parameters and work, through *conflictual* participation in crisis-induced national economic restructuring, to expand trade union power towards economic democracy? Almost everywhere, including in France, new advocacy of such a strategic posture can be heard. Or should they simply stand their ground defensively and resist crisis-induced restructuring, perhaps even to the point of advocating protectionist policies in their national settings? Here again one can find advocates of such positions in France.

Thus a broad range of choices confronts French unions. But whatever option or combination of options they might desire to choose in the renegotiation of the French political economy, they must face certain prior questions before they will be able to pursue any new course. Put bluntly, they must find ways to extract themselves from the self-destructive cycle of contradictions which has bedeviled them in the postwar period. To do so, they would have to develop radically new perspectives on their own identity and action orientations. As we have noted, the decisions of French unions have been critical in the past in recreating French union problems. Their decisions in the immediate future will therefore determine whether they can avoid repeating past mistakes. As the decade of the 1980s turned however, certain new decisions had already been made in the wake of the failures of the mid-1970s. 'Opposition force' unionism on the part of the CGT, and 'reformist' *recentrage* on the part of the CFDT, promised little but renewed problems in the future. As the crisis deepened, then, it seemed that French unions, stuck in outmoded perspectives, would refuse to take their fates in their own hands, transform themselves, and confront the changing world around them in up-to-date ways. The likely alternative was, therefore, that French unions would be transformed by this new world, despite themselves and perhaps to their detriment.

Part 7

Postscript: French Unions and the Events of May–June 1981

François Mitterrand, the Socialist candidate, was elected President of France on 10 May 1981, defeating the incumbent Valéry Giscard d'Estaing handily.[93] Then, in the legislative elections called by the new President for 14 and 21 June, the Socialist Party by itself won 38 percent of the vote and, as a result of the workings of the electoral system, emerged from the runoff with an absolute majority in the new Parliament.[94] In the immediate aftermath of the legislative elections President Mitterrand invited four Communists to join his Left unity government, albeit in subordinate positions.[95] Thus almost from one day to the next the entire political situation of France changed. Up until late April 1981 it had been assumed by analysts, politicians, and most of the French people that France belonged politically to the Right–Center majority which had dominated the Fifth Republic since its inception. After 10 May a completely new political game emerged. This game had profound implications for French unions. For the first time in more than three decades they faced a government which was not anti-labor and which had a guaranteed tenure in power long enough to implement far-reaching reform. Even though, at the time of writing, the exact outlines of such reform, and its implications, were not yet clear, we could not conclude without some reflection on the meaning of the events of May–June 1981.

What made May–June 1981 occur? Three interconnected processes can be cited. First, and most important, critical segments of the French electorate rejected the policies, and particularly the economic policies, of Giscard and Raymond Barre. A great deal has recently been made of the ineluctable Rightward drift of Western electorates—based on evidence drawn from Sweden in 1976, the UK in 1979, and the USA in 1980. France in 1981 demonstrates that if there is any general trend it is not 'to the Right' but rather towards the rejection of governments which have failed in coping with the contemporary economic crisis, whether the methods used were Keynesian/Social Democratic or 'neoconservative.'

The Giscard–Barre policies qualified, in fact, as the first 'neoconservative' responses to crisis to be implemented anywhere. Their shortrun goal was to promote exports and French international solvency at the expense of expansion in the domestic market. This choice was part of a longer-term strategy of increasing the profits, and, if all went well, the investments, of those sectors of French capital which were in a position to make new breakthroughs in the international market. Corollaries of this strategy were lowered growth, high unemployment, and a willingness to allow a significant amount of foreign control over French economic destinies through the further insertion of France in the complex international division of labor.

After five years, the results of such policies were mixed. Exports were maintained, the franc held solid, reserves remained adequate and (excepting the period following the second oil shock of 1979–80) the balance of payments was manageable. Other indicators were less satisfactory. Profits went up, but investment in France did not follow. Growth stuck at mediocre levels which did not allow any significant reflation of the domestic market. Inflation proved intractable, never falling below 10–12 percent and flashing upwards at the slightest provocation. Unemployment continued to rise, to nearly two million in 1980 (almost 8 percent). Record numbers of plant closings and bankruptcies occurred, making it obvious to everyone that much of this unemployment was structural—jobs were being lost which might never be replaced. Everything considered, the balance sheet of the Giscard–Barre stewardship over the French economy went a long way towards explaining the sudden turn of events of 1981. The French electorate had been told over and over again that the government's policies were the only conceivable way to face international crisis, that austerity and sacrifice were necessary to ensure felicity in the future. Yet, even after the French had undergone a great deal of austerity and sacrifice, crisis persisted. Given a choice in 1981 to register their opinions about what appeared to be both a painful and unsuccessful policy course, French voters—or at least the critical middle strata voters whose shift Leftwards made the difference —voted to try something new.

The second process contributing to the sea-change in French politics of 1981 was growing division in the Right–Center majority itself between the partisans of Giscard and those of neo-Gaullist Jacques Chirac. Undoubtedly disagreements about economic policies were central to such divisions. The 'deindustrializing' sides of Giscard–Barre policies plus the apparent willingness of Giscard to sacrifice French economic integrity in the interests of advancing French multinationals in the world market were direct affronts to what remained of Gaullist nationalism. Fears about the disintegrative social effects of high unemployment were also important. Superimposed upon such things was a bitter struggle between political clans. After coming to power in 1974 Giscard had moved to dispossess Gaullists from key positions in the state apparatus and had attempted to establish his own political party to compete for hegemony over the existing majority. The Presidential election of 1981 came after two years of deepening conflict between different segments of the majority, during which the Gaullists had often threatened to vote down Barre's government in Parliament (although they had never done so). The acrimony which Jacques Chirac expressed in the primary round of the election demonstrated how deep intramajority ill-feeling had gone. In effect, in May 1981 the Gaullists and the social groups which backed them faced an ominous decision. The reelection of Giscard for another seven years would, in all likelihood, have meant the destruction of any future chances for Gaullist hegemony over the Right–Center, and, quite possibly, the ultimate destruction of the Gaullists as a force. Jacques Chirac therefore chose to withhold full Gaullist support from Giscard in the Presidential runoff. A substantial number of Gaullist electors (15 percent) voted instead for

Mitterrand, while an equal number abstained. Giscard lost, of course, but it is unlikely that Chirac and his *état-major* had predicted the full consequences of the event. Instead they probably theorized that a Mitterrand victory would be neutralized by the perpetuation of a Right–Center parliamentary majority (whose leader M. Chirac would become). In this they dramatically failed to foresee the 'dam bursting' phenomena which followed 10 May.

The third process which underlay the events of May–June was that which caused the drastic electoral decline of the PCF. The primary campaign for President was as marked by bitter division on the Left as on the Right, with PCF candidate Georges Marchais attacking François Mitterrand as a 'reformist' whose ambitions were to 'manage the capitalist crisis' and who belonged to a 'gang of three' composed of Mitterrand, Giscard, and Chirac. In the 26 April primary, however, Marchais obtained only 15 percent of the vote, compared to 27 percent for Mitterrand, a decline of more than 25 percent from recent PCF electoral scores (20–21 percent in 1978 and 1979). The effect of this Communist decline was electrifying. With the Socialists tremendously strengthened, the Communists weakened and perhaps moving towards marginality, middle-of-the-road voters could vote Mitterrand and Socialist without much fear that the Socialists in power would be beholden to the Communists. As a result the last, and often best, defense of the Right–Center against a Left victory, anti-Communist hysteria, lost its utility.

Why had such a dramatic shift in the balance of power between the PCF and PS occurred? The two major parties of the Left began an extremely complex process of gambling when they decided to unify their forces after 1972 with the signature of the Common Program. Both foresaw Left unity leading to a Left majority and Left electoral victory. But each bet that new growth in support for the Left would work to its own advantage and lead to a power balance within the Left alliance in its favor. The PCF reasoned that because it was the most powerful party on the Left at the outset of Left unity, because it had been the earliest and most ardent advocate of Left unity, and because it was willing to change itself within certain limits to expand its appeal, that *it* would benefit primarily from the accretion of new support for the Left. The Socialists, in contrast, reasoned that were they to rejuvenate their party to appeal to Leftward shifting parts of the new middle strata and develop tactics to gather up working-class votes they could construct a cross-class electoral alliance which would allow *them* to reap the benefits of *Union de la Gauche*.

In this the Socialists turned out to be correct, for by the mid-1970s it was clear that the balance of new support for the Left was going to the PS. The reasons why it was able to appeal to 'new middle class' elements were clear. French socialism had always been a middle-class phenomenon. Moreover, the Party's attempts to reformulate the identity and scope of French socialism in the 1969–71 period proved remarkably skillful at tapping the rebellious sentiments of May–June 1968 and at opening up the new PS to penetration by the generation of new middle-class radicals revealed by the 1968 crisis. The reasons why the PS proved ultimately successful at acquiring a degree of working-class electoral support were more complicated. François Mitterrand, the architect of the PS' Left unity option, firmly believed that the party had to face resolutely Leftwards both in program and rhetoric in order to accomplish the complex task of appealing both to middle strata and workers. The Party's signature of the Common Program in 1972 was meant to demonstrate this Leftward stance. Mitterrand theorized that as long as the PS lacked credibility on the Left as a genuine agent for change it would be vulnerable to criticism from the PCF and unable to penetrate the working-class electorate. Thus as *Union de la Gauche* became consecrated as a serious alternative to the Right–Center majority, the Socialists began to win new credentials as a party of change. Then, when, with the accretion of new voting strength from new middle strata, the Socialists began to redress the balance of forces on the Left and appear as the more powerful party in the Left alliance, it began to sap the PCF's own working-class base, gathering up 'protest' voters whose allegiance was less to the PCF than to the idea of Left purity.

These trends had become quite clear by 1977–8. The Left was about to become an electoral majority in the country, while the PS was taking the lion's share of new electoral support for the Left due to the success of its cross-class appeal. In response the PCF shifted its own tactics in ways which, ironically, furthered the PS' goals. In essence, the PCF decided that rebalancing forces on the Left was more important to it than a Left victory which would allow the Socialists to dictate policy in government. Thus the PCF broke off Left unity and changed its own course towards sectarian *ouvrièrisme*. The purpose of this shift—which we have already discussed in its trade union manifestations—was to demonstrate to workers that only the PCF had their interests at heart. This demonstration, plus the PCF's exaggerated polemics against the Socialists for their alleged 'Right turn,' was designed to deprive the PS of its Left credibility. Were the PCF able to stabilize its own working-class support by such tactics, the Party leadership thought, the Socialists' cross-class, catch-all scenario would be stymied. This, in time, would force the PS into a real 'Right turn' either towards compromise with Giscard or towards new Centrist moderation. Either choice would have played into the PCF's hands. The rupture of 1977–8, and Georges Marchais' 1980–1 Presidential campaign were both parts of this 'scorched earth' Communist strategy.

The Socialists blinked, but only momentarily, in the face of this Communist onslaught.[96] After reflection, the PS decided to hold its strategic course through the 1981 Presidential elections, reasoning that, since the Socialist candidate was likely to make it through to the runoff round, the PCF would ultimately face a dead end. If the Communists failed to deprive the Socialists of their Left cachet through sectarian *ouvrièrisme* before the electoral campaign, they would face a choice between sabotaging the Socialist candidate's chances openly in the runoff, or of supporting the Socialist, despite itself. In fact, the PCF's 'go it alone' line failed badly. The major reason for this was that critical segments of the French electorate really wanted change (a desire which the PCF, in the years of *Union de la Gauche*, had done much to foster) and would not be deterred by PCF attempts to block such change if it were led by Socialists.

The Socialists' first months in power proved very clearly that they were not the Northern European Social Democrats which PCF propaganda had portrayed. Very quickly they moved towards major reforms which dramatically recast French approaches to crisis, in ways which were of great potential importance to French unions. Indirectly, the new regime's civil libertarianism and its desire to decentralize French political life were significant to unions, because they promised new union rights and points of access to decision-makers. But it was the new regime's approach to economic policy which was of greatest salience for the unions.

One dimension of this policy was classically 'reformist.' The new Socialist government immediately announced that it would act to stop any further rise in unemployment, in part by giving a mild Keynesian push to domestic demand. It raised the minimum wage, increased certain social welfare benefits (family allowances in particular), created several tens of thousands of new public sector jobs, extended Giscard's youth employment programs (the *pactes d'emploi*), and, perhaps most importantly, gathered up a large number of dossiers on bankrupt or about-to-be-bankrupt firms which might be subsidized or otherwise prevented from closing their doors. This new Keynesianism, however, was quite moderate, designed primarily to stop the coming of new unemployment and, very mildly, to stimulate growth (by about 1 percent in 1981–2). Moreover it was announced in a language which stressed 'rigor' and 'responsibility' by a Minister of Finance, Jacques Delors, who was to be taken at his word.

On top of such mild Keynesianism, however, the Socialists moved very rapidly to nationalize the financial and industrial groups which they had pledged to nationalize in their election manifesto. And here it was that they departed from ordinary reformist paths. France already possessed a public sector comparable to most of those existing in the rest of Europe— including much of commercial banking, public services and utilities, and a few industrial concerns confiscated from collaborators after World War II (Renault, parts of the aviation industry). Throughout the postwar settlement years, of course, this public sector had constituted the public side of the mixed economy upon which the French postwar boom had been constructed. In 1981, however, the Socialists moved to change the mix in the mixed economy, reaching beyond traditional public sector areas to bring a number of major, and profitable, private-sector industrial groups under public control. Eleven industrial concerns were targetted. In armaments Dassault and Matra were taken over. The only real 'lame duck' on the list, iron and steel (which was already owned *de facto* by the state), was next. After iron and steel were five successful oligopolistic conglomerates —CGE (French General Electric), Péchiney–Ugine–Kuhlman (metals), Rhône–Poulenc (France's largest chemical firm), St. Gobain–Pont-à–Mousson (glass/metals) and Thompson–Brandt (Europe's third largest electronics group). Another cluster of firms, where foreign capital held major shares, were scheduled for slower nationalization after negotiations with their foreign owners. These included CII–Honeywell–Bull (computers), ITT France and Roussel–Uclaf (chemicals/pharmaceuticals).

Such an expansion of public ownership into the core of profitable private activity was enough, in itself, to distinguish French Socialist policy from that of the PS' Northern European colleagues—indeed from any other political formation in advanced capitalism. What was most intriguing about this unprecedented step was, however, the way in which the Socialist leaders presented it. There was little or no 'revolutionary' or transformative rhetoric in the new government's propositions. Indeed, nothing was clearer than that the Socialists did not consider themselves to be revolutionaries, initiating a rupture with capitalism. Rather they said they were reformists, interested above all in jobs, growth, a just distribution of resources, and improving prospects for French economic success. They clearly had a Welfare State–Keynesian vision of what social justice was. But the bottom line for them was employment and growth. Without employment and growth, social justice was impossible. Pierre Mauroy's remarks as he introduced the nationalization program to parliament were indicative:

> The central objective of our industrial policy is simple. It seeks to create conditions for regenerating investment . . . for there cannot be a prosperous economy without powerful industry [and] no powerful industry without an investment and research effort.
> We want the State, through nationalizations, to acquire control over those industrial 'poles' which appear to us to provide the key to a dynamic investment and employment policy.[97]

The basic policy options of the Socialists represented, then, a 'third way' strategy in crisis. The 'return to the free market' school—of which Giscard–Barre policies partook—advocated remedies to solve the profits squeeze-investment problems which would grant private capital every conceivable opportunity to increase profits, even if this meant a return to certain pre-Great Depression policies and social arrangements (which it did under Thatcher in the UK). The second position was classically Social Democratic. Here the problems were diagnosed in similar terms—a profits–investment squeeze—but the proposed remedies were different. Workers, rather than being beaten down by market forces, were asked to accept some form of open or *de facto* corporatism (incomes policies and the like) in order to allow profitability and investment to regenerate.

The 'French road' announced by the Socialists' early measures, was different. Here the new government sought to endow the French state, through nationalizations, with new policy tools to regenerate the investment and technological change needed to bring France out of crisis while preserving democracy and social justice. Underlying this was a unique analysis. The Socialists agreed that France could only move out of crisis by regenerating investment and economic activity in ways which would enhance its international competitive position—the international logic of the crisis did not escape them and they refused to extract or unduly shield the French economy from its harsh international environment. Yet, the PS had concluded, French capital, even with the ample aid furnished to it by the Gaullist–Giscardian regime, had proven completely unequal to the tasks at hand. Moreover, under Giscard, it had proven itself quite unwilling even to try without inflicting intolerable social costs on French society. Further, one major consequence of its trying had been growing deindustrialization: French capital, on its own, could not make it internationally without undermining the basic integrity of the French economy and abandoning much of the French domestic market. The Socialists concluded from this that new nationalizations were necessary in the name of national economic rationality. To the Socialists there existed a clear contradiction between the goals of major sectors of French capital in crisis and the overall success of the French economy. Big French capital was, quite simply, no longer capable of national economic rationality. There was a certain nationalist/Gaullist ring to this. There was more than a bit of Colbertism in it as well. Nationalizations were not primarily to empower 'the people' or 'the workers.' Rather they were to enhance France's international economic position and to 'reconquer the domestic market.'

What did all of this signify for French unions? At time of writing— summer 1981—only speculation was possible. It is, of course, essential to note that the union movement had virtually no role in making the events of May–June 1981 occur. As of 10 May 1981, the state of the unions was as we described it in the preceding essay—division, acrimony, strategic conflict both within and between unions, declining resources and mobilizational capacities, and weakness. In their different ways both the CGT and the CFDT had behaved in the 1970s so as to abdicate any central agency in change. This meant, of course, that the new regime had few obligations to the unions. Rather than shaping its policies to take account of long-standing union demands, it was free to devise policies to shape—or reshape —the union movement itself.

Much in what the Socialists initially did did coincide with what the unions had said they wanted in the 1970s. Pumping up domestic demand, raising the minimum wage, creating public sector jobs and the like had long figured in union proposals to 'relaunch' the economy by 'relaunching domestic consumption.' The regime's proposal to reduce the length of the working week, ultimately to 35 hours, was a cherished union proposal as well (indeed, negotiations began towards this end immediately after the elections were over), as was lowering the retirement age. The government's promises to expand industrial democracy, trade union rights and union prerogatives in the public sector—old and new—were also long-standing union demands. Moreover, the government's leaders pledged to promote serious collective bargaining in France, a step which would also have to involve increased union power at firm level, a pledge which was made more credible by the presence of Jacques Delors at the Ministry of Finance (Delors having been the architect of the *Nouvelle Société* program, the last attempt to encourage serious collective-bargaining innovations in France). In all of this there existed the possibility of a vastly changed industrial relations system in France, where unions, armed with new shopfloor rights and privileges, would become *interlocuteurs valables* in real, regularized negotiations. There also existed possibilities for greatly increased industrial democracy. Needless to say either development, or both, would dramatically alter the environment within which French unions lived.

Given the freedom which the new regime initially had to define developments in the union movement through its policies, it was quite possible that the Socialists might try to use their power to alter the balance of forces between unions, probably to favor the CFDT at the expense of the CGT. Such an attempt would be quite consistent with parallel PS strategy to weaken the PCF: with the PCF in at least short-run decline as an electoral force, its major remaining asset was its control over the CGT. The Socialists would be foolish indeed not to attempt, through astute policy design, to undermine this asset. At the point when Socialist victory intervened, the CGT was deeply compromised in the PCF's post-1978 sectarianism, as declining CGT votes in professional elections in the spring of 1981 indicated. Were the new regime to use its resources in ways which did favor the CFDT, a breakthrough in CFDT power was not inconceivable. For this to occur, the CFDT would have to behave intelligently and the CGT foolishly.

CFDT *recentrage*, with its renewed stress on contractualism, put the Confederation in at least the right frame of mind to work with a regime which believed in expanding contractualism. Moreover the movement of several high CFDT officials into government posts indicated that lines of communication did exist between the regime and the CFDT which were absent between the regime and the CGT.[98] For the CGT, acting foolishly would involve engaging in oppositional posturing in the face of progressive new attempts to change the French industrial relations system. Were the new regime to prove willing to grant real institutional and material concessions to unions—which seemed likely—while the CGT stood aloof and denounced these concessions as 'reformism' or 'class collaboration', the field would be open for the 'recentered' CFDT. While it is *a priori* difficult to understand how the CGT could be so inflexible, evidence existed at the time of writing that currents favoring such oppositional posturing were quite strong in both the PCF and CGT.

Thus the events of May–June 1981 brought with them the possibility of the first substantial changes in French industrial relations in decades. They also brought with them, in an interconnected way, the possibility of a rebalancing of forces in the French union movement in ways which might undermine PCF power over labor. The great freedom of action which the new regime possessed towards the industrial relations system and the union movement faced a limit of time, of course. Much depended upon the success of the regime's economic policies in combating crisis. But everyone knew that there were no quick fixes, that the regime's longer-term goals would take years to bear fruit. Probably sooner rather than later the regime would need, and ask for, more formal trade union cooperation in maintaining economic stability through some form of corporatist agreement. At this point what it would be willing to offer the unions in exchange would become critical, especially in determining the balance between the CFDT and CGT. We cannot anticipate on events, however. It is enough to note that the accession to power of the Socialists in 1981 granted the PS the resources and the space to make more change in industrial relations, in the shape of the union movement and in the dynamic of class relations in France than any alliance of the Left has ever before had. Much of what we describe earlier in this chapter is likely to be challenged and reshaped. Perhaps French unions will be rescued from outside from the consequences of their mistakes in the 1970s.

Notes and References

1   In English, for the CGT in this period, see George Ross, *Workers and Communists in France* (Berkeley, Cal.: University of California Press, 1981), Chapters 1–3. In French see René Mouriaux, *La CGT* (Paris: Seuil, 1981).

2   On French Catholic unionism see Gérard Adam, *La CFTC* (Paris: Armand Colin, 1964). See also Stephen Bornstein, *From Social Christianity to Left Socialism: The Itinerary of the Catholic Labor Movement in France* (Cambridge, Mass.: Ph.D. dissertation, Harvard University, 1979).

3   See Ross, op. cit., chapter 2. On the PCF and CGT and their wartime goals, see Stéphane Courtois, *Le PCF pendant la guerre* (Paris: Ramsay, 1979) and Philippe Robrieux, *Histoire intérieure du PCF*, Vol. 1, (Paris: Fayard, 1980). The official policies of the CGT are well laid out in the collection of articles by Benoît Frachon, CGT Secretary-General, *Au Rhythme des jours*, Vol. 1 (Paris: Ed. Sociales, 1967). Texts of important intra-union documents are to be found in the Appendices of Jacques Capdevielle and René Mouriaux, *Les Syndicats ouvriers en France*, 2nd edition (Paris: Armand Colin, 1973). On broader issues of the period see Georges Lefranc, *Les Expériences syndicales en France de 1939 à 1950* (Paris: Payot, 1950), the same author's much later *Le Mouvement syndical en France, de la Libération aux évènements de mai–juin 1968* (Paris: PUF, 1969). In English see Henry Ehrmann, *French Labor from Popular Front to Liberation* (New York: OUP, 1947) and Val Lorwin, *The French Labor Movement* (Cambridge, Mass.: Harvard University Press, 1954). General treatises on French unionism worth referring to are Guy Caire, *Les Syndicats ouvriers* (Paris: PUF, 1978) and Jean-Daniel Reynaud, *Les Syndicats en France*, 2nd edition, two volumes (Paris: Seuil, 1975).

4   See, for union action in this period Jean-Louis Guglielmi and Michelle Perrot, *Salaires et revendications sociales en France, 1944–52* (Paris: Centre d'Etudes Economiques, 1954), also André Tiano and Michel Rocard, *L'Expérience française du syndicalisme ouvrier* (Paris: Editions Ouvrières, 1956).

5   Interestingly enough this was one major accusation leveled both at the PCF and the PCI at the founding meeting of the Cominform in October 1947, see Lilly Marcou, *Le Kominform* (Paris: Armand Colin, 1977), chapter 2.

6   See Ross, op. cit. chapter 3. On *Force Ouvrière* see Alain Bergougnioux, *Force Ouvrière* (Paris: Seuil, 1978).

7   The modern French industrial relations system which resulted is perhaps best described in François Sellier, *Stratégie de la lutte sociale* (Paris: Editions Ouvrières, 1961). See also Gérard Adam and Jean-Daniel Reynaud, *La Négociation collective en France* (Paris: Editions Ouvrières, 1972), Jean-Daniel Reynaud, *Les Syndicats, les patrons et l'état* (Paris: Ed. Ouvrières, 1979), Janice McCormack, *The Role of Collective Bargaining in French Industrial Relations* (Cambridge, Mass.: Ph.D. dissertation, Harvard University, 1979).

8   Here see Henry Ehrmann, *Organized Business in France* (Princeton, NJ: Princeton UP, 1957), p. 439 et seq., also Bernard Brizay, *Le Patronat* (Paris: Seuil, 1975).

9   Here we are, of course, referring to the interesting renaissance in political science of the concept of corporatism. See Philippe C. Schmitter and Gerhard Lehmbruch, eds. *Trends Towards Corporatist Intermediation* (Beverly Hills, Cal.: Sage, 1979).

10   There is a huge literature on planning and French economic development. Perhaps the best introduction in English is still Stephen S. Cohen, *Modern Capitalist Planning: The French Model* (Cambridge, Mass.: Harvard UP, 1969).

11   For the original texts of Maurice Thorez' 'pauperization' articles, see Maurice Thorez, *La Paupérisation des travailleurs français* (Paris: Editions Sociales, 1961). For the CGT, see the *compte rendu in extenso* of the 1955 *Congrès Confédéral*, especially the introductory report of Benoit Frachon, p. 44 ff., and the new Action Program, pp. 397–411.

12   For a broader discussion of PCF–CGT relationships see George Ross, 'The PCF and CGT . . .' in Donald L. M. Blackmer and Sidney Tarrow, *French and Italian Communism* (Princeton, NJ: Princeton UP, 1975).

13   This shift from a 'transmission belt' to a 'relatively autonomous' party–union relationship

is difficult to describe abstractly. From 1944 until the later 1950s 'transmission beltism' meant that the CGT's trade union activities were directly subordinated to the PCF's political goals such that union activity in the labor market was submitted, to the extent possible, to the direct rhythms of politics as defined by the PCF in its day-to-day political activity. With the shift to 'relative autonomy' the CGT gained some new room to maneuver as a trade union. It was henceforth given new space to decide upon its course of action after due consideration of the various strategic possibilities which were discernable from the climate in the labor market itself. Only after some reflection on the range of possibilities available did the Confederation leadership then seek out that strategy most compatible with PCF political goals. The CGT's shift to 'relative autonomy' first became apparent at its 1955 Congress, but was not fully implemented until the early 1960s.

14 On Gaullist strategy in English see Cohen, *Modern Capitalist Planning*, Volkmar Lauber 'The Gaullist Model of Economic Modernization,' and Bela Belassa 'The French Economy in the Fifth Republic, 1958–1978,' in William Andrews and Stanley Hoffmann, eds. *The Fifth Republic at Twenty*, unabridged hardback edition (Albany, NY: SUNY Press, 1981). In French see Alain Cotta, *La France et l'impératif mondial* (Paris: PUF, 1978) pp. 154 et seq, and Christian Stoffaës, *La Grande menace industrielle* (Paris: Calmann Lévy, 1978), chapter 3.

15 Here see Suzanne Berger, 'Lame ducks and national champions: industrial policy in the Fifth Republic,' in Andrews and Hoffmann eds., op. cit.

16 Change in the CFTC–CFDT is the subject of Bornstein, op. cit. See also Gérard Adam., 'De la CFTC à la CFDT,' in *Revue Française de Science Politique*, No. 1, 1965 and René Mouriaux, *Document du travail sur la CFDT*, Paris: Centre d'Etudes de la Vie Politique Française, 1978.

17 Perhaps the most accessible and interesting general review of trade union events in this *belle époque* of modern French labor is by a CFDT researcher, Michel Branciard, in his *Société française luttes de classes*, Vol. 3, 1967–77 (Lyon: Chronique Sociale de France, 1977). See also Jean Bron, *Histoire du mouvement ouvrier français*, Vol. 3, *La Lutte des classes aujourd'hui, 1950–1972* (Paris: Editions Ouvrières, 1974), and Ross, op. cit., chapters 6–8.

18 For the text of the accord and commentary on its origins, see Benoît Frachon, *Au Rythme des jours* (Paris: Editions Sociales, 1969), p. 498, and Branciard, *Société Française*, Vol. 3, p. 262.

19 The reader will note that we have ceased discussing *Force Ouvrière* in any detail. The reason for this is that by the mid-1960s the CGT and CFDT had become the central trade union actors in France, while FO pursued a very different and subsidiary course. The CGT–CFDT accord resulted in the self-exile of FO from the mainstream of French unionism. FO refused to collaborate in any official way with the CGT, which meant that no official FO cooperation with the CGT–CFDT alliance was possible. From this point onwards, then, FO became a professional contract signer. This choice stemmed in large part from the strategic options of both the CGT and the CFDT. Neither were eager contract signers and both were more concerned with promoting maximum mobilization for the best settlement. In such a context—once again the effects of trade union pluralism were demonstrated—FO proved willing to step in earlier than the other two to sign contractual agreements with employers, in the hope that FO would thereby gain some of the credit for union struggles which had essentially been promoted by the CGT and/or the CFDT. This was especially the case in the public sector and in public services within this sector, where FO's base was primarily located. During the period of rising militancy, from 1965 to 1973, this FO strategy to stake out a monopoly claim to union moderation did not work terribly well except to give employers and the state a bargaining edge which they might not otherwise have had. Afterwards, in the difficult mid-1970s, it seemed to be more successful.

20 The literature on the May–June strikes is immense. In English, see Ross, op. cit., chapter 7. In French, the most systematic review is to be found in Pierre Dubois *et al.*, *Grèves revendicatives ou politiques?* (Paris: Anthropos, 1971). See also *Le Peuple* 15 mai–15 juin 1968, for the CGT's review of the strikes. Both Eugène Descamps, Secretary-General of the CFDT and Georges Séguy, his CGT counterpart, subsequently published memoirs reviewing May–June. See Eugène Descamps, *Militer* (Paris: Stock, 1971) and George Séguy, *Le Mai de la CGT* (Paris: Julliard, 1972). For a good general review of the entire May–June crisis, see Lucien Rioux and René Backmann, *L'Explosion de mai* (Paris: Laffont, 1968).

21 On strikes in the early 1970s, especially CFDT-led actions, see Claude Durand and Pierre Dubois, *La Grève* (Paris: FNSP, 1975), a systematic review of 1971 strikes, Jacques Capdevielle et al., *La Grève au Joint Français* (Paris: Armand Colin, 1975), Danièle Kergoat, *Bulledor* (Paris: Seuil, 1975), Pierre Dubois, Claude Durand, Sabine Erbès-Séguin, 'The contradictions of French Trade Unionism,' in Colin Crouch and Alessandro Pizzorno eds. *The Resurgence of Class Conflict in Western Europe Since 1968*, Vol. 1 (London: Macmillan, 1978). Bornstein, op. cit., p. 215 ff., is especially good on this period.

22 See Pierre Dubois, *Mort de l'état patron* (Paris: Editions Ouvrières, 1974), Pierre Dubois, 'Stratégie syndicale et négociations salariales dans le secteur public,' *Economie et Humanisme*, March–April, 1973, and George Ross, 'Gaullism and organized labor: two decades of failure,' in Andrews and Hoffmann, op. cit.

23 Strike statistics—individual days lost—for the Fifth Republic until the crisis (1974), taken from *Statistiques du Travail*, France, Ministère du Travail et de la Particpation, Supplément 55, 1978:

Year	Days Lost (millions/year)	
1959	1,938	
1960	1,070	
1961	2,601	
1962	1,901	
1963	5,991	(Year of the miners' strike)
1964	2,497	
1965	979	(Year of Giscard Stabilization Plan)
1966	2,523	
1967	4,203	
1968	150,000	
1969	2,223	
1970	1,742	
1971	4,388	
1972	3,755	
1973	3,915	
1974	3,380	

CGT Membership, as reported at each CGT Congress beginning in 1961:

Year	Membership
1961	1,602,322
1963	1,722,294
1965	1,939,318
1967	1,942,523
1969	2,301,543
1972	2,333,056

From this date onwards, CGT membership first stagnates, then begins to decline. The CFDT membership followed a similar curve, if it rose a bit more rapidly in the 1960s and declined more slowly in the 1970s. At the beginning of the 1960s the CFTC–CFDT was about 1/3 the size of the CGT. By the early 1970s the ratio was about 1 to 2½.

24 See Crouch and Pizzorno, op. cit., two volumes.

25 The PCF first decided to shift to a modified United Frontism in 1962–3, in the aftermath of the Algerian War. Quite astutely, the party leadership foresaw the consolidation of a polarized party system in the new Fifth Republic, in which a Right–Center majority would crystallize around General de Gaulle, leaving the Socialists without access to power except through Left Unity with the Communists. Because the new Republic promised new success, the PCF began to tidy up its image to turn itself into a more palatable ally, jettisoning some of its more rigid Stalinist doctrinal legacies in the 1960s and 1970s. On this process, in English, see Jane Jenson and George Ross, 'The PCF and the Uncharted Waters of DeStalinization,' in *Politics and Society*, volume 9, no. 3. In French see Philippe Robrieux, *Histoire intérieure du PCF*, Vol. 2 (Paris: Fayard, 1981) and, for the latest in PCF interpretations, Roger Bourderon *et al.*, *Le PCF, étapes et*

problèmes (Paris: Editions Sociales, 1981), especially chapters 9 and 10, by Bourderon and Jean Burles, respectively.

26 *CGT Congrès Confédéral*, compte rendu *in extenso* du 37e Congrès de la CGT, Vitry-sur-Seine, 1969, p. 50.

27 For a full exposition of the PCF's variant of State Monopoly Capitalist theory see PCF, *Traité d'économie politique (le capitalisme monopoliste d'état)* two volumes (Paris: Editions Sociales, 1972).

28 CGT 1969 Congress, pp. 473–481.

29 For the specific list, see CGT 1969 Congress, p. 471.

30 Bornstein, in his dissertation and in an article, 'The CFDT and economic policy, changing perspectives,' in the *Council for European Studies Newsletter*, March–April 1978, asserts that in the 1964–6 period the CFDT was a ripe candidate for corporatist cooptation, had the regime been willing and able to take the proper initiatives. I doubt this, since the CFDT at the time was weak and divided organizationally and would have been unable to withstand the CGT onslaught upon it which would have followed. As a counterfactual exercise, however, Bornstein's notion has the merits of underlining the flaws in the Gaullist regime's approach to social issues.

31 *CFDT Syndicalisme-Hebdo*, 'Le Débat CFDT–CGT, pour un socialisme démocratique,' No. 1366, 1971, pp. 4–5.

32 In the early 1970s the CGT and CFDT had an extended public confrontation on the nature of socialism desired by each organization and the kinds of trade unionism necessary to lead to this new socialist society. See Henri Krasucki, *Syndicats et socialisme* (Paris: Editions Sociales, 1972), and Edmond Maire in *CFDT Syndicalisme-Hebdo*, 15 May 1973, for the best summaries of the discussion.

33 OECD, *Perspectives Economiques*, 24 December 1978, p. 140.

34 See Stoffaës, op. cit., p. 204.

35 ibid., pp. 204–205.

36 ibid., p. 205.

37 Cotta, op. cit., p. 128.

38 ibid., pp. 128–143, Stoffaës, *Grande Menace*, pp. 208–211.

39 Cotta, *L'Impératif mondial*, pp. 147–149.

40 ibid., p. 151. See also Gilbert Mathieu, 'Pourquoi avoir échoué dans tant de domaines,' *Le Monde*, 22 August 1979. For very useful overviews see *Le Monde*'s annual *Bilan Economique et Social* for 1978, 1979, 1980.

41 Stoffaës, op. cit., was by far the most influential and important of the economic polemics along such lines. Stoffaës, an extremely able young technocrat, was in charge of developing industrial policy in the Barre government.

42 ibid., pp. 213–214, Mathieu, *Le Monde*, 22 August 1979.

43 On this period in PCF and Left history see Jenson and Ross, *Politics and Society*, Vol. 9, no. 3, 1979.

44 For the original PCF outline see PCF, *Manifeste du Parti Communiste Française, pour une démocratie avancée, pour une France socialiste* (Paris: Editions Sociales, 1969)—the famous *Manifeste de Champigny*. In 1971 the Parti Socialiste and the PCF put out fuller programs in rapid succession, which formed the basis of final discussions. See PS, *Changer la vie* (Paris: PS, 1971) and PCF, *Changer de cap* (Paris: Editions Sociales, 1971).

45 *Programme commun pour un gouvernement d'union de gauche*, PCF edition (Paris: Editions Sociales, 1972), Part 2, chapter 2, pp. 113–117.

46 ibid., Part 2, chapter 5, pp. 121–124.

47 Here see Pierre Juquin, *L'Actualisation à dossiers ouverts* (Paris: Editions Sociales, 1978, Juquin's notes from the actualization discussion. See also the recollections of Robert Fabre, Left radical leader at the time of the rupture of the Left, *Toute vérité est bonne à dire* (Paris: Fayard, 1979). Fabre was the most outspoken critic of the PCF's maximalism on the program. The PCF also published a *Programme commun actualisé* (Paris: Editions Sociales, 1978) which purported to detail the modifications to the 1972 program proposed by all parties to the fateful updating discussions.

48 It was, in fact, the Communists who made the most noise in all of this, trying to expand the list of nationalizable industries and arguing for the full nationalization of all of the properties of the companies listed (which, since most of the 'groups' were holding companies of one kind and another, led to a substantial list of economic activities to be nationalized). The Socialists were quieter, desiring to downplay the issue altogether if possible, leave the 1972 Program essentially as it was written and thereby gain policy

flexibility in the event of a Left victory. Perhaps the best public statement of some of the PS anxiety is found in Serge Christophe Kolm, *La Transition socialiste* (Paris: Cerf, 1977).

49 The following CFDT internal documents are most useful in tracing the evolution of the Confederation's reflections:

CFDT 'Etudes Economiques' no. 101, *Document du travail sur la crise économique*, December, 1974 (Paris: CFDT Secteur Economique, 1974).

CFDT 'Etudes Economiques' no. 106, *Reprise économique et crise du capitalisme français*, July 1976 (Paris: CFDT Secteur Economique, 1976).

CFDT 'Etudes Economiques' no. 107, *La Situation économique à l'heure du Plan Barre*, February 1977 (Paris: CFDT Secteur Economique, 1977).

CFDT 'Nouvelles CFDT,' no. 31/37, *Un An de Plan Barre* (Paris: CFDT Secteur Action Economique, Emploi, Education Permanente, 1977).

Among the CFDT's published materials see *CFDT Syndicalisme-Hebdo*, 3 March 1974 'Les travailleurs face à la crise;' 3 October 1974 'Giscard et la crise, qu'en pense la CFDT?' 13 March 1975 'La Crise, son histoire, ses mecanismes, les moyens de la combattre;' 16 June 1977 'La Plate-forme CFDT;' and '1978: ce que veut la CFDT,' in *CFDT Magazine*, October 1977. See also CFDT, *La Crise* (Paris: CFDT, 1976), CFDT, *Positions et Orientations de la CFDT* (Paris: CFDT, 1977). For the CFDT's post-1978 election reflections (including *recentrage*) see *CFDT Syndicalisme-Hebdo*, special number on 38th Congress, December 1978.

50 cf. CFDT 'Etudes Economiques,' no. 101, *La Crise*.

51 CFDT, *La Crise*, p. 50.

52 ibid. p. 88.

53 ibid. p. 88.

54 Michel Rolant, 'La Riposte,' in *CFDT Syndicalisme-Hebdo*, 13 March 1975, p. 3.

55 ibid. p. 19.

56 See 'La Plate-forme CFDT,' *CFDT Syndicalisme-Hebdo*, 16 June 1977.

57 We will not discuss the PCF's own development of SMC theory in the crisis, even though the comparison between it and the CGT's views would be illuminating. For those desiring to do so, the following will be useful points of departure:

PCF collective, *La Crise* (Paris: Editions Sociales, 1975).

Anicet le Pors, 'La France et la stratégie des multinationales,' *Economie et Politique*, November–December 1978.

Anicet le Pors, *Les Béquilles du capital (les transferts état-industrie, critère de nationalisation)* (Paris: Seuil, 1977).

Paul Boccara, *Etudes sur le capitalisme monopoliste d'état, sa crise, et son issue* (Paris: Editions Sociales, 1974).

Jean-Claude Gayssot, 'L'Enlisement organisé,' *Economie et Politique*, January 1979.

Bernard Marx, *Comprendre l'économie capitaliste* (Paris: Editions Sociales, 1979), especially chapter 8.

Paul Boccara, Philippe Herzog *et al.*, *Changer l'économie* (Paris: Editions Sociales, 1977).

It is important to note that much of the economic theorizing and research of the PCF was coordinated through the PCF Central Committee's *Section Economique*, an official working group of PCF economists. Throughout the pre-1978 period the CGT's major economics writers and researchers, Jean-Louis Moynot, Confederal Secretary, Jean Magniadas, a member of the CGT Executive Committee and official research director at the CGT *Centre Confédéral d'Etudes Economiques*, and Philippe Zarifian, the CGT–CCEE's brilliant young economist, all participated regularly in the *Section Economique*.

58 Here perhaps the most useful CGT statements of this general perspective are to be found—in order of accessibility—in Jean-Louis Moynot and Philippe Zarifian 'Pour faire face à la crise,' *Le Peuple*, 15–28 February 1976, CGT, Centre Confédéral d'Etudes Economiques, *L'Industrie française depuis 1958, un bilan accusateur* (Paris: CGT–CCEE, 1978), Philippe Zarifian, *Inflation et crise monetaire* (Paris: FSM, 1976).

59 Important CGT documents include:

CGT, *Congrès Confédéral, 1972* (38e Congrès, Nimes), report of Georges Séguy and document d'orientation.

CGT, *Congrès Confédéral, 1975* (39e Congrès, Le Bourget), report of Georges Séguy and document d'orientation.

Jean-Louis Moynot, 'La situation economique en France et dans les grands pays capitalistes et la politique de Giscard,' *Le Peuple*, 1–15 October 1974.

Le Peuple, 1–15 April 1976, 'Le Patronat face à la crise, adaptation et continuité.'

Philippe Zarifian, 'La politique industrielle dans le VIIe Plan,' *Le Peuple*. 1–15 July 1976.

Options (journal of the CGT *cadres* union, UGICT–CGT), May 1977, 'Halte à la démission industrielle.'

Philippe Zarifian, 'La braderie de l'industrie, causes et conséquences,' *Le Peuple*, 15 November 1977.

Le Peuple, 15–30 June 1977, 'Les solutions et propositions de la CGT.'

60 'The core of the problem (and this is 'relatively' new) is that the pursuit of the general movement of capital accumulation is already largely centered on (and propelled by) the internationalization of capital.' Jean-Louis Moynot and Philippe Zarifian, *Le Peuple*, 15–28 February, 1976.

61 Here see CGT–CCEE, *L'Industrie française depuis 1958*, esp. chapter 3.

62 ibid. p. 40 ff.

63 ibid., p. 36.

64 ibid., p. 37.

65 On this question see Jean-Louis Moynot, 'La Crise sous nos yeux et son issue un peu plus loin dans les luttes,' *La Nouvelle Critique*, October 1975, CGT–CCEE, *L'Industrie française depuis 1958*, chapter IV, Section 4, and CGT–CCEE, *Des Manufactures à la crise du Taylorisme* (Paris: CGT, 1978).

66 CGT–CCEE, *L'Industrie française depuis 1958*, p. 220.

67 ibid., p. 227.

68 ibid., p. 228.

69 Jean-Louis Moynot and Philippe Zarifian, *Le Peuple*, 15–28 February 1975, p. 10.

70 See CGT–CCEE, *Imperialisme, solidarité avec les peuples du tiers-monde et lutte pour un nouvel ordre économique* (Paris: CGT, 1978), especially Jean-Louis Moynot, 'Indépendence économique et nouvel ordre international,' pp. 105–120.

71 See CGT 1972 *Congrès Confédéral*, pp. 441–466, 1975 *Congrès Confédéral*, pp. 595–630, and *Le Peuple*, 15–30 June 1977, 'Les Solutions et propositions de la CGT.'

72 *Le Peuple*, 15–30 June 1977, pp. 50–53.

73 Jean-Louis Moynot and Philippe Zarifian, in *Le Peuple*, 15–28 February 1976, p. 8.

74 *Force Ouvrière*, to the degree to which it had elaborated a general view of the crisis, had a 'working-class Keynesian' perspective, which stressed recovery through expanded domestic consumption to be won through collective bargaining victories.

75 For the text of the accord see *Le Peuple*, 15 July–15 August 1974.

76 This CGT shift was not unconnected with a prior and parallel shift in PCF tactics. At the party's 21st Congress in 1974 the leadership was obliged to acknowledge that *Union de la Gauche* had begun to strengthen the Socialists at PCF expense. Particular anxiety was expressed about the Socialists' newly energetic campaign to build up Socialist sections at firm and shopfloor level (See Georges Marchais' report to the 21st Congress in *Cahiers du Communisme*, November 1974). The Congress therefore put the party on alert to shore up its own shoplevel organization, in part by establishing a special *grandes entreprises* section attached to the Central Committee (chaired by Jean Colpin, a *Bureau Politique* member) which set up direct organizational ties between the PCF Central Committee and shopfloor party organizations in the forty-three largest factories in France. One immediate result of this was that Communists were prodded to take highly visible leadership positions in shopfloor struggles. Numbers of sharp actions led by Communists followed, designed to demonstrate that Communists, and not Socialists, were at the forefront of struggle. The CGT leadership was initially very uncomfortable about all this. Eventually, however, it absorbed the new militancy into its own tactics and under its own aegis.

77 Here see George Ross, 'The CGT in Eurocommunism,' in *Politics and Society*, vol. 9, no. 1, 1979.

78 It is now clear that not all of the CGT leadership was in complete agreement about this shift in focus. Certain members of the Confederal Bureau, for example, seem to have been aware of its potential costs, even if they were subdued in their objections. See Jean-Louis Moynot, in *La Nouvelle Critique*, October 1975, for a rare public expression of such awareness.

79 See, for example, *CFDT Aujourd'hui* November–December 1979, special number entitled *Classe Ouvrière Eclatée*. On the French 'black' sector, see *Nouvel Observateur*. 2 June 1980.

80   For a summary and references on new patronal strategies see Dominique Pouchin's excellent series of articles 'La Crise du syndicalisme,' in *Le Monde*, May 1980.
81   cf. Gilbert Mathieu in *Le Monde*, 22 August 1979.
82   cf. Le Monde, *Bilan Economique et Social, 1980*.
83   See Ross, *Workers and Communists*, chapter 10 and conclusions.
84   'Recentering' was first heard of in January 1978, in the heat of the electoral campaign, in a report to the CFDT Executive Commission authored by Jacques Moreau, then CFDT political secretary (and an avid socialist), see *CFDT Syndicalisme-Hebdo*, 12 January 1978. Its propositions were voted down at the CFDT National Committee meeting later that month, however. Reformulated, it was adopted by the same body in March 1978, to become the strategic core of the CFDT Confederal leadership's Congress Proposal in 1979 (see *CFDT Syndicalisme-Hebdo*, December 1978).
85   *CFDT Syndicalisme-Hebdo*, 17 May 1979, p. 14.
86   For the best general presentation of the 'proposition force' perspective, see Jean-Louis Moynot, 'Le Mouvement syndical en mouvement,' in *Dialectiques*, no. 28, 1979. See also the same author's 'Entre aujourd'hui et demain' in *Le Peuple*, 1–15 May 1978, Philippe Zarifian, 'Restructurer ou non?' in *Dialectiques*, no. 28, 1979, Zarifian's 'Tactique de lutte dans la sidérugie,' in *La Nouvelle Critique*, April 1979, and 'Reflexions sur la crise à propos de la sidérurgie,' in *Issues*, no. 7, 1980.
87   Perhaps the most succinct summary of this line is to be found in the documents for the PCF's 23rd Congress, published in *Humanité*, 13 February 1979. See also Anicet le Pors, *Marianne a l'encan* (Paris: Editions Sociales, 1980).
88   For the government's steel plan, consult *Le Monde* during the first half of December 1978. See also Philippe Zarifian in *La Nouvelle Critique*, April 1979.
89   See CGT, Fédération des Travailleurs de la Métallurgie, *Le Guide du Militant de la Métallurgie*, no. 136, November 1978, 'Face à la crise de la sidérurgie.' See also CGT–CCEE, *Crise et solution pour la sidérurgie* (Paris: CGT, 1979).
90   CFDT, Fédération Générale de la Métallurgie, *Avenir de la sidérurgie* (Paris: CFDT, 1979), also Georges Granger (the CFDT official closest to the steel issue), 'Produire, pour qui? pourquoi?' in *Dialectiques*, no. 28, 1979.
91   Conflict between 'proposition force' and 'opposition force' advocates in the CGT also broke out over the CGT's positions on Europe around the June 1979 elections to the European Assembly (whether the Confederation should endorse the PCF's line, which it didn't) and on unity-in-action with the CFDT (which 'proposition forcers' favored and 'opposition forcers' opposed).
92   This is especially significant given that, in both cases, upwards of 15 percent of official membership is of *retired* workers. In this light, by the end of 1980 the CGT was probably down to 1·5 million active members, while the CFDT was below 800,000. For the *Prud'homme* election results see *Le Peuple*, 16–31 December 1979. The CGT received 42·4 percent of the total vote, the CFDT 23·1 percent and FO (the real surprise result) 17·4 percent.
93   See Ross, op. cit., part 2.
94   Le Monde, *Les Elections législatives de juin 1981—la gauche socialiste obtient la majorité absolue* (supplement to the 'dossiers et documents du *Monde*,' June 1981).
95   Charles Fiterman became a *ministre d'état*, with a high protocol rank, but with a relatively unimportant functional attachment, transport. Jack Ralite, vice-mayor of Aubervilliers, became Minister of Health. The two others, officially secretaries of state, were Anicet le Pors, a high civil servant also a member of the PCF, and Marcel Rigout. Both had subordinate jobs, le Pors in charge of the civil service, Rigout in charge of adult education.
96   After 1978 there was an attempt made inside the PS to ditch François Mitterrand as potential presidential candidate in favor of Michel Rocard, an attempt which carried with it a very different strategic project for the PS, one which would have abandoned *Union de la Gauche* and the famous 'anchoring' of PS strategy to the Left in favor of a 'modernist' centrism. On these issues see the excellent book by Hugues Portelli, *Le Socialisme français tel qu'il est* (Paris: PUF, 1980). The Rocard offensive failed after a long and complicated factional battle in the PS. As a result of this episode Mitterrand was obliged to reconfirm his allegiance to a Left-facing program in ways which may have been responsible for some of the more surprising radicalness of the Mauroy government's behavior.

97 See *Le Monde*, 11 July 1981, for Mauroy's speech. For the Socialists' electoral manifesto see Le Monde, *Elections Présidentielles 1981*, p. 57.
98 Two members of the CFDT's National Bureau, Jeannette Laot and Hubert Lesire-Ogrel, went to the Elysée and Matignon staffs, respectively, while Hubert Prevòt (the author of much of the CFDT's recent economic writing and one of our informants) became *Commissaire au Plan*.

2 Strategy under Stress: The Italian Union Movement and the Italian Crisis in Developmental Perspective

Peter Lange and Maurizio Vannicelli

Part 1

Introduction

In comparison with other West European trade unions, Italian unions have responded to the political-economic crisis of the 1970s in a unique way. This uniqueness is not only the reflection of the peculiarities which have characterized Italy's economic and political development in the postwar period; it is also the product of the copresence in the Italian union movement of two strategic models which have been rarely found together in a single movement in other European countries. The first model is the 'conflictual model,' typical of unions which stress internal democracy, organizational decentralization, and active worker participation; in short, it is the form of unionism common to most countries of Western Europe's 'Latin belt' and which had its moment of greater popularity in Italy in the 'hot autumn' of the late 1960s. The second model describes unions which seek to participate actively in decision-making about macroeconomic policies and which are willing to adapt their strategy and demands to their interpretation (arrived at through consultation and bargaining with the other critical political-economic actors) of the requirements of the broader national and international economy.

Adding to the peculiarity of the Italian unions' behavior, the interplay between these two models of unionism has taken place alongside a process of strategic, if not organizational, union unity. This has not been, however, always the case. For much of the postwar period, organizational, ideological, and strategic fragmentation was the prominent feature of the Italian labor movement. A unified movement was created under the auspices of the political parties in June 1944, during the final stages of World War II, but it proved to be a sporadic episode. The outbreak of the Cold War and its repercussions on the Italian domestic scene led to the breakup of the union movement. Three confederations broadly reflecting the divisions in Italy's political system were formed: the CGIL (linked to the PCI and the Socialists), the CISL (sponsored by the Christian Democrats and the Church), and the UIL (supported by many of the minor political currents, primarily the Social Democrats and the Republicans). In view of the ideological and political polarization which characterized the first decade of postwar Italian history, it was all but inevitable that organizational fragmentation in the union movement rapidly evolved into an all-out confrontation among the three confederations. Throughout the 1950s, when the country's postwar economic development model was put in place, the union movement was lacerated by internecine competition. Interconfederal struggles based on divergent conceptions of the role of unions in society were bitter and unrelenting, often damaging the interests of the working class. Internal division and competition were, of course, not the only reasons for the weakness that crippled the effectiveness of Italian unions.

Nonetheless, they help explain the defensive market strategy and the often intense ideological and politicized character of the behavior of Italian unions.

In the early 1960s, in coincidence with a temporary revival of working-class militancy and changes in the national political market, interunion competition began to abate. It was the explosion of worker militancy in the late 1960s, however, which led to dramatic changes in the power of the working class and in the structure of the labor movement itself. From 1972 onwards, the Italian labor movement adopted a more unified structure and strategy. This should not suggest that internal divisions along ideological lines ceased to exist; rather, they were mediated inside a single movement, and they no longer inevitably manifested themselves in interinstitutional conflict. Fundamental agreement on strategic objectives prevailed, although disagreement on the means to be employed in the pursuit of such objectives continued to be present. Yet, not even the severe economic crisis of the early 1970s and the continuing problems posed by the developments in the political system, especially after 1975, have eroded the bases of union unity (until 1980). The resilience of union unity accounts for the success registered by the Italian labor movement in retaining the gains obtained during and after the 'hot autumn.'

The Italian union movement is, however, far from homogeneous. 'Unity in heterogeneity' is an appropriate formula for characterizing its present-day structure. The very birth of the unified Federation CGIL–CISL–UIL in 1972 was more a compromise among, or attempted synthesis of, different conceptions of unionism than a sweeping away of such differences. While its development has represented an improvement on the unity-in-action which had at various times characterized the behavior of the unions in the 1960s, it has been a far cry from the organic unity to which the most radical category unions and large segments of the working class had aspired. It is important to mention, however, that the foci of division inside the movement are no longer as clearly defined as they used to be before the 'hot autumn.' As acutely observed by Gino Giugni, the present unity of the Italian labor movement 'is the confluence of diverse ideological roots and historical traditions which are by now no longer identifiable with traditional labels, be they party or confederal.'[1]

Both the uniqueness of the Italian unions' strategy and the difficulties that they have encountered in implementing it reflect in part this tension-laden confluence. In a nutshell, this strategy consists of the attempt to combine the achievement of *both* transformative, classist political objectives and of associational, defensive, shopfloor objectives by acting simultaneously in the political and market arenas. Fundamental to this strategy is the preservation of union unity, autonomy from the political parties, and a real or potential high level of working-class mobilization.

This characterization of the Italian unions' strategy requires two qualifications. First, this strategy is the outcome of a long-term historical, ideological, and institutional evolution internal to the union movement, a process which is still evolving.[2] Second, the development of union strategy cannot be understood solely in terms of the internal workings of the union movement. It is also the product of factors in the environment in which the unions operate. This is not to say that union strategy is a mere response to what takes place in the political-economic milieu. With rare exceptions, Italian unions have enjoyed a certain freedom of strategic choice. External conditions, ranging from the character and pace of economic growth to the evolution of the political system, create obstacles, impose constraints, limit options, and, at times, offer opportunities for the unions. Yet, the types of response that the unions elaborate cannot be understood except by taking into account their own strategic orientation which, in turn, stems from the interaction among the various institutional, ideological, and strategic traditions of the different currents forming the union movement. What constitutes the strategic behavior of Italian unions consists of an intricate mix of internal and external factors—a mix which is seldom fully balanced, often the consequence of a complicated process of internal mediation, and always too nuanced to be explained to one's complete satisfaction.

The purpose of this chapter is to outline and appraise the strategy of the Italian unions in the changed and changing economic and political context of the 1970s. Three analytical categories will be employed: *objectives* (workplace or social reforms), political or market *arenas* for the pursuit of these objectives, and the relative role to be assumed by different *levels of organization* (workplace, federal, confederal) in the pursuit of these objectives. Central to our investigation is the analysis of the ways in which Italian unions have interpreted and responded to the economic crisis and— since in Italy the 'crisis' is as much political as it is economic—to the evolution of the political system, notably to the PCI's historical quest for participation in the government. For reasons that have been suggested in the preceding pages, our approach will be historical-developmental, and we will assess the strategy of the Italian union movement as it has evolved since World War II, paying particular attention to those 'critical junctures' which have greatly affected such an evolution.

In this way, we will single out those developments internal and/or external to the union movement (1) which have accounted for the changes that have occurred in union strategy in the last thirty-five years; (2) which have shaped the particular response that Italian unions have devised with regard to the challenges posed by the economic-political crisis of the 1970s; and (3) which have kept alive some of the old tensions and caused new ones inside the union movement.

Part 2

The Shaping of the Postwar Settlement

At the end of World War II, the Italian trade union movement gave all the appearance of considerable strength and great radical thrust. Reconstituted through the initiative of the major antifascist political parties with the Pact of Rome of 3 June 1944, the CGIL (Confederazione Generale Italiana del Lavoro) appeared relatively unified and brought under its umbrella the workers' organizations which had played an important part in the final years of the Resistance.[3] The wartime mobilization carried over into peacetime as did many of the institutions of workplace control and expectations of radical change which the workers and the Resistance movement had created.[4] These were the source for much working class militancy. Furthermore, the parties which had helped form the union were cooperating together in national government and maintaining close ties to the labor movement. Even the dire economic conditions of the country had an ambivalent effect on the strength and militancy of the workers, for a ban of dismissals obtained by the unions protected against drastic unemployment, and the crisis of the economy seemed to open vast opportunities for profound economic reform. It appeared that the CGIL would play a major part in the shaping of postwar economic reconstruction.

This was not to be the case. The postwar settlement which established the position of the union movement in Italian society from the late 1940s until the early 1960s was characterized by profound union weakness in both the market and political arenas. The once unified CGIL became only one of three confederations, divided among themselves by deep ideological and organizational rifts and competing with one another for support among the workers. The political parties (PCI and PSI) which primarily represented the working class were not only excluded from governmental participation but were considered illegitimate potential participants. As it emerged by the early 1950s, the development model reflected none of the radical ideals of only a few years before. It was premised on low wages, maintained a large pool of reserve labor and unemployment, was fundamentally oriented toward external rather than internal demand, and assigned only a small role to government and to the provision of social services.[5] The union movement had proven unable to play a major role in the determination of that model and was incapable of doing much to alter its basic characteristics and trajectory throughout the 1950s. The seeming strength of the immediate postwar years proved ephemeral, and the union movement, especially the segment tied to the Communists and Socialists, had to contend with more than a decade of isolation and exclusion.

It is not our intention here to describe in detail why the initial expectations of the union movement and working class were disappointed. At the general level two complementary factors were at work. On the one hand, the conditions brought about by the fall of fascism confronted the emerging Italian union movement with a set of economic, social, and political problems different from any in Italian union experience. The prefascist traditions of the movement with respect to union organization, immediate and long-term objectives, and how to pursue them were of little relevance to the problems posed by the collapse of the fascist economy and the need for reconstruction.[6] There was little—beyond lofty principles and sweeping long-term goals—in the ideological and strategic heritage of the movement which could provide guidance for the role it sought to assume in the postwar regime. On the other hand, both the partisan political origins of the movement at the end of the war and the enormous gravity of the economic problems faced by Italy continually conditioned the unions' choices. Unable to develop strategic and organizational autonomy and to define an economic policy which would strike a balance between global objectives and the short-run defense of the most pressing needs of the working class, the unions were able to do little to influence the course of events in either the economic and political arenas. These developments dovetailed with the emergence of a conservative economic coalition and design built around classical liberal economic principles.

While the specific developments of the initial postwar period are not of great importance to our analysis, the positions taken by the unions, and the underlying explanation of them, are, for it is in this period that the union movement developed the objectives, and many of the basic postures, which continued to characterize its behavior even into the 1970s.

The development of the CGIL was, from its origins in 1944, deeply conditioned by political factors. To a large extent this was the result of the reconstruction process of the CGIL which had been an expression of the will and actions of the parties. Moreover, the union's middle and top cadres were drawn directly from these parties. The partisan politicization of the Confederation, however, was only one of the causes of its politically oriented behavior. In fact, from the beginning the goals which it pursued were fundamentally conditioned by broader political problems, first the Resistance, then the construction of a mass democratic regime and the reconstruction of the economy.[7] While this more general form of politicization was undoubtedly linked to the partisan origins of the CGIL, it was also caused by the objective conditions of the country at the end of the war. The unions, like the parties, had to select as their first priority the development of democratic institutions after more than twenty years of fascism. A democratic constitution was fundamental to the unions' future, and their policies were and continue to be conditioned by this goal. The economic conditions of the country also contributed to the CGIL's orientation toward the political arena:

The state of the Italian economy at the end of the conflict was marked by: 1) a decided fall in industrial production . . .; 2) widespread and vast devastation of infrastructure and of agricultural and livestock. . . .; 3) growth in the state deficit paralleled by galloping inflation in the South and contained inflation in the North; 4) the collapse of the purchasing power of the working classes and those with fixed incomes along a curve which, when accompanied by the weak revaluations of wages and the decline of employment, dramatically posed the issue of the living conditions of the masses and led to a grave crisis of the internal market.[8]

In such a situation the unions could not hope to advance their interests and goals primarily through activity in the labor market; government intervention was essential, both in dealing with immediate problems and in establishing the conditions for economic reconstruction. This is not to suggest that the CGIL's policy choices were wholly determined by 'objective' conditions. The stress on particular options was clearly inspired by the Confederation's linkages to the political parties, most importantly the PCI. Nonetheless, the range of choices was severely limited, and reliance on action in the market arena was infeasible.

The partisan and politicized origins of the CGIL had a number of important consequences which were to leave their mark on the union movement. First, the foundation of the Confederation reflected both shared and contrasting purposes among the parties, incorporating the deep historical, cultural, and ideological differences between them into the new organization. In addition, from the beginning the Marxist and Catholic traditions of Italian trade unionism achieved an uneasy accommodation on matters of union policy and organization. The Confederation was thus simultaneously an organizational expression of unity of action and an arena of competition among the various currents of political and trade union ideology. As party unity broke down progressively, it is not surprising that this had a direct impact on the unions, eventuating finally in scission along partisan lines.[9]

Second, the union also was to a considerable extent an instrument of the parties and the policies which they were pursuing. After the war and until the splits of 1947 and 1948, this meant that the union movement was increasingly influenced by the Italian Communist Party (PCI). The Communists had for many years been the most active political force in the factories, and their cadres became the core of the newly constituted union movement, both at the grass roots and above. Thus 'the policy of the CGIL followed the general line of the Communist Party: a peaceful entry into the new bourgeois democracy which had replaced fascism.'[10] Communist policy goals were not immediately radical. Rather, they were characterized by moderation, the primacy of interparty relations and the search for the broadest possible social and political alliances. At least in the short run, the PCI sought not a socialist society but what it called 'progressive democracy,' a system which would enable Italy to establish a stable mass democracy, built around mass political parties, associations, and popular participation for the first time in its history.[11] Economic and social policies were to favor the interests of the working class and working strata more generally and assure such interests a pivotal role in the new democratic institutions, but 'the elaboration of an economic line was to be closely tied to an evaluation of the political situation which was emerging from the antifascist struggle.'[12] The PCI argued that the fall of fascism, the complicity of the bourgeoisie with the fascist regime and the leading role which the working class had taken in the Resistance meant that the laboring classes had to assume a *national* leading role and posture in contributing to the founding of a democratic system and to the rebuilding of the economy. We will see shortly how this Communist strategy became embodied in CGIL economic policy. What is important to stress here is that the Communist goals and the relationship between the party and the CGIL further shifted the focus of the union movement away from the factory and toward the political system and the state.

The relationship between the unions and the parties was, of course, not unique to the Communist Party. Before the breakup of the CGIL in 1948, the other major Resistance parties also sought to advance their political interests and ideologies within the CGIL. Furthermore, the Christian Democrats and Catholic Church created a flanking organization for Catholic workers, the ACLI, whose purpose was to promote Catholic trade union ideology. The ACLI was also seen by some DC leaders as a fallback should union unity in the CGIL prove undesirable.[13] The division of the union movement only exacerbated the unions' dependence on the political parties. In the years following, the basic weakness of the labor movement and the inability of any of the confederations to make much of a contribution to the improvement of the conditions of the workers tended to increase this dependence. It was only in the 1960s, when the unions gained in strength and the Cold War divisions had somewhat subsided, that greater union autonomy from the parties began to develop. Even then, and to the present day, however, the linkages between the unions and the parties, rooted in historical experience, ideology, and recruitment practices, remain important in explaining union behavior.

The third major consequence of the partisan and politicized character of the CGIL was centralization. This took both policy and organizational manifestations. At the level of policy, as we shall see, it meant that the unions concentrated on goals to be achieved through government action and sought to control agitation in the labor market. Until the breakdown of the Resistance coalition, in fact, there were almost no national strikes called by the CGIL despite the severe conditions faced by the workers and the growing social tensions due to the relative failure of government action to alleviate these conditions.

At the level of organization, centralization translated into weak implementation of those aspects of the organizational scheme adopted by the CGIL at the end of the war which might have shifted power away from the Confederation toward the category unions and which might have strengthened the presence of the union on the shop floor. The CGIL's organizational plan envisaged a combination of 'vertical' and 'horizontal' structures. The vertical structure was the category union whose purpose was to organize all workers within an industry. At the shop floor, however, the representative body of the workers was not to be a trade union organizational structure, but rather the *commissione interna* or workshop committee, which was to be elected by all, and not just unionized, workers and was to be responsible to them. The reason for this was the determination of the non-Catholic segments of the CGIL, rooted in their ideology and reflecting the Communists' desire to seek the broadest alliances, to represent all workers and to avoid particularistic union behavior. The horizontal structure had at its peak the Confederation and was organized at the local level into Chambers of Labor which grouped all the category unions in a city or province.[14]

The lagging development of the category unions was one reason for the weakness of the union at the factory level. Other reasons were also linked to the political role which the CGIL was adopting. Among these were the emphasis placed by the union on policies which required government action and which were best managed through negotiations between the Confederation and the government and parties, and the related reluctance of the Confederation or its lower-level organizations to utilize the strike and other forms of struggle at the shop floor. Bianca Salvati (Beccalli) argues that the diffidence which the Confederation showed toward the *commissioni interne* 'probably explains the ease with which the rights of the workshop committees were limited by collective contracts' after 1946.[15] Whatever the exact mix of reasons, the trade union organizations at the shop floor and in the industrial sectors were already weakened when the national political coalition split in mid-1947. As the growing political polarization was translated into competitive relations among the unionists on the shop floor, and as the centrist government implemented the first steps of its economic policy, this weakness became endemic. From the end of the 1940s until the early 1960s, the predominance of the confederations and the very weak presence of the unions at the shop floor were basic features of the movement. Thereafter, there has been considerable tension and debate about the most appropriate relationship between shopfloor power and category and confederal policy and about the relationship between the confederations and the category unions.

As so much else that we have discussed, the economic analysis and goals which the unified CGIL formulated in the first postwar years presages many of the principles which the later CGIL was to continue to promote in the following years. Despite the fact that the pre-1948 policy was intended to deal with the immediate problems facing the workers and to enhance political and class compromise, its general principles were in good part retained even after the conservative restoration.

The short-term goals of the pre-1948 CGIL were straightforward: the maintenance of employment, the protection of workers' purchasing power against inflation, and a battle against profiteering and speculation. These goals grew directly from the most evident problems at the end of the war. They were to be pursued through government action, agreements between individual employers and the workers' representatives in their factories, and more general agreements between the employers' associations and the CGIL. Emblematic of this perspective were the freeze on firings which lasted until February 1946, and the *scala mobile* (scheme of indexation) which was instituted in October 1946.[16]

The longer-term goals of the Confederation were less defined and reflected a combination of general ideological principles and an almost obsessive, though understandable, concern with unemployment. This problem had historically conditioned Italian industrial unionism, and it was no less prominent in the immediate postwar period. The number of unemployed in 1946–7 approched two million, there were large numbers of underemployed and there was a widespread perception that unemployment of this scale might be a longstanding feature of the Italian economic landscape.[17] The CGIL constantly and emphatically stressed the need to place the growth of employment at the top of the government economic agenda. This orientation, which in part was carried over from the prefascist years, contributed to the unions' general policy moderation, particularly with respect to wages. Union leaders operated on the assumption that undue wage pressure might hamper reconstruction and further contribute to the unemployment problem. Such an assumption, however, was not built into a more comprehensive analysis of the economy, nor was it linked to a coherent, systematic economic program. Instead, the Confederation's economic proposals amounted to a series of generic pronouncements and poorly linked demands which communicated more the unions' vision of the desirable future as they and the Left wished it to be than a concrete program for its realization. The result was that even at the peak of postwar union influence, with Communists and Socialists in the government and controlling key economic ministries and a highly mobilized working class at the shop floor, the CGIL and the Left were unable to have a significant impact on some of the decisions which in those years laid the bases for economic reconstruction.[18] There is no question that even had its economic policies been more precise, the Left would probably have been unable to force the government to implement them. Domestic and international pressures were already shifting the political and economic balance of power to the right. Nonetheless, the failure to analyze correctly the economic changes underway and how these were influenced by specific governmental measures, and the absence of a concrete economic program, left the unions on the defensive and ever less able to defend even the gains and positions they had already acquired.

It was only in 1949 that the CGIL, now split by the Catholic and Social Democratic defections, developed a full-fledged economic program which was presented as the *Piano del lavoro*.[19] It is one of the paradoxes of Italian trade unionism that the development of such a program had to await the exclusion of the Left from effective governmental influence. In explaining this paradox, four factors can be cited. First, by 1949 the government, with the help of the Marshall Plan, was implementing its own economic program. The Left had to offer a counterprogram. Second, and relatedly, such a counterprogram was indispensible to maintaining the support and enthusiasm of the union base in the face of the lack of union power in the market and political arenas. The *Piano* served much the same function for the PCI. Third, both union and party could use the program to seek support beyond their existing constituencies. Finally, the ability of the CGIL to develop a program was, ironically, improved by the internal split. No longer needing continuously to balance the traditions and political interests of the different union currents, the CGIL could proceed to develop an identity more consistent with its own traditions and political ties.

Like the earlier fragmented proposals, the *Piano del lavoro* was moderate and continued to reflect the absolute priority of the problem of unemployment.[20] The basic policy measures which it advocated were: nationalization of basic industries, agrarian reform and modernization, especially in the South, price control, distribution of essential consumer goods and rigorous use of taxation policy to create social savings which would then be directed through government policy to productive investment. All of these measures were intended, through the articulated use of government intervention, to assure that there would be significant and steady growth of the employed work force in all regions of the country. It is worthwhile at this point to note that, with the exception of the call for nationalization, all of the measures called for in the *Piano* of 1950 reappear in the unified unions' program in the decade of the 1970s.

Beyond the specifics of these measures, what is interesting for our purposes are the principles of political economy which underlay them. First, the basic capitalist framework and a major role for private economic initiative were accepted and thoroughgoing national planning was excluded, echoing in this the position of the PCI. As early as 1945, Palmiro Togliatti, Secretary General of the PCI, declared that 'even if we were today alone in power . . . we would call on private initiative for reconstruction.'[21] This theme was repeated consistently in the following years, even after the party was no longer in government. No matter how instrumental one's interpretation of the reasons for the Communist assumption of this stance, it reflects moderation and a partial commitment to try to maintain links with private capital.

Second, the model was premised on internal demand and public spending as the primary sources of stimulus for reconstruction and further economic development. It was purchasing power generated within Italian society which would be fundamental. The CGIL did not share the optimism of the liberals about the role of free trade and international demand. As a consequence, of course, the union placed heavy emphasis on the expansion of employment and the growth of salaries. The coincidence of this emphasis with the specific policy measures being promoted, with the CGIL's ideological commitment to class unionism and with its institutional interests, is obvious.

Third, none of the preceding should be taken to suggest that the Confederation was advocating a 'free market' solution or relying on the spontaneous generation of internal demand. Rather, its model was heavily reliant on an active government role in the creation and direction of demand. One author has written of the 'Keynesian flavor' to the CGIL's proposals,[22] while noting at the same time that the emphasis on nationalizations, particularly in basic industries, and on the close direction of public spending, moved in the direction of 'lessons' drawn from the Soviet experience. Be this as it may, the specific goals advocated resembled to a considerable degree the programs one might expect of an activist and interventionist welfare state: stimulus for public consumption, the development of a broad structure of social services (housing, hospitals, schools, transportation), public ownership and investment in basic industries (e.g., steel and machine tools), agrarian reform and income redistribution through the tax system.[23] Taken together, these measures would require a set of structural reforms which, while respecting the capitalist framework and role of private initiative, were to hedge them in by advancing popular control of the economy in a democratic framework.

To argue that the CGIL's proposed development model was relatively moderate should not suggest that it implied an acceptance of the model of economic reconstruction being implemented by the government after the exclusion of the Left. In fact it took an approach potentially hostile to the choices adopted by the dominant classes. The fundamental postulate of the *Piano*, that is, a relaunching of the development mechanism through a major expansion of the domestic market, was in radical contrast with the model of development effectively adopted after 1947 by the entrepreneurs and the government.[24]

Furthermore, the emphasis on government direct intervention rather than on simply using state spending as a stimulus to the private sector indicates that the CGIL's proposal was to combine redistribution and social service spending with a direct government interventionist role. Nonetheless, this was well short of planning. In addition, the union gradually gave up its call for the implementation of mechanisms of workers' collaboration in managerial decision-making in the factory. Finally, the emphasis throughout the proposal was on the role of the political system and the government. In order to promote the appropriate political alliances, in fact, 'the union, for its part, commits itself to assure that the wage push will not be in contradiction with the awareness of the national and leadership role of the workers in promoting the general development of the nation, even at the cost of sacrifices.'[25] In this posture we see once again how union positions tended to deprive grass-roots organizations of the kind of mobilizing role around concrete, factory-level demands which might have encouraged decentralized organizational development.

In concluding this discussion of the CGIL's political-economic stance, it is useful to examine briefly the premises which lay behind it. Some of these are retained in only slightly modified form to the present day. Others were abandoned after the mid-1950s when the Confederation's expectations about the development of the Italian economy proved incorrect and the CGIL suffered a series of sharp organizational setbacks due, in part, to its failure to adjust policy to the economic reality, especially the rise in productivity and introduction of new technology.

The CGIL's economic theory was relatively unsophisticated, a pastiche of Keynesian-like and traditional Third International assumptions.[26] Foremost among the latter was the view that Italy was caught up in the 'inevitable crisis of capitalism' due to the growing dominance of monopoly capital. This crisis was said to take the form of an increasing underutilization of productive resources, both in terms of capital stock and labor. From this it followed that relaunching of the economy and its long-term future depended primarily on utilizing this existing reserve and that the private sector, dominated by monopoly capital, could not be expected to take up the task. It was, therefore, up to the government to ensure the use of these reserves. Furthermore, it followed that major capital infusions were not a top priority and that what was instead required was creation of the conditions which would allow for steady growth of internal demand. In this analysis we see the bases of that 'flavor of Keynesianism' in specific recommended policy measures mentioned earlier, but here three caveats need to be introduced. First, as is evident, the underlying theory was not Keynesian. Second, the CGIL wanted to pursue 'the expansion of the market not so much through salary increases as by pushing for a growth of the base of salaried workers.'[27] Third, the Confederation's approach paid little heed to the need for technological development and to the place which Italy was to assume in the international economy. In fact, the CGIL's economic proposals had a protectionist and autarchic potential, for they would have led to a growing gap between Italy's technological base and that of its international competitors. Finally, the Confederation's theory showed little sensitivity to the effect on productivity which an aggressive, factory-level wage policy might generate and to the general economic benefits which might derive therefrom. It

> was more concerned to assure that its policy would reinforce class solidarity (among the employed and between them and those seeking employment) and would help develop broad class alliances. To these ends, the CGIL wage strategy aimed at uniform wage determination, relatively low wage differentials within industry and wage rates which would protect employment levels. The result was 'a claims strategy . . . which brought with it a rigid centralization of contractual initiative with the systematic repression of autonomous initiatives at the factory level' and a wage geared to what could be paid by the less efficient producers.[28]

This brings us to the political premises of the Confederation's position. Here two points need to be highlighted. First, the interpretation of the Italian economy as dominated by monopolies provided the rationale for the pursuit of alliances extending as far as small and medium capital. If monopoly capital was suffocating economic growth, a program which gave room to private initiative, which sought to limit or eliminate monopoly and which would stimulate the internal market could provide the basis for a very broad antimonopolistic alliance while seeking to meet the immediate needs and demands of the working class for employment and a decent standard of living.[29] Secondly, if the preceding provided an economic rationale for the program, its political necessity once again derived from the Communists', and the Confederation's, commitment to a broad alliance policy which would prevent the isolation of the workers' movement. Even after its exclusion from government and the implementation of the conservative economic design, the PCI retained its basic commitment to this policy. The CGIL was supposed to be one of its major instruments and the *Piano del lavoro*, like earlier statements of political-economic policy, was its concrete manifestation.[30]

Of course, in its expectation of permanent crisis, the economic analysis proved incorrect and the hoped-for alliances did not materialize. Instead, the Left was expelled from the government in 1947, the unions split shortly thereafter and the government rapidly imposed a conservative economic policy based on tight credit, deflation, high unemployment, and openness to the international economy. By the early 1950s this policy produced the premises for the particular character and tempo of the Italian economic takeoff (what was to become known as the 'economic miracle'). As we shall see in a moment, the union movement, and especially the CGIL, was slow to react to the changing economic conditions. Even when it did react, much of earlier policy and of the premises underlying it, continued to mark its behavior. On the one hand, basic objectives and orientations formulated in the initial postwar phase retained their hold: stress on the need for state action in the economy, the search for influence in the political system and sensitivity to the ways union action could foster or hinder desired political action, a concern to maintain class unity and to represent, and build alliances with, social strata outside the organized working class. On the other hand, organizational developments which had occurred in this period and were in part an effect of this policy—in particular, the unions' fundamental weakness on the shop floor and in direct negotiations with individual employers—continued to condition union choices and possibilities for action. It is, therefore, in the context of the choices and analyses of this initial period of postwar union development that subsequent responses to changing conditions need to be evaluated.

Part 3

The Postwar Settlement—The Early 1950s to the Hot Autumn

The onset of the Cold War, the exclusion of the Left from the Italian national government, the division of the trade union movement, the elections of 1948, fought around the theme of the 'choice of civilizations' and won by the Christian Democratic Party and its allies, the American commitment to European recovery and the Marshall Plan, these and other events at the end of the 1940s created the context in which Italy launched the economic development model which was to result in the so-called 'economic miracle.' Many of the traditional structural flaws remained—the developmental gap between North and South, the backwardness of the agricultural sector, the fragmentation of the work force—but were generally neglected in the face of large and accelerating growth rates. The relationship between political conditions and economic decisions was close, and it remained so in the years to follow.[31] Yet, in the 1950s economic development took on a dynamic of its own, the government assuming the role of facilitator and political guardian and using the public sector to enhance the character of the development process being set by the private sector. In the early 1960s, however, things began to change. The Christian Democrats shifted their governing coalition to the left, dropping the Liberal Party and bringing in the Socialist Party. At the same time, the success of economic development began to have the effect of tightening the labor market and of increasing the economy's sensitivity, if not vulnerability, to international conditions and competitive pressures. Some of the old structural flaws as well as some new social problems also gained public attention. The result was a tentative, but eventually unsuccessful, attempt to restructure the relationship between the trade union movement and society.

If there were two phases in the development of the political economy and of the consolidated postwar settlement, roughly separated by the changes in the political and economic situation around 1960, there were also two phases in the evolution of the union movement. As we shall see, change in the unions set in earlier, around 1955, but this change remained largely at the level of intentions and initial reorientations until the political and economic transformations at the turn of the decade. Thereafter, the unions too sought to restructure their strategies and policies, but they too failed to establish new relationships with their members, employers, political parties, and the state until the hot autumn. It is only then that events, largely unforeseen by any of the major institutional actors, exploded the postwar settlement and forced a radical rethinking of basic political-economic assumptions and strategies in an attempt to find a new equilibrium in a changed and changing domestic and international political economy.

The Phase of Labor Exclusion

Once the Left was excluded from power and a variety of other domestic and international political developments had provided Italian capital and its political allies with a strong hand, the government set about implementing a liberal economic design which was perhaps the most stringent in Europe.[32] The first phase of this design was a sharp deflationary policy, so sharp, in fact, that much of the entrepreneurial class objected to the tightness of the credit policy and to the degree to which it exposed the Italian economy to international competition. The initial impact of this policy was a substantial fall in investment and steep increases in unemployment, reflecting not only the structural weakness of the economy but the tight money policy and strict budget balancing of the government as well. By the early 1950s, also as a result of the Korean War, the initial shock of the policy had been overcome and the economic recovery began along the lines of the development model which was to characterize the Italian economy until the hot autumn.[33]

The main features of the model can be rapidly reviewed. The basic economic premise was liberalism, both with regard to the internal economy and to its place in the international economy. The market was to be ascendant, economic priorities were to be set by its discipline. Government's role was to insure that this discipline was adhered to by exercising budgetary restraint, both in terms of expenditures and credit policies. The decision for openness to the international economy was particularly important, for, in the context of governmental restraint and a general low-wage policy, it meant that international demand would be a primary stimulus to growth and that Italy would have to develop the means to compete effectively with its trading partners. This required a significant upgrading of productivity and technology and elimination of the many low productivity zones in the domestic economy. More generally, there had to be a compression of production costs sufficient to make Italian goods competitive on the open market. Italy's energy dependence further reinforced the need to be internationally competitive and to emphasize international demand.

Part and parcel of this approach to development was the maintenance of low labor costs, the intense utilization of labor in the factories, and relative freedom to employ and lay off workers. Here, of course, the general political conditions and the weakness and divisions of the trade unions were of major significance. The latter meant that the unions were ineffective in countering the policies of employers. The former insured that government action would not interfere with, but would rather support, entrepreneurial decisions and would not strengthen the unions. Furthermore, liberal economic principles and the contours of the development model itself assured that the government would not embark on policies which might stimulate domestic demand, thereby creating a safety valve from international competitive pressure.

The signals that this model was having the desired effects began to appear in the early 1950s. Industrial production rose, as did productivity.[34] The latter was not paralleled by commensurate wage gains. In fact, unemployment remained high, for growth in international and domestic demand was insufficient to compensate for initial unemployment. It was only in the latter part of the decade that employment began to rise sharply, fed by a massive growth in internal migration to the northern industrial centers. Even this change, however, did not alter the basic features of the development model. Heavy reliance on international demand, a relatively weak internal market, competitiveness achieved through the utilization of medium and low-level technology, low wages and the intense exploitation of factory labor (the latter two facilitated by the weakness of the labor movement) remained the hallmarks of the, now increasingly successful, Italian economy.

The trade unions, the CGIL much more than the others, were slow to acknowledge the growing success of the economic development underway, much less to elaborate a response to it. We have already seen that the CGIL's analysis was based on premises which denied the possibility of economic success with a development model like that being implemented. As late as 1952, when 'the symptoms of a recovery of production and an enlargement of the industrial base'[35] were already evident, Giuseppe Di Vittorio, General Secretary of the CGIL declared:

> We must confirm the reasoned and documented judgement which we have already made for some time: the Italian economic situation is a situation of depression, by now of chronic character, a situation of crisis in which one finds oscillations in some economic sectors but with an accentuation of the symptoms of an ever more general and ever deeper crisis.[36]

Consistent with this analysis, the union continued to pursue its goals much as it had in the past. Thus, it placed absolute priority on increasing employment, and retained its fundamental belief that this goal, and class solidarity, were best promoted by centralized bargaining and 'great struggles to obtain results applicable to all workers, whatever their industry, firm or region.'[37] More generally, the CGIL continued to operate as if only sweeping political change (a victory of the Left) could resolve Italy's economic 'crisis' and to favor action in the political arena (general strikes on political issues, especially international ones) above action in the market arena.[38] It was only in 1955 that the CGIL undertook a severe self-criticism and began to revise its posture.

The reasons for the CGIL's tardy reaction to the changes in the economy are in part attributable to the intellectual presuppositions which we sketched earlier. It should also be noted, however, that in the situation of political and market exclusion in which the Confederation found itself, the emphasis on crisis and on the principles of the *Piano del lavoro* had two more practical functions. Firstly, it served as a mobilizing mechanism in a situation in which the union had little other than ideological resources to offer its members. Stressing the complete bankruptcy of the economics and international alignments of the dominant classes maintained the spirits of the Confederation's supporters.[39] Secondly, the old position remained consistent with the policies and goals of the PCI, and the CGIL was, if anything, even more dependent on the party than it had been before. The utility of the CGIL position for the party was of two sorts. On the one hand, it was consistent with the Communists' alliance policy, a policy which was muted but not abandoned in these years.[40] On the other hand, maintaining the mobilizational capacity of the union was important for the party because the PCI promoted a number of mass demonstrations on national and international issues (e.g., anti-Nato, against the 'swindle' electoral law of 1953). The CGIL was called on to play an active role in these demonstrations and, like the ideology of crisis, they probably helped in the short run to maintain morale among the Confederation's members.[41] In fact, despite the severity of the attacks against the PCI and the CGIL in the early 1950s, the union held its own and the party recovered somewhat from its electoral losses in 1948.

Whatever the immediate utility of retaining the analyses, rhetoric, and policies of the late 1940s and early 1950s, however, by the middle of the decade the CGIL was faced with a severe organizational crisis. Its clearest manifestation was a series of sharp setbacks in elections for *commissione interne* in major northern factories in 1954–6. The most dramatic of these was the loss of the CGIL majority position in Fiat in late 1954.[42] More generally, the CGIL was suffering a decline in membership; its capacity to mobilize was being systematically damaged by exclusion from union–employer negotiations at the factory and national level; it was facing systematic repression of its activists on the shop floor; and, by its own admission, it was increasingly out of touch with and failing to adjust to the changing situation in the factories.[43]

The losses suffered by the CGIL must in considerable part be attributed to the position of profound economic, organizational and political weakness of the Confederation. It is unlikely that even a more rapid adjustment to the changing economic conditions of the 1950s would have enabled the union to avoid severe setbacks. The high rates of unemployment, the repression of its activists in the factories by employers who could be assured of political support, the vitriolic anti-Communist propaganda of the period and the inevitable loss of collective enthusiasm among members would undoubtedly have contributed to severe problems.[44] Nonetheless, the heritage of the Confederation, more precisely its politicization, centralization, and wage strategy also played an important role.

The basic issue which the CGIL faced was the adjustment of its strategy to an economy which was becoming increasingly successful and heterogenous. This required, according to the self-criticism undertaken by the Confederation in 1956, breaking away from positions

> which no longer corresponded to the needs which emerged from the profound process of differentiation between places of work, between regions and between productive sectors, in order to engage the problems raised by the new forms of productivity and of the organization of production and the new wage systems at the factory level.[45]

Adjustment was necessary because the process of differentiation underway and the relative success of the economy meant that there were many firms with high profitability. These firms, in the absence of effective union action, were able to pursue policies, including the calculated and discriminatory use of wage increases, which ostensibly filled one of the functions of unionism and further weakened the already weak unions. An effective union strategy, however, would have to be devised to allow and facilitate bargaining on a factory level.

Because of its previous positions, the CGIL was ill-equipped to make the appropriate adjustments. Its politicization and centralization led it to continue to stress macroeconomic issues and the failures of government action, and to pursue policies intended to reinforce the PCI's general strategy. The same factors had also contributed to the weakness of union organization on the shop floor and to an emphasis on the intersectoral character of the Chambers of Labor, which were poorly adapted to pursuing a highly differentiated wage strategy. The weak shopfloor presence helps explain the union's delayed recognition of the changes taking place in the factories and its inability to devise responses to those changes.[46] The wage strategy of the CGIL, with its emphasis on equal gains for all and on maximizing employment, even at the expense of workers in more productive sectors of the economy, was in conflict with an effort to tie wages at the factory level to productivity and profitability. It also was linked to the failure of the Confederation to recognize that struggle at the factory level, and not just general political-economic conditions, might make an important contribution to the reinforcement and growth of the union. Thus, the shift in perspective and strategy which the CGIL would have to undertake was great. At the same time, it was unlikely to abandon entirely the principles with which it had been operating. It is not surprising, therefore, that what emerged was a mediated posture, reflecting old, and continuing, objectives and the new economic realities.

Before indicating the basic outlines of this new position, it is important to introduce one further factor in our discussion: the emergence of the CISL as a competitor on the shop floor and as a source of an alternative conception of the role of unionism and of union strategy.[47]

The CISL had been born as a Catholic and anti-Communist union closely linked to the Christian Democratic Party. As an expression of a Catholic tradition of trade unionism, Church policy, and of the Cold War divisions, it has been subordinate to the DC: 'In the Catholic area the convergence between the objectives of the party and the union was no less close [than in the Left]: anticommunism . . . became the ideological cement of the new organization.'[48] The philosophy of unionism which accompanied ths was 'social Christian,' seeing the union as an instrument performing an important role in the harmonization of society around Christian values. It was, therefore, not primarily a philosophy of conflict and certainly not of class conflict.

Increasingly, however, another current of thought became influential in the CISL: trade unionism in the American style. (Many CISL cadres were trained at this time at the Florentine trade union school closely tied to the American trade union movement.) While the practical effects of this new style of unionism did not appear until around 1960, it represented from the beginning a sharp break with the politicized and centralized traditions of Italian trade unionism and a direct challenge to many of the precepts of the CGIL. Its fundamental premises were that the union ought to act as an association of its members (not as an agent of the working class as a whole), that the factory was the prime arena in which the union should pursue its interests and develop its organization, and that

> it was possible to orient the economic and production choices of the individual firms as of the system as a whole by using the contractual instrument in a new way, different both in content and structure from Italian union tradition.[49]

The impact of the Florentine school has had an unexpected and ironic twist. While the original intention of the confederal leaders was to train cadres who would use American union practices to promote a social vision inspired by Catholic humanism and to defeat the unionism of the Left, these cadres eventually became the promotors of a kind of unionism which has been antagonistic both to social conservation and Christian Democratic predominance over the union. By the 1970s, the CISL's insistence on political autonomy and on aggressive shopfloor demands and action (both of these paralleling the American union tradition) had made the CISL, especially its metalworker federation (FIM), a radical force in Italy's system of industrial relations.[50]

With the new conception of Catholic unionism in the 1950s came a wage strategy which at the factory level would be extremely aggressive, seeking to keep up with or even exceed productivity gains. Such a strategy would 'favor the process of capitalization, essential for effective economic development and for the increases in productivity which were the inevitable result of technological innovations.'[51] The aggregate effects of such a policy would maximize the interests of the workers and of the economic system as a whole:

> It would have the double effect of guaranteeing the workers employed in the productive firms a share of the income produced greater than that possible on the basis of wage claims based on the average yield of the system, and, on the other hand, by blocking the creation of super-profits for the large firms . . . would constitute a stimulus for the attainment of higher levels of productive efficiency.[52]

This policy was not immediately implemented. Throughout the 1950s, the wage demands of the CISL were consistently below productivity rates. The Confederation's close links to the ruling Christian Democrats and its special relationship with the country's entrepreneurial class prevented it from translating its revised conception of wage policy into practice.

Finally, at a more general level, the ascendant faction of the CISL espoused a pluralist, rather than classist, conception of society and viewed the conflict of interests within the pluralist rules of the game as the key to, and best guarantee of, democracy and social progress. Whereas the CGIL continued to be concerned to maintain compatibility between its actions and a broader (and more abstract) understanding of the interests of the working class and sought to gauge its policies in terms of the broader political conditions necessary to promote democratic cohesion, consent, and change, the CISL felt no such constraint and argued that it was nefarious to proceed as if it existed.[53] The differences between these positions, whatever their philosophical bases, cannot be separated from the fact that the CISL was linked to the DC, the entrenched party of the government, and the CGIL to the PCI and PSI, the parties excluded from government and continually concerned to establish their democratic credentials and to prevent their further isolation. In subsequent years, despite the drawing together of the CGIL and the CISL, these philosophical differences, and their political correlates, recurrently conditioned the two confederations' platforms and strategies and led to differences of substantial importance.[54]

It is worth mentioning that the third union confederation, the UIL, did not make a significant contribution to the process of reappraisal and innovation in the union movement which we have been describing:

> The UIL did not elaborate an autonomous conception of its own role, preferring to maintain a position equally distant from what it considered to be the Communist union and what it defined as a pro-government union.[55]

In practice, the UIL often tended to follow the policies of the CISL. It also frequently behaved as a company union. This behavior and the absence of an autonomous union doctrine and strategy was to haunt the UIL even into the 1970s when it was firmly aligned with the other confederations.

The challenge of the CISL along the lines suggested, fed into the crisis of the CGIL and influenced the response of the Left confederation. The CGIL looked on the CISL with disdain, characterizing it as a 'yellow-dog,' collaborationist union. It could not, however, fail to recognize that there were merits to a strategy directing greater attention to the factory, both in terms of contractual strategy and organization. This is, in fact, what was done. Maintaining its commitment to employment, the CGIL reversed its approach to the factory, placing it at the center of its revised strategy: 'The struggle for employment—which begins with the defense of existing jobs—must be guided by the employed workers who, with their demands, can contribute to determining, to orienting new investments which will give life to new production units.'[56] In subsequent years, the CGIL would devote significant resources to the rebuilding of its organizations at the factory level and to competing with those of the CISL. The grand rhetorical themes of the confederation did not change, but a much greater linkage between national and political themes and the power and demands of the union in the factories and at the sectoral level (through the category unions) was recognized. This did not mean that the tension between national objectives and grass-roots objectives was eliminated. This tension has continued to animate debate within the CGIL and between it and the CISL to the present day. For the first time, however, the fundamental subordination of factory and wage strategy to political and central confederal concerns partially was redressed.

This development had another important effect: it set in motion a process by which the CGIL gained increasing autonomy from the PCI. The Communists had, in fact, abandoned the 'transmission belt' conception of the union movement in 1956, but this only began to take on real meaning as the Confederation rebuilt its organization and strategy along the new lines and sought publicly to assert its autonomy in order to promote this rebuilding (e.g., the CGIL took a more positive position toward the formation of the European Economic Community than did the PCI in 1957–8 and began to disengage from the Moscow-controlled international trade union movement [WFTU]).[57] There is also an irony here. In a sort of 'reverse transmission belt' the CGIL was instrumental in stimulating the PCI to revise its economic thinking, a process which culminated in the 1962 party conference on 'Tendencies of Italian Capitalism.' Again, the pace of the development of autonomy was slow and should not be exaggerated. At the same time, its importance cannot be underestimated, for it created the bases for the increasing convergence between the CISL, which was also abandoning its ties to the DC (*collateralismo*), and the CGIL first in action and then in more general strategy in the 1960s and 1970s.[58]

This brings us to a final point in our examination of this critical period. The changes both in the CGIL and in the CISL did not bear immediate fruit.[59] Neither of the revised strategies succeeded in securing major gains for the workers, with the exception of a few contracts, in the slack labor market of the 1950s. Nor did the partial convergence of positions lead the unions to greater collaboration; the rhetorical hostilities between them continued and instances of CISL and UIL signing contracts from which the CGIL had been excluded recurred. Finally, none of the confederations succeeded in translating the principles of its strategic perspectives into practical action, although both the CISL and the CGIL underwent a major organizational renewal. Only the dramatic, and largely unexpected, shift toward a tight labor market and the entrance of the Socialist Party into national government in the early 1960s created the potential for effective union action for its factory and larger social reform goals. Only under these conditions did the most important consequences of the shifts of the mid-1950s emerge.

The Phase of Blunted Change

The 1960s were years of hope and disappointment for the union movement.[60] The great promise of developments at the outset of the decade was largely frustrated, and by 1968 it appeared that little had changed in the movement's basic status in the society. Behind this cycle of promise and frustration, however, there were more subtle but important developments.[61] On the one hand, many of the changes set in motion by the debates and shifts of the 1950s were consolidated: category unions were reinforced and took on a significant role, the factory and articulated bargaining at the shopfloor level assumed importance, the strategies of the CGIL and the CISL continued to converge, the major confederations engaged in more systematic consultation and cooperation, party tutelage continued to decline. On the other hand, the experience of the 1960s demonstrated both the degree to which union strength in the market arena could help promote broader political goals of social reform and, conversely, the extent to which the balance of power in the political system, and the dominant social coalition which it expressed, continued to have critical consequences for the ability of the unions to operate effectively in the market and in pursuit of political goals.

The successes of the economy, the waning of the Cold War and changing governmental political alliances began in the early 1960s to alter some of the conditions which had contributed so much to framing the contours of the unions' strategies and actions in the preceding decade. The labor market became tighter, especially for skilled labor, and the flow of migrants added a new, potentially militant, component to the work force.[62] The easing of Cold War tensions created a context in which greater contact between the center and non-Communist Left could take place. The entrance of the Socialist Party (and exit of the Liberals who had been militantly liberal in their economic philosophy) into the governmental area and then the formation of 'organic' Center–Left governments, including the Socialists and the Christian Democrats (1963), held out the promise of governmental support for policies of reform. In particular, it appeared that there would be a systematic attempt to provide for the collective needs of the working class through government action, that there would be an expansion and socially progressive use of the public sector of industry, and that an effort to introduce systematic planning would be undertaken. The fulfilment of this promise would represent a significant redefinition of the development model, with a more active and interventionist government, a markedly expanded role for domestic demand, and, potentially, an economy oriented by planning procedures which were to include significant trade union participation.

The changed economic conditions at the beginning of the decade had a rather dramatic immediate effect: a major burst of militancy around the demands of the confederations and federations (especially those of the metalworkers) in the 1961–2 contractual round. The results were also noteworthy. The unions made major wage gains and for the first time in many years seemed to be the protagonist in negotiations with the employers. In addition, the industries in the public sector took a progressive role in the contract negotiations, thereby institutionalizing an organizational division between public (Intersind) and private (Confindustria) employers which had existed since 1956. In some ways, however, the process of bargaining in 1962 was less innovative. There was some factory-level bargaining, whose scope was limited by the constraints set by the confederations. Thus, 'factory-level bargaining . . . did not succeed in becoming the primary structure of the system of industrial relations, capable of guaranteeing a new type of autonomous impulse to the union movement.'[63] Furthermore, the category unions did not exercise a major role; power still remained concentrated in the confederations. Finally, the union movement did not succeed in implanting its organizations more deeply in the factories. These themes—articulated factory bargaining, the continuing weakness of union organization on the shop floor, the degree of strategic autonomy to be granted to shopfloor organizations and the role of the category unions—remained central in the union movement throughout the decade and even in the 1970s. This is symptomatic of some enduring difficulties faced by the unions in formulating their strategy: what are the appropriate arenas (market and/or political) for pursuing what objectives; and what roles are to be assigned to different levels of organization in the pursuit of these objectives? It was to take the far more intense and prolonged mobilization of the hot autumn before the unions would succeed in consolidating extensive gains in any of these areas. The continuing relative weakness of the union at the shop floor and in factory negotiations was a function both of its structural position in the market, which remained fragile, and of its tardiness in developing factory organization. Ironically, this same weakness contributes to the explanation of the degree to which the hot autumn disrupted the entire political economy and the development model to which it was linked.

The militancy, strikes, and contracts of the early 1960s represented the high point of strength until 1969. Thereafter, the unions were forced back on the defensive, unable to influence government macroeconomic policy and the basic decisions of firms and therefore the general path of economic development. This was not at the time a general expectation, nor can it be said in any simple way to have been inevitable. The strikes and contracts of 1962–3 indicated that major changes were underway in the economy and the labor market: for the first time in the postwar period wage gains won by the workers threatened to upset the economic equilibrium of the postwar economic settlement. The changes seemed to signal that Italy was in the process of becoming a mature industrial economy and society. It appeared to many that the unions could not—and should not, if wage pressure was to be kept within limits deemed 'reasonable' for the further development of the economy—be excluded in the market and political arenas.[64] Instead, it was maintained, a stable industrial relations system and the integration of the union movement into the political process was called for. This would, of course, entail changes in government policy, most importantly a systematic program of social reforms which would satisfy the collective needs which had been becoming ever more pressing as industrialization proceeded. Only in this way could the unions be expected to cooperate in assuring that development continued smoothly by maintaining wage claims within appropriate limits. In view of its stated objectives and composition the Center–Left government seemed the ideal instrument to undertake a policy of labor integration. Such a policy would not only be functional to the economy and consistent with the explicit ideology which had been expressed by both the Socialists and the Christian Democrats to justify the coalition. It would also be in the most immediate political interests of the coalition partners, for it would enhance the likelihood of isolating and weakening the PCI which was argued to be profiting (its electoral strength was steadily growing) from the failure of government to address the social consequences of the country's development. Thus, it seemed the time was ripe to end the union movement's exclusion and to make it an integral part of a social coalition to reform the Italian political economy.

This was not to occur. In 1968 the unions' status in the society was, from an institutional standpoint, little changed from what it had been in 1962. We cannot here dwell at length on why this was the case. At the most general level, it can be observed that the progressive elements within the Center–Left coalition (who held only the slimmest of political majorities) proved unable to put together the social coalition which would have augmented their strength and enabled them to impose a reformist design. Most important, they failed to enlist the full support of the unions. Instead, a vicious cycle was set in motion: the tentativeness of the government's reformist commitment fed the confederations' understandable (given their past experience and their strategic orientations) diffidence, leading to further weakening of the political strength of reformist political forces and, in turn, to greater diffidence and hostility from the unions. As we will see, this cycle was in considerable part repeated in the 1970s, although to some extent the critical actors and political and economic conditions were changed, greatly complicating the problem. In order to set the context for these later developments, however, two policy episodes from the 1960s need to be mentioned.

The first is the government's response to the threats of inflation and balance of payments problems (only in part due to the contract gains of the early 1960s) in 1963–4. The response was of the most traditional kind, designed to foster once again the necessary conditions for the effective pursuit of the postwar development model: tight credit and restrictive monetary policy.[65] The resultant reduction in economic activity and increase in unemployment was expected to discipline the wage process and create the conditions for a relaunching of investment and for renewed gains in productivity, in other words, to restore economic 'health' through a disciplining of the unions. The policy was only partially successful. The recovery of the economy was slower and less vibrant than anticipated.

The continuing structural weaknesses of the unions, however, were brought into sharp relief. At the shop floor, they were unable to counter the employers' use of the recession to reorganize production and to intensify work rhythms. In the contractual process, the recession was translated into rather poor contracts in the 1965–6 round of bargaining. The only innovations were the growing attempts of the category unions, especially those of the metalworkers, to establish their autonomy from the confederations, and the increased unity of action among the unions at the federal and shopfloor level. The former produced considerable tension with the confederations which continued to try to control the bargaining process. The latter only highlighted the extent to which the contracts were poor and the weakness of the unions in the market and political arenas was a fundamental restraint on their ability to make significant gains. Finally, at the political level, the unions proved incapable of gaining any significant influence over the development process.

The second policy episode is related to this last point. Some might believe that recession was the only way to restore economic equilibrium, but this was not a commonly shared assumption at the time. There were, in fact, a number of prominent leaders from the parties of the Center–Left who advocated a combination of planning, with direct union participation, incomes policy, and social reforms. It was argued that this would not only restore economic growth but would also allow the gradual removal of distortions in development (e.g., the unequal development between North and South, the weakness of the internal market, the social costs produced by the failure to address the collective needs of the working classes in a developed and urbanized economy) which were already causing problems and which might well undermine economic growth in the future.

The development of a plan was begun in 1963–4 and the unions' cooperation was sought. The effort failed: for different reasons both the

CGIL and the CISL refused to agree to a self-limitation of wage demands, much less to a legally sanctioned one;[66] both confederations, again with different motivations, were diffident toward the planning process, although the CISL eventually agreed to it. The UIL, in contrast to the other two confederations, accepted the planning process with alacrity. Despite its failure to bring about the incorporation of the unions, two things about the planning episode are, however, of more lasting interest. First, although a five-year plan was passed and some of its provisions enacted, it did not function as a means to correct the structural flaws of the Italian economy to which it had been originally addressed. It became, instead, another mechanism for the general expansion of government which went on in Italy in the 1960s. Second, the postures which the unions assumed toward planning were themselves of significance for future developments.

With respect to the first point, it must be emphasized that despite the fact that the basic contours of the development model were retained throughout most of the 1960s, the role and size of government expanded significantly. The plan of the mid-1960s was only a stage of this process which had begun earlier in the decade.[67] This expansion, however, did not have the 'rationalizing' impetus which was supposed to be part and parcel of the effort to provide for the needs of the industrial working classes and thereby to help integrate the unions. Rather, it generally served to extend and deepen clientelistic and narrow interest group linkages between the government parties (especially, but not exclusively, the Christian Democrats) and a vast array of social strata other than the organized working class. The long-run effects of this development would make themselves felt in the 1970s when these linkages, and their importance for the political power of the DC, became major impediments to the implementation of effective policies to deal with the political-economic consequences of a much stronger and more militant union and workers' movement. It should also be noted that the expansion of clientelism and narrow special interest politics under the Center–Left further eroded the autonomy of state institutions and undermined the credibility of the Socialist Party as a potential agent of social reform.[68] Again, these consequences were to have a major bearing on developments after the hot autumn.

Both the CGIL and the CISL had reasoned arguments for their diffidence toward the planning process. In both cases, these arguments were direct descendants of the basic union positions hammered out in the 1950s.[69] The CISL seemed, at a general level, favorable to a planning process. It certainly coincided with the interclassist and potentially liberal corporatist traditions of social Christianity, now minoritarian but still important within the Confederation. At a more practical level, however, the dominant wing of the CISL was opposed, on principle, to any form of planning which included, implicitly or explicitly, an agreement by the unions to limit wage bargaining and claims: it violated 'the tendency to accentuate evermore the pure contractual role of the union, especially at the factory level.'[70] The centralization and planned wage policy of even a loosely programmed economy would deny the union of precisely the role and levers of power which the CISL had been promoting for more than a decade. It would also require the union to adjust its policies to exigencies over which it had only partial control and which were not in the direct, immediate interest of its members and thus would be in contrast with the 'associational' unionism which the CISL advocated. Finally, it would be in contradiction with the pluralist conception of society which the CISL majority held.

The CGIL was more hostile to the planning process as presented by the government. Yet both at the level of principle and at the level of internal and external confederal politics, the Confederation was cross-pressured. The CGIL did not in principle reject the idea of planning as a means to rationalize the economy. Its ideological traditions made the CGIL receptive to the idea of planning and even, in contrast to the CISL, to the theoretical possibility that it might be appropriate to exercise some wage moderation in the context of a systematic and long-term process of planning which would use resources to eliminate structural economic flaws (especially the southern problem) and would assure productivity growth. In practice, however, the Confederation considered the plan as it evolved as placing too much emphasis on incomes policy and as being too vague with regard to the implementation of planning goals.[71]

The politics of the CGIL's stance on the plan were similarly complex and contradictory. On the one hand, the Confederation's ties to the PCI encouraged full opposition. Since the Center–Left was, in part, an effort further to isolate and weaken the Communist Party, CGIL cooperation in the coalition's reformist designs was unlikely. On the other hand, there was an implicit threat that the Socialist Party might encourage a split by the Socialist minority current in the CGIL (which had already begun to develop autonomous views on issues of overall CGIL strategy) if the Confederation failed to keep open the possibility of cooperation in planning.[72] For the Communists in the CGIL, therefore, both principle and politics encouraged moderation. The result was that, although the PCI voted against the legislation enacting planning, the Communist and Socialist parliamentarians belonging to the CGIL abstained. This was the first time in the postwar period that the vote of CGIL parliamentarians did not follow the vote of the party.

The distinctions between and within the CISL and CGIL positions on planning and incomes policy which emerged in these years were to retain their importance in the 1970s when similar issues confronted the union movement. Nonetheless, the issue of how to respond to planning set in motion a debate on ideological and practical issues between the confederations. For the CGIL, this debate accelerated the abandonment of the 'revolutionary' rhetoric which had colored its economic pronouncements in the 1950s. For the CISL, the debate encouraged its acceptance of the idea that the union movement should concern itself not just with shopfloor issues of importance to its membership but also with general political-economic policy and reform. Thus, the two major confederations established a terrain of shared concerns, removed from the impact of conflicting ideological positions, which offered the possibility of strategic convergence in the early 1970s.[73]

Before turning to the dramatic events of the hot autumn and its consequences, a brief survey of the union movement at the end of the 1960s is called for. The decade did include some developments which were to prove of major importance for the coming years. In terms of the internal affairs of the unions, two developments are worthy of note. First, co-operation increased among the federations, especially the metal and chemical workers, at the federal and shopfloor levels. By 1969, in fact, the metalworkers had developed a shared conception of how unification of their federations and of the union movement as a whole should proceed. Second, the growth in power of the category unions and the growing commitment to articulated bargaining and to the strengthening of organiz-ation at the factory level raised the issue of the appropriate responsibilities of different organizational levels of the trade union movement. In terms of external relations, the most important development was the growing autonomy of the confederations from the political parties. In short, the changes initiated in the mid-1950s began to bear real fruit.

There were also a number of negative lessons learned. Foremost among these was the keen awareness of the continuing structural weaknesses of the unions, both in the market and political arenas and of the consequences of these for the unions' ability to carry out both their market strategies and their pursuit of broader social reforms. In addition, the unions also became acutely aware of the need for political change beyond that which the Center–Left had embodied. Taken together, these lessons produced what Alessandro Pizzorno has referred to as a basic pessimism, more pro-nounced in the CGIL than in the CISL but present in both, about the results likely to be gained by action in the market arena alone.[74]

If viewed in a longer perspective, it can be argued that by 1968 the union movement was confronted with a series of problems many of whose roots lay in the immediate postwar period but which had matured to the point that they now posed fundamental strategic dilemmas. These problems were: what relationship to strike with the party system and with political parties (e.g., favor specific partisan outcomes, only political policy goals or maintain strict autonomy from politics); what should be the proper relationship between confederations and category unions; what should be the relationship between union leadership and the mass base of unionized and nonunionized workers; what should be the balance between con-federal, category and factory-level bargaining; what should be the dynamic between wage bargaining, broader economic goals (employment, develop-ment, productivity) and the need for social reform; how should the confederations relate to one another.

As is evident, these problems were the expression of themes which had been present almost from the moment of the rebirth of Italian unions after World War II. They concerned the objectives which the movement was to seek to attain, the arenas (market and/or political) within which specific objectives were to be pursued, and the roles which were to be assigned to the factory, federal, and confederal structures. What had changed was that the ways these problems might be resolved were less clear to the individual confederations than had been true in the past. The old certainties had been eroded as the unions had been compelled to confront the changes in the political economy, the party system, the state, and their relationships to one another. Real strategic choices were now recognized where in the past only theoretical alternatives had been acknowledged. At the same time, however, the continuing structural weakness of the union movement in both the market and political arenas made choices with respect to these strategic problems difficult. The unions' ability to control their own fate was severely constrained, and thus no strategy gave great promise of being effectively implemented or of producing significant, lasting results. The unions remained on the defensive and no amount of strategic innovation seemed likely to alter this state of affairs. The hot autumn, unexpected by all including the union leaderships, dramatically changed this situation, projecting the union and workers' movement to the center of the economic and political stage and making decisions about these strategic problems of vital importance, both for the movement and for Italy more generally.

The End of the Postwar Settlement and the Search for a New Model of Development: Union Analyses and Strategy after the Hot Autumn

Introduction

The hot autumn—more accurately, the period of intensive social and labor mobilization from the student demonstrations and mass rallies for pension reform in 1968 until the conclusion of the contractual round in early 1970—overturned established patterns of economic, social, and political relations in Italy.[75] Traditional economic expectations were disrupted and the usual economic policy instruments lost much of their efficacy. Longstanding social relationships within the working class and between it and other social strata were uprooted, and the search for new linkages begun. Political alliances among the parties and between them and diverse social actors including the unions were disrupted and the search for new relations between the parties, political institutions and society initiated. In contrast to what followed the 'May uprising' in France, in Italy the older order was not quickly and effectively reestablished. Instead, the hot autumn marked the onset of an intense process of conflict and compromise—not yet concluded—as critical economic, social, and political actors sought to define the basic characteristics of a renewed social and political-economic order.

The union movement was an essential protagonist in this process.[76] This status derived (and derives) from the centrality assumed by the movement in the Italian political economy as a result of the changes which took place during and after the hot autumn, and from the strategic choices adopted by the movement itself. Our focus will be on the latter, and on the economic and political analyses to which they were linked. In particular, we will examine how the analyses and choices made in 1969–70—themselves linked to the pattern of developments already described—affected the unions' subsequent responses to the deep national and international crisis which began after 1973. In order to do so, however, we need first to look briefly at the most important direct effects of the hot autumn.

The hot autumn and its immediate consequences destroyed many of the workplace, internal union, economic, and political conditions on which Italy's postwar development model had been built and sustained. In doing so, it also broke the pessimism of much of the union leadership and gave impulse to significant strategic innovations which were to set the parameters of union policy for the remainder of the decade.

At the shop floor, the most visible feature of the hot autumn was the intense and seemingly inexhaustible mobilization of the workers. Associated with this mobilization was an incipient new worker culture. The themes of egalitarianism (reduction of wage differentials and elimination of many levels of the job hierarchy both within the blue-collar workforce and between blue-collar and white-collar workers) and of meaningful participation by wage earners in production decisions and in the organizations which represented them became both the slogans and the measures of the transformation underway. Strike rates soared and remained very high, assemblies of workers within the factories multiplied, street demonstrations became common, new forms of struggle (articulated strikes shop by shop, for instance) were tried, worker participation in many forms of union and nonunion organization and meetings was extensive. At the same time, long-established shopfloor institutions and practices were overturned. The *commissioni interne* gave way, first spontaneously in some large factories and then through union initiative and legislation (the *Statuto dei lavoratori* or Workers' Statute), to the election of delegates shop by shop and the creation of factorywide Delegates' Councils.[77] The *Statuto* also vastly extended the unions' ability to control and affect the discretionary power of employers at the shop floor.[78] The pace of the line and work procedures, the introduction of new technology, the mobility of the workers within the work place, and layoffs became issues for continuous bargaining between the delegates, workers, and management. As a result of these and other changes, substantive collective bargaining over work conditions became the norm in large and medium factories. The era of employer discretion to reorganize rapidly at the shop floor in order to meet economic contingencies came to an end.

Within the unions themselves, marked changes also took place as a consequence of the hot autumn. The most important of these were the aforementioned implantation of far more representative and effective organizational structures in the factories and the drive toward union unity. The delegate and factory council structures were particularly noteworthy because they were not purely union institutions: all workers, whether members or not, could vote and become delegates. This characteristic helped to reinforce the push for unity among the CGIL, CISL and UIL and their associated category unions and to broaden the appeal of the unions among workers. This push came simultaneously from below—from the workers and the federations—and from the confederations. We will see below that the type of unity pursued differed and that the overall drive for unification, in any form, did not entirely succeed. Nonetheless, after the hot autumn and the negotiations on unification which followed it, there was a qualitative increase in the cooperation among the unions at all levels, not only in shopfloor and sectoral bargaining but also in the relationships established between the unions and the government. When dealing with others, whether employers, political parties, or the government, the unions began to present themselves as a united, single front, regardless of the continuing differences between them.[79]

The economic consequences of the hot autumn were enormous and will not be detailed here. From the standpoint of the development model, two major effects need to be emphasized. Firstly, there was an enormous wage push—the wages of Italian workers were brought into line with those of other workers in advanced industrialized Europe—accompanied by a significant shift in the share of GNP going to labor.[80] Prices rose, profits were squeezed, and the pressure on employers markedly increased. Secondly, the mobilization and organizational changes at the shop floor meant that the employers were unable to respond to these pressures with the mechanisms which had served them so well in the past. Increasing productivity through work reorganization became extremely difficult, and in many cases impossible. At the same time, the continued mobilization of the workers served to sustain their demands over a protracted period of time and even in the face of stagnation of the economy in the early 1970s.[81] Unlike the period of the mid-1960s when employers were able to restore profitability and control in the work place through the combined use of work reorganization and increased unemployment, this time the new strength of the workers and unions made such a response impossible.

Political changes also worked to preclude earlier solutions. With the hot autumn, the era of the Center–Left effectively (if not in terms of government coalitions) came to an end. The Socialist Party had already seen its attempt to merge with the Social Democrats founder and had suffered severe losses in the 1968 national elections. The mobilization of the workers now pushed the Socialists significantly to the left. In general terms, this shift posed the question of whether the collaboration between Socialists and Christian Democrats could survive and what coalition might follow (i.e., the 'Communist question' was put on the political agenda). More specifically, the continuing participation of the Socialists in the coalition (no immediate alternative was available) meant that the government could not undertake effective policies of economic restraint like those which had been utilized in the 1960s, especially since the new strength of the workers meant that such measures would have to be all the more severe. On the other hand, as we shall see, the debilitated Center–Left coalition also proved unable to implement reform policies which would have responded to some of the unions' demands and which might have created the possibility of a return to greater economic stability.

From even this brief overview, it should be evident that the hot autumn and its consequences brought an end to the conditions on which the Italian development model had been erected. The low-wage, high-export premises of the model were challenged and the mechanisms which in the past had served to meet such challenges and to restore stable growth were rendered ineffective. These changes, in addition to other domestic and international factors which have tended to augment economic difficulties and further preclude traditional responses, have been reflected in Italy's economic performance in the last decade.

There is clearly an irony in this. Italy's development model had been hoisted on its own petard:

In almost no other European advanced industrial country were the unions so organizationally weak, participation so limited to a narrow strata of politicized and skilled workers, base level bargaining over wages and conditions of work so absent from the daily practice of the union [prior to 1969]. Paradoxically, such relative weakness—the limited unionization of the work force—was to become a factor of disequilibrium; this was so because in few other countries were the conditions so favorable for a radical change.[82]

With the hot autumn, largely unanticipated even by the union leaderships, enormous opportunities were created for the union movement. Many of the conditions which had made the unions both economically and politically weak rapidly disappeared, and they found themselves in a position to impose or at least to think of imposing their objectives on the larger political economy. At the same time, however, this new power, and its effective utilization, also required the unions to come to terms with many of the strategic and organizational problems with which they had long been contending and to devise analyses and strategies appropriate to the new context within which they were operating and which they appeared to have much ability to influence. Luciano Lama describes the situation as follows:

> The gap between words and facts is less than what it once was . . . therefore rigor in choices and in the linkage between this or that choice and the rest of the strategy of the union and the situation in which the union operates and the reflection on all of this, become more pertinent, up to date and careful than they once were.[83]

The immediate need of the unions was to capture control and simultaneously respond to and utilize the mobilization in the factories to worker and union institutional advantage. They managed this with considerable skill. In a relatively brief period, they succeeded in incorporating the new values and demands and placing themselves at the head of the militancy. Through their contractual policy and the *Statuto*, they also succeeded in generalizing many of the gains made in sectors and factories where the movement was strongest. Progress toward union unity also accelerated. Beyond the gains in wages, workplace power, and political influence already mentioned, another measure of this success is that, between 1969 and 1971, membership in the CGIL and the CISL (the only two confederations for which data are available) climbed by 20 percent.[84]

The unions' new power, however, was perceived by their leaderships to require, and to offer the opportunity to undertake, strategic and organizational innovations which could overcome the strains and contradictions that had marked their strategies in the past and that had become ever more evident in the 1960s. We have seen that these strains were over the relative emphasis to be given to different *objectives*—workplace or social reforms, *arenas* for the pursuit of these objectives, political or market—and over the roles to be assumed by different *levels of organization*—workplace, federal, confederal—in their pursuit. With the hot autumn, the unions, now operating in closer concert, sought to develop a strategy which might overcome the tensions and fluctuations of the past. The fundamental premise of this strategy was that the unions should not confine their concerns and use of their new power to the pursuit of workplace objectives, no matter how innovative, through action in the market arena by all levels of the union structure. Rather, such objectives had to be systematically linked to broader sociopolitical objectives representing the interests of a constituency beyond the unionized work force—structural reforms of the Italian political economy; the unions had to take the initiative in the political as well as the market arena; and all levels of the union had to be involved in and gear their goals to this strategic perspective. The union movement was to be both a market and political protagonist. Its capacity to stimulate, channel and control mass mobilization was to be used as a resource in contractual negotiation and as pressure on the political institutions in the pursuit of broader political objectives. Combined action in the market and political arenas was to be melded into a global strategy of political-economic change.[85] Lama described the strategic perspective of the CGIL, and to a considerable extent of all three confederations after the hot autumn, as follows:

> It clearly maintained the commitment of the union on questions of contractual policy . . . and on the other hand, it forced the contractual policy of the union out of the mold of the status quo determined by factory situations, by sectoral situations, by the general economic situation, as if these were static components which could not be 'forced' by the initiative of the union and of the movement of struggle.
> This, however, was only possible if one established, as we did, a certain parallelism between this type of position on contractual policy and the commitment of the union at the level of society.[86]

This attempt to merge market and political action to attain contractual advantage for the work force and transformative political outcomes for the benefit of broad strata of the population is the unique characteristic of Italian trade unionism in the 1970s. It is the source of many of the innovative proposals made by the unions and of many of the strategic dilemmas faced by them in the decade.

The reasoning behind the unions' adoption of this perspective will be examined in detail below. At a more general level, several factors contributed to it.[87] First, it was in many senses a synthesis of elements which had been present in the strategies of the two major confederations and some of the federations in the past and which in the 1960s had become matters for discussion and debate. The CGIL's conception of class unionism and its emphasis on action in the political area and on alliances and global political objectives were incorporated. So too were the CISL's stress on shopfloor issues, aggressive and articulated wage policy, and egalitarianism. More generally, the new strategic perspective brought together some of the major strands of historical Marxist and Catholic union doctrine in Italy. In short, in the heat of the struggles and pressure for unity, a fusion of many of these elements seemed to be achieved. This trend was reinforced by the evolution which the UIL, Italy's third largest confederation, had experienced in the late 1960s, especially among its metalworkers. Both its rabid anti-Communism of old and its pro-capital leanings became attenuated, while the themes of egalitarianism and social reforms came to occupy a central position in its strategic orientation.

Second, the new strategy was the product of a perception on the part of the unions that social change was occurring more rapidly than political change and that the party system was incapable of responding effectively to the demand for structural reform coming from society. The unions themselves had to become agents for the mediation of these demands, rather than, as in the past, delegating this role to the parties.[88] In this connection, two consequences of the enormous gains in union strength (rise in membership, sustained mobilization, organizational implantation and control on the shop floor, steps toward unification) need to be underlined. On the one hand, the growth in power gave the unions legitimacy based on their own organizational resources, making them less reliant on legitimacy derived from partisan affiliations. On the other hand, the unions' new strength sharply increased their capacity to disrupt the economy and to challenge the legitimacy of the existing governmental coalitions and of the political and party system more generally. The challenge before the unions, therefore, was to utilize this capacity in a manner consistent with their strategic objectives. If they failed to do so, they risked weakening their ability to represent and aggregate working-class demands, undercutting their status in the political arena and setting in motion a chain of economic developments which would erode their power in the market arena. In short, if the unions did not succeed in contributing to the emergence of a new political-economic development model, they risked becoming trapped once again by the limits of the old one.

Third, this autonomous political role for the unions allowed them to accelerate their withdrawal from the tutelage of the political parties—which was indispensable to the development of union unity—without abandoning many of the goals which they had come increasingly to share in the 1960s. The strategy, therefore, was both a product of and a factor contributing to union unification. Fourth, it also served the internal institutional needs of the unions, for it assigned important functions to all levels of the union structure, while it simultaneously was intended to provide guiding principles which might link the initiatives and objectives pursued at the different levels into a more organic design. Finally, the strategic perspective was supposed to enable the unions to serve their members while also pursuing goals which would tie the movement to a broader range of social strata.

These can be identified as the central factors contributing to the development of the new union strategic perspective in the wake of the hot autumn. Potentially this perspective offered a synthetic plan of action which might resolve the tensions with respect to objectives, arenas, and institutional instruments which had plagued the unions in the past.[89] As we shall see, many of these tensions reappeared in subsequent years in the face of political and economic conditions which made implementation of the initial design impossible and of renewed internal conflicts between the confederations and between levels of the structure of the confederations. The basic principles of the strategy, in particular the tight linkage between market and general reform objectives, were, however, to be retained. In this sense the hot autumn marked not only a breakdown of the development model but a breakthrough in union strategy. Nonetheless, many of the old tensions, rooted in the history of the movement's evolution and the character of Italy's economic and political system and the place of the trade unions within them, continued to provoke disagreements and strategic revisions.

From the Hot Autumn to the Oil Crisis: The Policy of Social Reform

The years from the hot autumn through the winter of 1973–4 represented the highpoint of sustained union militancy and initiative in the last decade. It was in this period that the unions consolidated their organizational hold, through new institutions, in the factories, made substantial advances toward unification, and sought to capitalize on their new power to implement the various components of their reformulated strategy. Tensions with regard to objectives, the emphasis to be given to action in the market and political arenas and the relationship to be struck between the two, and the role to be assumed by the shopfloor, federal and confederal structures remained, but they were largely obscured, for the first two years, by the optimism and sheer collective enthusiasm which pervaded the union movement. Only toward the end of 1972 and in 1973, did the problems with the new strategy emerge and begin to lead to a closer examination of priorities and how they were to be pursued.

Before turning to the substance of the unions' strategic response following the hot autumn, a brief discussion of the movement toward union unity is necessary.[90] Along with the development of the factory councils and the consequent implantation of the unions in the factories, this is undoubtedly the most important institutional development of the last decade. The process by which partial unification of the confederations was attained is enormously complex and intricate and is worthy of an essay (or book) on its own. Here we intend simply to indicate the general features of the process.

We have seen that unity of action among the unions had been developing throughout the 1960s. The most advanced forms had occurred in the factories and among the federations, especially the metalworkers. The latter, in fact, had already begun to move toward 'organic' unity in 1966. The confederations lagged behind. Even at this level, however, the debate over planning in the second half of the 1960s had opened the way toward the possibility of greater cooperation and, with the benefit of hindsight, toward the unity which was attained in 1970.[91]

The conceptions of unity being promoted 'from below' and 'from above' had significant differences. The pressure from below, coming from the factories, especially the large ones in the North, and from the most advanced federations, were for an 'organic' unity which would create a single, trade union structure in which the traditional divisions on political and confederal lines would be abandoned. One united confederation would be the peak of one united movement built from the bottom up with new structures which would break down all the old barriers. The confederations, in contrast, were more cautious. The conception of unity which they eventually came to espouse was one of bringing the previous confederal and federal structures under a single institutional umbrella while maintaining, at least for some time, their separate identities and right to institutional expression of position on issues faced by the union movement.

These divergences should not be surprising. The federations were more directly an expression of the workers on the shop floor, many of whom were not affiliated with any union or who had not lived through the 1950s, and who saw the power which unity might confer. The transformation of the working class, particularly in the large factories of the North, was a potent force in the unitary process, as was the renewal of cadres which had taken place in the industrial confederations in the 1960s. Many of the new activists, fervent believers in the need to build the union in the factory, saw unification as indispensable to this end. It should also be noted that unification on the shop floor was a potentially powerful tool in the hands of the federations in their efforts to wrest more independence from the confederations.[92] These latter had always been, and continued to be, much more closely linked to the party system, and most of their leaders were also important figures in one of the political parties. It is not surprising, therefore, that they were more sensitive to the impact union unity might have on partisan politics, more susceptible to the expressions of concern voiced by the parties as the unity process proceeded and more cognizant of how that process, if it proceeded too far too rapidly, might create a partisan backlash which could not only bring an end to the drive for unity but also might eliminate the gains in autonomy which the unions had been making.[93]

These latter points highlight the issue which was, from the beginning, the critical problem which any form of union unity had to resolve: the posture of the union toward politics and the political parties. Among those who favored any sort of unity (there were important dissenters both in the CISL and the UIL, usually vehement anti-Communists and often linked to non-industrial unions), neither the 'radicals' nor the 'moderates' questioned the idea that a more unified union movement would have to maintain a commitment to political goals and develop a fully autonomous posture with respect to the political parties. Even in the CISL, which on past experience might have been expected to want an 'apolitical' union movement, those who favored unification did not hold such a position.[94] Despite these shared assumptions, however, there were sharp differences which strongly influenced the process of unification and affected its outcome. These continue to the present day to condition the posture assumed by the movement.

A detailed chronology of the events which by mid-1972 led to the creation of a federation of the confederations and of the confederally linked federations in a variety of sectors is impossible here. Basically, the process can be divided into two phases. In the first, on the heels of the hot autumn, the forces in favor of 'organic' unity seemed to have the upper hand, braked only by the caution of the 'moderates.' In the second, beginning in late 1971 and concluding with the Pact of Federation in July, 1972, it was the more moderate interpretation which became the best option in the face of ever stronger opposition from the anti-unity forces within the unions and from the political parties, especially the Christian Democrats.

The first phase rode on the wave of collective enthusiasm and optimism rising from the factories.[95] A major accomplishment in this phase was the implementation by all three confederations of an incompatibility rule: all trade union officials at any level who also held positions of responsibility within a political party or in an elective assembly had to choose between union and political office. The importance of the rule was brought home by the rapid resignations of CGIL and CISL leaders from their positions in Parliament and, subsequently, from their party (e.g., Lama who resigned from the Central Committee of the PCI) or union (in the case of Agostino Novella who resigned as CGIL General-Secretary and returned to the PCI) posts.[96] At the same time, in July 1970 the CISL abandoned its commitment to the notion of the union as an association of its members, thus opening the way to agreement with the CGIL on the conception of the union as a class institution.[97] With these stances, the confederations resolved one of the most symbolically important questions with respect to union autonomy, while at the same time clearing away obstacles which might have interfered with agreement among them about the political, but nonpartisan, posture to be assumed by a unified movement.

The more general thrust of this phase can be identified in two developments. First, throughout 1969 and 1970, the federations of metalworkers, always the vanguard in the unity process, adopted a series of measures which were premised on the prospect of the rapid creation of a 'new union implying the dissolution of the existing confederations and the generalization of the concilar structures' to the entire union movement. The metalworkers thus foresaw the creation of a new movement 'from below' which would reflect a 'unitary class unionism, expression of the totality of salaried masses, profoundly rooted in civil society and powerful in political life'.[98] The drive for unity by the metalworkers in this phase culminated in the agreement on the rules of a unified federation in March 1971 to be established one year later.

At the confederal level, developments toward unity also moved quickly, if always constrained by the factors already cited. In early 1970 the three confederations held congresses which implemented the incompatibility rule and which called for rapid progress on unification. In October 1970 the leading deliberative bodies of the confederations met jointly for the first time. In November 1971 the three approved a document which set the end of 1972 as the date on which they would, after holding individual congresses of dissolution, create 'a new unitary organization of Italian workers.'[99] The character of the new union was also stipulated. It was to be 'the class organization of all workers' which would assume a directly political role promoting economic and social reform. Political currents were ruled out, incompatibility would apply at all levels and all officers would be elected (not designated by parties). The stage had been set for the organic unification of the Italian union movement twenty-eight years after the Pact of Rome.

Organic unity was not to be attained. Instead, less than a year later the federated structure alluded to earlier was established. While it did not exclude the possibility of further development toward organic unity, the Pact of Federation of July 1972 brought a halt to the process of unification. The Pact included a number of provisions and principles drawn from the more 'radical' plank: the councils, for instance, with elections open to all workers whether in the union or not, were designated as the basic workplace structures. However, the unions in the factories were assured participation in the directorates of the councils. Furthermore, organic unity was excluded as a violation of the principle of federation. The halt in the process of unification was also evident in the manner in which the leadership organs of the newly constituted federation of confederations were to be chosen. On the one hand, their members were to be nominated by the general assemblies of each confederation, a rule which assured continued representation of the political currents of which each confederation was composed. On the other hand, the Directing Committee and Secretariat of the new federation was to give equal representation to each confederation, and all lower structures were to employ the same rule. Four-fifths of those voting or a majority of each organization was required to adopt a position, thereby effectively giving a veto to any major political current.

From even this brief review of the rules of the Federation CGIL–CISL–UIL, it is evident to what extent the organization which emerged in July 1972 differed from that foreseen in November 1971. It is also clear that the thrust of the rollback was to continue the role of the political currents within the union movement, albeit in sharply reduced form from that which had prevailed even in the 1960s. If we ask what factors contributed to this outcome, several can be cited. The first is contextual. By late 1971 the wave of mobilization of the hot autumn had crested. In the factories, the enthusiasm of the preceding two years began to decline, particularly in light of the situation of general economic stagnation which prevailed. This is not to argue that the workers became docile; activism, strike activity, and the like remained high. Nonetheless, the pressure from the base lessened. At the same time, a political reaction to the hot autumn had set in. The electorate appeared to be shifting to the right, the government attempted to impose a recessionary policy and then, in early 1972, Parliamentary elections were called one year ahead of schedule. Thus, just as the confederations seemed determined to create an organic unity, both the labor-market and political conditions which provided so much of the energy for such a policy began to weaken.

In this context, it should not be surprising that those elements within the union movement and on its margins who were either skeptical about or wholly opposed to unification and which had been an ineffectual minority in the preceding three years should be able more effectively to assert themselves. In the unions we have already noted that there were groups of this sort. They existed in the parties as well, particularly in the Christian Democrats who saw themselves faced with the prospect not only of losing one of their most effective social arms but also of having to deal with a union movement in which the social opposition to Christian Democratic policies and the Communist Party might have a predominant role. In the other parties, including the PCI, there were also groups which had their doubts about the advisability of a union movement which was totally autonomous from the parties and insistent on playing an explicitly political, and potentially destabilizing, role. As the forces opposed to unity of any sort became more vocal, those who wanted a more moderate form of unification were also reinforced. The union leaders, especially those at the confederal level, became more sympathetic to a limited, federated structure as the best outcome possible in a situation in which the tensions within the political system and within the unions might threaten most or all of the gains of the preceding three years.[100]

The less than maximal result of the unification process, however, should not leave the reader with the impression that no progess was made. The union movement which emerged with the Pact of Federation was dramatically different from that which existed prior to the hot autumn. It was more unified than at any time since 1947, and perhaps since 1944. Since 1970, the unions at the confederal, federal, and firm levels, respectively, have bargained together on the basis of agreed-on platforms. It was also more autonomous from the political parties: incompatibility, the federated structure, the commitments of the leaders to unity, and the experience of working together eroded some of the old party–union linkages. The federated union movement was, for the first time in its postwar history, strongly and unitarily organized on the shop floor, thus creating not only a more powerful base from which to promote its positions but also a further continuing pressure against falling back into old divisive behaviors. Finally, and it is to this that we now turn, the union movement was, for the first time in its postwar history, unified on a number of key orienting principles and was able to devise and seek to implement, in common, a strategy which sought to mediate many of the tensions which had afflicted the movement in the past.

We will not devote extensive attention to the policy of the union with respect to workplace issues.[101] In general, the militancy and demands which characterized the hot autumn were retained. Strike rates remained extremely high and the forms of strike behavior which were 'invented' during the most intense period of conflict continued to be utilized. The union movement, however, now established a dominant role and the more spontaneous sources of worker action receded. In terms of demands, the militancy of the base was translated into 'salary increases markedly above productivity growth, decidedly egalitarian demands in terms of job classifications, opposition to forms of economic incentivization' (e.g., piece rates), 'strong controls on overtime, work hours, and labor mobility.'[102] The unions broke out of the 'functional constraints' of the development model of the past and pursued with vengeance demands which percolated up from the shop floor and were, sometimes, redefined and added to by the union cadres.

These demands were accompanied by significant institutional innovations as well. On the one hand, the unions won the right to factory contracts and to collective bargaining over a broad span of issues. This was part and parcel of the definitive consolidation of union rights at the factory level, assured in part through the passage of the legislation which became known as the *Statuto dei lavoratori*. On the other hand, changes also occurred in the role assigned to different levels of the union in contract policy. There was, in Gian Primo Cella's term, a 'polarization' of contractual functions, as the councils of factory delegates and the national federations assumed the leading roles at the expense of the provincial, horizontal structures. At the same time, the confederations lost most of their contractual prerogatives: salary and work condition issues became the responsibility of the federations and the councils—the latter assumed a broad scope of initiative within the context of the federal contracts, normative issues became covered by the *Statuto*.

These institutional shifts appear to reflect the reality of the bargaining process as well. Most observers are agreed that in this period contractual policy was set through a complex interaction between workers and delegates—many of whom were not effectively controlled by the unions or even, in some cases, union members—and the federal cadres and leaders.[103] The indirect control of the confederations does not appear to have been extensive. Thus, contractual policy became the province of the vertical structures, its objectives were 'implicitly antagonistic' to prevailing economic relations and the role and autonomy of bargaining at the factory level was great.

This is not to suggest that, beyond their role in the unification process, the confederations lost all practical importance. Rather, their objectives and arena of initiative, and thus their role in the overall pattern of union activity, became redefined. Whereas the federations and factory councils were predominant in the pursuit of shopfloor goals in the market arena, the confederations were the agents for the attempt to utilize the unions' strength, both in the market and as a mobilizer of consent, to achieve extensive socioeconomic reform in the political arena. The policy of reform, intimately linked to the aggressive contractual policy, became the primary terrain of the confederations and the hallmark of union strategy in this period. It was also the terrain on which the unions attained the most meagre results.

This policy involved promotion of a global program of measures to be undertaken by the government and state institutions. Its overall goal was to transform radically Italy's development model, shifting much more demand onto the internal market and public consumption, through a set of public policies which would vastly improve and rationalize social services, repair the structural weaknesses of the economy, create the conditions for full employment, especially by dealing with the economic problems of the *Mezzogiorno*, and develop a fiscal policy which would more equitably distribute the costs of government. Never before, in Lama's view, had the union movement achieved a similar capacity

> to see all aspects of the political–union situation as tied together and, above all, the interdependence between contractual policy [wages, hours, etc.] and the problems of development, and also the relationship between the questions of employment and the South and the problems of economic development.[104]

The policy did not involve only general principles. In the early 1970s, the confederations detailed a series of prelegislative proposals covering the following areas:

• full employment to be achieved without further internal or external waves of migration through public control of private investment and expansion of public spending with the goal of economic restructuring, the rationalization and end of clientelism in public spending;

- the modernization and restructuring of agriculture with special concentration on the South, on the use of the public sector and on the development of industries linked to agricultural production;
- fiscal and tax reform to make taxes truly progressive and to simplify the administration of public and bank finance;
- major expenditures for housing, especially through a restructuring of the public housing agencies, easier conditions for land expropriation in urban areas;
- creation of a full and effective public health insurance system which would include public participation and which would be restructured around decentralized public health units linked to the communes and regions;
- reform of the school system with a reduction of class size, an end to tracking and the creation of greater autonomy for teachers in the classroom;
- extensive reform of the radio–television system.

These proposals were accompanied by detailed analyses of their linkage to existing conditions and by financial data.[105]

It should be evident that many of the proposed measures, and more particularly their general thrust, had been an integral part of the CGIL's policy perspective for many years. The echoes of the *Piano del lavoro*, and, to a lesser degree, of the more reformist orientation of many of the CISL's statements on economic development in the 1950s, are obvious. Several major differences with the past need, however, to be noted. First, all three confederations supported the reforms and acted in concert and with a single front to promote them. The gradual development of the CISL and the UIL in the 1960s toward a strategic outlook which included socioeconomic reform through action in the political arena thus reached a new stage. Second, the reforms were not posed as goals which might replace objectives pursued at the factory level. Rather,

> for the first time . . . the action of the confederations in the political market is characterized by its own objectives which do not play the simple role of substitution or compensation for short-term objectives handled in the contractual market.[106]

The confederations were neither proposing, nor even suggesting the possibility, that passing reforms would bring about an immediate easing of tension in the labor market. Trade-offs, if they were to result, should be more gradual and a product of 'spontaneous' processes. Third, and relatedly, the unions' power in the market was to be used as an instrument to advance the ability of the confederations to bargain directly with government over the content of reforms. In contrast to most periods in the past, the unions sought for a period to deal directly with government without the mediation of the political parties, and to some extent bypassing them.[107] The unions thereby attempted to carve out an autonomous place for themselves in the political process. It is for this reason that some have referred to this period as the 'pan-syndicalist' phase in Italian union behavior.[108]

Why did the confederations assume these objectives and redefined responsibilities in their overall strategy? At one level, they can be viewed as the natural outcome of the shifts in power between organizational levels of the union which had accompanied the hot autumn. The mobilization at the base, institutionalization of shopfloor organization and strength and demands of the workers in the market could be expected to shift power and influence over workplace and contractual policy away from the con-federations and toward the federations and councils. There is, of course, centralized bargaining in other countries with strong labor movements, although rarely in the presence of shopfloor strength and organization like that which had developed in Italy after 1969. Furthermore, the longstand-ing recognition within the unions, and pressure from the federations (especially the metalworkers), of the need to place greater emphasis on workplace issues and decentralized bargaining made such a shift almost inevitable once conditions were right. This was all the more the case as a result of the greater unity of the unions. The new posture of the confederations and their relationship with the federations was a logical synthesis of the past positions of the CISL and UIL, on the one hand, and the CGIL, on the other.

Beyond this 'natural' reason, other factors also can be cited. The stress on reforms to be pursued by the confederations in the political arena expressed the union movement's skepticism about the old economic development model and about the capabilities of adjustment of the political party and governmental system if left to its own devices.[109] The unions argued that Italy had a schizophrenic political-economic system: a highly industrialized economy with a backward agricultural sector, a modernized North and underdeveloped South, a vast public sector and administration with great capacity for intervention but riddled with inefficiency, waste and clientelism, and unable, therefore, to contribute to rational economic development, growth of employment and social equity, or even to respond effectively to changing conditions in the economy. This critique reflected as well profound doubts about the political parties, both in the government and in opposition, and their ability to institute change or respond to the new demands emanating from society. The Center–Left, for reasons already indicated, was largely discredited, and the prospects for dramatic political change, including Communist participation in government, did not seem great. Again, factors internal to the relationships between the unions in a period of growing unity played a role. By seizing the political initiative on their own, the confederations could avoid having to reach judgments about specific political parties or governmental formulae and, more generally, could insulate themselves from some of the pressures of partisan politics.

The policy of reforms had two further motives. It embodied the unions' (especially the CGIL's) long aspiration, and immediate need, to achieve class representation.[110] The new strength at the workplace brought with it the danger that the union might isolate itself as it pursued goals which would benefit only those who were working in the factories. Advocacy of a broad set of reforms could establish ties to all the laboring strata and overcome divisions which the entire development process and the recent mobilization had tended to exacerbate. Finally, the reform policy served the institutional needs of the confederations. In a situation in which much power had flowed to the periphery, it served to reconfirm their leading role, both as negotiator with government over critical questions of reform and, implicitly, as arbiter of strains between the different reforms and the priorities they were to be accorded, between contractual objectives and the policy of reforms and between the intention to serve the unions' immediate constituencies and the perceived need to develop and maintain broader alliances.[111] Thus, the redefinition of the leadership role of the confederations gave them two critical 'political' functions, one external and one internal. The external one was to operate as a political agent for the reform policy.[112] The internal one was to assure that the general objectives of the union strategy did not become submerged by narrower concerns. Difficulties in carrying out these functions and changes in the broader economic context were soon to lead to further redefinitions of the confederal role and of union objectives and how they might best be achieved.

The economic objectives of the reform policy were not modest. Their implementation would have required a transformation of Italy's pattern of development: a marked increase in the role of internal demand, a distinct shift from private to public consumption, and a rationalization of the public sector.[113] Furthermore, this transformation was to occur not through a social pact including wage restraint, but in the context of continuing pressure at the base of the economy deriving from the wage demands of the workers and the reduced margins of flexibility available to employers in the workplace. Viewed in this light, it is evident that while the explicit issues were social reforms in a framework of redistribution of money and power at the point of production, what was truly involved was a political struggle over which social and political forces, in what coalition, would direct the efforts of the country to readjust to the changes brought on by the hot autumn.

At the shop floor, the unions were able, in this first phase, to consolidate, and even make further, gains. The contracts concluded at the end of 1972 and in early 1973 assured increased real wages despite a rising rate of inflation and gave up nothing in terms of working conditions and shopfloor control.[114] These advances, however, rested almost entirely on the continued mobilization of the work force and on the success of the unions in organizational reconstruction in the workplace.

In the political arena, success was not forthcoming. Instead, the policy of reforms foundered on the unions' inability to transform market power into political power capable of changing the basic lines of government policy. Throughout most of 1970–1, the confederations sought to engage the government in negotiations which would begin the process of legislating the desired reforms. They did so without the direct mediation of the political parties with which they had been traditionally tied (of course, the Socialists and Christian Democrats were in the government). They promoted their positions through general and regional strikes and mass demonstrations in favor of specific policies. They sought to present their proposals as means by which a wide array of reform-oriented social groups could finally break through the resistance which efforts at reform had encountered in the past.

The effort proved largely fruitless. After an initial responsiveness (the passage of the *Statuto*), the government proved increasingly unable and/or unwilling to commit itself to reform. Detailed negotiations on housing and health reform between the unions and the government were undertaken but the results were disappointing. The former resulted in an agreement, but the accord was gutted in Parliament, in part as the result of the lack of support of members of the governmental parties. Health reform never reached the stage of concrete agreement. More generally, during this period the government underwent an involution, shifting its policy focus to the right and undertaking a series of macroeconomic policies which, although largely ineffective, signalled an attempt to deal with the strains in the economy through traditional measures rather than new ones based on different political-economic priorities.

The rightward shift of the political system and the political inefficacy of the unions were also evident in electoral terms. A series of elections in 1970–2 were marked by an increase of votes for the most conservative parties and very conservative campaigns on the part of the Christian Democrats. The national elections of 1972 were called a year ahead of schedule for the first time in the postwar period. This was due in part to the government's inability to deal with the unions and to establish an internal agreement among its coalition partners. The elections confirmed the rightward shift.[115] At the same time, they demonstrated that the militant and leftward shift of the unions did not necessarily have an impact on the electoral preferences of the unionized work force: Christian Democratic workers still appeared to vote for their party as before. Thus, the unions were confronted with the fact that they could not 'deliver' votes or punish their enemies and reward their friends. Their strength in the market, their capacity to mobilize and to impose a political agenda, their ability to negotiate directly with government and to assure that they would be consulted prior to any major governmental initiatives were not translated into political currency which could be used to obtain the desired measures from the political system.[116] This failure in the political arena, which culminated after the 1972 elections in the formation of a Center–Right government, could not fail to rekindle tensions within the strategy developed at the beginning of the decade. The objectives and division of responsibilities between confederations, federations and grass-roots organizations which had been part and parcel of the consolidation of the new union structure were inevitably to undergo rethinking and revision in the face of a political system in which the unions found themselves unable to exercise the influence necessary to attain policies which they deemed essential to their overall success.

This process of rethinking and strategic realignment began in 1973. The debate in the unions remained within the basic framework of principles and objectives with which they had been operating and around which the united front of the confederations had been built. With these as a given, however, several problems had to be confronted. The first was that of the *mobilization of resources* for the unions' programs. The period 1970–3 had shown the difficulty of counting on rationalization of governmental commitments as a means to mobilize resources for reform. Furthermore, the tension between an aggressive strategy in the market and sustained and stable economic growth had also emerged with increasing clarity, especially in the context of the inefficacy and waste of governmental political-economic policy. The unions, therefore, had to reevaluate the linkage to be established between their strategy in the market and for contractual objectives of the traditional type, and their commitment to socioeconomic reform.[117] Second, and relatedly, they had to contend with decisions about the *appropriate instruments* of pressure to be used to try to achieve their market and political objectives: strikes and, more generally, their capacity to disrupt the economy increasingly threatened to be counterproductive because of the seeming inability of the Italian economy to make the appropriate readjustments and to achieve full employment. Demobilization of the workers, however, threatened to deprive the unions of the sole instrument which they could use to pressure for the changes they deemed indispensable and might open the way to reestablishment of the old development model. Third, the problem of *strategic coherence*, in several forms, loomed increasingly large: how to avoid 'sectoralization of advantage' in the strongest sectors and federations by developing a contractual policy which would redistribute the benefits of strength;[118] how to link contractual policy over workplace issues to the objectives of the reform policy; how to assure that the reform policy would be an instrument benefiting not just union constituencies and the workers of the North but serving to build alliances with non-blue collar groups and with the poor of the South, especially in light of the rightist drift in the country (concentrated in the South) and the danger of isolation of the union movement; how more effectively to establish priorities of objectives now that the enthusiasm about the possibility of attaining everything, and right away, had passed. More generally, how to assure that the day-to-day practice of the unions at all levels was consistent with its explicit principles and goals and realistic in terms of the economic and political environment in which the movement had to operate.[119]

It should be evident that these were problems which went to the heart of the union strategy and that their resolution would necessarily require renegotiation of the compromises with respect to objectives, arenas, and the appropriate responsibilities of different levels of the union structure which had been reached in the preceding three years. This process had already begun when the oil embargo and subsequent drastic rise in energy prices dramatically altered the economic context. With this changed context, however, the problems became both more pressing and more difficult.

Part 5

The Years of Crisis

Introduction

Since 1974, Italy's economy has seemed to many to be in a permanent state of crisis. With the change in the prices of energy, most of the already existing problems of the economy were exacerbated, new ones appeared and the authorities charged with management of the economy have often appeared unable to implement short-term policies of stabilization, much less longer-term policies of readjustment to the altered international economic context, shift in energy costs, as well as the already existing problems linked to the dramatic changes in the labor market and cost of labor. One prominent economist and former American ambassador to Italy went so far as to refer to Italy as a potential economic Bangladesh of the West.

This picture, even in its more measured form, is not entirely accurate. Both short- and longer-term problems have been severe, among the worst in the advanced industrial economies, and conjunctural difficulties have increasingly interacted with structural problems to make stable recovery a problematic prospect. Italy has also suffered, in the winter of 1975–6, one of the worst balance of payments crises of the postwar period. At the same time, however, there have also been periods of surprising growth, there has been no economic collapse, and there have been sporadic signs that even a more concerted policy to attack the structural problems afflicting the economy might be undertaken.[120] As with the forecasts of doomsayers about a number of other aspects of Italian life, the image of an Italy in economic dissolution has been confounded by the reality of an Italy which has somehow muddled through.[121]

This is not to diminish the problems which the economy has encountered, to suggest that political management of the economy has been effective or to dismiss the difficulties which the unions have faced in attempting to formulate and implement a strategy in a condition of economic stagnation, crisis, and occasional spurt. Rather, what we wish to highlight is the often contradictory developments of the political economy in the last six years. While accepting the notion of an economy in deep trouble, one's analysis of the situation depends to a considerable degree on which factors and indicators are highlighted: conjunctural problems or structural ones, growth rates or shutdowns and crises in major firms, the 'visible' economy or the 'invisible' one, practically full employment among adult males in the North or severe unemployment in the South and among youth, and so forth. The relevance of this observation is that it underlines the importance of the particular analysis given to the crisis by the union movement and the strategic consequences of this analysis.[122] Options, both in terms of how to analyze the development of the economy and of what strategy to follow, were available. The ones selected by the unions cannot be understood as an 'inevitable' or 'logical' outcome of the political-economic 'facts' but only in the context of the strategic principles which had been developed subsequent to the hot autumn. What we see is a union movement, with all the tensions already indicated, seeking to adapt, rather than abandon, its strategy in a complex, contradictory and ever-changing political-economic environment.

A general profile of the economic development of Italy in the years since 1973 is presented in the appendix to this paper. Here only a few points which are not evident in these data but which have an important bearing on union policy need to be highlighted. The first is the unevenness of the impact of the crisis.[123] Unemployment has for the most part been concentrated outside of the core work force of the industrial sector. Its major impact has been felt in the South and among youth in search of their first employment. More generally, one can say that the crisis has tended to exacerbate long-existent uneven development between the North and *Mezzogiorno*.[124] Second, most of the data fail to capture one of the most significant developments of the 1970s to which many economists attribute much of Italy's economic resilience: the growth of the 'invisible' economy. We cannot here go into a lengthy description of this phenomenon. Basically, the term is used to describe a vast network of production which escapes the payment of taxes and social security benefits and is not unionized, and which therefore has significantly lower costs of production than the core industrial sector.[125] Analysts are agreed that employment in this invisible economy has grown sharply in the last decade. There is far less agreement about the technological and manpower composition of this economy, the rates of wages paid and to what extent those employed also hold another job. It has become increasingly clear, however, that many of the firms in this economy are quite dynamic, that they produce a significant portion of real, as contrasted to measured, GNP and that they are not concentrated only in the less industrialized zones of the country but in the industrial heartland as well.

The third point to be made is that the crisis has had a differential impact, even within the 'visible' industrial economy of the North.[126] Its effects have tended to be more severe in large industries with a considerable labor force than in industries with greater capital intensiveness and/or smaller size. The layoff or potential layoff of large numbers of workers in one plant or firm has tended to contribute to the crisis symbolism, but this has not always reflected the general situation of the economy.

Fourth, unionized workers have been very well protected throughout the period.[127] Indexation has protected real wages, laid-off workers have continued to be paid almost their entire wage, firings have been almost impossible, labor mobility within plants, much less between them, has been rigidly controlled. It needs once again to be emphasized, however, that these benefits and protections have applied to workers in the industrial, unionized core of the work force.

When taken together with the more statistical data, these features of Italian economic development in the period since 1973 highlight the problematic context within which the unions have sought to develop their strategy.[128] On the one hand, they have retained much of their strength and many of the traditional mechanisms by which the government and capital might have attempted to reduce such strength, have been ineffective. The unions have done well in defending their core constituencies. On the other hand, a number of developments have pointed to the danger of economic decay of such magnitude that even this situation might not be sustainable in the long run. Furthermore, it has been clear that the division between the core industrial sectors and work force and other sectors of the economy has grown, a factor which might contribute to the economic and/or political weakening of the union movement. Thus, the unions have often appeared, to themselves and to others, like a cap on an increasingly heated and potentially explosive situation.

How to stimulate the venting and restructuring of this situation while not suffering a decline in real power and opening the way to severe setbacks for the unionized work force has been the central problem with which the union movement has wrestled. The unions' political-economic analysis and strategic rethinking has gone through two distinct phases with a long period of transition between the two. The general pattern which spans these phases is an increasing emphasis on a narrowed set of priorities with respect to objectives, a development which Lama has directly linked to the objective problems the union movement was facing:

> Does this situation have a relationship to the structural crisis and to the specificity of the conjunctural situation? . . . the crisis, on the one hand, underlines the necessity of reforms, that is, if one examines the real causes of the crisis; it also, however, makes a policy of reforms more difficult, if one thinks of means, of the resources which are required for a policy of reforms.[129]

In the first phase (1973–6), however, the unions seek to pursue both their reform objectives and those related to wages and conditions of work more through action in the market arena than in the preceding years, although this does not prevent a partial restoration of the primacy of the federations and confederations in the setting of union policy at all levels. Furthermore, this phase is marked by renewed, if subdued, partisan tensions within the union movement. In the second phase (1978–present), the phase of the so-called 'EUR line,' political-economic reforms become the absolutely primary objectives, a measure in terms of which other union objectives, and even possible concessions in terms of wages and the conditions of work, are to be gauged. The focus of action returns to the political arena and the confederations reassume their centrality. While the confederations remain united, internal tensions become more acute. By the end of our examination, the union movement retains many of the strategic principles first developed after the hot autumn and much of the strength acquired in that period but still unable to translate its strength in the marketplace into the structural changes in the political economy deemed ever more pressing if a crisis of the movement itself is to be avoided.

Economic Thought after the Oil Crisis

We have already stressed that the years since the oil crisis have been ones in which the union movement has had significant options, both with respect to how it analyzes the crisis of the economy and with respect to the strategy to be pursued. It is important, therefore, to examine in detail the unions' economic thought, highlighting those features of the political-economic situation to which they have paid greatest attention, the explanations they have offered for the appearance of these features and the understanding they have reached about how these manifestations of crisis might affect the future of the Italian political economy and the place of the union and labor movement within it. This examination will allow us better to evaluate the unions' strategic development.

The unions' belief that the hot autumn spelled the start of an irreversible erosion of the Italian development model has always been part and parcel of their commitment to a strategy including efforts to promote reform of the political-economic system.[130] Prior to the oil crisis, however, this analysis remained primarily on a national basis. The union movement was concerned with the immediate consequences of the hot autumn for the *Italian* political economy and their implications for strategy. The hot autumn was interpreted as fundamentally a national event, the impact of which was understood in national development terms. With the oil crisis, the scope of the explanation of the national crisis was broadened and Italy's economic development was more firmly placed in an analysis of inter-national crisis and change.

The oil crisis, with its effects on both the international and national economy, reinforced the unions' conviction that Italy was suffering not just a severe perturbation of a basically sound system, but a crisis of the system itself.[131] This crisis was attributed to the interplay between the sharp dislocations, readjustments, and crisis tendencies in the international economy and the structural faults of the Italian national political economy. The postwar international economic system, and consequently all of the advanced industrial capitalist economies, were viewed to be facing severe difficulties. Italy's, however, were more profound due to the heritage of the postwar development model and the place Italy had assumed in the international division of labor, and due to the domestic political, social, and institutional crises which, while linked to the country's economic problems, had other causes as well. In this perspective, for the unions, the oil crisis was more a precipitant than cause of the Italian crisis.[132]

The unions did not view the quadrupling of oil prices as the sole source of disruption in the international economic order. They explicitly rejected the 'shock' interpretation.[133] Accentuated competition among advanced in-dustrial countries, competitive challenges from the new industrial pro-ducers of the Third World, the growing power of multinational corpor-ations, the collapse of the Bretton Woods system and practice of com-petitive devaluations—these are some of the other features of what the Italian unions interpreted as the structural decay of the American-dominated international economic order established after World War II. The imputed response to this decay—redistribution of roles within the international division of labor including the assignment of secondary status to countries like Italy and efforts to reestablish a technological gap between the advanced economies and those of the Third World—were interpreted as part of the design of international capital to 'solve' its own crisis by resorting to the classical instruments of imperialistic policies: unequal distribution in the international division of labor, unjust terms of exchange, and 'technological coercion.' Thus, the unions' analysis was decidedly 'radical' in tone and substance, rejecting piecemeal, *ad hoc* or conjunctural interpretations.[134]

Much the same picture emerges from the unions' analysis of the relationship of the crisis to economic theory. We have seen that in the past the unions adopted a critical, but grudgingly accepting, view of Keynesian policy, if not of Keynesian theory.[135] With the oil crisis, however, they have argued that the principles of the Keynesian model have broken down. This model, they maintain, was based on three imperatives: maintenance of global demand at a level capable of supporting high utilization of capacity; promotion of investment through incentives intended to counterbalance the tendency toward the underutilization of savings; institution of mechanisms for the creation of monetary liquidity sufficient to respond to recessionary spasms. For two decades after World War II this model seemed triumphant. Economic cycles appeared to be no more than conjunctural mishaps, employment grew steadily and growth seemed to have no limits. As part of this process, the state became one of the fundamental regulators of economic activity. Through central banks and public expenditures, it contributed to the creation of the financial liquidity necessary to maintain high levels of growth in investments and employment. Increasingly, however, this outcome was achieved at the price of a relatively uncontrolled monetary policy. Enterprises, freed from financial constraints and under growing union wage pressure, sought to maintain their profit margins through further expansion of demand, an outcome partially attained through governmental support of private consumption. The result was a constant and progressive increase in production costs, now endemic to the system, a strong upward pressure in government expenditures and a growing inflationary push. Thus, the contradictions of capitalist accumulation, which in the past had resulted in conjunctural ups and downs, became explosive. Regardless of their intensity and duration, cyclical fluctuations have become structural crises. Again, the unions adopted a 'radical' interpretation. While not necessarily accepting a catastrophic view of the outcome of such structural crises, they rejected any possible 'solutions' based on Keynesian principles.

The breakdown of the postwar international economic order and collapse of the principles on which it was founded could be expected, according to the unions, to have dire effects on the Italian political economy, especially in the form of simultaneous recession and inflation. The crowding of the international market, particularly by low-cost, low- and medium-technology products, has exposed the structural flaws of the country's economic system: limited industrial diversification with concentrations in precisely such products, sectoral and regional disequilibria, a backward agricultural sector, source of a constant drain in the balance of payments, emphasis on a few 'pulling sectors,' notably the auto industry. These, of course, have long been targets of the unions' criticism, but with the oil crisis, it is raised to a new level. A country with such an economic structure, they argue, is peculiarly unable to respond effectively to the changes in the international system. Thus, it was inevitable that of all industrially advanced countries, Italy should have suffered most. Her past economic advantages have disappeared, her structural vulnerability to the altered international context is acute.[136]

The unions' crisis interpretation has, as one would expect, not been confined to a focus on economic factors. Although the conviction that what is occurring is a breakdown of the postwar capitalist model of accumulation remains at the core of their perspective, the unions' analytical horizon has broadened to include political, institutional, social, and even 'moral' factors.[137] Failure of the Italian state to use the powers at its disposal to act autonomously from private capital in order to counter structural flaws, the inability of state institutions to attain levels of efficiency consonant with the requirements of an advanced industrial economy, the neglect of R and D and general technological backwardness and dependence of the country—these are just a few of the many noneconomic factors included in the unions' appraisal of the crisis. Together with those previously indicated, they constitute an almost unbroken, structurally based indictment of Italy's political economy.

The union judgment of those charged with the responsibility of responding to the crisis is no less harsh. Government and capital are accused of aggravating its impact. 'Freezing' the economy has been, the unions argue, the guiding principle of the government's economic policy, diverging little from the directives of the EEC and the IMF; a first phase of sharp restraint of the volume of internal demand, severe monetary and credit policy, strict budgetary controls, and a reduction of public expenditures; a second phase of 'tempered austerity' with limited investment programs in agriculture, energy, and construction in support of internal demand.[138] Even this policy, however, has been ineffectively implemented according to the unions. Demand restraint and tight money have been undertaken, but neither the controls on wasteful public expenditures nor the stimulative policies supposedly part of the second phase have been undertaken. At the same time, the government has sought to have the unions accept an incomes policy. The result has been to slow the economy and to seek restraint on the part of the working class without stimulus or longer-term response to the country's structural economic problems, or even the realistic hope thereof.

The unions' characterization of the employers' policy is similarly drastic: 'restructuring in stagnation.'[139] Entrepreneurial strategy is argued, in general, to have followed the traditional patterns of response to Italian cyclical downturns: support for compression of internal demand and pursuit of exports. The latter is sought primarily through the reduction of production costs, above all labor costs, by reductions in manpower. In the entrepreneurs' view, the unions claim, restructuring requires a more mobile labor force, on the one hand, and an economic system liberated from what capital refers to as union and industrial 'restraints,' on the other. In short, capital seeks to reestablish Italy's full integration in the international economic system on much the old basis and to reaffirm the centrality of the firm and entrepreneurial prerogatives.[140]

The logic behind governmental and entrepreneurial policy is interpreted by the unions to be one and the same: to bring about, through a dose of both inflation and recession, a drastic redistribution of income in favor of profits, entrepreneurial and governmental recovery of power lost to the workers in the late 1960s and early 1970s and a restriction of union action to primarily factory-oriented issues. In other words, what government and employers are seeking is a rollback of the hot autumn by using the crisis to blackmail the labor movement, force it into moderation and passivity and thereby create the conditions for a restoration of Italy's traditional position in the international economy.[141] Deep recession, the government and employers are said to believe, will create (or recreate) the conditions for new expansion. The unions instead argue, on the basis of the analysis presented above, that it can only aggravate the already existing tendencies toward crisis, structural disequilibria, growing unemployment and the general impoverishment of the Italian economy.

Before turning to an appraisal of the specific manifestations of crisis in the Italian economy to which the unions have devoted greatest attention, it is worthwhile pausing for a moment to reflect on their global analysis and its strategic implications. It should be evident that the criticism of the unions in this phase is drastic and sweeping. The image of crisis is pervasive and the sense of closure with respect to past principles and policies complete. This mode of analysis is largely consistent with the pattern of argumentation in earlier periods, particularly that of the CGIL in the early 1950s, but with at least one major difference: there is no image here of catastrophe, only of stagnation and decay.[142] Other similarities with the past are also worthy of note. As before, the unions do not have an alternative economic theory to offer; theirs is a global criticism, but appears to be largely a theoretical one. To some extent, however, this reflects the unions' willingness (no matter how grudging) to accept the basic rules of capitalism as a given and to seek to operate accordingly. It is for this reason that we have not offered an analysis of the *unions*' economic theory. In contrast, for instance, with the CGT and its 'state monopoly capitalism' theory, the Italian unions are far more eclectic and, some might say, practical. Relatedly, the Italian unions' focus is on the more concrete problems raised by the crisis, on their implications for the Italian economy and on their impact on workers, and on the union movement and its strategic objectives.[143]

This should not suggest that the analyses of the crisis we have thus far sketched are not of practical importance for union strategy. On the contrary, they have significant implications for the strategic options likely to be chosen. First, they lead to a rejection of *ad hoc* conjunctural policies as prospective palliatives, an important rationale in union rejection of measures which would seek from them economic and other sacrifices in the short-term simply in exchange for 'trickle-down' benefits in the future.[144] The former are too limited for the latter reasonably to be expected. Second, the global condemnation of government and entrepreneurs contributes to the unions' conviction that they must be full and active participants in any process of developing a policy which would effectively address the structural underpinnings of the crisis. The others have contributed to political-economic failure and continue to do so; the union movement must have a prominent policy role, for only thereby will discredited premises be abandoned and structural blockages be broken.[145] Third, the characterization of the linkage between international and national crisis which the unions make has a twin importance. On the one hand, the stress on national factors, and not solely economic ones, suggests that to a considerable extent it is in the national context—through national policies designed to alter economic, political, and institutional features of the Italian political economy—that resolutions to the crisis must be found. The international economy cannot be expected to provide solutions. On the other hand, the arguments about the crisis tendencies in the inter-national economy, while underlining the preceding, also further reinforce the notion that limited change is likely to be ineffective. Only structural change which adjusts Italy's economy to the emerging international economic order offers the possibility of a return to stable growth with high wages and full employment.[146]

We have indicated that Italy's development in recent years has been uneven and contradictory. The unions focus unequivocally on the elements of crisis. Beyond this general perspective, however, there are particular manifestations of the crisis to which they have directed their attention and which have had the greatest bearing on the premises and practices of their strategy. These are inflation, the balance of trade, dualisms in the Italian economy, and the labor market.

The union movement's interpretation of the fundamental causes of inflation has already been discussed. It should be added that beyond the generalizations indicated, their position on inflation has never been well articulated. For much of the postwar period the unions regarded inflation as a symptom of the dysfunctions in the Italian process of economic growth rather than as a sign of growing contradictions in the capitalist system. This is the source of their inclination often to regard inflationary trends as little more than a maneuver by big capital in its effort to reinforce its position in the market (as the result of compensatory devaluation), to diminish the power of the working class and to impose monopolistic pricing practices.[147]

The neglect of specific analysis of the inflation phenomenon prior to 1974 may also be explained by the unions' unwillingness to recognize that their own policies may have contributed to the inflationary push. They re-peatedly rejected such an analysis—made repeatedly by employers and government—arguing that wages be treated as 'an independent variable' in the national economy. This view was to persist until the second post-crisis phase and the development of the EUR line. Nonetheless, after 1973 the unions developed a more detailed argument about the causes of inflation.

The core of this view was that inflation is not—as was charged—a product of unceasing demands for wage increases made without taking into account the ups and downs of the business cycle or the growth of productivity. Rather, the unions argued that the driving force of inflation was the reduction of levels of production, which created disequilibria between demand and supply. Widespread reduction of production volumes and underutilization of productive capacity caused high production costs, and hence inflation. This domestic inflationary tendency was further aggravated by the worsening terms of exchange between imported and exported goods.[148]

Severe price controls and industrial reconversion designed to alter the quantity and quality of industrial and agricultural production were the policies offered by the unions for dealing with inflation. They recognized, however, that such measures would be ineffective unless the fundamental problem of Italy's economy—the character of her import/export balance— was successfully addressed. What was required was to break out of the cycle, particularly characteristic of the 1970s and most severe in the winter of 1975–6, in which industrial growth had periodically to be sacrificed to the need to reequilibriate the balance of payments. Due to the 'transformative' nature of Italy's economy, a veritable vicious cycle was argued to be at work: the greater Italy's economic activity, the greater her demand for raw materials from abroad (and for food) and hence the necessity further to increase exports in order to maintain balance of payments equilib- rium.

For capital and government, this problem can only be redressed by further increasing exports. The unions consider sole reliance on this solution unrealistic, symptomatic of big capital's design to divide Italy's economic structure into two parts, one fully integrated into the inter- national economy, the other catering almost exclusively to the domestic market. This is illusionary from the unions' standpoint, because the worldwide trend toward stagnation and a declining rate of growth can be expected to continue. International competition will sharpen and pro- tectionist tendencies, already evident, are likely to grow. Italy will also face growing competition from those developing countries producing 'tra- ditional' industrial products. Hence, in addition to increasing exports, a fundamental measure for dealing effectively with the problem of the balance of payments is to 're-qualify' imports, reducing the volume of some imported goods. (Some unions, for instance, the Federation of Metal- workers, openly favor rationing those imports—oil, alimentary products— which most heavily weigh on the country's balance of payments.)[149] They also advocate improving economic and political relations with developing countries in general, and with oil-producing nations in particular. Italy should in fact engage in direct agreements with oil-producing nations, thereby circumventing oil companies.[150]

The issue of the balance of payments is recognized to pose several further problems for the unions' strategy. In the past, especially at the time of the Marshall Plan, trade deficits could be kept within limits through the securing of foreign loans and aid. In present circumstances, the inter- national system is no longer propitious for such a solution. On the one hand, the stronger capitalist countries (United States, West Germany), affected by the crisis themselves, do not intend or are unable freely to guarantee loans that would permit Italy to sustain a prolonged deficit in the balance of payments. On the other hand, the system of political alliances and of economic relations of which Italy is part does not allow her to turn directly to those developing countries from which she imports raw materials. In the unions' view, it is therefore necessary to make Italy less dependent on the international economic system by solving the domestic problems of the balance of payments, above all, the problem of the agricultural sector. This is not to say that Italian unions have an autarchic vision of the country's economy; rather, although they acknowledge the inevitability of Italy's dependence on the international economic system, and perhaps even the potential benefits of interdependence, they also want to attenuate the external constraints on the country's economic performance.[151]

Equally worrisome for the Italian unions is another manifestation of the crisis: the sharpening of old dualisms and divisions in the economy and the emergence of new ones.[152] What has been happening, the unions argue, is precisely the opposite of what they have advocated. The economic structure has become more divided and fragmented rather than more integrated and harmonious.[153] This process takes several forms including sharper conflicts between very large firms and some small and medium ones, growing tensions between those firms which operate extensively in the international market and as multinationals and those which cater almost exclusively to the domestic market, and an increasing gap between an industrial sector which has managed, even in the 1970s, to grow and an agricultural sector which is ever more backward and inadequate for the domestic needs. The dualistic development which has most preoccupied the unions, and to which they have devoted the greatest attention and concern, is the ever increasing gulf between the North—industrialized, unionized, enjoying close to full employment, with at least marginally efficient social services—and the South—weak industrially, highly tertiarized, poorly organized except through clientelism, suffering from severe unemployment and inadequate or nonexistent social services, in economic decline and increasingly socially fragmented. For the unions, this situation is the most clamorous example of the failure of governmental policy to counter the effects of Italian capitalism and the country's traditional development model. It has created a South which is in social and economic disintegration, a reservoir for political reaction and a constant drain on the Italian economy.[154] We have seen that the problem of the *Mezzogiorno* has played a prominent place in Italian union strategy for many years and especially after the hot autumn. After 1974, even more than before, the unions made the shifting of resources to the South a major criterion in determining their strategic and policy priorities.

The fourth manifestation of the crisis on which the unions have focused their attention is the growing fragmentation of the labor market and heterogeneity of the work force.[155] Few already employed workers have lost their jobs in recent years. The combination of rigid and highly protective rules with regard to temporary layoffs and a seemingly full-employment economy in most of the industrial North has meant that the core of the union constituency need not fear loss of job. Growth of official employment, however, has been slow or nonexistent when corrected for those on layoff. Instead, two phenomena, both of deep concern to the unions, have been developing. On the one hand, there has been an increase in unemployment, especially among youth, women, and in the poorer regions of the country. On the other hand, there has been an increasing, if only partially documented, 'invisible' work force of nonunionized workers operating in firms which escape the tax and social security system. The character of these firms—the types of products they produce, their relationship to the 'official' economy, the type of workers they employ and the types of work these workers carry out—varies considerably. From the studies which have been done, it is clear that they cannot all be assumed to be low-wage, low-technology shops exploiting the unemployed. Many appear to be producers of more advanced goods and to employ skilled workers at relatively high wages. Some of these workers, particularly in the North, may also be employed in the visible economy, holding double jobs. Whatever the exact case, the unions have consistently denounced both the growth of unemployment and the expansion of the 'invisible' economy as further signs of the fragmentation of the Italian economy and labor force.[156] At the same time, they have come increasingly to recognize that the spread of the invisible sector poses profound and contradictory problems for them, both because some of their own constituents may be involved and because this economy has acted as a shock absorber in a situation in which the visible economy has been under severe strain. Thus, the unions have been loathe to promote a frontal assault on the invisible economy, desiring instead gradually to reintegrate it into the visible one.

Not surprisingly, the unions stress that all the manifestations of crisis indicated above have causes in and effects on the political system. The various forms of fragmentation and the constant corrosive impact of inflation and recession are a product, in part, of the failure of the political system to address adequately the fundamental structural problems of the political economy. They also tend to contribute further to the deterioration of state institutions, ever more caught up in a clientelistic or entirely defensive welfare effort to ameliorate the worst damage or to satisfy the most powerful impacted groups. This, in turn, feeds a credibility and delegitimation crisis of the state and of the political system and parties, promoting further difficulties in the development of the social consent necessary to undertake any policy which might effectively address the underlying structural causes of the crisis. The rending of the social fabric and decay of political legitimacy bring with them not only the menace of further economic degeneration but the possibility as well of a political turn in an authoritarian direction.[157]

Strategic Responses in the First Phase: 1974 to the EUR Line

The unions' analysis of the crisis sketched out in the preceding pages obviously has important implications for their strategy and for how they might deal with some of the tensions and problems which had reemerged by 1973. In analyzing the crisis as they did, the unions brought into sharp relief those of its features which they felt most dangerous, either directly or indirectly, for their newly attained economic and political power. The image which emerged is a paradoxical one. On the one hand, the conditions for implementing the strategy were recognized to have significantly worsened: resources for reform had become even more limited and there was little prospect for recovery; the economy had become even more vulnerable to aggressive labor market action, and the potential consequences in terms of economic performance, further economic and societal fragmentation and political reaction greater; the fragmentation of society and economic pressure on social groups had increased, with a resultant growing danger of narrow sectoral defense both within the working class itself and among other social groups, making alliance politics around a policy of structural reform more difficult.[158] On the other hand, precisely these conditions, and the failures of the entrepreneurs, the government and the political system and parties more generally, made it ever more necessary that the unions assume an active political role in favor of a design of structural reform. The rather drastic picture of the crisis, in fact, served on the one hand to magnify the difficulties and dangers of the situation and at the same time to provide a rationale for the intensification of the unions' efforts successfully to pursue a strategy whose premises, they would argue, were already attuned to the problems which the crisis had aggravated.[159]

The evolution of strategy after 1973 reflects this view. The union movement was slow to abandon the cardinal principles formulated after the hot autumn but sought continually to adjust its policy objectives and the arenas and instruments through which they were pursued in order to respond to the problems and tensions which had already emerged before the crisis and to those growing out of or accentuated by it. In this phase the objectives of reform were narrowed and sharpened and contractual policy over shopfloor issues became more defensive. Decisional power shifted back toward the top in both the federations and between them and the confederations. Despite these changes, however, there was considerable oscillation with respect to the emphasis to be given to the labor market and political arenas and the objectives to be pursued in each.

If we look first at objectives, the most notable developments in this phase were a shift to a defensive posture with regard to shopfloor issues and an effort to move from the somewhat generic package of reforms sought earlier to the elaboration of a more precise set of priorities and proposals. Both of these developments are linked to the changes brought on by the crisis and the unions' analysis of them.

On the shop floor and in more centralized bargaining in these years, the unions' chief efforts were directed to defending gains made in the preceding years. The unions sought to use the contractual process: to prevent or reduce layoffs and block firings, to exercise close control over labor mobility both within and between factories, to try to contribute to greater employment through the restriction of overtime and, especially among the metalworkers, through a reduction of the work week, and to defend real wages against the ravages of inflation.[160] The last is particularly noteworthy because it involved an innovation, the introduction in the 1975 contract between the Confindustria and the confederations of 90 percent or more indexation of all wages in industry.[161] Indexation and the specific rules through which the raises were to be determined, was to become a major issue of contention between the unions and government (the employers have been more divided on the question) in subsequent years. Nonetheless, the unions managed largely to defend the positions earlier attained, a major success in light of the degenerating economic situation, but a success with potentially severe consequences.

We have noted that these objectives were defensive, but this should not obscure the fact that in a decaying economic situation they represented an ongoing source of pressure in the political economy and an obstacle to efforts to restore economic equilibrium on the basis of a rollback of labor gains. Production costs, to which most of these objectives have a relationship, were in fact the major issue over which capital (often allied with government) and labor fought. For capital, production costs, and the wage increases demanded and successfully obtained by labor were the fundamental cause of the inflationary spiral and thus of the crisis. Therefore, a continuous effort to achieve a reduction of production costs was necessary, the argument being that only thereby could investment be revived, productivity increased, and the crisis begun to be resolved. Central to the employers' and the government's position was an emphasis on the formula 'lower wages = accumulation = investments = employment.'

The battle over production costs was fought on several fronts.[162] One target was the size of the entire wage bill. The unions were pressured to agree to a socialization of the social overhead costs paid by employers. (These are very high, certainly more than 50 percent above the take-home pay of the workers. The effect of such a change would be to shift costs from employers to the national tax system and thus to tax the nonwage portion of the employees' gross pay.) Capital and government also sought to get the unions to moderate their wage policy and to agree to changes in the *scala mobile* (the indexation system) which would have the effect of reducing the degree of protection it provided for workers' wages.[163] In the first postcrisis phase the unions' response to all these proposals was blunt: a refusal to entertain any significant changes. The issue became most focused on the *scala mobile*. The unions refused all but the most minor revisions because indexation was argued to defend the poorest strata of the industrial work force and to tend toward greater equalization of pay. The *scala mobile*, they emphatically stated, 'should not be touched!'[164]

A further source of conflict was the issue of working hours. On this question, the union movement was divided and remains so after the EUR line. The confederations were inclined to accept the existing ceiling of forty hours (in all but metalworking) per week. Some federations, chief among them the Metalworkers and Chemical Workers, favored further reductions. Despite this disagreement, however, many at both levels of the unions shared a belief that lower working hours would have beneficial effects on employment. Their disagreements arose over whether a reduction of hours was opportune and whether, as the confederations claimed, it might not introduce further divisions within the labor force between those in stronger and weaker sectors without creating more jobs in the areas of severe unemployment.[165]

A third issue of conflict was the mobility of the work force. In the unions' view, the most important precondition for the successful realization of capital's strategy of industrial restructuring at labor's expense was a highly mobile work force—the possibility to transfer workers from one sector of the production process to another, from one factory to another of the same firm, possibly even to fire workers. The gains following the hot autumn with respect to labor mobility represented the most effective tool which the unions had to counter this design. Nonetheless, this was the area in which the unions were least effective in devising a policy. While their rhetoric in the first phase was totally opposed to mobility, they were not able entirely to block the transfer of workers at the level of the factory. Employers succeeded in gaining their agreement to some shifts. Furthermore, the *cassa integrazione* (the state-financed mechanism which pays the salaries of 'temporarily' laid-off workers) increasingly became an extended holding pen for 'unproductive' or 'superfluous' workers. Management also was able to rely more heavily on subcontracting, 'outwork' and on the variety of other forms of production which constitute elements of the 'invisible' economy.[166] Thus, the unions found themselves largely unable to hinder the decentralization of the productive process by which the employers sought in part to counter the wage pressure and rigidities introduced by union policy in the core economy. The irony is obvious. The policy designed to block restructuration and protect the work force partially failed to accomplish this goal while at the same time contributing to further fragmentation of the work force.

From the preceding, it is evident that in this first post-1973 phase the unions did not relieve the pressure which their gains at the shop floor with respect to wages and working conditions applied to the economy. They explicitly rejected any notion that the deepening crisis should be accompanied by a willingness to agree to rollbacks of past gains and instead sought steadfastly to defend acquired positions. To do otherwise, they maintained, was simply to give capital the margins to restructure on the basis of old principles and to avoid addressing the underlying structural crisis of the economy. Action in the market arena with respect to these objectives, however, did undergo several major changes. First, there was a shift of initiative toward the federations and confederations. The former exercised greater control over the factory councils in the setting of the platforms for factory contracts. Confederal contracts once again took on a major role, as in the bargaining over the *scala mobile*.[167] These changes were coupled with institutional ones. The delegates at the factory level came under greater control of the federations (the percentage of delegates who were union members increased) and partisan political criteria also exercised more sway. Third, the forms of struggle also reflected greater centralization. Spontaneous actions and the highly articulated strikes of the hot autumn and early seventies gave ground to more traditional forms—general strikes, category strikes—managed by the federations and confederations. The overall level of militance remained high, but the composition altered: the number of actions declined, their dimensions increased. In general, it can be said that the higher levels of union organization tended to assume greater control over those below and that divisions within these higher levels, on partisan or confederal lines, made themselves more felt throughout the union structure.[168]

From the hot autumn onwards, the reform policy of the unions had been seen as an indispensable complement of the contractual policy. The new power of the union movement conferred on it responsibilities which it could avoid only at its peril. If the unions did not become active in the struggle for structural reform, the possibilities of a degeneration of the political-economic system and an undermining of the unions' own position were great. This was all the more the case because of the imputed inability of the parties and political system to address the problems and because the policy of reforms enabled the unions to find a nonpartisan but political terrain for compromise and synthesis of their traditions. The problems encountered by the reform policy after 1972 did not alter these basic premises and conditions. The crisis and the unions' analysis of it after 1974 only strengthened the conviction that an aggressive union role in promoting structural reforms was required. At the same time, both past experience and the features of the crisis necessitated that the reform policy be revised.

The fact that this had to occur in the heat of an intensifying political-economic crisis did not facilitate the effort, nor did it encourage radical departures from already established premises. In examining the policy of reforms in this first post-1973 phase, the continuities with the preceding years deserve, in fact, to be underlined. Objectives remained much the same but were reordered and given priorities. Similarly, the unions retained the principle that reforms had to be viewed as a general objective, not as a currency with which peace and concessions in the labor market could be purchased. The unions' determination not to compromise on the objectives of their reform policy gradually weakened, however, as the economic crisis became more severe. By the mid-1970s, social reforms had lost much of their centrality in the unions' strategic agenda. Finally, there was no wavering with respect to the strategic autonomy which the union movement must exercise (although in reality there were problems in this regard). Where the most marked changes occurred was with respect to how structural reforms were to be pursued—what emphasis was to be given to the market and political arenas, and how to operate in the latter, especially after 1976 when the Communist Party assumed a greater role in national governance. As we will see, however, no matter how implemented, the policy of reforms produced little better result in this phase than it had in the preceding years, and by 1977 the unions began to recognize that they faced a real impasse with respect to that part of their strategy deemed most essential to resolution of the country's deepening crisis.

The objectives of the unions' reform policy in this phase became more specific and priorities and criteria more defined. The unions came to accept the charge that their earlier proposals had reflected an unwarranted 'globalism' of demands, and identified more clearly the issues on which they thought action was most urgently required.[169] Unemployment, defense of real wages and reform of the structure of the economy assumed priority; expansion and reorganization of social services tended to recede. In addition, the union accentuated its emphasis on assuring that the problems of the South were stressed, and it sought to assure that the reforms proposed would have the effect of linking the industrial working class to other social strata rather than accentuating divisions and a process of fragmentation and competitive mobilization. In this sense, the criteria to be applied in evaluating proposals of reform were both economic—creating the bases for a durable exit from the crisis—and social, contracting the effects of the crisis on the social structure in order to prevent disaggregation and encourage the development of consent around the unions and their program.

According to the unions, reform of the economic structure and thus the planting of the roots of a new model of economic development were to proceed along four lines: a sectoral policy whose overriding purpose should be to favor industrialization in the South; a strategy of industrial re-conversion, not just restructuring; a plan for development of the agricultural sector (again with special emphasis on the South); and a new program of investments favoring productive activities and public, rather than private, consumption.[170] The logic behind these proposals was simple indeed. In order to overcome the crisis, it was necessary to change the modes of capital formation on the one hand and the criteria directing investments and expenditures on the other. The sectors which had been sacrificed and pushed to the margins by the employers' restructuring in the 1960s and 1970s had to become the targets of reconversion and investments. Hence, the unions requested that priority be given to the development of alternative sources of energy, development of the South, an emergency plan for agriculture and intense investments in public works, mass transportation and the construction sector. As envisioned by the unions, such programs would have a twin effect: to bring about recovery of these sectors and areas, and, at the same time, to remove some of the most damaging structural flaws in the economy.

As the preceding proposals suggest, the unions viewed the key problem of escaping the crisis to be that of investments and of breaking out of the historical tendency to underinvest, to direct investments to the satisfaction of private consumption and to the North, and to transfer productive resources, especially capital, abroad. Resolution of these problems required a reordering of the relationship between the state and the accumulation process, and consequently a reform of state activity in the economy was also called for.

During this phase, there were several proposals which the unions made in this regard. First, they stressed the need to reorganize the system of *partecipazioni statali* (enterprises fully or partially owned by the state). This system, they claimed, offered the state a potentially powerful instrument for assuming a more active role in directing the economy.[171] To do so, however, management of the public sector had to be reorganized in order to break the traditional pattern in which the public firms supported or simply followed the lead of the private sector. Second, the unions called for new and more stringent mechanisms designed to assure that the state would have the resources necessary to carry out a structural investment program. Among the measures advocated were reform of the tax structure to end evasion and increase its progressive character, a more selective credit policy intended to encourage productive investments, especially in the sectors and areas deemed of highest priority and a change in the criteria used by the state in elaborating its budget in order to make the process more transparent and facilitate investment initiatives.[172]

A third key feature with respect to the role of the state was the demand for a new planning initiative. In contrast to the 1960s, the unions came to see planning both as critical to the efficient utilization of available resources and as a potentially effective instrument in a structural reform effort. The deepening of the crisis and the unions' analysis that the existing model of development had irremediably failed, led them to call for a 'guided and programmed' economy to replace the spontaneity of the market.[173]

We have seen earlier that in the 1960s whatever disposition there was on the unions' part toward planning was eroded by their doubts about their ability to play a meaningful role in the planning process. These doubts remained in this period, but under the new conditions the unions went further in proposing ways in which they might participate in the formulation and implementation of a program of investments. In doing so, they also recognized that how the unions interacted with the planning process would affect all aspects of their internal organization and of their relations to government, the political parties, and capital; in other words, their role and status in the economic and political systems.

In discussing this issue, the unions were quick to reject three foreign 'solutions'. The British pattern of semi-institutionalized 'social contracts' was vehemently rejected, although the UIL favored establishing regular tripartite meetings between government, the unions, and the employers. The German pattern of *Mitbestimmung* was equally opposed, seen more as a means of granting legitimacy to capital for its policies than as a means for the workers' movement to achieve effective control of the development process. Finally, French *autogestion* was held to be no more than a transitional choice, perhaps a useful instrument for expanding the unions' power inside the workplace (although not in the Italian situation) but with no potential as an instrument for transforming society.[174]

The formula finally devised by the Italian unions was and remains workers' control over investments through an uninterrupted process of negotiations with government and capital.[175] The unions are to participate in formulating the direction and content of investments by bargaining at all levels from national government to the individual factory. Workers' organizations inside the factory are delegated the task of supervising the implementation of the investment programs, factory by factory or zone by zone.[176] Even organizations outside the factory (territorial councils) are to be involved in this task of supervision, especially in the agricultural sector. A critical aspect of this proposal has been the demand for the inclusion of contractual provisions giving the unions the right to have access to information on the firms' economic condition and investment programs. This was agreed to in some important 1975 contracts and has been expanded subsequently.

In essence, the thrust of the unions' planning proposal is that control of the investment process must be linked to and a result of the acquisition of greater industrial democracy.[177] This is supposed to allow the unions to have decisive input into the fundamental decisions governing the general directions to be taken by the economic system, while avoiding (and the unions strongly affirm their desire to do so) laws which would regulate industrial relations. The union movement's conception of 'democratic planning' (programming is the word used in Italian in order to distinguish from state planning of the Eastern European varieties), then, is one based on continual negotiation, state incentives but not directives and the direct involvement of the unions' own organizations at all levels and during all phases of the programming process.

A program of objectives as ambitious as the one just sketched out was seen by the unions to require a broadening of their traditional constituency or, at least, a policy of alliances with a broad range of working strata and of the poor unemployed. This had been a part of the policy of reforms from its formulation after the hot autumn and had always been instrumental in how the content of that policy was developed. With the onset of the crisis, however, building and maintaining alliances was, as we have seen, deemed more difficult, and failure to do so more dangerous.[178] Thus, the unions intensified their insistence on catering their policies to the development of alliances. The CGIL spearheaded this policy thrust. As early as 1973, Lama had argued for a more aggressive pursuit of allies. The CISL and UIL went along with this emphasis, although with less enthusiasm. These differences are to be explained, in part, by the CGIL's longstanding linkage to the PCI and the fact that much of its leadership remained Communist. The point here is not that the Communist Party imposed an alliance perspective on the CGIL's leadership; this seems very unlikely in the circumstances of the 1970s. Rather, the Communists had long stressed the importance of social alliances between the Party and working-class and other social strata, especially to reduce what they perceived as the everpresent danger of reaction. The PCI had intensified this argument in the 1970s.[179] It seems probable that those of Communist background within the union leadership shared this perspective. The agreement of the other two confederations to increase the union movement's stress on alliances, in contrast, is more likely explained by concern to maintain the newly achieved union unity and by the fact that the unions, by their own analysis of the crisis and its effects, did see a danger of isolation.[180] Finally, the ideology of the union as representative of the working class and not mere association of its members (always the case for the CGIL and accepted by the others since the early 1970s) undoubtedly also played a role. How the search for social allies was to be integrated into the union strategy at the practical level remained, however, a contentious and problematic issue and one of the major inputs into the EUR line.

In our discussion of the objectives of the unions' reform policy in the first post-1973 phase, we have stressed the continuities with the previous period. We will see that there were also no great changes with respect to objectives in the second phase, that of the EUR line. What changes there were primarily involved a reordering of proposals in terms of priorities, a sharper delineation of the criteria to be applied in formulating and judging proposals for structural reform and, consequently, a greater stress on economic reforms and of the means by which they might be achieved (here the new commitment to planning represents a break with the past) at the expense of social welfare reform. These continuities, however, should not suggest that the unions also maintained their pre-1973 conviction that reforms were best pursued by the confederations in the political arena. In fact, the failure of this approach to secure significant victories in the 1970–2 period led to an attempt in 1974–5 to pursue the most pressing reform priorities, investments in the South, and to expand employment in the market arena and, through the contractual process, at the sectoral and workplace level.

Such an approach was a major break with Italian union traditions. On the one hand, the CGIL had always viewed the political arena as the one through which reforms were likely to result. On the other hand, the CISL and UIL in giving priority to workplace bargaining had always regarded the contractual process as one through which the workers in the individual factory could improve their lot with respect to wages and working conditions. They had not generally, until the late 1960s, accepted a more 'political' conception of the union, and certainly not one which encompassed using the contractual process to pursue 'political' ends. Thus, there was no precedent for the fact that in contracts with, among others, Fiat and Montedison in 1975, the unions demanded, and won, guarantees that the companies would invest in the South.[181] It should be noted here, however, that this was a Phyrric victory, its value being more symbolic than practical: virtually no investments in the South ensued from these contractual agreements. We will return in a moment to an explanation of this innovation, but before doing so, we need briefly to discuss other developments in this phase with respect to the arenas of union struggle and the relationships between the levels in the union structure.

The pursuit of some reform goals through the contractual process did not, of course, exhaust the union movement's action with respect to its reform policy. The proposed program required, and explicitly called for, a broad range of governmental initiatives. In seeking to apply pressure to the government to do so, the confederations retained their leading role. There were numerous consultations between government and the unions about a wide range of measures, primarily, however, those concerned with dealing with conjunctural problems and the unions' contractual policy with regard to wages and working conditions. On specific reforms called for by the union movement, discussions were less concrete than those of 1971. Furthermore, a subtle change took place. Whereas immediately after the hot autumn the unions sought, and the government acted as if, direct negotiations between them could produce reforms, with the parties and Parliament acting primarily as a rubber stamp, this was no longer the case. Instead, it was clear that the parties had to have a critical mediating role, and the unions presented their proposals to them.[182] Thus, the parties reasserted their political function with respect to the unions which, while still operating in the political arena, reduced the scope of the political functions which they sought to assume for themselves.

We have already noted in discussing contractual policy in this phase that the confederations had once again become more important and that, in general there was a recentralization of initiative and control within the union movement. The revised policy of reforms had somewhat contradictory effects in this regard. On the one hand, the decision to pursue the investment objectives through the contractual process tended to shift some initiative to the federation level, although for goals which were not directly to benefit those already employed in the sector or firm. On the other hand, the unions' analysis of the crisis and its effects tended to underline the necessity of centralized coordination of all union policies and thus the importance of the confederations. No other level of the union movement could assure that the stronger sectors and factories did not make gains at the expense of the weaker, coordinate the reform policies, intervene with government to try to get the best possible conjunctural policy, and make sure that reforms and other policies pressed for by the movement were consonant with the alliances being sought. That is to say, only the confederations could manage the array of policies which the crisis had made increasingly impelling.[183] Finally, to the extent that the mediation of political parties became more necessary, only that level of the union movement with the best linkages to the parties, once again the confederations, could be expected to operate effectively. One further development needs to be noted: the growing political tensions within the unions, especially at the confederal level. Throughout this phase, there was increased disagreement and bickering among the confederations, and the final agreements reached, especially with regard to how best to pursue the reform policy, came after often difficult negotiations. While a number of factors contributed to this, one deserves special mention because of the importance which it has assumed to the present day. Until 1975, the possibility of Communist governmental participation had not been an issue of practical concern, although it certainly occupied much attention. In the administrative elections of that year, however, the PCI made a major electoral leap forward, one which was largely repeated in the national Parliamentary elections one year later. With about one third of the seats in Parliament, control of almost all of the major northern cities, the Socialist and Christian Democratic parties in considerable disarray and momentum on its side, the PCI (in the framework of its 'historic compromise' strategy) demanded, and was able to gain, a greater role in national governmental decision-making.[184] The arrangements were Byzantine, the actual power relationships not always visible, but there was little doubt that, for the first time since the immediate postwar years, the major party of the Left with the strongest representative base in the working class and the trade union movement was a daily participant in the major decisions of the national government, especially those concerned with the management of the political economy.

The problems posed for, and within, the union movement by these developments were of two sorts. The first concerned the attitude to be assumed toward the composition of the government and the participation of any particular party in it.[185] It had been evident since the failures in the early 1970s to get the government to undertake reforms that its composition —which parties were in and which factions of those parties ascendant—had a major bearing on the success of the reform policy of the union strategy. Power in the market and society did not translate directly into political power; the balance of strength within the government and Parliament and the social linkages of the dominant groups were critical. It was also clear, however, that the newly unified union movement could not hope to maintain its unity if it were to declare its preference for any particular government. The old partisan linkages remained too strong. This potentially highly divisive issue, however, could much more easily be kept in the background as long as the Communist question was not a practical concern.[186] The unions had not, for instance, had great difficulty in making clear their opposition to the Center–Right government which had ruled for a short period after the 1972 elections. After 1975, this was no longer possible. Every action of the union movement, from their policies at the shop floor to their efforts to use strike actions to promote national reforms or block efforts to roll back past gains, became part of the considerations about whether and how the PCI should be brought into 'the governmental area.'[187] This was all the more the case because the Communist Party presented itself, among other things, as the only party which, by its presence in government, might provide the guarantees to the unions necessary to gain their cooperation in both conjunctural and structural policy to break out of the crisis. The result was that, even without declaring a preference for one government over another (something which would have irreparably destroyed union unity), the unions became deeply involved in partisan maneuverings. That under such conditions the old political divisions within the movement should once again become more prominent is not surprising.[188]

The second problem for the union movement derived from the content of government policy once the PCI was more deeply involved in the policy-making process. Since the mid-1970s, the PCI had been presenting itself as a moderating force in political economy. It declared its concern with the questions of inflation, productivity, investments, and the balance of payments, and its opposition to a politics of 'the worse, the better.'[189] Implicitly, and sometimes explicitly, it criticized the unions for inconsistency between their broad policy objectives and their day-to-day conduct, particularly with regard to contractual policy. By late 1976, it was evident that the PCI felt that with appropriate guarantees, the union movement should be willing to ease its pressure on the economy (accepting some forms of wage restraint, greater labor mobility, and the like) in exchange for significant efforts at structural reform, especially with regard to the development of a national plan of investments and the shift of significant resources to the South. In early 1977, PCI Secretary-General Enrico Berlinguer sought to formalize this posture in calling for a 'politics of austerity' which would distribute sacrifices across the social spectrum (including the working class) as part of a national policy of structural reforms. The crisis, he argued, represented a great danger of reaction, but also a great opportunity to restructure the nation's political economy with the full cooperation of the labor movement in both its political and union components.[190]

The difficulties raised for the unions by this posture on the part of the Communisty Party exercising major governmental influence are evident. Much of what the PCI was calling for in terms of structural reforms was parallel to the unions' own program. Furthermore, Communist influence at the level of national government could be argued to provide guarantees that the reforms would actually be implemented, and in ways the unions could accept.[191] Given the priority which the unions placed on reform, the dangers they saw in a further degeneration of the economic situation if effective measures were not undertaken and the failures of their past efforts with other governments, this might be the best, and last, hope. Thus there were strong arguments on the side of those who favored greater co-operation. On the other hand, there were also significant arguments in the opposite direction. A union turnaround on the question of trade-offs would appear like a political subordination of the union movement and would inevitably tend to reinforce the PCI's political position. The political autonomy of the movement (or the image thereof), which had been so basic to the process of unification, would be undercut, and the appearance of subordination of the CISL and the UIL to the CGIL would be difficult to avoid.[192] In addition, a turnaround would likely generate considerable resistance from sectors of the unions' base unwilling to accept the 'sacrifices' which would follow, or who had an ideological commitment to a policy in which contractual demands should never be limited by 'political' considerations, whether justified by partisanship or the promise of reforms. Such discontent at the base would provide resources to those at higher levels of the unions who opposed a change in policy. In light of these contrasting arguments, it is hardly surprising that political tensions should have risen within the union movement. Those who retained partisan linkages to either side of the political battles on the Communist question could be expected to feel pressure from the political forces with which they were linked; and they could expect to find allies who took either side for reasons which had little to do with direct partisan preferences. Thus, both the structure of the new political situation and the specific content of the policies being advocated by the Communist Party tended to aggravate longstanding partisan and ideological divisions within the union movement. They also brought to the surface tensions more closely related to judgments about the policies followed by the unions since the hot autumn and the onset of the crisis.

In concluding this discussion of the first post-1973 phase of union economic analysis and strategy, it is worthwhile briefly examining the record, seeking, in terms of the goals set out by the unions themselves, to highlight some of the major outstanding issues. As a general judgment, we would argue that the unions found themselves increasingly entrapped in a series of interrelated dilemmas growing out of their continuing, and even growing (due to the crisis) disruptive power in the market arena but their ongoing inability (in their own terms) to have a significant policy impact in the political arena.

In terms of objectives, at least three dilemmas can be identified. First, could the unions continue to maintain maximum pressure with respect to wages and working conditions, or should they make concessions? Already after 1974, they had sought to restrain the demands made by the strongest federations and factories in order to reduce internal differentiation within the labor movement. This remained an important problem as the crisis deepened, but the issue of the relationship between the entire organized working class and the economically and politically weaker strata of the working population loomed increasingly large. The unions' own analysis suggested the gravity of a split.[193]

Second, if concessions were to be made, how could the unions assure that the accumulated resources would benefit those on whose behalf they had been made? The technique of attempting to use contractual agreements to direct investment funds to the South, for instance, was clearly only a very partial response, and even that technique raised questions about the unions' real control of the agreements they reached with employers. Given the drastic judgments which the unions had reached about both the employers and the government, effective mechanisms of control were indispensable.[194]

Third, what relationship should be struck between objectives related to wages and working conditions and the policy of reforms? Since the hot autumn, the unions had rejected the notion of a trade-off or any form of social contract, arguing, among other things, that it would only create margins for capital to restructure on its own terms. Yet, this posture had produced few results with respect to the reforms which the unions had sought and the deepening of the crisis made reforms, in the unions' own view, ever more necessary. The problem was further complicated by the PCI's entrance into the governmental area and its accommodative position on this problem. The pressure on the union movement to agree to some sort of self-imposed limitation on its demands as part of an implicit or explicit social pact was increasing. So too was the danger of the political isolation and/or redivision of the union movement on this issue.

The preceding dilemmas obviously had implications as well for the arenas in which the unions were to pursue their strategy. We have seen that, since the hot autumn, the unions had sought to carry out their reform policy in both the market and the political arenas, and in neither had major successes been attained. These failures raised significant questions about the capacity of the unions to pursue the reform component of their strategy. Yet, in their own analysis, the deepening of the crisis made reforms increasingly necessary and the pressure of the union movement indispensable to assure that such reforms addressed the underlying structural causes of the crisis. Thus, the unions had little option but to continue to use the political arena to pursue reforms, but at the same time they faced the problem of what new approach might make that pursuit more effective.[195] Here again, the questions of how to relate to government and the political parties became crucial, and potentially highly divisive.

Looking finally at the internal structure of the unions, we have seen that throughout this first phase there had been a tendency toward the centralization of initiative within the movement. Here too, however, there were dilemmas. On the one hand, such increased centralization was an almost natural by-product of the problems intensified by the crisis and of the decline in the mobilization of the base. On the other hand, it was accompanied by two potentially serious problems. First, it was undoubtedly contributing to a decline of the politicization (not in the partisan sense) of the workers. Such a decline tended to accentuate the tendency toward sectoralization of the movement, workers becoming more concerned with their own immediate interests and less with the broader objectives (alliances with, and reforms intended to benefit, the weaker and poorer strata). In a period in which the unions were feeling pressures to make concessions and in which their own analysis pointed to the dangers of isolation, this was not a congenial development. Second, centralization and a decline of mass mobilization at the base tended to reduce the flexibility of the unions, to underline internal conflicts and to give greater voice to those at the base who were the most active, and often also the most closely linked to the old political divisions within the movement.[196] A greater concentration of initiative in the confederations, furthermore, made the reemergence of old partisan conflicts at that level more likely (they were less conditioned by the unitary thrust from the base), especially in the fluid and heated political context in which the unions were operating.

It is apparent that by 1977 the union movement had reached somewhat of an impasse. Its strength and disruptive power remained great but were menaced by demobilization and division. At the same time, exercise of this strength in the market arena (which might contribute to remobilization) threatened to deepen the crisis, might produce even more internal division (on sectoral bases) and could contribute to the isolation of the movement.[197] Exercise of this strength in the political arena had proven ineffective, and here too internal division was increasingly menacing. Thus, the strategic continuity which had characterized the movement since the hot autumn was becoming not an element of strength and unity but a potential source of failure and conflict. As perceptively remarked by Giorgio Ruffolo,

the unions must fear their strength as much as their weakness. The 'syndical paradox' lies in the unions' capacity to destabilize a system on which they continue to depend, and which they cannot change, neither alone nor in the short run.'[198]

Strategic Responses in the Second Phase: The EUR Line

The impasse came increasingly to preoccupy the trade unions during 1977. Once the severe balance of payments and inflation crisis of 1975–6 had been contained, the movement could redirect its attention to its broader strategic concerns. Yet the crisis itself, and the unions' basically *ad hoc* and defensive responses to it, only served to underline the difficulties which they were encountering in implementing their strategic aims and to highlight their inability to achieve an effective linkage between their short-run policies, both in the market and political arenas, and their longer-term objectives.[199] These problems, and the internal debates which they provoked, were aggravated by two developments. On the one hand, the structural problems in the economy which the unions saw as most damaging to their long-term prospects were not effectively being addressed either by government or by the employers themselves. While the economic situation was somewhat improved, its structural foundations were considered ever weaker. On the other hand, the PCI was now playing a major role in the formulation of government political-economic policy, and this development was interpreted by many as a major step in its full integration into the political system and toward full cabinet participation. The implications of this change will be discussed extensively below.[200]

The EUR line—denoted as such because the critical meeting of the Federation of the confederations at which the basic tenets of the policy were accepted took place at the EUR conference center outside Rome in January 1978—must be evaluated in the context of these developments. At the same time, however, the new line represented a further step in a longer process: the adaptation of strategy as the outcome of the interplay of union traditions, accumulated experience, organizational needs, and the impact of the conditions created by the hot autumn and the subsequent political-economic crisis. The stragegy of EUR was more moderate than what had come before, and it did mark a significant shift in some of the principles which had guided the unions in the 1970s. The shift, however, should not be overstated. The EUR line, like its predecessors, incorporated important elements of continuity from the traditions of the three confederations and from the synthesis of these traditions which had been hammered out as part of the process of unification. As such, it was as much a reordering of priorities and further effort to develop a policy which would allow the unions to resolve the problems they were facing in achieving their unchanged goals as a basic change in perspective. The unions did not suddenly abandon their will to be agents of political-economic transformation, nor their determination to defend the gains which had been made by the working class in the 1970s.[201] They did not give up their ambitions in the political arena, nor their understanding of the importance of struggle in the market. They did, however, seek to restructure the relationships among these features of their strategy. We have seen that in the past the attempt to combine these features in one strategy produced tensions within the union movement, particularly in light of the vulnerability of the Italian economy and the unresponsiveness (in the unions' view) of the Italian government. These latter conditions changed little after 1978. It is therefore not surprising that many of the tensions with respect to objectives, arenas, and internal organization which existed prior to EUR continued—and continue —to plague the union movement.

The EUR line did not introduce significant new objectives of political-economic reform, nor did it abandon any. The policy goals stipulated in earlier positions were retained. Thus, in the document laying out the basic demands of the new strategy, the unions called for:

- a policy of full employment based on noninflationary growth and paying particular heed to the needs of the South and of unemployed youth;
- democratic programming with the intention of establishing a rigorous relationship between program goals and available resources;
- agricultural reform and investments;
- housing reform through a ten-year program to build 250,000 new residential units per year;
- reform of energy policy;
- reform of transportation and the development of necessary transportation infrastructure;
- reform of state finance;
- implementation of an effective and efficient policy to improve the economic situation of financially strapped firms;
- reform of the tax system to assure an end to evasion, to make taxes more progressive and to shift the tax base away from indirect and toward direct taxes;
- general rationalization of public spending to reduce waste and make more efficient the use of public monies.[202]

If there was little change in the general objectives of the unions' reform policy, however, there were significant new emphases and, relatedly, a new orientation toward the relationship between reform objectives and shop-floor contractual demands.

We have seen that, since the onset of the economic crisis in 1974–5, the unions had begun to focus their priorities with regard to reform objectives. The admitted 'globalism' of the years immediately following the hot autumn had given way to an increasing emphasis on reforms of the political-economic structure over reform of social services. Nonetheless, there still had been little systematic selection of priorities among structural reforms and even less concrete commitment in day-to-day policy to the priorities which were expressed in the unions' programmatic statements. The discussions of the EUR line acknowledged this, and the new policy sought to correct it: absolute priority, at least in the short run, was assigned to creating the conditions for full employment.

> The fundamental objective, to which all the specific demands of the unions should be subordinated, is to set in motion a process leading to full employment. This process should permit, in particular, the entrance into the work force of the unemployed in the South, youth, and women.[203]

The new jobs were to be concentrated in the South, and special efforts were to be made to employ young workers. Furthermore, the Federation CGIL–CISL–UIL recognized that a policy of full employment was critically dependent on an increased, stable rate of economic growth:

> The maintenance of a low growth rate for a long period of time and the related stagnation of employment in the face of a predictable further increase in the size of the work force threaten to aggravate the problem of employment in an intolerable manner, to make chronic the low investment levels, to stabilize stagnation and to deprive the human and productive potential of any innovative drive and of any commitment to the necessary structural changes.[204]

The rhetoric of full employment, the South and growth was, of course, not new to the Italian union movement.[205] The focus on youth was greater than in the past, largely due to growing youth unemployment. In addition, the unions had treated the recent disruption of a speech by Lama at the University of Rome as an extremely serious event, pointing to the need to pay greater attention to the specific problems of new entrants to the labor force. Nonetheless, had the EUR line been nothing more than a narrowing and sharpening of priorities and a greater verbal commitment to a very few reform objectives, it would have amounted to a continuation of trends which had been present for several years. It would certainly not have constituted the 'turning point' which even the unions claimed it to be.[206] Nor would it have represented a new approach to the strategic dilemmas which had emerged since the hot autumn and especially since the crisis.

Yet, at least in principle, the EUR line was both of these, for it abandoned the unions' simultaneous commitment to gains in wages and work conditions won through action in the market and to reform of society to be achieved through action in the political arena which had been a strategic hallmark since the hot autumn. Instead, the unions accepted the need for a policy of sacrifices and of austerity in which the working class, along with other social strata, would have to participate. In other words, in contrast to the past, all other union objectives and policies, including those incorporated into contractual policy, would have to be adjusted in light of their contribution to the attainment of full employment and the creation of jobs in the South for youth and for women.[207] In one bold stroke, the union movement acknowledged that there might be an inverse relationship between their contractual demands and their reform policy, a reversal of the understanding with which they had operated for almost a decade. We will see shortly that there were important qualifications to this new posture. In particular, the unions made systematic programming of investments at the firm, sectoral, and national levels, other government interventions, and a direct and continuing union role in the formulation and implementation of programming objectives at all levels the conditions for their cooperation in an austerity policy. Nonetheless, austerity and sacrifice were to become the watchwords of the better-off northern industrial working class.[208]

In undertaking this revision, the unions established a new standard against which the coherence of their strategic implementation could be measured.[209] This should not suggest that there was agreement about the precise meaning and implications of the new union strategy. Most industrialists, while expressing pleasure over the unions' decision to be 'reasonable,' maintained that the concessions 'did not go far enough.'[210] The government, while also assuming a very moderate interpretation, sought guarantees that the confederations, and especially the federations, would remain faithful to the new directives. Most important for our purposes, there was significant discord among unionists themselves about the precise significance of the new line and a good deal of reinterpretation in reaction to the appraisals of others within and outside the union movement.[211] Thus, while the fundamental shift of the EUR line—the new relationship between contractual and reform policy and the new reform priorities—was agreed on, its specific details and policy consequences were continually reformulated in response both to the conceptions which others sought to impose on the unions and to economic and political changes in the unions' environment. As we trace the EUR strategy, it must be kept in mind that we are dealing with a moving (and still moving) target.

The extent to which the EUR line represented a turning point in the union movement's strategy can be captured through the discussion of two of its principle features: the revised understanding of the sources of the economic crisis and of the conditions necessary to restore stable growth; and the specific content given to the themes of austerity and sacrifice.

We have seen that in the past the unions had rejected the charge, widespread among entrepreneurs, the government and, to some extent, even among the parties of the Left, that the unions' own gains with respect to wages and control over the conditions of work had contributed to Italy's economic problems and crisis. The union movement had focused its analysis of the crisis on the historical roots of Italy's postwar development model, on the errors and intransigence of employers, on the inefficacy and lack of autonomy of government policy (from the narrow interests of capital and the clientelistic practices of the government parties), and on changing conditions in the international political economy. This analysis had been permissive of a highly aggressive policy in the market arena for shopfloor goals and had also enabled the unions to defend themselves against the charge that the *scala mobile* was a source of inflation and not just a protection against it. The hallmark of this approach had been the unions' treatment of wages as if they were an 'independent variable' in the economy.

In a highly controversial interview which anticipated formal union acceptance of the EUR line and caused heated debate within the movement, Lama abandoned this approach to wages, and more generally, the understanding of the relationship between union wage and work condition policy and the overall state of the economy with which the unified CGIL–CISL and UIL had been operating since the hot autumn. His elaboration of the new approach was noteworthy not just for the change it signaled but also for the bluntness of its critique of the past:

> We have become aware that an economic system cannot sustain independent variables. The capitalists maintain that profit is an independent variable. The workers and their union, almost as a reflex, have in recent years sustained that wages are an independent variable and the size of the employed work force another . . . one established a certain wage level and a certain level of employment and then one asked that all other economic quantities be fixed in such a way as to make possible those levels of salary and employment. . . . It was an absurdity, because in an open economy the variables are all dependent upon one another.[212]

Lama also delineated a series of other specific areas of union policy which had failed to take proper account of the relationship between shopfloor gains and economic performance and which the EUR line would, under appropriate conditions, seek to correct:

- excessive rigidity with regard to the mobility of workers within factories and even between them;
- 'Imposition of excessive numbers of workers on firms' is a suicidal policy. 'We retain that the firms, when it is determined that they are in a state of crisis, have the right to fire.'
- use of the *cassa integrazione* as a form of 'welfare.'

Instead, Lama asserted, the unions were asking their core constituencies to play their part in a societywide policy of sacrifices which would be critical to a program to employ all national resources in pursuit of one objective: to increase employment and decrease unemployment; it was necessary to sacrifice all other objectives to the problem of eliminating the existence of 1,600,000 unemployed. This, in turn, would require that:

> wage policy in the coming years be greatly contained . . . the entire mechanism of the *cassa integrazione* be reexamined from top to bottom. We can no longer oblige the firms to maintain at their cost numbers of workers exceeding their productive capacities, nor can we continue to require that the *cassa integrazione* permanently aid the excessive work force. . . . [There must be] an effective mobility of the work force and an end to the system of permanent subsidized work.[213]

All of this, particularly in Lama's unexpectedly blunt and self-critical tone, had an enormous shock effect on public and union opinion. It looked to many, within the union movement and outside it, like a full-scale retreat from the ramparts which had been won in the hot autumn and after, and which had been tenaciously defended since. Yet it rapidly became clear that such an interpretation was off the mark. In focusing on the general things which the unions were saying they were willing to give up or change, it failed to take account of the limits of such concessions and, more importantly, of what the union movement required in return. The unions were not, in fact, abandoning most of their earlier objectives—although priorities with respect to the timing of measures to implement such objectives were now far more explicit. Rather, they were seeking—in the face of past failures, growing problems, and perceived opportunities— different means to attain these objectives. Having found it impossible to impose reforms, and seeing a government potentially more willing to undertake reforms, the union movement was not proposing a general retreat but an extremely hard bargain which, if struck, would protect many of the gains which had been made at the level of the shop floor while giving the unions a major role in the formulation and implementation of structural reforms of the economy.

The essential condition of the unions' participation in a politics of austerity was assurance that the resources freed would be effectively implemented for productive investments which would contribute to stable growth of the economy and employment.[214] We have seen that in the past, the unions had rejected the notion that growth could be left to the entrepreneurs and to the spontaneous decisions of the market. They had also increasingly lost confidence that government, unless under unrelenting pressure, would commit itself to structural reform. These negative judgments were now combined with proposals which, if implemented, the unions felt would justify their asking their supporters for sacrifices.[215] The core elements of these proposals were three: (1) bargaining at the firm and sectoral level over investment plans, with the unions acquiring a contractual right to sufficient information about the financial situation of the firms or sector to enable them to reach informed contractual agreements with respect to the levels and location of investments; (2) more rational and efficient implementation of the vast array of existing government instruments for economic intervention in pursuit of a delimited set of investment goals attuned to the unions' reform objectives; and (3) a major government effort to reduce waste, to make more of existing public resources available for productive purposes and to rationalize and make more equitable the chaotic and patronage-ridden system of social services and public sector wages. Let us now consider these three core elements in more detail:

(1) Characterized by some union leaders as the 'Italian road to comanagement,' the demand for control over the levels and location of investments has become a major strategic objective of Italian unions.[216] From the mid-1970s onwards, the unions have sought to include this demand in their contractual platforms.[217] Only in recent months, however, have unions, notably the CGIL,[218] developed a full-fledged plan concerning the specifics of this demand, the *Piano d'impresa*. According to this plan, firms should be requested to present every year a plan specifying their programs with regard to projected production and employment levels, location of productive activities and their eventual decentralization, and intended modifications of the organizational structure of the firms and of the organization of work. All levels of union structure and state agencies involved in planning should receive this plan and discuss it with management. Sanctions should be applied to those firms which refused to present such a plan.[219]

We have already discussed the reasons that make the search by Italian unions for a direct, active role in investment programs quite unique when compared to the experience made by unions in other European countries. However, there are a few aspects of the demand for control over investments which are worth stressing.[220] First, this demand is perceived by the unions as being part of their more general demand for a 'new model of economic development.'[221] By acquiring control over investments, unions would be able to exert influence on how, where, and what should be produced, thereby shifting the direction of economic growth away from private consumption to collective consumption patterns. Second, this demand reflects the unions' historical concern with the problem of unemployment and of the South. The agreements that unions have so far concluded with management over investment programs have in fact attempted to channel investments towards the creation of new jobs in the South. Third, control over investments is seen by unions as a means for creating the conditions favoring the implementation of planning (at the national, regional, and sectoral levels), in which unions and workers would have a direct role.[222] Fourth, this demand, especially in the ways in which it has been elaborated in the *Piano d'impresa*, points to the historically rooted tendency by Italian unions to accept the capitalist framework of economic development while, at the same time, wanting to change it. The aim is not to deprive management of its decisional power over the firm. Rather, unions want to force firms to act more rationally by coordinating their initiatives with the other economic actors. On the other hand, for the unions the acquisition of control over investments is a step toward the achievement of industrial democracy and of social reforms. Fifth, the 'concessions' that unions are willing to make in order to establish a system of controls over investments underscores their sense of responsibility, that is, their willingness to assume certain responsibilities (wage restraint, commitment to increased productivity) in order to reduce unemployment and to overcome regional and sectoral disequilibria. Finally, the demand for control over investments is largely an expression of the traditional aspiration of Italian unions, especially pronounced in the CGIL, to link particularist demands with global demands, to go, as argued by Bruno Trentin, 'beyond the confines of the firm by tying themselves directly to nationwide economic policies, to dynamics of the labor market, and to economic planning at the regional and sectoral level.'[223]

(2) For Italian unions, the crisis of investments which afflicts Italy is largely the problem of the relation between state action and accumulation. This is why in recent years they have demanded with growing insistence that the role of the state in the process of economic development be increased. It should be stressed, however, that Italian unions are not in favor of further nationalizations. In this, they share the view of the forces of the political left, including the PCI. According to the unions, the problem is not to nationalize further Italy's industrial sector but rather to make the existing presence of the state in the economy more rational and efficient and more consonant with the need for structural reforms. The unions' demand that the system of *partecipazioni statali* be reorganized, especially with respect to its investment patterns, has already been mentioned in the preceding pages. Three other dimensions of the union view on the role of the state in the economy deserve to be singled out. First, unions demand the elaboration of a nationwide plan comprising specific plans for industrial sectors which are in a situation of crisis or which have been historically backward, and of regional plans for the

more underdeveloped regions of the country.[224] Second, decentralization of state action in the economy is viewed by unions as fundamental to the successful implementation of regional and sectoral plans. Greater autonomy should be granted to regional and local governments, particularly with regard to the allocation of resources.[225] Third, the government should commit itself to the implementation of legislative measures. Unions have pointed repeatedly to the fact that the government has consistently failed to act upon the decrees that it has promulgated in recent years. (See, for instance, the '*Piano verde*' for the agricultural sector, the special law for reducing youth unemployment, the law for industrial reconversion, etc.)

(3) Though Italian unions recognize that existing public resources are limited and that they cannot be expanded overnight, they also argue that the government is largely responsible for the paucity of resources. The government's failure to stall the rapidly expanding public administration and to make it more efficient is the target of much criticism by the unions. They have constantly demanded its reorganization and decentralization. The wage policy actuated by the government in the public sector has also been criticized by the unions as being inherently clientelistic and a source of much iniquity.[226] Although many of the systems of social services, notably the system of social security, are managed, if not virtually controlled, by the unions themselves, they argue that government attempts to wrest such a control from them and its unwillingness to introduce reforms are the basic reasons for the continued inefficiency of these systems. Finally, unions have been very critical of the government's use of the *cassa integrazione* as a means for favoring large firms' uncontrolled processes of restructuring and reconversion.

From the preceding, it is evident that the union movement's availability for a policy of sacrifices and austerity was conditional on its ability to exercise what it considered to be the necessary influence on the process of investment. It is important to note, however, that, unlike the case in some other European countries, this 'social contract' was not to encompass the unions' institutionalized participation in the making of government decisions either with, or without, the parallel participation of employers. Institutionalized arrangements were to be confined to the contractual process, to the setting of investment decisions in firms and within sectors. The unions wished to retain their autonomy with respect to government and their role as a source of pressure on government to implement its commitments. This role, in fact, was deemed essential to the success of contractual agreements over investment policy at the firm and sectoral levels. Such agreements would have to be premised on the government undertaking compatible policies, and the unions would have to apply pressure to assure this. Becoming enmeshed in institutionalized relations with government would compromise their ability to do so. The overall thrust of this union stance, therefore, was that management of the 'surplus' produced by sacrifice would have to include a major but noninstitutionalized participation of the union movement.[227]

A further contrast with some other European cases appears when we examine in detail the 'concessions' which, the unions argued, the policy of austerity and sacrifices was to compromise. As would be expected, the unions demanded that the sacrifices be distributed equitably across the whole society and not concentrated in the working class and the poorer strata. Beyond this, however, the EUR line also did not fully abandon the idea—determinedly maintained since the hot autumn—that pressure on the shop floor was essential to any process of reform and reconversion. No general retreat was being sounded from this view—based on a profound pessimism about the decision which would otherwise be taken by employers and the government—nor from the gains which had been made.[228] Rather, the unions were proposing a series of limited changes which, while making economic change and growth more possible by removing unwarranted restraints on decisions, would maintain pressure on capital and protect the fundamental gains made by the working class.

The cautious and limited character of the rollback proposed in exchange for a more effective and participatory investment process can be illustrated with examples of specific proposals relating to wages, the *scala mobile*, worker mobility, reduction of the work week and wage egalitarianism. In briefly discussing each of these, we will indicate the limits on the concessions, how the changes were argued to contribute to the achievement of growth and the reduction of unemployment, and also some of the differences which appeared within the union movement. It was, in fact, over the specific content of the policy of sacrifices that many differences among the three confederations and between them and some federations emerged. These differences have proven of some consequence subsequently.[229] They also demonstrate the extent to which the EUR line was the product of a tentative consensus in which longstanding differences of tradition and everpresent tensions within the movement remained only barely beneath the surface. It is, of course, not surprising that the EUR line, with its premise that choices had to be made and priorities set and effectuated, should have brought these close to the surface.

Wages

The wage policy of the EUR line called for moderation and self-restraint. It rapidly became evident, however, that many union leaders did not accept Lama's wages and work conditions theory of the crisis.[230] This was especially the case for leaders in the CISL and for the non-PCI Left in the unions, a not unexpected finding in light of the traditional stance toward wages and wage pressure of these groups.[231]

Far more important, in calling for moderation, the EUR strategy did not accept the notion of legal limits on wages (all restraint was to be *self-imposed*), and it did not foresee the possibility that—in contrast to the position of British unions, for instance—wage restraint would lead to an absolute decline in working-class living standards. Rather, wages were to be set at levels compatible with

> stability of the cost of labor. In other words, the wage dynamic should: (1) assure coverage of inflation through the *scale mobile*; (2) assure growth of real wages in proportion to the growth of productivity.[232]

This was in contrast to the position of employers and the government who wanted all productivity gains to go into profits. The record since EUR shows results which fall between these two standards: wage gains have been below productivity growth but above the absolute stability of real wages. In any case, the union position in the EUR policy for the first time since the hot autumn accepted the notion of productivity bargaining while continuing to seek to maintain a significant degree of wage pressure and, in the unions' view, stimulus to reconversion.

Scala mobile

The EUR line accepted the notion that some revisions of the system of calculating the cost of living escalator were possible, thus abandoning the former slogan that the escalator was 'not to be touched.' The unions did not, however, specify the changes which might be made. They also made it clear that such changes could not result in less real protection for workers against inflation. What was basically being suggested was a 'technical' revision of the escalator mechanism which would eliminate anomalies which had accumulated over the years and which tended to inflate the actual benefits paid.

Again, however, important differences of view have emerged within the movement. The UIL, in the person of its Secretary, Giorgio Benvenuto, has argued openly that the *scala mobile* should, in fact, be abandoned or its degree of automatic protection reduced. The argument is interesting, for it reveals the presence of organizational concerns already visible before EUR and potentially aggravated by it. Expressing a view shared by many in the unions, Benvenuto maintains that, especially in light of the wage restraint proposed by EUR policy, the 'automaticity' of the escalator means that little of the traditional function of the union to fight for the incomes of workers remains. This, in turn, weakens the unions' ability to mobilize and even to maintain its membership.[233] To date, the UIL position has been rejected by the other two confederations, but it points to important problems within the unions.

Worker Mobility

One of the major assumptions of the EUR line was that the lack of mobility of the industrial work force could impede effective industrial reconversion,[234] increases in productivity, and sustained economic growth. The unions did not, however, accept a general and complete return to work-force mobility, much less employer discretion in allocating the workers. Instead, the unions stated that they were willing to accept mobility and even firings when firms are in crisis, and when such measures are demonstrated (to the unions) to be necessary to reconversion. Furthermore, the unions have demanded direct participation with employers in deciding which workers will be relocated and how reconversion will be accomplished.[235] No restoration of traditional employer prerogatives with respect to personnel is envisaged, even in situations of crisis. Work-force mobility and union participation in firms' decisions are to be two sides of one coin.

Reduction of the Work Week

The EUR declaration represented a significant change from the traditional union position that a reduction of the length of the work week was an objective of union policy. Instead, the unions stated that such a reduction would not contribute to employment growth and that reductions, if they were not to damage Italian international competitiveness, would have to be coordinated with similar reductions in other European countries. It rapidly became clear, however, that there was little real unified conviction behind this position.[236] The CISL—once more as would be expected in light of its traditions—did not accept this position but rather continued to adhere to the principle that 'all must work, but fewer hours,'[237] which had been a product of the hot autumn. The metal, chemical, and construction federations also did not accept a general veto on further reductions of the work week. The former two were already below forty hours and had been pressing for further reductions for a number of years. In subsequent contracts, these confederations demanded, and partially attained, an additional decline of the work week over the objections of the confederations and heated declarations in the press by nonunionists that this decline represented the end of EUR.[238]

Egalitarianism

The reduction of wage differentials had been a constant slogan in the union movement since the hot autumn. The EUR line called for a reappraisal of this objective, arguing that it was potentially damaging to productivity and that it contributed to organizational problems of internal union cohesion, especially between the more and less skilled and between blue- and white-collar workers.[239] Both the CISL and the metalworkers have expressed opposition to abandonment of the goal of further compression of wage differentials, while the CGIL and UIL have defended it.[240] Once more, the weight of different union traditions appears to be making itself felt on this issue.

In explaining and justifying the EUR line, one union leader stated that it exemplified the unions' commitment to be a movement 'which does not limit itself to preaching from its bunker.'[241] There is considerable truth, if also much self-congratulation, in this characterization. In offering to participate in a policy of austerity and sacrifices in exchange for a more efficacious role in the process by which investment decisions are reached in the society, and in narrowing the immediate objectives of the movement to the directed growth of the economy and employment, the unions were, in fact, stepping out from the ramparts which they had built in the hot autumn. These had at first seemed a bridgehead from which the unions could launch a further battle for reforms of the economy and society. They had increasingly become, the EUR line recognized, a defensive position which might actually be impeding the unions' ability to affect the larger process of political-economic decision-making.[242] The new strategy, therefore, sought to establish a different relationship between power at the shop floor and in society and at the same time to link short- and long-term goals, conjunctural and structural measures, in a more systematic and coherent manner.[243] How well this has been accomplished to date will be taken up in the Conclusion. Here we wish briefly to indicate what particular factors contributed to a change of strategy in 1978 and how the new EUR line fits into the general pattern of union strategy which we have examined in this essay.

The adoption of the EUR strategy, as was the case with the development of Italian union strategies in the past, appears to have been the result of a combination of economic, political, and internal union institutional factors, all of them filtered through a general strategic perspective hammered out within the union movement throughout the postwar period and especially after the hot autumn. It was this general perspective which gave the other factors salience. It was these same factors which pushed the unions to revise their strategy.

The main economic concern of the unions was not a sudden or precipitous crisis but rather continued and gradual deterioration. 1977, in fact, had witnessed a significant recovery after the severe problems of 1975–6, and even during the latter, the unions had made only limited and *ad hoc* adjustments of their policies. Nonetheless, by 1977 the union leadership was becoming increasingly concerned that there was no improvement in those features of the economy which were deemed threatening to long-term economic performance and to the unions' own strategic position.[244] Unemployment stayed high, and the problem was, if anything, even more concentrated in the South and among new entrants to the labor market. The gap between long-employed, well-employed and well-protected workers and the rest of the labor force appeared to be growing. This situation was only aggravated by the still high rates of inflation (no longer at the levels of the worst months of 1975–6) which tended to draw attention to the differences between those protected by the *scala mobile* and those without such protection. Inflation also encouraged particularistic defense of income both within the union movement and in groups outside it, the latter often decrying the unions' escalator as a source of their woes. Another unsettling continued trend was the growth of the 'invisible' economy and of forms of 'black' or hidden labor. Finally, the unions were also threatened with the closure of a number of major unionized firms suffering from severe financial problems. Taken together, and viewed in the context of what was perceived as economic stagnation, these conditions seemed to signal further and worsening problems for the union movement in just the areas—relations with other social groups, internal coherence, protection of the already employed, danger of isolation and of being 'blamed' for the country's economic difficulties—which the strategic perspective since the hot autumn had assumed to pose the greatest dangers to union influence in the society and, in a narrower perspective, to the union constituencies and organization.

As indicated, none of these problems was new, nor were the unions' anxieties about them. Since the early 1970s, the union movement had sought to relieve these difficulties by using pressure on firms and the government to get them to undertake policies which would initiate a process of structural reform. By 1978, however, it was increasingly apparent that this approach was a failure. Very little in the way of the structural changes—much less political-economic transformation—which the unions deemed essential to resolving the problems of the political economy had been undertaken. Furthermore, the failure to initiate such change was deemed to be one of the major causes of the continuing deterioration of the situation. The attempt to maximize pressure in the market arena to force political reform was not working. This might be attributed to the character of the governments which had come before, but the unions, as we have seen, also came increasingly to see that their policies too might be contributing to the degenerating situation. Thus, a change in policy might be called for, and the entrance of the PCI into the governmental area could not fail to encourage some within the union leadership that such a change might produce results.

Here an important question arises: how was the relationship between the PCI's new governmental influence and the unions' strategic revision to be understood? There certainly was considerable similarity between the EUR line and the policy recommendations which the PCI had been making for a number of years. This similarity was especially apparent in the interpretation of the EUR policy which had been made by Lama and other CGIL Communist leaders.[245] Was the new line, then, an expression of a revival of the 'transmission belt' in which the Communist Party was using the unions to reinforce its political gains?[246] Such an explanation seems to us unlikely for at least three reasons. First, as already indicated, it fails to acknowledge the degree to which the entire union movement was aware that the success of its strategy was dependent on a shift to the Left of government policy. There is no doubt that all the ideological and political currents of the unions were not in agreement that such a shift should encompass Communist participation in the government; but the experience of the preceding years left little question that a change in the balance of strength in the government toward forces more sympathetic to and capable of structural political economic reform was necessary. After 1976, that change seemed to be underway—in the form of PCI presence in the governmental area— and despite their misgivings, most of the strands of the union movement had to see this as opening improved prospects for their strategy of reform. Thus, showing greater flexibility in order to encourage and consolidate this development—once undertaken by the political parties—is entirely understandable.

Second, the theory of the 'restored transmission belt'—with its implicit notion that the unions are infinitely flexible—underestimates the degree to which the decisions of the unions, given the power and influence which they had achieved and wished to maintain in society, were necessarily the product of an intricate process of mediation among a large number of pressures (the PCI's positions among them). It can, in fact, be argued that the 'logic of action' of the unions and the party had become somewhat similar, due, on the one hand, to the political posture which the union movement had assumed and, on the other hand, to the importance which the Communists assigned to union strength.[247]

The third reason why the simple notion of the unions as instrument of the party seems incorrect is more prosaic, but tends to reinforce the others: the continued existence of confederal, ideological, and political divisions within the *unified* union movement. Both sides of the equation are important. The divisions made it unlikely (by the formal rules of the Federation of Confederations, impossible) that one political current would be able to impose its policies on the others. The unity of the movement, and the commitment of the leadership to that unity and to the partisan autonomy on which it was premised, meant that no group was likely to risk seeking to impose a partisan policy on the entire movement.[248] It would, therefore, appear that to the extent that the EUR line was similar to that of the PCI and tended to reinforce the Communist quest for a position in government, this was the product of a complex process of internal union decision-making in which the PCI's positions undoubtedly were an influence, but only one, and not the predominant, influence.

Economic and political factors promoted change in the unions' strategy. So too did organizational developments. The years since the onset of the economic crisis had witnessed a growing tendency toward fragmentation within the union movement. Some federations had been under increasing pressure from the base to abandon any commitment to the policy of reforms and to pursue entirely particularistic policies, beneficial only to the workers within their sectors.[249] There had also been a growth of 'autonomous' unions, unaffiliated with the confederations.[250] These were also extremely particularistic in their demands and often used the strike weapon in ways which were highly disruptive for the general public.[251] There were, of course, a number of explanations of these developments, but the unions tended to concentrate on those for which it deemed itself most responsible: the inability to develop an effective strategy to achieve structural reform. This failure fostered frustration on the shop floor and undercut the legitimacy of the ideals which were to hold the movement together. Through its effects on the economy, it fueled particularistic drives; and through its effects on the political attitudes of masses of the population, it fed the base of political groups which were fundamentally opposed to reform of the political economy. Thus, as with the other factors we have indicated, organizational pressures, perceived through the lens of the union movements' longstanding strategic principles, seemed to push in the direction of strategic change.

Identification of the pressures for change, however, does not entirely explain the policy adopted. We cannot offer a complete explanation. The EUR line was necessarily the product of an extremely complex process of internal negotiation within the union leadership about which we may never have the full story. Nonetheless, we would argue that much of the EUR line can be understood as an expression of continuities in union strategy since the hot autumn and of the ongoing effort—fundamental to the maintenance of union unity—to balance and find a synthesis among the traditions of the currents of the movement. To the extent that this is correct, it underlines once again the fact that the major shift of EUR was one of means—what was the appropriate relationship between shopfloor demands and reform objectives, and between action and pressure in the market arena and in the political one—rather than ends. It also would mean that the EUR line was not a radical change in union policies, breaking out of the parameters immanent in the strategies of the past, but rather a new attempt to pursue constant objectives more effectively while remaining as much as possible within those parameters. If this is correct, we would also not be surprised to see the reappearance of many of the tensions which characterized the years before 1978. This is a point which will be taken up in the Conclusion.

Several continuities with past strategy are worthy of note. The first is the attempt to come to terms with the dynamics of capitalist accumulation—thereby implicitly accepting the basic capitalist framework—while at the same time seeking to find ways to alter the outcomes of the capitalist process to make them more consistent with the objectives of societal transformation of the union movement. The EUR line, like the strategies preceding it after the hot autumn (and for the CGIL earlier as well), represents the unions' effort to transform through reform.

The second continuity is the determination to find a means to use the power of the organized working class to pursue objectives which would benefit not only the unions' immediate constituencies but the entire working class and other working strata. The EUR line, like its pre-decessors, is a class strategy premised on the need for class alliances. The former is considered unachievable without the latter.

The third continuity, clearly related to the preceding ones, is the effort to combine work place and political action to pursue union objectives. EUR, as we have stressed, did not abandon the idea that only through pressure in the market arena could the indispensable political change be advanced. Nor did it renounce the necessity for change achieved through the actions of government and the state. Rather—consistent with the unions' critical stance toward the past actions of both capital and the state—the unions sought to promote their own indispensable role in assuring that both the market behavior of entrepreneurs and the actions of the state be constantly conditioned by the participation—autonomous and with the constant threat of conflictuality—of the unions.

Fourth, EUR is expressive of two post-1968 organizational continuities in union strategy. On the one hand, it is a strategy premised on the fundamental conviction that union unity must be preserved. This, in turn, also means that union autonomy from partisan political purposes is to be maintained.[252] The continuity of union objectives, the detailed character of the entire spectrum of union reform proposals and the unions' unwilling-ness to be drawn into institutionalized relations with government are all expressive of this orientation. The unions can only act (or appear to act) autonomously in the political arena to the extent that their program is their own, and it is only thereby that union unity might be preserved. On the other hand, the EUR strategy also takes account of the continuing need to assign an important role in the overall pursuit of the strategy to the different levels of union organization. EUR, like its precedents, attempts to define the strategic functions of the shopfloor structures, the federations, and the confederations, while at the same time seeking, through general strategic objectives, to make action at these levels coherent and re-inforcing.

Finally, underlying all of the preceding points is a more general continuity with past union strategy: the determination to exercise a general societal leadership role while continuing to represent the core interests of the working class. Lama expressed this point in its most ideological form when he spoke of the Gramscian roots of the unions' strategic perspective, arguing that in accepting sacrifices and assuming a political function in the making of decisions which are to be measured in terms of the benefits which accrue to the society as a whole, the class becomes 'the state' and 'hegemonic.'[253] It is certain that the other confederations' leaders, and probably even some within the CGIL, did not adhere to this rather exalted notion of the origins of the EUR line. Nonetheless, this formulation underlines the extent to which EUR was intended to continue the unions' commitment to strategic ends which would encompass a broad range of interests, enable the union movement effectively to promote these, and thereby enable the working class to become the critical agent of societal transformation.

Part 6

Conclusion

The strategy of the Italian trade union movement in the 1970s with respect to objectives, arenas, and division of internal roles and responsibilities has made the movement singular in Europe. The combination of societal policy objectives in the name of transformative class unionism and of aggressive shopfloor union objectives; the expressed desire both to participate in general political-economic management and to retain an autonomous posture of conflictuality; the effort to pursue strategic objectives through autonomous action both in the political and the market arenas, using resources in the latter to promote the former; and, the attempt to assign roles to all levels of the union structure in the advancement of both prongs of the strategy are features which set the Italian movement apart from its European counterparts, especially those which have not had a close relationship with a steadily governing political party. Gino Giugni has spoken of a 'lacerating contradiction' in two models of Italian unionism of which these features would be the expression. He has also noted, however, that 'irremediable contrasts at the conceptual level . . . can become resolved at the level of concrete behavior.'[254] In concluding this essay, it is important to reiterate the sources of these distinctive features, to examine the extent to which the EUR line has represented an effective resolution of the tensions which they embody and create and thereby to suggest some of the possible paths which Italian unionism might take in the decade of the 1980s.

We have argued throughout these pages that the particular characteristics of the Italian movement and its strategy in the 1970s in the face of economic crisis are the product of the dynamic interaction of two sets of factors. On the one hand, they express the dialectic among the diverse and often historically antagonistic ideological, political, and organizational currents of Italian unionism as they have sought to build a unified movement while also seeking to insert their particular outlooks and values into that movement. On the other hand, these characteristics represent the response of the individual currents and of the unified movement to the external changes (and/or lack thereof) which the unions have confronted and partially been responsible for. These changes, in turn, have assumed importance not only because the Italian unions are responsive to environmental influences to which all unions must react out of institutional necessity, but also because some of these influences take on particular importance in light of the movement's own strategy.

The EUR strategy has been the most recent step in the process of strategic development. Many of its general characteristics were drawn from previous union strategy. It was, also, however, an effort to break out of the strategic impasse which became increasingly apparent to the unions by

1977: their continued strength, as measured by their ability to defend their gains on the shop floor and to disrupt the political economy, but their ineffectiveness in translating their market and political strength into the structural political-economic change which they deemed essential to their long-range interests, especially in a situation of growing internal tension and deepening societal crisis.[255]

At the time of this writing—two years after the announcement of the EUR strategy—it is still too early to judge with any certainty the success or failure of that strategy, either in terms of its resolution of tensions within the movement or in terms of its external objectives. Nonetheless, an initial evaluation would necessarily be negative. Few, if any, of the structural reforms sought by the unions have been accomplished or even undertaken. The instruments through which the unions have sought to promote these objectives—at the firm and political levels—have been found wanting. Internal tensions have increased and become more manifest. The general political climate has shifted in a direction less favorable to the unions' policies. The economic situation appears once again to be in a phase of more rapid deterioration. The unions have retained their ability to defend their core constituencies but seem to find themselves ever less able to positively influence the evolution of the political economy.

Rather than illustrating these points through a number of examples, we want in these closing pages to examine a critical policy event which took place in the summer of 1980, the proposal to develop a 'fund of solidarity.'[256] A brief discussion of the proposal, how it emerged and why it failed will enable us to indicate the current situation of the unions as well as to reflect on the ongoing tensions which the kind of strategic development which we have described has bequeathed to the union movement, and on the critical factors in the unions' environment which seem most to condition their behavior.

A repeated theme of the Italian government since the mid-1970s has been the reduction of factors which, it maintained, contributed to cost–push inflation in the Italian economy. One of the major targets of this policy was the agreement on the *scala mobile* which the unions won in their 1975 contracts. During 1977–9, however, the attempt to get the unions to agree to changes in the escalator had subsided. Improved economic performance, the presence of the Communist Party in the governmental majority, and the general effort, following EUR, to develop a more general program—which would engage the commitment of the unions and which would modify the escalator only in the context of a general set of political-economic reforms—all led to a less antagonistic relationship between the unions and the government.

By the spring of 1980, however, conditions had changed. There were renewed signs of impending severe economic difficulties, e.g., high inflation rates, proposals for mass firings at Fiat, major problems in large public sector firms. Politically, there had been a significant turn to the right. The PCI had withdrawn from the government majority in early 1979 saying it wanted cabinet seats or would return to the opposition. In both the 1979 Parliamentary and the 1980 administrative elections the Communists had suffered sharp setbacks with respect to their gains of 1975–6. They had then returned to a posture of full opposition. At the same time, the Socialist

Party had entered a coalition with the Christian Democrats (and small Republican Party) and seemed to be oriented, as was the internal majority in the DC, to building a successful government without Communist cooperation. Thus, as the economic situation gave new signs of deterioration, the government had strong reasons to try to show that it could govern the political economy without the help of the PCI.

It was in this climate that the government proposed a series of measures intended to increase government revenues, mildly dampen demand, and bring inflation under control. Included among these measures was a proposal to alter the *scala mobile*. Three things about these proposals need to be noted. First, they were to be implemented by decree rather than being put into law by Parliamentary procedure. Second, there was no prior consultation with the Communist Party about the content of the measures. Third, the government sought union agreement to the package, entering into direct negotiations with the Federation CGIL–CISL–UIL about them. Thus, the government was seeking at one and the same time to bypass the mediation of the PCI with the union movement and to get the unions to agree to a measure—the reform of the escalator—which had been a symbol of the unions' ability to defend their past gains.

The unions did not, however, agree. Instead, a protracted negotiation ensued, ending in the wee hours (as per Italian practice) of the morning before a final policy announcement was due. The outcome of the negotiation was that once again the *scala mobile* would not be touched; the government withdrew its proposal of modifications. In exchange, the unions agreed to a 0.5 percent withdrawal from the paychecks of industrial workers which would go into an investment fund which would be used to promote industrial investment according to criteria established by a board on which the unions would have significant participation. This so-called 'solidarity fund' was also to be instituted by decree. The provisions for the securing of the monies were clear; those about how it was to be distributed, less so. Aside from these details—which were to take on great importance in subsequent weeks—the other noteworthy feature of the fund proposal was that its origins were unclear. Neither the government nor the unions had discussed it publicly prior to the negotiations. It appears, in fact, that it was a rather extemporized idea developed once it was clear that no agreement could be reached on the *scala mobile*. This, of course, meant that there had been no debate within the unions about the merits of the proposal, nor had there been any discussions between the unions and the political parties, including the PCI.

The initial reaction to the solidarity fund proposal was cautiously positive. The unions defended the idea as an expression of the principles of the EUR line because it embodied the idea of sacrifices by industrial workers of the North for investments which would aid other strata of the working population, and because it offered the unions the opportunity to participate directly in the administration of the investment process. The government and, to a lesser extent, the employers also appeared pleased, although the conservative wing of the Christian Democratic Party indicated its continued preference for modifications of the escalator, a preference which was treated as undermining the accord reached. The Communist Party, however, after two or three days of deliberation, came out vehemently against the 'solidarity fund' both on substantive grounds—that it was vague and possibly unconstitutional—and procedural ones—that the decree process was not the appropriate way to introduce so important a shift in investment policy and procedures. More ominous than the Communist opposition in principle was the fact that the PCI also declared its intention to 'go to the workers' to gain their support for opposition to the fund.

It is unnecessary here to detail the *iter* of the fund proposal. After a few weeks of intensive political infighting, the government withdrew the decree, promising to reintroduce the idea of a fund as a legislative proposal in the late fall of 1980. Several aspects of the process leading to the collapse of the fund proposal, however, need to be noted. First, Communist opposition to the fund resonated with a significant portion of the working class in the factories.[257] It is impossible to say in what percentage workers were opposed, but it rapidly became clear that there was significant opposition in major northern factories. Whether this opposition was based on the PCI's objections or instead on narrower economic considerations is not of great consequence for us and is, in any case, unascertainable. What is important is that the opposition of the PCI created 'space' for opposition at the union grass roots sufficient to make the confederations rethink their support. Second, the PCI's position on the fund led to a major split with the union movement and to some bitter words between Lama, who defended the fund, and the party's economic spokespersons.[258] This was the most dramatic divergence since the hot autumn and perhaps in the entire postwar period. The union argued that the fund was coherent with the EUR strategy, a strategy which the PCI had enthusiastically supported. The party questioned the procedural features of the fund and its vagueness with respect to the disposition of the monies collected. It also argued that pressing for the proposal would lead to an erosion of the ties between the union leadership and union supporters.

Third, the government majority, which initially took responsibility for gaining passage of the fund proposal during the sixty days allowed for by the decree process, collapsed. This involved an intricate set of maneuvers, both among the parties and in Parliament, but its basic thrust was that the conservative wing of the Christian Democrats as well as other groups within the majority abandoned the proposal, reaching the judgment, not dissimilar from some of the claims of the PCI, that features of the fund proposal might well be unconstitutional. Finally, as the government was about to decide whether to proceed with the fund decree or to withdraw it, the confederations announced that they too wanted more time than the decree process would allow to evaluate the fund proposal and to discuss it with their base. The initiative for this decision was taken by the UIL which sent a letter to the other two confederations asking for a change in position. The CGIL agreed with alacrity, leaving little possibility, if union unity was to be preserved, for the CISL to take a different position. Thus, a little more than a month after the solidarity fund had been proposed as an alternative to reform of the *scala mobile*, almost all of the support for the fund had disappeared, and the escalator remained intact. The losers in the fight were many; the big winner, at least in the short run, was the Communist Party.

The brief but dramatic history of the fund proposal (at least to date) is of great interest for any student of Italian political affairs and, more generally, for anyone interested in the spreading attempts in the European political economies to find mechanisms to draw the union movement into the process of investment and more general political-economic decision-making. Whether or not these attempts are interpreted as efforts to install forms of neo- or liberal corporatism, there is little question that the Italian solidarity fund can be linked with proposals in other countries by which the unions are drawn—and willingly enter—into processes in which they are to participate with employers and/or government in the making of crucial political-economic decisions in exchange for an easing of wage and other shopfloor pressures. That tendencies in this direction were present in Italy in the mid-1960s and throughout the 1970s should be evident from this essay and has also been noted by a number of scholars; so too have many of the obstacles to a successful achievement of a stable neocorporatist arrangement in the Italian setting. Again, many of these obstacles are evident in the brief history of the solidarity fund.

In the present context, however, we do not intend to discuss these general issues. Rather, we want to indicate how the unions' agreement to the proposal of a fund, and the ultimate failure of the proposal to be enacted, fit with the general picture of strategic development, tensions, and constraints presented in the preceding pages. We will do so by discussing a series of dualities which have characterized union strategy and activity. Most of these dualities have been present throughout the postwar history of the union movement, first with elements embodied in the strategies of the different confederations and then incorporated into the united movement, although with important innovations reflecting the unification process itself and the changed and changing environment in which the unions operate.

Coherence of Principle/Pragmatism. In principle, the proposal of the solidarity fund was, as the union argued, a logical and coherent, if not inevitable, step in the effort to find mechanisms to implement the EUR strategy. The fund embodied the notions of sacrifice and austerity for those workers relatively better off and with greater job security and of participation by the unions in the direction of investment funds to objectives intended to benefit the South and expand employment. At the same time, however, the proposal was vague in regard to how the latter would be undertaken, and the way it came into being raised serious questions about the commitment of the government (and the employers) to full implementation of the agreement. Nonetheless, the unions accepted the proposal and then defended it in terms of its consistency with past strategic pronouncements and principles. The historically rooted ideological orientation of the Italian movement and its concern to maintain and raise the class consciousness of its supporters seem here to have acted as constraints on its ability to maneuver with agility in a highly fluid and politically charged situation. This is particularly noteworthy, and of potential significance for future developments, because of the fact that, in the hot autumn, these same characteristics of the movement had helped it to innovate and to capture and direct the mobilization of the workers. The contrast suggests the extent to which the gains of the hot autumn, and the principles on which they were based, have become institutionalized and a potential constraint on the unions' ability to adjust to the changing political-economic circumstances in which it is operating.

Institutional Autonomy/Participation. We have seen that throughout the history of the Italian unions in the postwar period there have been differences of view about the degree to which the unions should become participants in the making of political-economic decisions.[259] The unions have wished in recent years to fill such a role while also maintaining their institutional autonomy and thus their ability to act with independence with regard both to employers and the state. The proposal of the fund high-lighted the inherent difficulties in this posture. The fund would have represented an institutionalized presence of the movement in tripartite structures, albeit structures intended to manage only a restricted and clearly defined set of monies. The unions could not avoid accepting such an institutionalized role if they wished to exercise control of the 'surplus' created by austerity. Yet to commit themselves to austerity without such control would leave the disposition of the fund to others, those whom the unions had repeatedly denounced as incapable of undertaking effective structural reform. Thus, in the concrete proposal of the fund, the unions for the first time had to come to terms with the practical implications of the heart of the principles of EUR. If the story of the fund is taken as exemplary, it would suggest that the unions have little choice but to enter increasingly into arrangements which will have a constraining effect on their autonomy.

State/Firm as Site of Reform Initiatives. Throughout the postwar history of the union movement there had been internal differences about the extent to which the state, rather than the firm, should be the site of political-economic initiatives for change and reform. These differences had been incorporated into the union strategy in the 1970s by arguing that both sites must be utilized. The EUR line had continued this principle. At the same time, however, EUR had also expressed the unions' growing understanding that without reform at the state level, firm initiatives could not be effective, even if they could be assured (which was also unclear). The proposal of the fund was a further expression of the tendency to focus increasing attention on the state as the priority site of reform initiatives.

State/Market Arenas as Sites of Union Action. Again, the union move-ment's postwar history had expressed a constant attempt to utilize and combine action in the political arena and in the market to promote the objectives of union strategy. We have already noted that under the impact of the crisis this had become more difficult. The fund proposal and the manner in which it was arrived at underlined the extent to which the political arena—in particular, direct bargaining with the government—was assuming priority. Yet, the resistance to the fund at both the union base and in some of the federations (the metalworkers primary among them) and the eventual impact of that resistance on the confederal leaderships indicate the degree to which a focus on political bargaining among top élites remains constrained by traditions of market action with deep roots in the movement and with strong organizational roots in the federal and shopfloor strutures of the unions developed in the 1970s.

Centralization/decentralization. The preceding two points simply express a more general tension which has existed within the union movement since at least the mid-1950s and which was accentuated by the hot autumn and its effects: the attempt to operate as a centralized and decentralized move-ment at the same time. We have seen that union strategy has continually sought to assure a strategic role both to decentralized and centralized structures and that both have been assigned responsibilities in the pursuit of most of the objectives of the movement. The EUR strategy, however, was a clear expression of the fact that under the impact of the economic and political crisis, greater centralized control over the process of the form-ulation and implementation of union objectives was necessary. The fund proposal expressed this logic. Its failure indicated, in part, the difficulties encountered by the union movement in following this logic.

Political Autonomy/Partisanship. Union autonomy in the formulation and implementation of strategy was the hallmark of the process of union unification and the indispensable condition for the effective pursuit of unified union policy in the 1970s. Political autonomy meant not only the formal distancing of the unions from their prior political affiliations but also the attempt to keep the unions and their actions out of the partisan struggles among the political parties. As the unions' strategy became increasingly dependent on governmental policy, however, the latter became more difficult: the composition of government, and therefore its likely contribution to a policy of structural reform, became increasingly central to the overall success of union strategy. The problem was only complicated by the PCI's entrance into the governmental area, and its exit therefrom did not really facilitate matters. The incident of the fund enables one better to understand a number of the complexities of the relationship of the union movement and its strategy to the government and party system.

First, the initial attempt to get the unions to agree to changes in the escalator was itself an expression of the changed political composition of the government; and the proposal of the solidarity fund was clearly a defensive or fallback position for both the unions (which probably would have preferred simply to see the government abandon the escalator changes) and for the government in a situation in which both felt a full rupture would be damaging to their interests. Second, the effort to deal with the unions directly was a partisan maneuver on the part of the government, and party factions within the majority, to try to reach agree-ments which would entirely bypass the unions and thereby show that the PCI was no longer an important actor in political-economic decision-making. Thus, the unions were immediately drawn into direct partisan maneuvers but over questions important to the unions and impossible to ignore. Third, the reaction of the PCI, with its consequences for the unions, cannot be understood except in light of the attempts to exclude it. Again, however, this was of enormous and unavoidable direct consequence for the unions and their ability to pursue an effective and autonomous policy. Fourth, the intra-union maneuvers which developed as the fund en-countered resistance at the base and from the PCI and, as factions of the majority also indicated their hesitancies, showed the extent to which union unity remains conditioned by longstanding partisan (as well as ideological) preferences within the movement. Finally, the collapse of the proposal due to these various pressures and disagreements highlighted the extent to which the unions' ability to pursue their strategy was critically related to partisan relationships among the parties and within them. In sum, the history of the solidarity fund brought once more into sharp relief the degree to which the unions' political autonomy remains indispensable to union unity but continues to be conditioned by longstanding partisan linkages and traditions and, more importantly, by contemporary party conflict in which the union movement and its policies are critical resources.

The preceding discussion has outlined the ways in which the debate over the solidarity fund can be taken as indicative of the continuing tensions which remain within the union movement. These tensions have deep origins—their roots in large part lie in the period prior to the hot autumn.[260] It is the hot autumn, the unification of the movement and the resultant attempt to create a synthesis among the various union traditions and experiences which led to the incorporation of these tensions—or dialectic, if one prefers—into a single strategy with two prongs: conflictual and participatory, macro and micro, shopfloor and societal, decentralized and centralized, autonomous and political, associational and class, unionist and alliance oriented. In the 1970s the union movement had sought to maintain both prongs of the strategy while adjusting it to changing environmental conditions, most critically political realignments and economic crisis.

In attempting to adjust to these changes, however, the fundamental constraints on the unions' ability to implement their strategy have become increasingly apparent, contributing to the emergence of the tensions we have discussed. On the one hand, the economic crisis has made the unions' attempt to combine aggressive shopfloor demands and market arena action with structural reform demands and political arena action ever more contradictory. The EUR strategy accepted this to be the case and has sought to establish a new relationship between the strategic prongs. Nonetheless, the continuing economic crisis, and its social and political effects, represent an ongoing threat to the unions' overall strategic posture and the internal compromises and agreements on which it is built. On the other hand, the unions have also had little success in attaining the political-economic reforms which they have sought. Instead, they have found that government action (and/or the absence thereof) and partisan conflict among the parties have become increasingly costly for the union movement, for they have meant that the unions could expect no effective compensation, either in terms of control or reform, for greater moderation. Thus, the Italian union movement finds itself increasingly squeezed between a rock and a hard place.[261] It is evident that it could escape this uncomfortable position by abandoning the strategic principles which have guided its actions throughout the last decade, but this would require the abandonment of long and deeply rooted union traditions and might possibly destroy union unity. Or the union movement could attempt, as it has for a number of years, to experiment with new positions within existing frameworks, hoping in the meantime that political change will allow for the undertaking of the kinds of structural reforms which might relieve the pressure on the economy.[262] To date, the unions have been able successfully to defend themselves through such a process. Whether they will be able to continue doing so in the 1980s, however, seems increasingly problematic.

Appendix: Italy

	1969	1970	1971	1972	1973	1974	1975	1976	1977	1978
Growth of Real Gross Domestic Product at Market Prices (Percentage Change from Previous Year)	5.7	5.0	1.6	3.1	6.9	4.2	–3.5	5.7	1.7	
Consumer Prices (Percentage Change from Previous Year)	2.6	5.0	4.8	5.7	10.8	19.1	17.0	16.8	17.0	
Current Balances (Millions of Dollars)	2,340	1,133	1,902	2,043	–2,662	–8,017	–751	–2,816	2,465	

Source: *OECD Economic Outlook* (December 1979)

	1969	1970	1971	1972	1973	1974	1975	1976	1977	1978
Unemployment (as Percentage of Total Labor Force)	3.4	3.1	3.1	3.6	3.4	2.9	3.3	6.6	7.1	7.2

Source: *Labor Force Statistics* 1969–72 (May 1975), 1973–5, (May 1976), 1976–8, (November 1979)

Notes and References

1 Gino Giugni, 'Il rebus dei due sindacati,' *La repubblica*, 28 July 1980. p. 8.
2 General literature on Italian unions available in English is surprisingly limited and often outdated. For some major works, see Daniel L. Horowitz, *The Italian Labor Movement* (Cambridge, Mass.: Harvard University Press, 1963); Joseph LaPalombara, *The Italian Labor Movement: Problems and Prospects* (Ithaca, NY: Cornell University Press, 1957); John Clark Adams, 'Italy,' in Walter Galenson, ed., *Comparative Labor Movements* (New York: Prentice-Hall, 1952); Peter R. Weitz, 'Labor and politics in a divided movement, the Italian case,' *Industrial and Labor Relations Review*, no. 2, 1975; Pietro Merli Brandini, 'Italy: creating a new industrial relations system from the bottom,' in Solomon Barkin, ed., *Worker Militancy and Its Consequences, 1965–1975*, (New York: Praeger, 1975), pp. 82–117.
3 For a discussion of the characteristics of the Pact of Rome, see Georges Couffignal, *I sindacati in Italia* (Rome: Editori Riuniti, 1979), pp. 48–54. An excellent analysis of the strategies and thinking of the 'unified' CGIL in the 1944–8 period can be found in Adolfo Pepe, 'La CGIL dalla ricostruzione alla scissione,' *Storia contemporanea*, no. 4, December 1974, pp. 591–635.
4 The *Consigli di gestione* were the most important of the workplace control institutions which emerged during the Resistance and in the immediate postwar period. Their functions and powers were never clearly defined, and they became a major source of controversy among the parties of the coalition government and among the various union currents. For an overall, detailed assessment of the *Consigli di gestione*, see Liliana Lanzardo, 'I consigli di gestione nella strategia della collaborazione,' in *Problemi del movimento sindacale in Italia, 1943–1974*, Annali Feltrinelli, XVI (Milan: Feltrinelli editore, 1976), pp. 325–366. For works on the institutional aspects of post-World War II Italian unionism, see Aldo Forbice and Riccardo Chiaberge, *Il sindacato dei consigli* (Verona: Bertani, 1974) and Piero Craveri, *Sindacato e istituzioni nel dopoguerra* (Bologna: Il Mulino, 1977).
5 The historical and political traditions of Italian trade unionism are discussed by Daniel L. Horowitz, *The Italian Labor Movement*, op. cit., esp. pp. 10–127.
6 For a retrospective analysis of the features and premises of the economic model which developed in Italy in the late 1940s, see Laura Pennacchi, 'Economia, politica, e sindacato, (1947–1955),' *Quaderni di rassegna sindacale*, no. 70, January–February 1978, pp. 5–37. Ricciotti Antinolfi, *La crisi economica italiana* (Bari: De Donato, 1974), esp. pp. 11–77, offers an interesting interpretation of the ways in which the process of economic reconstruction set the stage both for the economic 'miracle' of the early 1960s and for the severe economic crisis of the 1970s.
7 This second aspect of the unions' politicization had also the effect of reinforcing their dependence on the political parties. As convincingly argued by Alleo Riosa, in the immediate postwar period, 'the distinction between parties and unions tended to become blurred because of the presence in the unions' sphere of action of a political dimension which was only indirectly linked to traditional unions' actions.' See 'Le concezioni sociali e politiche della CGIL,' in *I 30 anni della CGIL, 1944–1974* (Roma: ESI, 1975), pp. 89–157, here p. 129.
8 Massimo Legnani, 'Il dibattito sulla ricostruzione e le scelte economiche,' in *Problemi del movimento sindacale in Italia*, op. cit., pp. 292–3.
9 Virtually all analyses of post-World War II Italian trade-unionism stress the correlation between the breakup of the Resistance-caused coalition among the antifascist parties and the splits in the unified CGIL. There are, however, differences in emphasis. For instance, Giorgio Amendola has argued that the fragmentation of the trade unions movement was due largely to the outbreak of the Cold War and to the divisions among the antifascist parties. 'Anche l'unità ha la sua storia,' *Rinascita*, 23 April 1971. Bruno

Trentin has, on the contrary, stressed the lack of close and 'democratic' links between the Confederation and the working class which made the former particularly 'receptive' to national and international events. 'Dal Patto di roma all'autonomia sindacale,' *Rinascita*, 14 May 1971.

10 Bianca Salvati (Beccalli), 'The rebirth of Italian trade unionism,' in S. J. Woolf, ed., *The Rebirth of Italy, 1943–50* (London: Longman, 1972), pp. 181–211, here p. 195.

11 Started with the famous 'svolta di Salerno,' which set the stage for the transformation of the PCI from a party of opposition to the system into a party of opposition within the system, the strategy of 'progressive democracy' was officially enunciated at the V Congress of the PCI (29 December 1945 to 6 January 1946). See Palmiro Togliatti, 'Rinnovare l'Italia,' *Report to the V Congress of the PCI*, (Roma: Soc. Ed. 'L'Unità,' 1946), *passim*.

12 Massimo Legnani, op. cit., p. 304.

13 Giuseppe Rapelli, who played a major role in the Catholic current's secession from the CGIL, has admitted that the ACLI played a decisive role in bringing about the splits within the CGIL. As he argued in 1955, the ACLI gave the CISL 'the power necessary to assume a position which was increasingly autonomous and self-sufficient.' *I sindacati in Italia* (Bari: Laterza, 1955), pp. 229–275. Or, as argued by Giancarlo Galli, with the foundation of the ACLI Catholic unionists 'were able to rely on an organizational and ideological hinterland (to use as a base) for building a new union.' 'I cattolici e il sindacato,' *Quaderni di rassegna sindacale*, No. 33–34, pp. 47–57. For a general analysis of the behavior and attitudes of Catholic unionists and of the DC with regard to the issue of union unity, see Sandro Fontana, *I cattolici e l'unita sindacale 1943–1945* (Bologna: Il Mulino, 1978), esp. pp. 9–35. For an overall assessment of the ACLI's role and evolution in the panorama of the Italian labor movement, see 'Le ACLI tra inter-classismo e scelta di classe,' special issue of *Relazioni sociali*, no. 5–6, September–December 1973, esp. the essay by M. Giacomantonio, 'Dalle origini confessionali alla critica dell'interclassismo,' pp. 10–33. The evolution of the relationship between ACLI and CISL is effectively analyzed by Ruggero Orfei, 'ACLI and CISL,' in Guido Baglioni, ed., *Analisi della CISL* (Rome: Edizioni Lavoro, Vol. 1, pp. 77–95.

14 In its implementation, the formation of the category unions lagged behind the develop-ment of the Confederation and the Chambers. The Confederation had been re-constituted by the parties. The Chambers had emerged at the end of the Resistance as mechanisms to coordinate political activities. The category unions, in contrast, required the initiative of the Confederation once the war had concluded. That this lagged behind should not be surprising, given the enormous problems faced by the union movement at the war's end. It is also to be noted that the horizontal structures corresponded closely to the political role which the union was taking on.

15 Bianca Salvati (Beccalli), op. cit., p. 199.

16 For an appraisal of the structure and evolution of the *scala mobile* system, see 'La scala mobile da dopo guerra ad oggi,' *I consigli*, no. 6, August 1974, p. 19.

17 Giuseppe Di Vittorio to the Directing Council of the CGIL, 15 July 1946, quoted in Walter Tobagi, 'La fondzione della politica salariale della CGIL,' in *Problemi del movimento sindacale in Italia*, op. cit., p. 424.

18 Sergio Turone, *Il paradosso sindacale* (Bari: Laterza, 1979), pp. 142 ff.

19 As convincingly argued by Gino Giugni, the *Piano* was *not* a new model of economic development, and it was intended to serve short-term strategic and tactical needs. See Atti del Convegno di studio, Ariccia, 3–5 March 1975, published as *I 30 anni della CGIL*, op. cit., p. 326. The short-term and emergency character of the *Piano* was stressed already in 1949 by Vittorio Foa at the II Congress of the CGIL. *I congressi della CGIL*, vol. 3 (Rome: ESI, 1970), pp. 128–30.

20 Giuseppe Di Vittorio, op. cit., p. 96. For a general discussion of the problem of unemployment in the immediate postwar period, see Giuseppe Regis, 'Considerazioni sulla disoccupazione in Italia nel biennio 1946–47,' *Critica economica*, May–June 1948, no. 3.

21 Palmiro Togliatti, *Ricostruire. Resoconto del convegno economico del PCI* (Roma 21–23 August 1945), (Rome: Edizioni dell'Unità, 1945), pp. 269–283.

22 Giorgio Amendola has argued that at the heart of the *Piano del lavoro* 'there was a Keynesian inspiration and the idea, typical of the Labour Party, of a policy of austerity as a means of promoting full employment,' 'Lotta di clase e sviluppo economico dopo la Liberazione,' in *Tendenze del capitalismo italiano*, Vol. 1 (Roma: Editori Riuniti,

1962), p. 181. The 'Keynesian flavor' of the *Piano* is also stressed by Vittorio Foa, 'La ricostruzione capitalistica nel secondo dopoguerra,' *Rivista Italiana di storia contemporanea*, 1973, pp. 453 ff.

23 See Giuseppe Di Vittorio's report to the II Congress of the CGIL (Genoa, 4–9 October 1949) in *I congressi della CGIL*, vol. 3, (Rome: ESI, 1970), pp. 54–60 and pp. 375–6. The proposal underwent modifications in subsequent years, with growing emphasis on the issue of monopoly capitalism and on the political implications of the Plan. See, for instance, Conferenza economica nazionale, Roma, 18–20 February 1950, *Notiziario CGIL*, no. 5–6, February 1950, and Convegno sindacale nazionale per l'industria e il Piano del lavoro, Milan, 2–4 June 1950, *Notiziario CGIL*, no. 16, 10 June 1950.

24 Renzo Razzano, 'I modelli di sviluppo della CGIL e della CISL,' in *Problemi del movimento sindacale in Italia*, op. cit., p. 536.

25 Renzo Razzano, ibid., p. 532.

26 For an excellent, general overview of the evolution of the CGIL's economic thinking throughout the post-World War II period, see Gian Primo Cella, Bruno Manghi, Roberto Pasini, *La concezione sindacale della CGIL: Un sindacato per la classe* (Milan: ACLI, Collana Ricerche No. 9, 1969). The authors' conclusion is that, more than its specifically Marxist heritage, what has decisively and consistently influenced the ideological stance of the CGIL has been its 'classist orientation.'

27 Renzo Razzano, op. cit., p. 536.

28 Renzo Razzano, ibid., p. 537.

29 In presenting the *Piano del lavoro*, Giuseppe di Vittorio emphasized that by adopting the *Piano* the 'CGIL demonstrated once again to be concerned not only with the everyday, though fundamental problems of the workers, but also with the solution of the great national problems' and that 'the well-being of the entire Italian nation was dependent on the solution of the great national problems.' In *I congressi della CGIL*, vol. 3, op. cit., p. 60.

30 The immediate response of PCI leaders to the *Piano del lavoro* was not too enthusiastic. Togliatti, in particular, expressed perplexities about the overtly economic reasoning of the *Piano* and argued 'that in order to effectively plan the Italian economy it was necessary to replace the existing capitalistic government with a government representing the working class.' Palmiro Togliatti, 'Piano del lavoro,' *Rinascita*, no. 2, 1950, p. 57. Later elaborations of the *Piano* by CGIL leaders tended to stress the issue of its political implications too.

31 For an analysis of the evolution of the interaction between the DC and private capital, see Giancarlo Provasi, *Borghesia industriale e democrazia industriale* (Bari: De Donato, 1976), esp. chapters 2–3, pp. 91–174.

32 Marcello Di Cecco, 'Economic policy in the reconstruction period,' in S. J. Woolf, ed., *The Rebirth of Italy*, op. cit., pp. 156–180. Michele Salvati, 'Ricostruzione e disegno capitalistico,' *Italia contemporanea*, no. 3, 1974.

33 For an overview of the debate among political leaders and economists during the period of economic reconstruction, see the documents collected in Augusto Graziani, ed., *L'economia italiana 1945–1970* (Bologna: Il Mulino, 1972), part one, 'Il periodo della ricostruzione (1945–1950),' pp. 99–154. Also, Pasquale Saraceno, *Ricostruzione e pianificazione 1943–1948* (Bari: Laterza, 1969).

34 From 1948 to 1955, industrial production increased by 95 percent. There were still, however, about 2 million unemployed. The rate of productivity per worker increased by 89 percent. From 1950 to 1955, profits in the industrial sector increased by 86 percent, while real wages increased by only 6 percent. Acli, *Incontro*, 2 April 1957. Norman Kogan has noted that 'while (in the 1950s) there was some increase in nonagricultural employment, more of it probably went into the low-paid, small-scale artisan and distribution sectors than into industry . . . between 1950 and 1959, larger industry absorbed only about 120,000 workers, while construction and transportation accounted for 400,000 to 500,000 more.' *A Political History of Postwar Italy* (New York: Praeger, 1966), p. 67.

35 Renzo Razzano, op. cit., pp. 529–30.

36 Giuseppe Di Vittorio, Report to the III Congress of the CGIL (Naples, 26 November–3 December 1952), in *I Congressi della CGIL*, vol. IV–V, op. cit., pp. 11–12.

37 Bianca Salvati (Beccalli), 'The Rebirth of Italian Trade Unionism,' op. cit., p. 205.

38 A. Pepe, *Storia della CGIL* (Bari: Laterza, 1974), passim. A. Di Gioia, *La CGIL nei suoi congressi* (Rome: ESI, 1975), passim.

39 In Sergio Garavini's opinion, not only the *Piano del lavoro* but also the CGIL's politicization and organizational centralization played a positive role in the period of labor exclusion, since they provided 'ideological and political certainty' to the members of the CGIL. 'La centralizzazione contrattuale e las strategia del sindacato,' in *Problemi del movimento sindacale*, op. cit., pp. 673–684, here pp. 676–77.

40 As perceptively argued by Donald L. M. Blackmer, 'it seems less important, however, to evoke the well-remembered confrontation of the Cold War years than to recall that beneath this aggressive façade the PCI was in fact struggling to keep alive the essence of its earlier (alliance) strategy.' 'Continuity and Change in Postwar Italian Communism,' in D. L. M. Blackmer and S. Tarrow, eds., *Communism in Italy and France* (Princeton: Princeton University Press, 1975), p. 21–68, here p. 47.

41 Mario Ricciardi has argued that the CGIL's emphasis on international issues such as that of the 'defense of the peace' was not accompanied by an emphasis on the specific values of socialism. And this at the time when the CISL was presenting itself as the champion of democracy and freedom on the shop floor. 'Conflitto ideologico e pluralismo sindacale,' in *Problemi del movimento sindacale in Italia*, op. cit., pp. 589–608, here p. 598.

42 At the FIAT the position of the CGIL suffered a veritable collapse. In fact, while in 1952 the CGIL enjoyed 68.7 percent of the votes for the *Commissioni interne*, by 1957 its share of the vote had shrunk to 21.1 percent. See Angelo Di Gioia, *La CGIL nei suoi statuti* (Rome: ESI, 1975), p. 13. For analyses of the factors behind the mid-1950s defeats of the CGIL and for the impact that such defeats had on the strategy of the CGIL, see Aris Accornero, *Gli anni cinquanta in fabbrica* (Bari: De Donato, 1973) and Emilio Pugno and Sergio Garavini, *Gli anni duri alla Fiat* (Turin: Einaudi, 1974).

43 As reported by Daniel L. Horowitz, at its 1956 National Congress the CGIL claimed that 674 members of *Commissioni interne*, 1,128 activists and 'thousands of workers' had been discharged during 1955 alone because of their CGIL activity. *The Italian Labor Movement*, op. cit., p. 291.

44 For the support given by the United States to the antilabor repression carried out by some of Italy's major enterprises, see Gian Giacome Migone, 'Stati Uniti, FIAT, e repressione anti-operaia negli anni cinquanta,' *Rivista di storia contemporanea*, April 1974, no. 2.

45 Secondo Pessi's report to the IV Congress of the CGIL (Rome, 27 February–4 March 1956), in *I congressi della CGIL*, op. cit., vol. 4–5, pp. 53–4.

46 Franco Momigliano, *Sindacati, progresso tecnico, programmazione economica* (Turin: Einaudi, 1966), pp. 30–90. The PCI was even slower in understanding and adapting its strategy to the technological changes taking place in the factories. See, for instance, Sergio Leonardi, *Progresso tecnico e rapporti di lavoro* (Turin: Einaudi, 1957).

47 For detailed analyses of the nature and role of the CISL in the 1950s, see Guido Baglioni, 'La CISL e l'esperienza sindacale nella società italiana,' *Prospettiva sindacale*, no. 1, April 1973, pp. 79–94, and 'La CISL, il mondo politico, il mondo cattolico,' *Prospettiva sindacale*, no. 3, December 1974, pp. 9–32; Lucio De Carlini, 'Indirizzi, scelte e dibattiti contrattuali della CISL,' *Quaderni di rassegna sindacale*, no. 19, June 1968, pp. 52–65. A recently published collection of essays on the historical, strategic, ideological, and organizational evolution of the CISL since 1945 fills an important gap in the literature on this Confederation. See, *Analisi della crisi*, op. cit., two volumes.

48 Umberto Romagnoli and Tiziano Treu, *I sindacati in Italia. Storia di una strategia* (Bologna: Il Mulino, 1977), p. 154.

49 Renzo Razzano, op. cit., p. 547.

50 For the influence of Selig Perlman and of the Wisconsin School on the CISL, see Gian Primo Cella, Bruno Manghi e Paolo Piva, *Un sindacato italiano negli anni sessanta* (Bari De Donato, 1972), pp. 7–47. The present leadership of the CISL has been, in one way or or another, influenced by the Florentine trade union school of the Confederation. See Claudio Torneo, *Il sindacalista d'assalto* (Milano: Sugarco, 1976), esp. pp. 32 ff. For a general assessment of the importance of the Florentine trade union school in the ideological and strategic evolution of the CISL, see Benedetto DeCesaris, 'La scuola CISL di Firenze negli anni cinquanta,' *Quaderni di rassegna sindacale*, no. 37, July–August 1972, pp. 80–95.

51 Renzo Razzano, op. cit., p. 548.

52 Renzo Razzano, ibid., p. 548.

53 Pietro Merli-Brandini, 'Una riflessione sulla CISL,' in F. Archibugi et al., *La questione sindacale oggi* (Rome: Edizioni Lavoro, 1978), pp. 30–46.

54 Many of the positions taken up by the CGIL in the 1960s and 1970s can be fully understood only if viewed as a response to those assumed by the CISL in the same years. Aldo Agosti and Dora Marucco have aptly pointed out that a comprehensive image of the Italian union movement in the 1970s can be drawn only from an analysis of the extent to which the theoretical elaboration of the CGIL was influenced by the strategies formulated by the CISL in the 1950s. 'Gli ultimi anni,' in *Il movimento sindacale in Italia* (Turin: Fondazione Luigi Einaudi, 1970), pp. 83–140, here p. 139.

55 Aldo Bonavoglia, op. cit., pp. 247–8. For general discussions of the origins of the UIL, see Italo Viglianesi, op. cit., pp. 197–228, and Joseph LaPalombara, op. cit., pp. 99, 136–7, and *passim*.

56 Fernando Santi's report to the IV Congress of the CGIL (Rome, 27 February–4 March 1956), *I congressi della CGIL*, op. cit., vol. 4–5, p. 350.

57 See Donald L. M. Blackmer, *Unity in Diversity. Italian Communism and the Communist World* (Cambridge, Mass.: The MIT Press, 1968), pp. 319–329, 276–292, and *passim*.

58 For a collection of documents outlining the various stages of the unions' disentanglement from their partisan ties, see F. Liuzzi, L. Morosini, and A. Perrella, 'L'autonomia sindacale dal Patto di Roma agli anni '70,' *Proposte*, no. 40–41, November 1976.

59 The practice of 'separate agreements' continued well into the 1960s. According to Daniel Horowitz, between 1954 and 1957 only 41 percent of all shopfloor agreements were signed by the CGIL too. *Storia del movimento sindacale in Italia* (Bologna: Il Mulino, 1970), p. 109. Trentin and Foa have argued that, while 'separate agreements' demonstrated the weakness of the CGIL on the shop floor, they were not signs of 'an autonomous capacity for theoretical elaboration and for action on the part of the unions which signed those agreements and were the results, therefore, of the entrepreneurial paternalism.' 'Le politiche rivendicative della CGIL negli anni '60,' *Quaderni di rassegna sindacale*, no. 31–2, July–October 1971, pp. 6–17, here p. 9.

60 Giorgio Amendola, 'La classe operaia nel decennio 1961–1971,' *Critica Marxista*, November–December 1973, no. 6. For a chronology of the major struggles undertaken by the unions and the Italian working class in the 1960s, see Aris Accornero, 'Le lotte operaie negli anni '60,' *Quaderni di rassegna sindacale*, no. 31–2, July–October 1971, pp. 113–139.

61 Alessandro Pizzorno has pointed out the following major developments in the period prior to the 'hot autumn': (1) the labor market became more favorable to the workers; (2) ascendant working-class combativity; (3) growing prominence of shopfloor contracts; (4) progressive disentanglement of the unions from the political parties and rapprochement among the three confederations; (5) growing emphasis on demands concerning work conditions. (Of course, in the period of recession from 1964 to 1966, the labor market became less favorable, and there was a decline in working-class combativity.) 'I sindacati nel sistema politico italiano,' in Paolo Farneti, ed., *Il sistema politico italiano* (Bologna: Il Mulino, 1973), pp. 117–146, here p. 119.

62 There was, however, a sharp decline in the rate of unemployment. According to CGIL estimates, from 1959 to 1963 the number of unemployed fell from 1,117,000 to 504,000. In this way, there was a weakening of what had been the major concern of the CGIL in the previous years, and the one factor which had decisively influenced its strategy. Alleo Riosa, op. cit., p. 149.

63 Gino Giugni, *Il sindacato fra contratti e riforme* (Bari: De Donato, 1973), p. 144.

64 Giuseppe Tamburrano, *L'iceberg democristiano* (Milan: Sugarco, 1974), p. 33 ff.

65 Michele Salvati, *Alle origini dell'inflazione italiana* (Bologna: Il Mulino, 1979), pp. 37–43.

66 Although Agostino Novella recognized at the VI Congress of the CGIL that the government's proposals for planning contained the elements for channeling the process of economic development in directions more favorable to the working class, he rejected the constraints that the implementation of the plan would place on the unions. See Relation to the VI Congress of the CGIL (Bologna, 31 March–5 April 1965), in *I Congressi della CGIL*, vol. 7, op. cit., pp. 22–9. Also see Bruno Trentin, 'Politica dei redditi e programmazione,' *Critica Marxista*, January–February 1964, no. 1. For a general appraisal of the unions' position on the issue of planning, see Franco Momigliano, op. cit., pp. 141–250.

67 For a discussion of Italy's various attempts at planning, see Percy A. Allum, *Italy—*

Republic Without Government? (New York: Norton & Co., 1973), pp. 168 ff.

68   Giuseppe Di Palma, 'The available state: problems of reforms,' in S. Tarrow and P. Lange, eds., *Italy in Transition* (London: Frank Cass & Co., 1980), pp. 149–165.

69   Massimo Bordini, 'I sindacati e il dibattito sulla programmazione (1960–7),' *Quaderni di rassegna sindacale*, no. 77, March–April 1979, pp. 3–16.

70   Franco Momigliano, 'Sindacato e politica di programmazione,' *Quaderni di rassegna sindacale*, no. 31–2, July–October 1971, pp. 93–112, here p. 94.

71   CGIL, documento presentato alla CNP, in *Rassegna sindacale*, 23 March 1963.

72   The extent and the nature of the influence exerted by the socialist current on the CGIL's strategic and ideological orientation is an issue which has so far received little attention among analysts of Italian trade unions. That the socialist current has made an original contribution to the evolution of the CGIL, and that it is possible to detect a socialist 'trade union conception in the CGIL,' is a view put forward by Aldo Forbice and Paolo Favero in their book, *I socialisti e il sindacato* (Milano: Palazzi Editore, 1968). This view is rejected by Gian Primo Cella, Bruno Manghi and Roberto Pasini, who argue that differences between the socialist and the communist currents within the CGIL have never been on fundamental issues of strategy, with the exception of problems of international politics, but rather on tactical issues, op. cit., pp. 20 ff.

73   Silvano Levrero, 'Sindacati e programmazione: primo bilancio,' *Quaderni di rassegna sindacale*, no. 17, December 1967, pp. 14–38.

74   Alessandro Pizzorno, 'I sindacati nel sistema politico italiano: aspetti storici,' *Rivista trimestrale di diritto pubblico*, XXI, no. 4, 1971, pp. 1510–59, here p. 1546.

75   The literature on the 'hot autumn' is simply monumental. For a good summary of the background, forms of struggle, and nature of the demands of the 'hot autumn,' see Dominique Grisoni and Hugues Portelli, *Le lotte operaie in Italia dal 1960 al 1976* (Milan: Rizzoli, 1977), esp. pp. 45–160. Also see the special issue of *Proposte*, 'Il sindacato e il '68,' no. 54–6, ed. Aris Accornero.

76   An excellent review of union responses in this period can be found in Ida Regalia, Marino Regini, and Emilio Reyneri, 'Labour conflict and industrial relations in Italy,' in Colin Crouch and Alessandro Pizzorno, eds., *The Resurgence of Class Conflict in Western Europe Since 1968* (London: Macmillan, 1978), chapter 4.

77   See Aldo Forbice and Riccardo Chiaberge, op. cit., 84–156. A general discussion of the evolution of shopfloor organizations is contained in Filippo Peschiera, *Sindacato e rappresentanze operaie* (Rome: Coines, 1973), esp. pp. 61–160, and in Leonardo Altieri, *Sindacato e organizzazione di classe* (Milan: Sapere, 1973), pp. 78–151. For an analysis of the evolution of the unions' contractual strategy after the hot autumn, see Gino Giugni, 'Recent trends in collective bargaining in Italy,' *International Labour Review*, no. 4, October 1971, pp. 307–328, and Edoardo Ghera, 'Linee di tendenza della contrattazione aziendale, 1967–1971,' *Quaderni di rassegna sindacale*, no. 35, March–April 1971.

78   For a comprehensive appraisal of the *Statuto dei lavoratori* and of its impact on unions' strategy, see Giuseppe Federico Mancini, 'Lo statuto dei lavoratori dopo le lotte operaie del 1969,' in Enzo Bartocci, *Sindacato classe società* (Padova: Decam, 1975), pp. 303–341, and Tiziano Treu, 'Statuto dei lavoratori: primo bilancio e linee di politica sindacale,' *Prospettiva sindacale*, no. 1, March 1972, pp. 5–36; and Emanuele Stolfi, *Da una parte sola. Storia politica dello Statuto dei lavoratori*, (Milan: Longanesi, 1978).

79   Luciano Lama, Report to the General Council of the CGIL, *Rassegna sindacale*, no. 194, 27 September 1970.

80   Jeffrey Sachs, 'Wage, Profits, and Macroeconomic Adjustment in the 1970s,' unpublished manuscript (September 1979), p. 54 and *passim*.

81   Ricciotti Antinolfi, *La crisi economica italiana*, op. cit., pp. 105–133.

82   Michele Salvati, *Alle origini dell'inflazione italiana*, op. cit., p. 65.

83   Luciano Lama, *Il sindacato nella crisi italiana* (Rome: Editori Riuniti, 1977), p. 227.

84   Ida Regalia, Marino Regini and Emilio Reyneri, op. cit., p. 317.

85   Alessandro Pizzorno, 'Due logiche dell'azione di classe,' in A. Pizzorno et al., *Lotte operaie e sindacato: il ciclo 1968–1972 in Italia* (Bologna: Il Mulino, 1978), p. 37.

86   Luciano Lama, 'Il sindacato di classe ieri e oggi,' in *Quaderni di rassegna sindacale*, no. 41, March–April 1973, p. 215.

87   See the special issue of *Quaderni di rassegna sindacale*, 'Sindacati e riforme,' no. 36, May–June 1972, and the issue of *Dibattito sindacale*, 'Lotta per le riforme,' no. 5, September–October 1970. For a review of the issue of reforms in the historical evolution

of Italian trade unions, see Adolfo Pepe and Gino Guerra, 'Riformismo e riforme nell'esperienza sindacale italiana,' *Proposte*, no. 9.

88 Luciano Boggio and Gian Primo Cella, 'Il condizionamento economico e il futuro dell'azione sindacale,' *Prospettiva sindacale*, no. 4, December 1976, pp. 53–71. Carlo Donolo, 'Istituzioni, società e movimento sindacale dentro la crisi italiana,' *Quaderni di rassegna sindacale*, no. 58, January–February 1976, pp. 101–115.

89 Guido Baglioni, 'La'azione per le riforme e la logica dell'esperienza sindacale,' *Prospettiva sindacale*, no. 3, December 1970, pp. 3–53.

90 For an excellent analysis of the various stages of the unification process, see Georges Couffignal, op. cit., pp. 257–297. Also see the special issue of *Quaderni di rassegna sindacale*, 'L'unità sindacale,' no. 29, March–April 1971, and Giorgio Lauzi, *Per l'unità sindacale* (Rome: Coines, 1974).

91 Aris Accornero, ed., *Dalla rissa al dialogo* (Rome: ESI, 1967), esp. pp. 85–159.

92 'La democrazia nel sindacato,' round table organized by *Sindacato moderno*, no. 2, February 1969.

93 For the positions of the major union leaders, see the series of articles published in *Economia e lavoro* in 1968.

94 Pierre Carniti, 'Verso l'unità sindacale,' *Problemi del socialismo*, no. 43, November–December 1969.

95 'Unità sindacale: rispondono 100 dirigenti di base,' *Rassegna sindacale*, no. 190, 21 June 1970.

96 For a perceptive analysis of the evolution of the relationship between the CGIL and the PCI since World War II, see Peter Weitz, 'The CGIL and the PCI: from subordination to independent political force,' in Donald L. M. Blackmer and Sidney Tarrow, eds., *Communism in Italy and France* (Princeton, NJ: Princeton University Press, 1975), pp. 541–571.

97 It is recognized by most analysts of the Italian trade union movement that the ACLI have played a decisive role in the CISL's transformation into a class institution and, even more tangibly, in the process of unification. See, for instance, the round table organized by the ACLI in the spring of 1966, 'Sindacato di partito o unità sindacale,' *Quaderni di azione sociale*, no. 1, January–March 1966.

98 Reprinted in Georges Couffignal, op. cit., pp. 264–5.

99 CGIL–CISL–UIL, *Riunione introduttiva dei consigli generali. Firenze, 22–24 Novembre 1971* (Rome: Seusi, 1972), pp. 1098–1107.

100 Bruno Storti's report to the Direction of the Fed. CGIL–CISL–UIL, 10–12 December 1974, *Rassegna sindacale*, no. 302, 15 December 1974.

101 For an analysis of the link between the policy of reforms and workplace issues, see Pietro Merli Brandini, 'Lotte nella fabbrica e azione per le riforme,' *Politica ed economia*, no. 2, September–October 1970, pp. 39–43.

102 Gian Primo Cella, 'L'azione sindacale nella crisi italiana,' in L. Graziano and S. Tarrow, eds., *La crisi italiana* (Turin: Einaudi, 1979), pp. 271–302, here p. 279.

103 Lauralba Bellardi, 'I sindacati,' in L. Bellardi and E. Pisani, *Sindacati e contrattazione collettiva nel 1975* (Milan: Franco Angeli, 1978), especially her analysis of the seminar on the economic crisis and contractual strategy held by the CGIL in July 1975, pp. 22 ff.

104 Luciano Lama, 'Il sindacato di classe ieri ed oggi,' op. cit., p. 211.

105 'Che cosa chiediamo al governo,' *Rassegna sindacale*, no. 286, 28 April 1974, pp. 4–8, R. Vanni's report to the Direction of the Federation CGIL–CISL–UIL, 23–24 September 1974, *Rassegna sindacale*, no. 297, 29 September 1974, pp. 9–11, and Luciano Lama, Report to the Direction of the Federation CGIL–CISL–UIL, *Rassegna sindacale*, no. 277–8, 30 December 1973, pp. 8–13.

106 Gian Primo Cella, *'L'azione sindacale nella crisi italiana,'* op. cit., p. 277.

107 Gino Giugni, 'Stato sindacale, pansindacalismo e supplenza sindacale,' *Politica del diritto*, no. 1, 1970, pp. 49 ff. Alessandro Pizzorno, 'Sull'azione politica dei sindacati,' *Problemi del socialismo*, no. 49, November–December 1970, pp. 867–896. Vittorio Foa, 'La frontiera politica del sindacato,' *Problemi del socialismo*, no. 39, March–April 1969, pp. 213–226. Elio Giovannini, 'Sindacato e forze politiche,' *Sindacato moderno*, no. 3, March 1970, pp. 14–15. Bruno Trentin, 'Fuori della dicotomia fra il politico e il sociale,' *Rinascita*, 14 February 1975.

108 Angelo Bonzanini has correctly noted that rather 'than of pan-syndicalism it would be more correct to speak of a different awareness (on the part of the unions) which makes

unfeasible a separation of the worker as a 'citoyen' and as a producer or a distinction between workplace-related issues and society-related issues.' *Il movimento sindacale in Italia. Temi e momenti* (Rome: Editrice Elia, 1974), p. 139.

109   Raffaele Morese, 'Politica economica e riforme,' *Dibattito sindacale*, no. 5, September–October 1970, pp. 29–33.

110   Umberto Romagnoli and Tiziano Treu, op. cit., p. 98.

111   For a discussion of the cruciality of alliances in the general strategy of Italian unions, see *Unità di classe e alleanze nella strategia sindacale*, a cura della CGIL della Lombardia. Seminario Olds (Bergamo), 1–2 October, 1976 (Rome: ESI, 1977).

112   Luciano Cavalli, *Il sindacato come agente di cambiamento*, Working Papers sulla società contemporanea, no. 1 (Bologna: Il Mulino, 1973), pp. 11–45.

113   Perhaps the most thorough elaboration of unions' demands is contained in the economic document prepared by the General Council of the FLM, *FLM-Notizie*, no. 60, 6 June 1974.

114   Carlo Dell'Arringa, 'Problemi dell'egualitarismo,' *I consigli*, no. 15–16, June–September 1975, pp. 26–27. Luciano Boggio, 'Sindacato, pressione salariale e crisi economica,' *Prospettiva sindacale*, no. 2, June 1976, pp. 23–33.

115   Alberto Spreafico, 'Risultati elettorali e evoluzione del sistema politico,' in Mario Caciagli and Alberto Spreafico, eds., *Un sistema politico alla prova* (Bologna: Il Mulino, 1975), pp. 25–84.

116   Bruno Trentin has argued that during the period of active pursuit of the policy of reforms, the unions failed to establish a successful rapport with the political forces. This led them to regard reforms as if they were contractual demands. 'Crisi della federazione e unità sindacale,' *I consigli*, no. 6, August 1974, pp. 6–10.

117   Session of the Direction of CGIL–CISL–UIL, 23–4 September 1974, *Rassegna sindacale*, no. 297, 29 September 1974, pp. 9–11.

118   Gian Primo Cella, 'L'azione sindacale nella crisi italiana,' in Luigi Graziano and Sidney Tarrow, eds., op. cit., pp. 287–8.

119   Nando Morra, 'Contributo al dibattito su sindacati e riforme', *Quaderni di rassegna sindacale*, no. 36, May–June 1972, p. 80.

120   Augusto Graziani, 'Aspetti strutturali dell'economia italiana nell'ultimo decennio,' in A. Graziani, ed., *Crisi e ristrutturazione nell'economia italiana* (Turin: Einaudi, 1975), pp. 5–73.

121   Michele Salvati, 'Muddling through: economics and politics in Italy in 1969–1979,' in P. Lange and S. Tarrow, eds., op. cit., pp. 31–48.

122   For an interesting overview of the Italian unionists approach to the crisis, see the 'tavola rotonda' in the issue of *Quaderni di rassegna sindacale* on 'Sindacato e crisi,' no. 58, January–February 1976.

123   Giorgio Benvenuto, *Austerità e democrazia operaia* (Milano: Sugarco, 1977), pp. 87–8.

124   Starting with the III CGIL National Conference on the South, the 'Southern Question' has increasingly become central to the strategy of Italian trade-unionism. *Quaderni di rassegna sindacale*, no. 11–12, December 1965.

125   Franco Bentivogli, Report to the General Council of the FLM, *FLM-Notizie*, no. 127, July 1977.

126   Giorgio Fuà, *Occupazione e capacità produttive la realtà italiana* (Bologna: Il Mulino, 1976), *passim*.

127   Luciano Boggio, 'Sindacato, pressione salariale e crisi economica,' *Prospettiva sindacale*, no. 2, June 1976, pp. 23–33.

128   Bruno Trentin, 'Il mestiere del sindacato di fronte alla crisi,' *Quaderni di rassegna sindacale*, no. 51, November–December 1974, pp. 231–9.

129   Luciano Lama, op. cit., p. 257.

130   Pierre Carniti, *L'autonomia alla prova* (Roma: Coines, 1977), pp. 12–14.

131   Ufficio economia e riforme CGIL, 'Sulla situazione economica e sociale dell paese,' in Ruggero Spesso, *Sviluppo e crisi dell'economia italiana*, Proposte no. 7, May 1974.

132   Luciano Lama, 'Report to the General Council of the CGIL, 25–26 November 1974,' *Rassegna sindacale*, no. 301, 29 November 1974, pp. 6–17.

133   This is not to say that Italian unionists overlook or downplay international and conjunctural aspects. They argue, in fact, that even the quadrupling of oil prices would not have had such negative consequences if international and Italian capital had not taken advantage of the oil crisis to restructure. See Pierre Carniti, Report to the General

Council of the Federation of Metalworkers, *FLM-Notizie*, no. 46, 6 February 1974, pp. 2–9. Some union leaders, especially in the more 'radical' federations (see, for instance, the Metalworkers) refuse even to consider the oil crisis as crisis, labelling it a maneuver by oil companies in the interest of American capitalism. Document of the Federation of Metalworkers on economic policy, *FLM-Notizie*, no. 64, 18 July 1974, pp. 4–8.

134 Luciano Lama, *Report to the IX Congress of the CGIL* (Rimini: 6–11 June 1977), (Rome: ESI, 1977), pp. 10 ff.

135 Giancarlo Meroni, *Sindacati e crisi in Italia e in Europa* (Rome: ESI, 1979), pp. 20–47 and *passim*.

136 Paolo Sylos Labini et al., *Prospettive dell'economia italiana* (Bari: Laterza, 1978), pp. 9, 66. Gianni Celata, 'Riconversione e ristrutturazione industriale,' *Rassegna sindacale*, no. 369, 21 October 1976, pp. 19–21.

137 Although the institutional, social, and 'moral' aspects of the crisis are emphasized more by CISL and UIL leaders, a multidimensional approach is common to all confederations and federations. Indeed, there is among Italian unionists no disagreement as to the causes of the crisis. See Luciano Lama, *Il potere del sindacato* (Rome: Editori Riuniti, 1978), p. 26. Giorgio Benvenuto, *Il sindacato tra movimento e istituzioni* (Padova: Marsilio, 1978), p. 6. Pierre Carniti, op. cit., p. 22. Bruno Trentin, Tavola Rotonda, *Quaderni di rassegna sindacale*, no. 68–9, September–December 1977, pp. 23–6. VII Congress of the UIL, July 1977, *Rassegna sindacale*, no. 28, 14 July 1977, pp. 39–47. Franco Bentivogli, Report to the IX Congress of the FLM, June 1977, *FLM-Notizie*, no. 127, 10 July 1977, pp. 5–25. Sergio Garavini, 'Autonomia operaia e nuove oggettività capitalistiche nella crisi economica,' *Quaderni di rassegna sindacale*, no. 58, January–February 1976, pp. 48–53.

138 Franco Bentivogli, Report to the General Council of the FLM, 5–7 December 1974, *FLM-Notizie*, no. 75, 17 December 1974, pp. 2–7. Giorgio Benvenuto, Report to the Assemblea Nazionale dei Quadri CGIL–CISL–UIL, 7–8 January 1977, *Rassegna sindacale*, no. 1, 13 January 1977, pp. 25–35.

139 See, for instance, Antonio Lettieri's report to the Convegno della FLM sulle lotte nelle aziende a PP.SS., in *FLM-Notizie*, no. 50–1, 7 March 1974, pp. 11–18; Giorgio Benvenuto, 'Dove va l'economia italiana,' *I consigli*, no. 13, April 1975, pp. 14–20; 'Investimenti e recessione. Una strategia contro la recessione e las crisi,' *Rassegna sindacale*, no. 310, 27 April 1975, pp. 14–17.

140 The notion of the 'centrality of the enterprise' was most fully elaborated by Guido Carli, then President of the Confindustria, in the fall of 1977. Basic to this notion was the argument that Italy's economic system must be liberated from the 'ties and constraints' imposed on it by the unions and the government. See, *Intervista sul capitalismo italiano*, a cura di Eugenio Scalfari (Bari: Laterza, 1977), *passim*. For union reactions to this argument, see Bruno Trentin, Report to the Directing Committee of the FLM, *FLM-Notizie*, no. 111, 26 September 1976, pp. 3–11.

141 Lucio Libertini, *L'industria italiana alla svolta* (Bari: De Donato, 1975), p. 13; Bruno Trentin, at the Conferenza nazionale dei delegati di azienda e delle strutture di base, March 1975, *Rassegna sindacale*, no. 313, 12 June 1975, pp. 15–21; Pierre Carniti, op. cit., p. 23.

142 For a systematization of the premises and elaborations that have colored the 'crisis theory' held by Italian unions in the post-World War II period, see Salvatore Bonadonna, 'Le idee della crisi nelle scelte e nei comportamenti del sindacato,' *Quaderni di rassegna sindacale*, no. 72–3, May–August 1978, pp. 5–21, esp. pp. 16 ff.

143 An excellent analysis of the different impact of the crisis on the CGIL and the CISL is contained in the essay by M. Colombo, 'I diversi effetti della crisi sulla CGIL e sulla CISL,' *Prospettiva sindacale*, no. 2, June 1976, pp. 103–110.

144 Luciano Lama, op. cit., p. 156.

145 Aris Accornero, 'Vero soggetto politico il sindacato nella crisi,' *Prospettiva sindacale*, no. 2, June 1976, pp. 110–118.

146 Pietro Boni, 'La gravità della crisi, l'impegno del sindacato, e le risposte del governo,' *Rassegna sindacale*, no. 336, 8 January 1976, pp. 2–3.

147 Ada Becchi Collidà, 'Egualitarismo e politica salariale,' *Proposte*, no. 59–60, November–December 1977, pp. 22–3.

148 Roberto Romei, interview, *Rassegna sindacale*, no. 379, 30 December 1976, pp. 30–2.

149 Document of the Executive Committee of the FLM, *I consigli*, no. 29–30, October–

November 1976, pp. 5–6. For the less 'radical' stand taken by the confederations, see Luciano Lama, Report to the Directing Committee CGIL–CISL–UIL, *Rassegna sindacale*, no. 277–8, 30 December 1973, pp. 8–13.

150 Luciano Lama, Report to the General Council of the CGIL, *Rassegna sindacale*, no. 301, 29 November 1974, pp. 6–17.

151 Italian unions have, for instance, opposed Italy's entry into the European Monetary Union on the ground that such a project has little to do with European integration. Rather, they see it as a maneuver by European big capital. See Paul Wittenberg, 'Sme e politica agricola,' *Rassegna sindacale*, no. 1–2, 11 January 1979, pp. 20–21; Massimo Bordini, 'Sme. La lira è divergente cronica,' *Rassegna sindacale*, no. 4, 25 January 1979, pp. 16–18.

152 Bruno Trentin, Session of the Direction CGIL–CISL–UIL, 23–4 September 1974, *Rassegna sindacale*, no. 297, 29 September 1974, p. 11 ff.

153 Doriana Giudici, 'Sindacato e decentramento produttivo,' *Proposte*, no. 62–3, January 1979.

154 See the special issue on the South of *Quaderni di rassegna sindacale*, 'Il Sindacato e lavoro nel Mezzogiorno,' no. 71, March–April 1978, especially the essays by Raimondo Cantanzaro and Roberto Moscati, 'Classi sociali e riproduzione della marginalità nel Mezzogiorno,' pp. 87–101, and by Mario Didò, 'Contraddizioni dello sviluppo economico e sindacato nel Mezzogiorno,' pp. 122–133.

155 Luigi Frey, 'La struttura dell'offerta e della domanda di lavoro, 1970–6,' *Quaderni di rassegna sindacale*, no. 61, July–August, 1976, pp. 43–4.

156 For a discussion of the manifestations of the 'invisible economy' and of its effects on the labor market, see Roberto Spallucci, 'Le prospettive a medio termine del mercato del lavoro in Italia,' *Contrattazione*, no. 4–5, July–October 1978, pp. 39–69; Luigi Frey, 'Dal lavoro a domicilio al decentramento dell'attività produttiva,' *Quaderni di rassegna sindacale*, no. 44–5, September–December 1975, pp. 34–56.

157 See Documento Preparatorio, IV Conferenza nazionale dei delegati FLM, *FLM-Notizie*, no. 123, 18 March 1977, pp. 3–14.

158 Guido Baglioni, op. cit., pp. 9 ff.

159 Angelo Bonzanini, *Il movimento sindacale* (Palermo: Palumbo Editore, 1978), p. 40.

160 Rino Caviglioli, 'Le ambiguità sono in noi,' *I consigli*, no. 32–3, January–February 1977, p. 3.

161 Elena Pisani, 'La contrattazione,' in L. Bellardi and E. Pisani, op. cit., pp. 77 ff.

162 Final Document of the Directing Committee of the CGIL, 26 November 1977, *Rassegna sindacale*, no. 47–8, 1 December 1977, pp. 61–3.

163 Some union leaders, especially those of the more advanced categories, have demanded the elimination of the wage ceilings (6–8 million lire per year) beyond which the mechanism of the *scala mobile* becomes either inoperative or loses about 50 percent of its effectiveness. Antonio Lettieri, 'Costo del lavoro,' *FLM-Notizie*, no. 133, October 1977, p. 3–13. Confederal leaders have, however, not shared this demand. Lama, among others, has declared himself willing to make the *scala mobile* fully operative only for wages inferior to 8 million lire. 'Sindacato e programma di governo,' *Rassegna sindacale*, no. 364, 9 September 1976, pp. 21–2.

164 The CGIL has been less 'uncompromising' on the issue of the *scala mobile* than the CISL. See Rinaldo Scheda, Report to the Directing Committee CGIL–CISL–UIL, *Rassegna sindacale*, no. 363, 22 July 1976, pp. 13–24. The CISL has been generally more unwilling to move away from the themes and demands of the 'equalitarianism' of the hot autumn. See Pierre Carniti, Report to the Directing Committee CGIL–CISL–UIL, *Rassegna sindacale*, no. 373, 18 November 1976, pp. 23–33.

165 Sergio Garavini, 'La discussione dentro il sindacato,' *Rinascita*, no. 43, 3 November 1978.

166 Moreover, capital has consistently violated agreements with unions. The case of Fiat is symptomatic. In 1974, the FLM accepted Fiat's requests to transfer workers from sectors producing cars to those producing industrial machinery. Although the FLM had made its acceptance contingent on two conditions (workers had to volunteer in order to be transferred, and the transfer was not to mean a greater amount of time needed by workers to reach their work place), Fiat succeeded in introducing mobility even within each assembly line. (Over the last six years, over 5 percent of Fiat's entire work force has been transferred each year.) A. M. 'Mobilità Fiat. L'altalena che piace,' *I consigli*, no. 14, May 1975, pp. 21–3.

167 'Confronto con la Confindustria, le trattative punto per punto,' *Rassegna sindacale*, no. 3, 27 January 1977, p. 7.

168 Enzo Mattina has observed that the confederations' return to a position of pre-eminence in the union structure has been the result of four factors: (1) the shift in the unions' strategic orientation from the workplace to the political arena; (2) the unions' pursuit of increasingly general and undefined political demands for structural change; (3) 'the lack of organizational structures which would have projected the actions of the Delegate Councils outside the shop floor'; (4) the rapidly changing economic and political context facing the union movement. Report to the General Council of the FLM, 21–22 December 1976, *FLM-Notizie*, no. 118, 17 January 1977, pp. 3–20.

169 Mario Didò, Roberto Romei, and Gino Manfron, 'Due domande sulla crisi,' *Rassegna sindacale*, no. 379, 30 December 1976, pp. 30–2. For a redefinition of unions' objectives, see Bruno Trentin, Report to the Directing Committee of the FLM, *FLM-Notizie*, no. 111, 26 September 1976, pp. 3–11.

170 Document (addressed to the political parties) of the Federation CGIL–CISL–UIL, 'Necessaria una svolta radicale nella politica economica,' *Rassegna sindacale*, no. 356, 27 May 1976, pp. 5–8. Document of the Fed. CGIL–CISL–UIL, 'Confronto su temi specifici,' *Rassegna sindacale*, no. 364, 9 September 1976, p. 27. Pierre Carniti's report to the Directing Committee of the Federation CGIL–CISL–UIL, *Rassegna sindacale*, no. 373, 18 November 1976, pp. 23–33. Giorgio Benvenuto, Report to the Assemblea Nazionale dei quadri CGIL–CISL–UIL (Rome, 7–8 January 1977), *Rassegna sindacale*, no. 1, 3 January 1977, pp. 25–35. Luciano Lama, *Report to the IX Congress of the CGIL*, op. cit., pp. 29 ff. Document of the Federation CGIL–CISL–UIL, 'Proposta sindacale sulla politica industriale,' *Rassegna sindacale*, no. 44, 10 November 1977, pp. 44–7.

171 See the issue of *Quaderni di rassegna sindacale*, 'Le Partecipazioni Statali,' no. 68–9, September–December 1977, especially the 'tavola rotonda' with the participation of F. Cavazzuti, M. Colitti, P. Leon, and B. Trentin, and the essays by S. Restuccia, 'Sindacati e partecipazioni statali negli anni '50,' pp. 62–74, and by P. Barcellona and G. Bolaffi, 'Riforma delle partecipazioni statali e nuovo governo dell'economia,' pp. 75–87. Also, see Sergio Garavini's report to the Assemblea Nazionale dei quadri e dei delegati CGIL–CISL–UIL (Rimini, 9–10 May 1977), *Rassegna sindacale*, no. 20, 19 May 1977, pp. 26–32.

172 Pierre Carniti, op. cit., pp. 240–1. For a general analysis of the many flaws which characterize the Italian fiscal system, see Paolo Sylos Labini et al., op. cit., pp. 120 ff.

173 Giancarlo Meroni, op. cit., p. 17.

174 The rejection of social pacts, Mitbestimmung, etc., is shared by all Italian unionists. See Roberto Romei, Report to the Executive Committee of the CISL, *Conquiste del lavoro*, no. 16, 17 April 1978, pp. 8–9; Franco Bentivogli, 'Dopo le grandi vertenze,' *I consigli*, no. 4, May 1974, pp. 15–19; Giorgio Benvenuto, *Austerità e democrazia operaia*, op. cit., pp. 132–3. On the issue of worker participation, see Atti del Convegno, 'La partecipazione dei lavoratori: cogestione e autogestione,' Fondazione Pietro Seveso, 19–21 September 1977 (Rome: Edizioni Lavoro, 1978), esp. the essay by Lorenzo Bordogna et al., 'Le esperienze del sindacato e il problema della gestione dell'impresa,' pp. 15–36.

175 Vito Scalia, Directing Committee of the Federation CGIL–CISL–UIL, 12–13 February 1974, *Rassegna sindacale*, no. 281, 18 February 1974, pp. 21–5. Bruno Trentin, 'Riconversione e democrazia,' in *Da sfruttati a produttori* (Bari: De Donato, 1977), pp. 336 ff. Claudio Torneo, 'Contratti e crisi economica,' *Sindacato Nuovo*, no. 2, February 1976, pp. 5–6. Agostino Marianetti, *L'autogoverno responsabile* (Venezia: Marsilio, 1979), pp. 82 ff. Also, see Atti del Covegno, *La partecipazione dei lavoratori: cogestione e autogestione*, Fondazione Pietro Seveso, 19–21 September 1977 (Rome: Edizioni Lavoro, 1978), esp. the essays by Lorenzo Bordogna, 'Le esperienze del sindacato e il problema della gestione dell'impresa,' pp. 15–36, and by G. Baglioni, G. P. Cella, B. Manghi, and T. Treu, 'Cogestione e autogestione: il ruolo del sindacato,' pp. 121–144; and the issue of *Quaderni di rassegna sindacale*, 'Sindacato e controllo degli investimenti,' no. 62–3, September–December 1976.

176 The territorial–regional level is seen by unions as the key to a successful control over investments. It is in fact at this level that regional planning and sectorial plans meet. This explains why one of the unions' most constant demands has been that regional governments be given greater autonomy over the allocation of investments. See Enzo Mattina, *Sindacato e controllo operaio* (Milano: Mazzotta, 1977), p. 92.

177   See special issue of *Quaderni di rassegna sindacale*, 'Sindacato e controllo degli investimenti,' no. 62–3, September–December 1976.

178   Luciano Lama, 'Una strategia unitaria per uscire della crisi,' *Quaderni di rassegna sindacale*, no. 58, January–February 1976, pp. 11–12.

179   Peter Lange, 'Crisis and consent, change and compromise: dilemmas of Italian Communism in the 1970's,' in P. Lange and S. Tarrow, eds., op. cit., pp. 119 ff.

180   Guido Baglioni, 'Ragioni ed orientamenti di una politica sindacale delle alleanze,' and Sandro Antoniazzi, 'Il problema delle alleanze e la necessità di rivedere la linea del sindacato,' *Prospettiva sindacale*, pp. 11–28 and pp. 95–100.

181   Elena Pisani, op. cit., pp. 103–4.

182   See, for instance, the meeting between the unions and the parties belonging to the 'governmental area,' including the PCI. 'Incontro Partiti-Federazione unitaria,' 21 December 1976, *Rassegna sindacale*, no. 379, 30 December 1976, p. 6.

183   As some leaders of the Metalworkers' Federation, which is the union most closely identified with Workers' and Territorial Councils, have admitted, Workers' Councils have become growingly bureaucratized, while Territorial Councils have practically failed to take off. See Bruno Trentin, report, XVI Congress FIOM–CGIL, *FLM-Notizie*, no. 130, 21 July 1977, pp. 3–29; Franco Bentivogli and Bruno Trentin, interviews, 'Per una rinnovata democrazia dei consigli,' *I consigli*, no. 36, May 1977, pp. 4–7.

184   Arturo Parisi and Gianfranco Pasquino, 'Changes in the Italian electoral behavior: the relationships between parties and voters,' in P. Lange and S. Tarrow, eds., op. cit., pp. 6–30.

185   This is probably the most divisive 'political' issue with which Italian unions have to deal, while there is virtually no disagreement on the necessity for the union movement to act in the political arena. As it is to be expected in view of its ideological heritage, the CGIL is less inclined to practice 'political agnosticism' with regard to the composition of the government and of the participation of any particular party in it, while the CISL and the UIL are in favor of 'political neutrality.' For statements typifying the positions of the three confederations, see Rinaldo Scheda, Report to the Executive Committee of the Fed. CGIL–CISL–UIL, Rome, 14–15 July 1976, *Rassegna sindacale*, no. 363, 22 July 1976, pp. 13–24. Giorgio Benvenuto, op. cit., p. 90. Pierre Carniti, 'Crisi politica crisi di prospettive,' *Conquiste del lavoro*, no. 1, 2 January 1978.

186   Editorial, 'La crisi del sindacato nel rapporto con i lavoratori,' *I consigli*, no. 31, December 1976, pp. 45–7.

187   Nino Pagani, Report to the VI Congress of the FILCA–CISL, *Sindacato nuovo*, no. 5, May 1977, pp. 11–16.

188   Pio Galli, 'Il ruolo del sindacato si ritrova nella lotta,' *I consigli*, no. 27–8, August–September 1976, pp. 5–8.

189   For the economic policy of the PCI, see *Proposta di progetto a medio termine* (Rome: Editori Riuniti, 1977).

190   Enrico Berlinguer, *Austerità, occasione per trasformare l'Italia* (Rome: Editori Riuniti, 1977).

191   Raffaele Morese, 'Autonomia del sindacato e quadro politico,' *I consigli*, no. 17, October 1975, pp. 27–9.

192   Bruno Trentin, op. cit., p. 124.

193   Bruno Trentin, ibid., p. 69.

194   Only in recent months, however, have the unions, notably the CGIL, been able to develop a concrete plan about the mechanisms that should be implemented for acquiring control over investments: the *Piano d'impresa*. See 'Democrazia industriale,' document approved by the Council of the CGIL, 10–12 October 1979, in G. Amato, B. Trentin, and M. Magno, *Il Piano d'impresa e il ruolo del sindacato* (Bari: De Donato, 1980), pp. 89–115.

195   In Guido Baglioni's and Tiziano Treu's excellent analysis of the reasons that have led to a shrinking of the unions' sphere of action after 1975, five major reasons stand out: (1) the economic crisis; (2) the reduction and transformation of Italy's productive base; (3) the growing interdependence between politics and economics, which increases the importance of state intervention in the economy; (4) weakness of the political framework; (5) the political polarization emerged after the electoral results of June 1976. 'I mutamenti politico-istituzionali e lo spazio del sindacato,' *Prospettiva sindacale*, no. 4, December 1976, pp. 29–52, here p. 37.

196   Pio Galli, 'I consigli e il rinnovamento del sindacato,' *I consigli*, no. 2, January 1974,

pp. 38–40. Bruno Trentin, 'Per una rinnovata democrazia dei consigli,' *I consigli*, no. 36, May 1977, pp. 4–7.

197 Carlo Maria Santoro, 'Dove va l'economia italiana,' *I consigli*, no. 13, April 1975, pp. 14 ff.

198 Giorgio Ruffolo, Introduction to Agostino Marianetti, op. cit., p. 8.

199 In the opinion of Enzo Mattina (one of the leaders of the metalworkers), it is 'from the outbreak of the economic crisis that the union movement has found itself in a contradiction, caught between the need to defend the old (wage gains and jobs) and the need to build up the new (economic recovery and development of the political-economic system). This in a political context which has tended towards the reestablishment of the old,' *I consigli*, no. 32–3, January–February 1977.

200 An attentive observer of the Italian trade unions has argued that one of the prices paid in order to permit the entry of the PCI into the governmental area, but not into the government, has been a gradual return of the unions to the confines of more traditional policies, with the consequent abandonment of the innovative fervor which resulted from the hot autumn. Sergio Turone, op. cit., p. 188.

201 Many union leaders have vehemently argued that the EUR line is *not* an 'emergency line' and that it is fundamentally a project for the structural transformation of society. See Agostino Marianetti, op. cit., pp. 62, 67.

202 Pierre Carniti, Report to the Directing Committee of the Fed. CGIL–CISL–UIL, Rome, 13–14 January 1978, *Rassegna sindacale*, no. 2, 19 January 1978, pp. 2–6. 'Proposte per una svolta di politica economica e di sviluppo civile e democratico,' same issue of *Rassegna sindacale*, pp. 5–15. Final document approved by the National Assembly of the Fed. CGIL–CISL–UIL, Rome, 13–14 February 1978, *Rassegna sindacale*, no. 8, 23 February 1978, insert.

203 'Proposte per una svolta di politica economica e di sviluppo civile e democratico,' *Rassegna sindacale*, no. 2, 19 January 1978, p. 5.

204 ibid., p. 41.

205 It has been argued that, with the EUR line, Italian unions have engaged in a 'new' *Piano del lavoro*, though there are strategic differences between the two. Luigi Agostini, 'Dibattito sul sindacato. Limiti e prospettive dell'Eur,' *Rassegna sindacale*, no. 10, 8 March 1979, pp. 18–20.

206 For a review of the various interpretations that have been offered of the 'turning point' of 1978, see Stefano Bevacqua and Giuseppe Turani, *La svolta del '78* (Milan: Feltrinelli, 1978), pp. 9–40.

207 Pierre Carniti, 'Dare lavoro a tutti,' *Conquiste del lavoro*, no. 6, 6 February 1978, p. 2.

208 All unions have accepted the theme of austerity, regarding it as an unavoidable necessity. See Pierre Carniti, op. cit., pp. 254–7. Carlo Truffi and other leaders of the FLC (the Federation of Construction Workers) at the II Conferenza nationale dei delegati FLC, in *Sindacato nuovo*, no. 2, February 1977, pp. 4–16. Document for the IV Conferenza nazionale dei delegati FLM (Federation of Metalworkers), in *FLM-Notizie*, No. 123, 18 March 1977, pp. 13–14. Final document, VII Congress UIL, July 1977, *Rassegna sindacale*, no. 28, 14 July 1977, pp. 39–47. It must be emphasized, however, that the CGIL began to speak about the theme of austerity well before other unions. See Luciano Lama, Report to the General Council of the CGIL, November 1974, *Rassegna sindacale*, no. 301, 29 November 1974, pp. 6–17.

209 Luciano Lama, *Il potere del sindacato*, op. cit., p. 11.

210 Guido Carli (then President of the Employers' Confederation), Conference on 'Worker participation in the management of industrial enterprises' (Gramsci Institute), Milan, 4–5 February 1978, reported in S. Bevacqua and G. Turani, op. cit., p. 111.

211 At the confederal levels, two major 'interpretations' of the EUR line emerged during and after the actual formulation of the line. The "Lama interpretation" and the interpretation elaborated by most leaders of the CISL. See Silvano Scaloja, 'Il sindacato dell'Eur. Ovvero delle due letture,' *Sindacato nuovo*, no. 2–3, May–June 1978, pp. 13–14. Among the federations, the FLM (Federation of Metalworkers) has been the most vehement in its criticism of the EUR line. See Enzo Mattina, Report to the Directing Committee of the FLM, 23–4 January 1978, *FLM-Notizie*, no. 136, 2 February 1978, pp. III–XV.

212 Luciano Lama, interview to *La repubblica*, 24 January 1978. For Pierre Carniti's criticism of Lama's positions, see 'Pieno impiego: vincolo non variabile,' *Conquiste del lavoro*, no. 5, 30 January 1978, p. 3.

213   Luciano Lama, ibid.
214   Giorgio Benvenuto, 'Posizione e iniziativa del sindacato di fronte alla crisi,' Report to the Assemblea Nazionale dei quadri CGIL–CISL–UIL, Rome, 7–8 January 1977, *Rassegna sindacale*, no. 1, 13 January 1977, pp. 25–35.
215   See, for instance, the final document issued by the meeting of the Directing Committee of the Federation of Metalworkers, 23–4 January 1978, *FLM-Notizie*. pp. III–XV.
216   Mario Didò, interview to *La repubblica*, 29 March 1979, p. 26.
217   For the gains made by unions with respect to control over investments in the contractual round of 1976, see 'I diritti d'informazione nei nuovi contratti,' *Quaderni di rassegna sindacale*, no. 62–3, September–December 1976, pp. 164–178.
218   The fact that the CGIL had gone further than the CISL and the UIL in the demand for control over investments is no surprise in view of its 'ideological traditions.' See M. Colombo, 'I diversi effetti della crisi sulla CGIL e sulla CISL,' *Prospettiva sindacale*, no. 2, June 1976, pp. 103–110. Giuliano Amato, 'Crisi di rappresentanza e governo del movimento: la proposta del Piano d'impresa,' in B. Trentin, G. Amato and M. Magno, op. cit., pp. 5–6.
219   'Democrazia industriale,' document approved by the General Council of the CGIL, Ariccia, 10–12 October 1979, in B. Trentin, G. Amato and M. Magno, op. cit., pp. 89–115.
220   For a more detailed discussion, see Lorenzo Bordogna et al., 'Le esperienze del sindacato e il problema della gestione dell'impresa,' op. cit., pp. 27 ff.
221   Luciano Lama, op. cit., pp. 33 ff.
222   As it has happened with the strategy of reforms, the failure of the state to devise coherent and effective planning has rendered futile many of the gains made by unions in the area of investments. This has happened, for instance, with the important agreements that unions concluded in the mid-1970s with some of Italy's largest enterprises (Fiat, Montedison, Anic) which, because of the lack of nationwide planning, 'have, in actual fact, become corporative agreements' failing to create a substantial number of jobs in the South. Mario Didò, round table, 'Una strategia unitaria per uscire dalla crisi,' *Quaderni di rassegna sindacale*, no. 58, January–February 1976, p. 6.
223   Bruno Trentin, round table, *Contrattazione*, January–April 1978, p. 46.
224   In August, 1978, the government elaborated the so-called *Piano Pandolfi*, a three-year year whose aim was to create 600,000 new jobs. Italian unions vehemently criticized such a plan, in particular the proposed measures to freeze real wages, to eliminate all constraints on worker mobility, and to limit public expenditures. For the unions' critique of the plan and for their counterproposals, see Document Fed. CGIL–CISL–UIL, Roma, 31 January 1979, in *Rassegna sindacale*, no. 6, 8 February 1979, pp. 40–3.
225   See Document, General Council CGIL, in *Rassegna sindacale*, no. 7, 15 February 1979. For a general appraisal of the growing importance that unions attach to the 'territorial level,' see Alfredo del Monte, 'Ruolo delle regioni nella politica industriale,' *Contrattazione*, January–April 1978, pp. 98–111. V. Onida, 'Le istituzioni regionali e la partecipazione del sindacato,' *Prospettiva sindacale*, no. 1, March 1976, pp. 12–35.
226   G. B. Chiesa, *Pubblico impiego sindacato riforma* (Rome: ESI, 1977), esp. pp. 49 ff., is an excellent illustration of the union demand for a reorganization of the public administration sector.
227   Bruno Trentin, op. cit., p. CXIX.
228   Enzo Mattina, Report to the General Council of the Federation of Metalworkers, *FLM-Notizie*, no. 118, 17 January 1977, pp. 3–20.
229   Due to the divergences in the interpretations of the EUR line offered by confederal leaders, the union movement has been unable, among other things, to obtain the support of the rank-and-file activists. As illustrated by a 'debate among factory delegates' organized by the journal of the Federation of Metalworkers, activists have found themselves caught between two different 'images.' On the one hand, the image of the 'conflictual union movement' of the hot autumn. On the other hand, the image of a union movement which seeks to become the privileged interlocutor of state institutions and which abandons a conflictual posture towards capital. *I consigli*, no. 46, April 1978, pp. 35–6.
230   For an illustration of the position of the CGIL on wage policy, see the report prepared by the confederation's 'ufficio studi,' 'Struttura del salario,' *Rassegna sindacale*, no. 7, 16 February 1978, pp. 41–7.
231   On the issue of wage policy, the position of the Federation of Metalworkers has been,

for instance, precisely the opposite of the one advocated by the EUR line. See Document approved by the National Direction of the FLM, 24 January 1978, reported in S. Bevacqua and G. Turani, op. cit., pp. 81–2.

232 Pietro Merli Brandini, 'Il nostro mestiere è di fare politica,' *Rinascita*, 7 March 1980, pp. 13–14.

233 Giorgio Benvenuto, 'Italian Unionism after the Elections of 1979,' speech delivered at the Center for European Studies, Harvard University, Cambridge, Mass., 10 December 1979.

234 For an excellent overview of the divergences which exist among the unions on the issue of worker mobility, see Aviana Bulgarelli, *Crisi e mobilità operaia* (Milan: Mazzotta, 1978), esp. pp. 58 ff. Also see the special issue of *Contrattazione*, 'Orientamenti del dibattito sulla mobilità,' January–April 1978.

235 Luciano Lama, op. cit., p. 39 ff.

236 For an appraisal of the debate among unions on the reduction of the work week, see Paolo Forcellini, 'Il dibattito sull'orario: elementi di analisi,' *Quaderni di rassegna sindacale*, no. 72–3, May–August 1978, pp. 66–78.

237 Pierre Carniti, 'Dare lavoro a tutti,' *Conquiste del lavoro*, no. 6, 6 February 1978. Luciano Lama has argued precisely the opposite, namely that 'it is no longer possible to realize the slogan "all must work, but fewer hours,"' *Il potere del sindacato*, op. cit., pp. 96–7. For the position of the Federation of Metalworkers, see Franco Bentivogli, 'La riduzione del tempo di lavoro,' *Conquiste del lavoro*, no. 7, 13 February 1978, pp. 1–2.

238 See 'Quattro piattaforme a confronto,' *I consigli*, no. 52–3, November–December 1978, pp. 36–42. The metalworkers, and to a less extent the chemical and construction workers, have also opposed the agreement between the Fed. CGIL–CISL–UIL and Confindustria concerning the abolition of seven holidays. See Richieste FLM, *FLM-Notizie*, no. 52, October 1978, special issue.

239 For Luciano Lama's position, see his interview to *La stampa*, 27 May 1978.

240 Of course, the controversy among the unions on the issue of egalitarianism precedes the formulation of the EUR line. See Ada Becchi Collidà, 'Egualitarismo e politica salariale,' *Proposte*, no. 59–60, November–December 1977, *passim*.

241 Eraldo Crea, 'Una nuova partecipazione,' *Conquiste del lavoro*, no. 4, 23 January 1978, p. 3.

242 Pietro Merli Brandini, 'Un sì che è un impegno,' *Conquiste del lavoro*, no. 8, 20 February 1978, p. 3.

243 Luciano Lama, Report to the General Council of the CGIL, 'L'impegno della CGIL per avanzare sulla linea dell'Eur con l'iniziativa unitaria di lotta,' Ariccia, 9–11 November 1978, *Rassegna sindacale*, no. 43–4, 16 November 1978, pp. 21–9.

244 Sergio Garavini, Report to the Assemblea Nazionale dei quadri e dei delegati, Fed. CGIL–CISL–UIL, Rimini, 9–10 May 1977, *Rassegna sindacale*, no. 20, 19 May 1977, pp. 26–32.

245 Indeed, the reading of the EUR line given by Lama and other Communist leaders in the CGIL and the economic policy of the PCI are strikingly similar. See, for instance, Giorgio Napolitano's report and Enrico Berlinguer's final statement at the VII Conferenza Operaia PCI, Naples, 3–5 March 1978, printed in *L'unità*, 4 and 6 March 1978.

246 Luciano Lama has vehemently argued that it is not true that the EUR line is an attempt to 'hook the CGIL to the PCI.' Op. cit., p. 17. For the PCI, the EUR line is to praise because it is based on a realistic assessment of the country's economic conditions. Ferdinando Di Giulio, 'Autonomia e quadro politico,' *I consigli*, no. 46, April 1978, pp. 4–11.

247 For a more detailed discussion of this point, see Peter Lange, 'Sindacati, partiti, stato e liberal-corporativismo,' *Il mulino*, no. 266, November–December 1979, pp. 943–72.

248 The need 'to preserve the pluralism' of the (unified) Italian trade union movement has been used by non-Communist union leaders, especially in the UIL, to explain their vehement opposition to the 'historic compromise.' See Giorgio Benvenuto, op. cit., p. 63 ff.

249 This has led not only to rather sharp controversies between the confederations and the federations, but also to rather paradoxical situations. During the 1979 bargaining over the renewal of the metalworkers contract, the representatives of the industrialists rejected the demands of the metalworkers, accusing them of 'having betrayed the EUR

line.' See Maria Grazia Bacchi, 'I metalmeccanici hanno o no tradito l'EUR,' *Rassegna sindacale*, no. 1–2, 11 January 1979, pp. 12–13.

250 The spread of 'autonomous' unions has been particularly visible among state and municipal employees, both white- and blue-collar. The tendency of the confederations, which have been generally unable to do very little against it, has been to hold the government, that is, the government's failure to implement reforms, responsible for the growingly frequent outbursts of disruptive actions by the 'autonomous' unions. See Rinaldo Scheda, 'Una forte iniziativa contro il corporativismo,' *Rassegna sindacale*, no. 318–9, 4–11 September 1975, pp. 2–3. Corrado Perna, 'Il contratto dei piloti,' *Rassegna sindacale*, no. 1–2, 11 January 1979, pp. 1–2.

251 Also because of their opposition to the actions of the 'autonomous' unions, the issue of the strike and of its utility as a means for achieving specific objectives has come to occupy an increasingly central position in the interunion debate. While the union movement has rejected government and capital proposals for introducing some form of legislative constraints on the right to strike, it is more and more inclined to think that workers must use their right to strike more moderately. 'Self-regulation' is the formula devised by Italian unions for achieving this. See Gianni Arrigo and Angelo Pandolfo, *Autoregolamentazione dello sciopero*, Interventi, No. 1 (Rome: Edizioni Lavoro, 1978), and Paolo De Luca et al., *Perché l'autoregolamentazione* (Rome: ESI, 1978).

252 Salvatore Bonadonna, 'Le idee della crisi nelle scelte e nei comportamenti del sindacato,' *Quaderni di rassegna sindacale*, no. 72–3, May–August 1978, p. 17.

253 Luciano Lama, statement to the VII Conferenza operaia of the PCI, Naples, 3–5 March 1978, printed in *L'unità*, 5 March 1978.

254 Gigno Giugni, 'Il rebus dei due sindacati,' *La repubblica*, 28 July 1980, p. 8.

255 Bruno Trentin, *Il sindacato dei consigli* (Rome: Editori Riuniti, 1980), pp. 180–212.

256 For more details about the negotiations between government and unions, the interunion debate, and the reaction by major political and economic leaders, see the July 1980 issues of *La repubblica* and *Il corriere della sera*.

257 For the position of the PCI on the *Fondo*, see the July 1980 issues of *Rinascita*, especially Luciano Barca, 'Ricatti da far cadere,' and Federico Rampini, 'Le lotte operaie contro la politica economica del governo,' 25 July 1980.

258 'Tra Lama e Berlinguer polemica ormai aperta,' *La repubblica*, July 8, 1980.

259 See *Sindacalisti nelle istituzioni*, research sponsored by the Fondazione Seveso (Rome: Edizioni Lavoro, 1979), especially the essays by Tiziano Treu, 'Forme, caratteri e direttivi dell'intervento sindacale nelle istituzioni,' pp. 5–18, and by Massimo Roccella, 'Sindacati e poteri pubblici; il quadro istituzionale,' pp. 19–47.

260 For an interesting analysis of the various ideological trends which exist in the leadership of the union movement, see Walter Tobagi, *Che cosa contano i sindacati* (Milan: Rizzoli, 1980).

261 Or, as suggestively phrased by Giorgio Benvenuto, 'today the unions find themselves in the position of a convict on parole: they can say what they want about how the country should be changed, but they can do nothing to bring about change,' op. cit., p. 65.

262 According to Bruno Manghi, author of one of the most insightful though not entirely convincing analyses of the behavior of Italian unions in recent years, this is one of the causes for the emergence of what he calls 'il sindacato dell'immagine': while waiting for major political changes which would allow the realization of their strategic goals, union leaders have become more and more concerned with the creation of 'images' through which they can continue to maintain the support of the working class and legitimacy in the political-economic system. *Declinare crescendo* (Bologna: Il Mulino, 1977), esp. pp. 23–46.

3 Conclusions: French and Italian Union Development in Comparative Perspective

Peter Lange and George Ross

Part 1

Introduction

France and Italy are very often paired in the comparative analysis of advanced industrial democracies as systems with much in common and important distinctive features setting them off from others. The pairing has had much merit. The postwar histories of the two countries have been similar and there do exist a number of obvious shared political and economic-institutional characteristics, among these the presence of powerful Communist parties excluded from participation in government, union movements divided along partisan and ideological lines and industrial relations systems which were weakly institutionalized and legitimated. This volume is both part of, and an argument for departure from, this traditional perspective.

The postwar political-economic settlements in the two countries were, in fact, remarkably similar. United Resistance–Liberation fronts which included Communists ruled in the immediate aftermath of war, implementing major programs of social and institutional reform. Union movements, within which Communists were very powerful, reached historic high points in terms of membership and social influence. After mid-1947, however, when Communists were removed from power in both countries, events took a dramatically different turn. The Cold War, which divided both societies and polities profoundly, completely halted the progress of reform and, ultimately, put in place the mixed economy from which the postwar boom was to emanate. At the same time, the Cold War break divided the union movements of both countries from top to bottom, with Communist-influenced unions, which retained substantial resources, opposing the pro-American policies of governments, while non-Communist unions supported the American side. One result of such dramatic union divisions was that the union movement as a whole proved less and less effective in protecting and advancing the interests of its members and supporters. Thus in both countries private sector employers and increasingly conservative governments gained the upper hand in politics and in the labor market. By the earlier 1950s, both union movements seemed headed on similar trajectories—they were weak, divided, highly politicized, and by and large excluded from any influence over the course of events. The marked similarity of the political and economic contexts in which the unions operated, of the structural and ideological features of the movements and of the unions' behavior in the first postwar decade suggests, then, the utility of grouping the French and Italian cases together for analysis.

This is all the more attractive as an approach because, as we have already seen, the subsequent evolution of the two union movements followed two distinctive paths, culminating in manifestly different responses to the economic challenges of the 1970s: what we would call, in the French case, 'maximalism,' and in the Italian case, 'interventionism.' This gradual, but eventually marked differentiation of development from common starting points should allow us to identify the factors which seem best to explain such differentiation.[1] Furthermore, to the extent that we are able to offer a broad analytical approach to the understanding of trade union behavior in advanced capitalist democracies, we may also be able to suggest how the factors which emerge in explaining the growing differences in these two cases might also operate over a broader range of cases. At a minimum, we would hope to grasp why two union movements, so similar twenty years earlier, responded so differently to the crisis of the 1970s.

The profound differences between French maximalism and Italian interventionism are clearly delineated in the separate country chapters. They involve all the features of union ideology, analysis, strategy, policy, and organization. *French maximalism* was marked by a belligerent and principled refusal to play any role in the 'management of the crisis' or to establish any type of cooperative relationship with those who had been and still were running the national economy and individual firms. For the French union movement, the choices posed by the crisis were basically no different than those which had been present before its outbreak: either general and non-incremental political-economic transformation or aggressively defensive trade union 'business-as-usual'; either fundamental change in national political leadership, without which all meaningful political-economic change was impossible, or continued confrontation at all levels of the political and economic systems. At the practical level, maximalism meant a focus of union action on the political center, a use of mobilization for national symbolic and electoral purposes and, because the CGT still dominated the union movement, a subordination of union policy to the strategic and tactical interests of the PCF. Support was built and maintained not primarily through the gains won by the unions themselves, but at least as much through a reliance on ideological appeals and the prospect for gains to be made as a result of the political victory of forces external to the union movement—political parties—to which the unions had linkages and from whose control of the state they could expect to be able better to deliver benefits to their supporters. Maximalism, in a nutshell, was a strategic approach to the crisis in which partisan political interests and ideological orientations determined to a considerable extent outside the union movement, and against the will of some elements within the movement, had primacy.

Italian interventionism, in contrast, was characterized by the efforts of the union movement to devise a strategic response to the crisis which entailed its direct intervention at the firm, sectoral, and national levels in the development of policies designed to relieve the crisis, to maintain and extend the unions' social alliances and, at the same time, to protect the gains made by their constituents in the preceding years. The Italian strategy was based on the idea that the unions' power could be used to initiate a process of incremental but structural change which would at one and the same time promote a gradual transformation of the political

economy and enhance the unions' own power and influence in the structures of political-economic decision-making at all levels. Like the French,
the long-term objectives of the Italian unions remained a structural transformation of the political economy. Italian union leaders, however, had a
different understanding of what would comprise such a transformation.
Furthermore, unlike the French, the Italians did not refuse, in principle or
in practice, to try to use their power both in the market and the political
arenas to attempt to steer the 'management' of the crisis. There was also no
assumption that the locus of power was entirely political and partisan and
that change had necessarily to be initiated at the center, through a partisan
victory of the parties sympathetic to the unions and the working class.
Change could come as well from below, incrementally, and through activity and negotiation in the labor market as well as in the political system.
All levels of the unions had an important role to play (their relative weight
would depend on the specific issues and economic and political conditions),
and union unity was critical to the success of the strategy. Support was,
therefore, built and maintained primarily through the ideals, programs and
activities of the unions themselves, operating in both the political and
market arenas of society. Interventionism, then, was primarily an autonomous and nonpartisan union strategy which aimed at giving the union
movement an important role in how the crisis was addressed at all levels; it
encompassed both political and economic objectives and was therefore
necessarily political and attentive to, and sometimes supportive of, the
positions of different parties, but whatever the influence exercised within
different unions by political parties, the interests of the unions as determined within the unified union movement were primary.

As this makes clear, in the crisis of the 1970s, the French and Italian
union movements—similar in strategic perspectives and structural characteristics in the first postwar decade—adopted sharply contrasting strategic
responses. Explaining this divergence in light of the common starting
points is the analytical task of this chapter. Our basic thesis is that the
outcomes of the 1970s can only be understood as the culmination of a series
of discreet responses which the two union movements and specific unions
within them made in reaction to challenges which they faced at identifiable
points during the preceding two decades. These responses were different in
the French and Italian cases because of differences in market and political
contexts within which the unions operated, in individual unions' relations
with political parties, in the character of interunion competition, and in the
specific ideologies and bases of support of the individual unions. What
occurred was a cumulative process of differentiation. The responses of
unions to each critical juncture had effects which, in turn, shaped and
limited how subsequent challenging conjunctures, and ultimately that of
the post-1974 crisis, were addressed. In order to make something more
than descriptive sense of this cumulative process of differentiation, however, it will be necessary, first, to address some general issues concerning
the comparative analysis of union movements. It is to this task that we now
turn.

Part 2

Unions as Objects of History and Unions as Actors

The predominant postwar theoretical approach to the development of trade unions in advanced capitalist democratic societies has been both economistic and historicist.[2] While explicitly challenging classical Marxist predictions about the specific outcomes of contemporary developmental processes, this approach—which we call 'liberal optimist'—has shared with Marxism a belief in the increasing convergence of trade union behaviors across nations due to the technological and economic 'logic' of the capitalist and/or industrial mode of production. Both in the French and Italian cases we have examined and more generally, however, this analysis appears inconsistent with reality. It is clear, therefore, that an alternative approach is necessary. To set the context for this alternative, we briefly focus on the chief characteristics of the liberal optimist analysis.

The Conventional Wisdom of Liberal Optimism

The use of the notion of an underlying 'logic' or set of functional requisites of industrialism and/or capitalism to explain the development of the institutions of modern industrial society has a long history in social theory and social science. The predominant classical version of this mode of thought has, of course, been Marxism. In the postwar period, however, a number of analysts took issue with Marxist predictions about the probable development of class relations—as embodied in trade union and employer behavior and the practices of industrial and labor relations—in advanced industrial society.[3] Where the Marxists foresaw increasing social polarization, the liberal optimists argued that a more pluralist society was emerging in which class was receding in importance and in which relationships between workers, employers, and the state were being broken down into an ordered and integrated set of subsystems, only partially interpretable through the prism of class. At the same time, however, many of the liberal optimists shared economistic and historicist assumptions with their Marxist adversaries, a fact which at least one of them acknowledged:

> In fact, history has validated a basic premise of Marxist sociology at the expense of Marxist politics. Marxist sociology assumes that cultural superstructures, including political behavior and status relationships, are a function of the underlying economic and technological structure. . . . Hence, as an unpolitical Marxist sociology would expect, instead of European class and political relationships holding up a model of the

United States' future, the social organization of the United States has presented the image of the European future.[4]

The shared postulates of the Marxist and liberal optimists are important, for they do much to explain why the latter's predictions about trade union behavior have not been borne out by events. The first of these postulates is fundamentally economistic, asserting that the motor of social change lies in economic development. The institutions of industrial society are thus products of changes in technology and of the economic practices accommodating those changes. Further, it is maintained that the changes in economic processes which, taken together, create industrial society, have a pervasive effect on all other social and political institutions. There is, on this view, a 'unitary character of industrial society' which derives from 'the processes of integration immanent in industrialization.'[5] Analyses of the sources of this unitary drive vary somewhat from author to author, although in all of them there is common an underlying economic functionalism and almost Darwinian understanding of institutional development: the economy has functional requisites and only institutions which are adapted to these can survive.

The process by which this functionalist logic asserts itself in any particular society is evolutionary and progressive. In the early stages of industrial development many institutions are likely to be out of step with the needs of the emerging industrial economy, but with time such institutions adapt or die. There are 'limited responses that are possible to certain functional problems intrinsic in industrial growth'[6] and 'an industrialized society is such a complicated mechanism with such interdependence of its parts that keeping it going without major disruption becomes an overriding concern.'[7] Thus, within any society, the industrial logic becomes evermore *the* logic underlying institutional development. Moreover, if this is the case for any particular industrial society, it follows logically that different industrial societies with similar and high levels of economic development will have increasingly similar institutions.[8]

Where, of course, the liberal optimists diverge from the Marxists is in the specific content of their predictions. For the Marxists, the development of capitalism promotes increasingly polarized, ideological, and politicized class relations. In the sphere of production, one should see increasing levels of militancy, radical goals which extend beyond the scope of industrial relations to call into question both property rights and the 'rules of the game' of 'bourgeois democracy' and a general decay of the mechanisms of social regulation which underpin capitalist class relations.[9] For the liberal optimists, the predicted pattern is almost the inverse. Relations between workers and employers will become more regularized, institutionalized, restricted in scope and autonomous from other, including political, conflicts in the society. The past 'superimposition of various lines of [social] differentiation' which promoted a 'hardening of the class fronts'[10] will give way to a diversification of roles, and softening and permeability of class barriers such that there will be a 'tendency toward decreasing intensity and violence in industrial conflict by virtue of the institutionalization of class conflict.'[11] Polarization around class will give way to integration due to pluralism and the cross-cutting character of social roles and interests.

This general standpoint is translated into a number of expectations about trade union behavior and labor relations in advanced industrial democracies, particularly about the intensity, scope, and issue content of conflict. There is widespread agreement that the duration and spread of conflict as well as the fervor associated with it should diminish. Liberal optimist authors are ordinarily careful to note that this does not mean that strikes will cease to occur, but only that they will lose the sense of intense confrontation along class barriers which characterized them in the past. The erosion of those barriers, the development of representative institutions for workers and employers, agreement on mechanisms for the negotiation and mediation of conflicts between those institutions, all are expected to lead to greater conflict regulation.[12]

As conflict moderates, its scope also narrows and the issues involved are depoliticized. Workers and their organizations will become ever less interested in issues which are not narrowly 'industrial.' Unions, acting as representatives for their constituents, will move away from broad programs of social and political change for which they seek extra-industrial social and political alliances. Instead, they will gradually become agents for the maximization of the relatively short-range interests of supporters who segregate their role as workers from other social roles (e.g. citizen, consumer) and who define their interests in terms of the legitimate issues of the industrial relations system.[13]

The analysis also anticipates a depoliticization of trade union goals and behavior. First, the industrial sphere and its conflicts will become dissociated from the political sphere: 'Industry and industrial conflict are, in post-capitalist society, institutionally isolated, i.e., confined within the borders of their proper realm and robbed of their influence on other spheres of society.'[14] Second, to the extent this is the case, issues which are 'political' will not be viewed as appropriate objects for union action, nor will 'industrial' issues be translated into political questions to be pursued through political instruments and action. Dahrendorf makes the analogy with the change in the role of the Church and religious issues, 'a process of confinement—that is, of delimitation of basically separate competences —takes place.'[15] As a result, and this is a point to which we shall return, the notion that trade unions have, or might choose to exercise, the option of pursuing the same goals either in the industrial or political spheres— depending on where they think they can best maximize their interests—is excluded. A third aspect of the depoliticization of trade union action concerns unions' relationship with political parties and movements. In time, the two will become separated: for Dahrendorf, 'the notion of a workers' party has lost its political meaning;[16] for Kerr and his colleagues, 'the day of ideological labor movements as we have known them will have passed' as the unions shift from being a part of a class movement to being a special interest group.[17]

Not surprisingly, all of these predicted changes are expected to have a conservatizing influence on trade unions. The narrowing and depoliticizing of their interests and concerns, the product of the more general institutionalization of industrial conflict, lead them to develop a stake in the newly developed institutions and modes of conflict regulation. Whereas in the past the unions were often part of revolutionary or at least radical movements for basic change, they are likely to become defenders of things as they are, or at least of the basic values and institutions within which such things are embedded, even as they seek to maximize interests within these confines. The unions 'aim, above all, at the maintenance or change of the industrial *status quo*, not the inclusive social *status quo*,'[18] for 'the consensus of a pluralistic society will have settled over the scene.'[19]

Whether we look at the recent behavior of unions in all of the European advanced industrial democracies, or just at France and Italy, there is little which supports the expectations of liberal optimist theory, and much which contradicts them. Convergence in trade union behavior has been much less than liberal optimists would expect, and where convergence has occurred, it has not necessarily been of the kind expected.

On the first point, the trade union movements of the major European countries were rather different in terms of their ideologies, strategies, organizations, and behaviors in the 1950s, and they still are so today. There was a period in the early 1960s when the rush to capture as large a share as possible of growing prosperity led many unions to act more similarly than had been their historical custom. Employers, prospering under conditions of sustained growth, were more willing to share some of their increased profits with workers, especially when higher wages might promote workforce stability and quality. Unions, strong in the labor market and on the organizational upswing, did not hesitate to utilize their strength to seek higher wages and better working conditions for their constituents. Yet, even in this period significant differences remained. British unions, for instance, were fitfully drawn into forms of incomes policies at the same moment when Italian unions refused to participate in schemes for economic and incomes planning and Swedish unions further developed their solidaristic wage policy.[20] Nonetheless, in the euphoria of growth and the assumption of its stable continuation, some convergence, supporting liberal optimist expectations, could be noted. From the late 1960s onwards, however, *these* signs of convergence gave way to others which were directly contradictory to the expected pattern. Furthermore, paradoxically it was also the case that as new trends developed, there was also a reafflorescence of older patterns of strategic orientation specific to different national unions.[21]

The first major shift was in the character of the demands made by unions. With the surge of militancy in the late 1960s, there was an expansion of the scope of demands to include not only questions of wages, health, safety, and the effects of the introduction of new technology —which had been traditional areas of concern for most unions—but also broader attacks on the wage structure (demands for reductions of differentials and greater wage egalitarianism between blue- and white-collar workers). More generally, the unions sought greater control of processes on the shop floor and a significant reduction of managerial power to enforce work discipline. The new demands extended beyond the shop floor as well to issues of social policy as it affected not only union constituents but broader groups as well. Further, with the deepening of crisis, unions sought a greater role in the making of national- and firm-level investment and other political-economic decisions, sometimes with explicit social goals in mind.

Insistence on greater union macro- and micro-influence in the making of political-economic policy became widespread. From the standpoint of liberal optimist theories, what was striking about this was not only that demands became broader, encompassing wider constituencies, but also that they invaded areas of responsibilities and prerogatives which had traditionally been those of employers or the state.[22]

The second, and related, shift in trade union strategy and behavior was toward an increased focus on the political arena, on the pursuit of union goals through direct relationships with the state and/or support for political parties. Throughout Europe, unions became more active in politics and in the state and were drawn into a web of political relations about substantive policy questions affecting not just the workplace but the society and political economy as well. Indicators of this include the manifold demands of unions which required direct or indirect partisan and state support or response, the growing impact of union actions on a broad range of political and social concerns, and the increased efforts of governments to reach out to the unions for help in implementing policies, all of which signalled increasing structural interpenetration of the unions with the state.[23] There has often, of course, been a relationship among these developments. The increase in the unions' focus on the political arena has been connected to tightening constraints on their ability to extract concessions in the market. The state's willingness to enter into systematic bargains with unions must be understood in light of the increasing damage which union action has been able to inflict on the overall political economy. These are points to which we will shortly return. What is essential to note, however, is that here again are trends running directly contrary to those anticipated by the liberal optimists: not increasing subsystem autonomy but increased union–state interpenetration[24] and growing politicization; not necessarily a basic acceptance of the rules of the game, but often a continual probing to rewrite those rules; not a narrowing of demands around bread and butter issues, but an expansion of them to encompass questions going sometimes to the roots of the prevailing postwar settlements.

These trends are common to most of the European cases. Their communality, however, does not amount to convergence in any 'historicist' sense. For the liberal optimists, convergence was expected not only on general union orientations but also with respect to the specific content of their policies and demands. For the trends we have sketched, however, each union gave specific and significantly varied content to its policies. Which new demands at the workplace were added varied significantly from country to country, as did the strategies which the unions adopted towards parties and the state, and the particular policies which they sought to pursue through action in the political arena. To cite but two examples, whereas the German unions sought to extend control at the shop floor through changes in and an extension of the *mitbestimmung* system, the British and Italians sought to do so through their autonomous power and through winning new rights in the collective bargaining process. The former, in other words, saw extended control linked to coresponsibility in the implementation of decisions; the latter did not. Similarly, whereas the British accepted, for a short period, the notion of a social contract, the Swedish contemplated linking future wage regulation to a gradual but massive extension of union involvement in the ownership of firms (the Meidner Plan).[25] And while the French unions sought a political transformation of the system through partisan change involving a massive extension of the state's economic role through nationalization, the Italian unions explicitly rejected this formula. The point here is not the detail of these differences but rather to stress that they existed and to suggest that in many cases they merely represented the continuation, under new conditions, of longstanding orientations in each of the union movements. Each union movement responded to the altered political-economic environment of the 1970s in some generally similar ways, but each did so in its own fashion.

The pattern of development of the French and Italian unions which we have detailed is exemplary of these developments and thus of the inadequacy of the liberal optimist approach. The two union movements were in many ways more similar in the 1950s than they were at the end of the 1970s. Then they shared structural characteristics and the individual confederations in each country had programmatic goals which were similar (in the case of the Communist confederations, very similar) to those of their counterparts in the other country. Today the differences are far greater. Instead of convergence, there has been divergence, a trend captured in their maximalist and interventionist strategic approaches to the crisis.

Here, an objection might be raised. It could be argued that the Italian and French movements, because of their historical characteristics, might be the last to conform to the pattern foreseen by the liberal optimists. The strong Communist union presence would promote a 'lag' of development. At some point, an argument based on the notion that it is simply a lag which explains the failure of a phenomenon to conform to expectations is incontrovertible but of no utility. Historicism and the notion of lag are, in fact, often found together. Furthermore, at least three points would suggest that a recourse to 'lag' is inadequate. First, at least in the case of the Italian movement, there have been significant changes. The Italian unions are not simply clinging to ideological, policy, and strategic positions which they have always held—although there is some continuity of very general principles—but have developed decidedly new proposals and strategic postures in the 1970s. Second, again in the case of the Italian movement, there are significant similarities between some of the orientations adopted in the last decade and those of other union movements in Europe. The Italians are today more like their European confrères (other than the French) than they were twenty years ago; these fellow unions, however, have not moved in the directions the liberal optimists would have led us to expect. Third, both the Italian and French movements are divided. If there were a logic which made non-Communist postures more effective as a basis for trade unionism, one would expect that the non-Communist unions would have adopted them and that the Communist unions, as a result, would have been forced to adapt or would have lost significant ground within the respective national union movements. This has not occurred, although there is some greater balance between the Communist and non-Communist union strengths than there was twenty years ago. Taken together then, these points suggest that simply the presence of Communist unions cannot explain the failure of the French and

Italian movements to conform to the expected pattern. And, when these arguments are combined with those made earlier about European union development more generally, they suggest that the causal factors and more general explanatory approach utilized by the liberal optimists cannot lead to an understanding of union behavior. An alternative is needed.

An Actor-Centered Alternative

It seems evident that the economistic and historicist postulates of liberal optimist theory are misleading and must be abandoned. As John Goldthorpe has pointed out, such postulates lead to perspectives on development and change which provide '. . . no explicit analysis of *why*—via what causal mechanisms—historical events follow the expected pattern'.[26] Thus not only does the functionalist 'logic of industrialism' line of argument fail to supply adequate predictions of events—as we have seen—it also fails to provide an adequate explanation of why events actually occur. Concluding that such a functionalist logic is less than useful is not enough, however. We are still left with an historical puzzle to solve. How can we account for the divergent paths of French and Italian unionism as represented in their very different responses to crisis in the 1970s? We are also left with a broader theoretical task: to attempt, in solving this puzzle, to develop an approach to the understanding of union strategic behavior which can be applied beyond these specific cases.

Our major explanatory suggestion is a simple one. If context-centric visions of the liberal optimist type do not work, perhaps a more actor-centric approach will prove more appropriate. Indeed, it is likely to be more fruitful to understand change and continuity in union behavior by starting with unions, rather than by assuming that unions are historical objects created and battered about by exogenous forces. Thus, at any given point in time, unions can be seen as agents with their own ideas, needs, and purposes, and not just as passive institutional entities responding to contextual forces which, in combination, determine how the unions will (and must) behave. Moreover, the ideas, needs, and purposes of unions cannot be reduced to simple notions such as the 'organizational self-maintenance' so dear to organization theorists. If union movements do resemble one another in some very general ways, their specific combination of outlook on the world, purposes, and interests springs from a long and complex historical process in which what is common to all unions plays only a part. Furthermore, this historically produced amalgam profoundly marks how unions can be expected to respond to change in their environments at any point in time or in any period. Thus, in our view, unions ought to be considered as strategic actors—with their own ways of perceiving the world and notions of what needs to be achieved and what is worth achieving —which analyze and respond to changes in the world around them through the prisms of such systems of perception and purpose. Our starting point is unions, understood as institutions with values and interests which they seek to promote. Seen in this light, unions have a degree of autonomy in their own internal, variable processes for maintaining and building support and making decisions. Outcomes ought, therefore, to be seen as a function of the interaction of these institutionalized values and interests—which will vary historically from one union (and union movement) to another—with relevant changes in the union's environment.[27] And the outcome at any particular historical conjuncture will have its bearing on the outcome at a subsequent conjuncture when environmental challenges or internal strains become sufficient to promote pressures for adaptation of the union outlook, strategy, policy, and organization.

Such a statement of general perspective, however, cannot alone suffice. We need to develop an approach to union strategy and behavior which, informed by this perspective, places unions systematically in the larger context in which they operate and identifies the character of the relationships between that context and the unions themselves understood as agents with historically and institutionally defined interests and goals. This should allow us to escape two polar types of analysis, both of which we reject: that unions are merely objects, or that they are purely subjects. Instead, what we will develop is an approach which understands unions as agents operating in contexts which, precisely because these contexts are important to the institutional interests and goals of the unions, constrain but do not determine the policies which the unions undertake to carry out. This approach, which draws heavily on theories of exchange and of organization, some of which have already been applied to the analysis of union behavior by others, is sketched in the next few pages. We do not here seek to develop and amplify upon all its theoretical and analytical implications. Rather, we simply wish to present its general outlines sufficiently to allow us then to apply it to the specific cases with which we are presently concerned.

We view unions as institutions which can best be understood as systems of mediation and regularized exchange. At the most basic level, these institutions mediate the relationship between individuals who need to sell their labor on a market and those who might purchase it. Performance of labor market mediation, or the attempt at it, is the common characteristic and minimal definition of all institutions which we consider unions. Unions can, and to differing extents most unions in the advanced industrial democracies do, however, also mediate relations in the political arena—between workers and the state and political parties. The strength or power of the unions resides in their ability to play these mediational roles in the market and in politics as effectively as possible. Furthermore, the two roles are generally complementary and reinforcing: union strength in the market arena augments strength in politics, and *vice versa*. The maintenance and improvement of mediational capacity in the two arenas, over time, therefore constitutes the primary institutional interest for unions and their leaders.[28]

The mediational capacity of unions is a function of two basic sets of relationships. On the one hand, it is a function of the extent to which the sellers of labor (workers) are willing to allow the union to represent and mediate for them in relations with the purchasers of labor (employers) and/or the state and other political actors, especially political parties; that is, the extent to which the workers will follow the lead and accept the bargains struck by the union. The strength and scope of this representational commitment can obviously vary cross-nationally, over time and according to a variety of circumstances. On the other hand, unions' mediational capacity will also be a function of the extent to which the employers or relevant political actors need, or find it useful, to accept the unions as mediators to achieve what they want from the workers.

In the light of these considerations, several more specific union interests contributing to overall mediational capacity can be identified. In the market arena, unions have an interest in acting for as many as possible of the workers who might be employed in the economic sector or sectors they wish to organize,[29] and in assuring that the workers have the strongest possible commitment to following the lead of the union. In the political arena, they have an interest in getting the workers to follow the unions' political guidance, thereby increasing the extent to which the union, rather than the individual worker, is the relevant unit from whom political actors seek support. Finally, in both arenas the unions have an interest in doing what they can to assure that they have the greatest possible ability to do damage or contribute to the interests of their market and political bargaining counterparts. Put succinctly, the mediational capacity of unions increases the more they achieve a monopoly of control over economic and political resources held by individual workers (the value of these resources, especially in the market arena, increases to the extent that they are collectively organized), and the more these resources are desired by employers, the state and political parties.

As this suggests, to function effectively the union must either be able to coerce support (or have some other institution, like the state, do such coercion) or be able to gain consent. In almost all unions in the advanced industrial democracies some degree of coercion is present, rules requiring the closed shop being one of the more obvious examples. The role of consent, however, is generally of great importance in most countries, especially in continental Europe.[30] To the extent that consent is important, it is the postulate of our approach that such consent is garnered through exchange between the union and its supporters and that, furthermore, the resources used by the union in these exchanges with supporters are primarily gained through a second set of exchanges between the union and other actors in its environment.

Each of these two sets of exchange relationships occurs on somewhat different terms. In the former, the union offers the supporter or potential supporter something which he desires in exchange for his consent—that is, his willingness to allow the union to act on his behalf in relation with other relevant actors—to follow the instructions of the union about what actions on the part of supporters are necessary in order best to pursue those relations and to contribute to the ability of the union to play this mediational role. In its relationship with other actors, the union offers the consent of its followers and its resultant ability to get them to behave as it deems appropriate in exchange for those things which, in turn, enable the union to gain, maintain or make more intense its base of support. In addition, some of the resources which the union can use in garnering support may be generated by the structure of the relationship with actors in the environment rather than by direct exchanges with them.

The medium of exchange between unions and their supporters—that which allows them to accumulate resources for action in their environment —is incentives, values which the union offers in exchange for support.[31] From an analytical standpoint, four types of incentives: material, purposive, identity, and sociability, can be identified:[32]

Material—'tangible rewards: money, or things and services readily priced in monetary terms.'[33] In the case of unions, this includes gains for workers in terms of hours of work, working conditions and the like;
Purposive—suprapersonal goals which are constituted as the ends for which the organization is maintained, are pursued through the 'rules of the game' and are open to compromise in order to increase the likelihood of at least partial success in the attempt to achieve them;
Identity—the privilege to identify and be identified with the set of principles and rights as expressed by and embodied in an organizational entity which claims to seek to promote those principles and rights over the resistance of other organizations and social and political forces;
Sociability—'intangible rewards created by the act of associating' and the interpersonal social bonds which come from feeling part of a relatively small and defined group.

All existing organizations employ some mix of incentives in generating resources from supporters. The particular mix or incentive system, however, will be of considerable importance for how any specific organization can be expected to behave and to react to changes in its environment.[34] In the case of trade unions, sociability incentives often play a significant role, especially in the early stages of union formation and in periods of high mobilization. This role, however, is one of solidifying the support generated by other incentives, and is only rarely a direct or intended outcome of union strategic behavior. Little of the following discussion will be devoted to them. Material incentives will always play a fundamental role in trade unions, given their functions in the society and the economy. This, however, will tend to be more the case once the unions are established and mediate the relationship between workers and employers. Furthermore, it must be underlined, and our following discussion will stress, that unions cannot be treated solely as institutions which exchange material incentives for support; both purposive and identity incentives can, and often do, assume an important role in the incentive structure of unions. With this said, some further brief discussion of the character of these incentives in trade unions is called for.

Material incentives are the direct or indirect monetary gains which the union supporter receives due to the action of the union. Increments in wages and improvements in hours and working conditions viewed by the supporter to result from the mediational role played by the union are the most obvious examples. The supply of material incentives available to the union will, in the most immediate sense, be a function of the success which the union has in prosecuting bargaining with employers and the state and thus delivering material benefits to workers. Purposive incentives are those which derive from the general policy goals which the union promotes in its relationships with employers and other environmental actors. These policy goals, while they may (but need not) be of direct benefit to the supporters of the union, generally have some wider constituency. They inspire support on the part of the worker because he wishes to see these policies undertaken and deems the union at least one of the possible agents to promote this. As has often been noted, purposive incentives are not, from the standpoint of 'rationalist' *homoeconomicus* assumptions about individuals, likely to induce support, for they create the possibility of 'free riding.' Nonetheless, especially in combination with other incentives, they may be a significant component in the incentive system of unions.

Identity incentives are inducements based on the supporter's ability, through his association with and commitment to the union, to identify with and receive gratification from a system of values for which the union claims to stand or with which it is associated. This system of values may be a broad *Weltanschauung*, as in the case of a revolutionary union. It can also be, however, a system of more limited scope down to the simple belief that unions are important institutions deserving recognition, as when a worker proudly declares himself a 'union man.' It should be noted, with regard to identity incentives, that their supply for the organization tends to increase when the prized values are under attack and, more generally, when there is more intense disagreement in the society about the worth and legitimacy of the values which the union is promoting, although not only then. Thus, for identity incentives, as contrasted to the other two types, there may be an inverse relationship between the supply of incentives which the union enjoys and the success or probability of success in actually achieving the relevant values. In many cases, open hostility on the part of actors in the environment to the values on which identity incentives are based increases the ability of the union to build support with those incentives. This has obvious implications for how a union wishing to rely on such incentives might choose to behave. It should also be noted that to the extent that a union can use purposive, and especially identity, incentives to attract support, its ability to deliver material benefits becomes less decisive in determining its level of support.

The relationships between the union and other actors in its environment are critical to the ability of the union to develop a structure of incentives capable of generating resources. The types of incentives which, ideally, the union seeks to use can be understood through a close examination of the goals, strategy, policies, and actions of the union. It is through these elements of its behavior that the union communicates its preferred structure of incentives. How successful these will actually be in generating support and thus what the effective (as contrasted to the ideal) incentive structure of the union is, however, will depend heavily on the character of the relationships which the union develops with environmental actors. Furthermore, these relationships, and how the union leadership anticipates their development, will affect the types of incentives which the union seeks to rely on and thus its behavior. It is, therefore, important to examine the kinds of relationships which the union can develop with the three other most important actors: employers, in the market arena, and the state and political parties, in the political arena.[35]

In dealing with employers, the union offers a degree of mediated social control of workers—or the promise thereof—in the form of regularity and therefore predictability of performance of work tasks. This potential of control can be exchanged for three types of incentives. The 'normal' exchange (as understood by liberal optimist theory and the literature in industrial relations more generally) is for material incentives in the form of wages, job security, and other benefits perceived by workers to have been gained for them from employers by the union. It is important to note, however, that the union's dealings with employers in the market arena can also generate identity and purposive incentives. Identity incentives have been the outcome of conflicts and bargaining with employers over issues of recognition and, more generally, over the delimitation of boundaries of control. These issues, whatever their long-range impact on material exchanges, are in the most immediate sense about identity: about what the difference is between 'us' (the union and its supporters) and 'them' (the employers), and what specific content, defined in terms of competencies and areas of legitimate control and prerogative, each of these identities is associated with. The issue in such conflicts is not the specific policies to be enacted, although they are undoubtedly also important, but the very right to set or have a recognized role in the making of policy. It is necessary to note, however, that once any specific area of competency is recognized, it loses some of its importance as a source of identity incentives: there is a shift from rights to substance, from whom to what.

Purposive incentives also can be generated by relations between union and employer. This is the case to the extent that the union seeks to use its bargaining power with employers to promote goals which extend beyond the immediate confines of the firm or sector or whatever the bargaining level and the material welfare of the workers in the relevant unit. Examples might include things like getting the employer(s) to make certain kinds of investments in regions of the country where there are high levels of unemployment or to contribute to community services. As should be evident these types of issues, to the degree that they seek to force the employers to do things which they have not traditionally done, will often serve to develop identity incentives as well. This raises a more general point about relations in the market arena which needs underlining. No struggle to arrive at a bargain in the market arena produces uniquely material incentives, for even the narrowest of contractual negotiations has some reinforcing effect on union identity. At a minimum, it reaffirms the right of the union to act as agent for the workers; every negotiation is a recognition of the union as mediator of relations between workers and employers. To the extent that the bargain is difficult to attain and the hostility between the parties to the bargain high, it will tend to generate more identity incentives. It is also the case, however, that the degree to which these identity incentives serve to maintain, extend or intensify the support for the union will depend on the degree to which union supporters are loyal to the union and willing to accept its mediational role for reasons of identity and not just material gain. It should also be noted, as this discussion suggests, that no union demand or policy and no specific interaction between the union and other actors need necessarily generate only one kind of incentive.

In its relationship with the state, the union offers the general political-economic consent of its supporters, understood in terms of their willingness to grant legitimacy to the regime *and* to refrain from actions which would threaten to undermine its overall political-economic performance.[36] Again, the union is offering mediated social control of its supporters; and again the union can derive several types of incentives through the relationship. The specific policies necessary to do so, however, will differ from those employed in the market arena. The relationship with the state can produce material incentives in the form of policies which the unions are able to take at least partial credit for getting the state to adopt and which improve the material condition of the union's supporters, either directly (by state policies which transfer money, greater job security, etc. to them) or indirectly (by policies, or the anticipation of them, which make employers less resistant to union demands). Two factors, however, potentially mitigate the effectiveness of this type of relationship as a source of material incentives. First, under most circumstances in a pluralist democratic system, the ability of the union to present itself as *the* agent which caused the government to introduce the policy is significantly limited by the complex political processes which lead to governmental action. The less direct the bargaining process between union and state institutions, the less visible the union's role in winning the gains and/or in distributing or implementing them, the less willing the government and state bureaucracy to acknowledge the role played by the unions, the less able the union is to take credit with its supporters for the improvements in their material condition.[37] Second, except under peculiar conditions, the programs which are implemented do not deliver benefits to union supporters alone, but to nonunionists as well. As a result, the 'logic of collective action'[38] suggests that winning concessions on programs from government will bring only limited returns of union support, at least from those who are willing to support the union *only* for the material benefits they thereby derive.

The union can also derive identity incentives from its relationship with the state. The most direct of these are developed through the struggles with the state for recognition and about the definition of the legal standing and competencies of the union in the labor and political arenas. Historically, however, it is clear that the relationship between the unions and the state has included as well a number of broader issues which have also provided the unions with identity incentives. The advocacy by unions of values of general economic, social, and political transformation and the presentation of conflicts with the state as struggles over such values are examples. More recently, unions have also increasingly come to include issues concerning the role and control of unions in the process of governmental economic policy-making. This has been part of the 'blurring' of the lines between public and private in the advanced industrial democracies which many have commented on. These questions of control, while they are often not presented in grand ideological but rather in narrower 'pragmatic' terms, nonetheless can represent sources of identity incentives, for they often involve deep conflicts over the prerogatives, rights and standing of unions, as contrasted to other actors, in the political/economic process.

The identity incentives which the union derives from such issues will be a function both of the process by which they are fought for and gained and by the result, of the difficulty and degree of mobilization necessary to arrive at a bargain and the actual content of the bargain. The point here is much like that made by Lipset and Rokkan when they argue that the height of the 'thresholds' which new entrants into the political process in the late nineteenth century had to overcome is associated with the degree of enduring loyalties to particular organizations of these new entrants which ensued.[39] As should also be evident, however, the degree to which the identity incentives derived actually help the union to build support will depend as well on the extent to which potential supporters of the union are attracted by such incentives.

The relationship between unions and the state is more likely to produce purposive incentives than is that between unions and employers. It is, after all, the state which in the advanced industrial democracies primarily bears responsibility for the implementation of the kinds of reforms which are embodied in the relevant union proposals. For these proposals to be an effective source of purposive incentives, however, the union must be able credibly to argue that it can, or might soon be able, to get government to implement the relevant programs. Furthermore, it should also be recognized that the efficacy of purposive incentives as inducements to support lies solely in the commitment of supporters and potential supporters to the programs regardless of the direct benefit which they may derive therefrom. To the extent the latter is important to them, the problems associated with the logic of collective action will again be relevant.

The third major exchange relationship in any union's quest to deliver incentives to and generate resources from supporters is with political parties. Here the union may offer votes (i.e., its ability to get its supporters to support a particular political party) and activism to the party. It can also offer to behave in a manner which will improve the party's ability to develop broader political support (for example, to make wage demands deemed consistent with the maintenance of business confidence) and/or to refrain from behavior which would damage that ability (for example, to agree not to strike). In exchange, it may receive material, identity or purposive incentives. The character of possible exchanges with regard to material and purposive incentives should be evident. The association of the union with a party or parties which, in turn, are able to get government to undertake programs which either materially benefit the union's supporters or their broader goals will serve to build the pool of material or purposive incentives on which the union can draw. Again, of course, it is important that the union be able credibly to take significant credit for the parties' actions. It should also be underlined that the ability to garner such incentives does not necessarily entail the establishment of a close and seemingly permanent linkage to any particular party. The principle of 'rewarding one's friends and punishing one's enemies' is entirely compatible with a union's efforts to develop material and purposive incentives through its relationships with political parties.

The party–union relationship can also be a source of identity incentives, the result of a relatively close identification of the union with a party which itself is characterized by a distinct ideology or outlook. Such identification is generally of long historical duration and is indicated by a number of shared symbols, explicit enunciations of common principles, overlapping leaderships, and signs of mutual solidarity. The historical relationship between unions and parties, within the class and denominational movements which developed around the struggles for the expansion of the suffrage and democracy more generally at the turn of the twentieth century, exemplify this. It should be noted that the degree to which the union can derive identity incentives from its relationship with a party will in part depend on the ideological fervor of the party itself and on the extent to which the context in which both union and party operate is such that it underlines, rather than blurs, the identity which the two share. Put in its simplest terms, to the extent that the party is embattled because of its identity, the flow of incentives will be greater.[40]

The relationships between union and party can extend beyond those indicated to include as well direct transfers of resources from the latter to the former. There are a number of ways such transfers might occur. The ones of greatest interest to our present concerns are the transfer of militance and of leadership. On the one hand, the party, itself a repository of militance, may direct its militants to work for the union; or it may simply make clear that those committed to the party should extend that commitment and related activism to the union. In this sense, the union 'borrows' support and militance from the party and the primary reference point for these activists remains the party and not the union.[41] On the other hand, the party may directly provide leadership for the union, directing some of its own cadres to fill union positions. Again, such union leaders nonetheless remain primarily loyal to the party. In both these cases, the party makes these loans because it deems the union—its strength, its strategy, policies, behaviour, and its reliability—important to the success of its own strategy. It is also the case that such loans make the union much more directly dependent on and subservient to the party.

The preceding pages have sketched an alternative perspective on trade unions (see Figure 3.1) intended to help us to explain their strategic behavior. Our perspective represents a marked departure from that implicit in the liberal optimist theories. There is no theoretical reason, we maintain, to assume that unions will necessarily restrict their strategic focus to the market arena. The incentives necessary to maintain and extend and/or intensify resources can be captured through action in either the political or market arenas. There is also no theoretical reason to assume that unions will necessarily strive to maximize their reliance on market arena material incentives and minimize their reliance on purposive and identity incentives. Material incentives will likely always play a major role in any established union's incentive system, but other types can be of importance as well, and the union may seek to make them so because of its broader strategic outlook and goals without fearing it will necessarily lose support thereby.

It is also clear that there is no theoretical reason to assume that any specific union will pursue a strategy and policies similar to those of any other union. In any national situation, the types of incentives on which any particular union desires, and is able, to draw, and the degree to which these incentives can be generated through relationships with actors in the political and market arenas will vary. The strategy of any union, we postulate, will reflect these different availabilities as union leaders—with their own ideas, maps of the social world and goals—attempt to maintain,

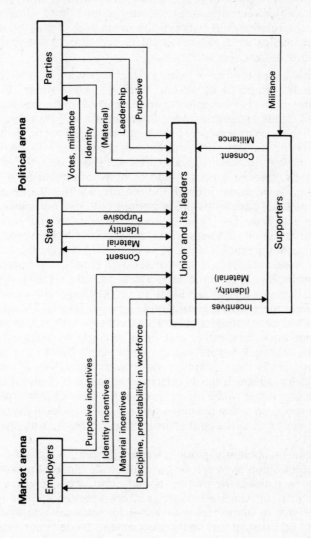

Figure 3.1 The strategic behavior of trade unions

extend or intensify institutional resources and thus their mediational capacity, given the contextual conditions in which they operate and the kinds of incentives to which supporters and potential supporters might be responsive. Thus, union strategy and policies can be understood as a reflection of the analysis by union leaders of the costs and benefits of different courses of action in light of the union's point of departure, of the particular conditions in which the union must operate, of how those conditions are reflected in the relationships between the union and various actors in its environment, and of what policies would be necessary to derive different types of incentives from those relationships.

This general understanding of union strategic behavior and policy needs, however, to be tempered by several further considerations. First, we assume autonomous decision-making on the part of union leaders, but as we have seen, union leadership and/or militance is not always autonomous but can be directly conditioned by linkages to a political party. In this case, strategic behavior may deviate from what would be expected—on the basis of assumptions that the leaders seek to maintain and, if possible, extend or intensify purely unionist support—due to party command or a priority accorded to party interests. Second, the context in which the union operates in any national case limits union options but does not wholly determine union behavior. The *same* contextual conditions can permit and suggest different union strategies. Here, the ideology of the union leadership—its sense of the union's identity, its map of the world, its goals—and the leaders' sense of what its supporters and potential supporters will respond to will play an essential role. Third, like almost all institutional leaderships, those of unions are likely to be relatively risk aversive and satisficing. Thus there will be considerable strategic inertia. Union leaders will tend to pursue existing strategies and policies rather than innovate unless existing lines seem rather certain to be costly or changes likely to pay off. This tendency toward inertia is not solely due to the fact that organizational leaderships generally reproduce themselves ideologically and strategically (although this is certainly the case). It is also due to the fact that the supporters of the union tend, on the basis of past experience, to develop expectations that the union strategy and policies of the past, and the flow of the types of incentives which these brought with them, will continue.[42]

These remarks obviously point towards the central question of this essay. Different union movements, given the wide range of possible variations between national environments and experiences, reach a certain point of maturity in which a balance is struck between specific types of incentives offered to supporters in exchange for resources which allow the movement to act satisfactorily on its environment. Under what conditions, then, are the incentive and resource systems of such union movements liable to change? In general, change becomes probable when the real or potential support/resource costs of strategic continuity are sufficient to overcome the inertial tendencies discussed earlier. Any exhaustive discussion of factors promoting such change and its conceivable vectors would be impossibly long, however. In any case, it should be clear from what we have already said that we do not believe it feasible to make rigorous, general 'if . . . then' statements about union choices. In the actor-centric focus which we propose, actual unions—which, of course, face the present with a preexisting system of incentives and resource generation—may confront challenges from a number of different environmental or internal sources, separately or combined, and may respond to them in a number of different ways. They may choose to stress the production of new resources by intensifying any of the types of incentives which we have defined, singly or in combination, and they may choose to do so by changed emphases on the market and political arenas. Thus, at best we might provide a long catalog of statements of the 'if X, then, *most likely* Y, but *possibly* Y + Z *or* Y + Z + Q' variety. In other words, we believe that it is only possible to produce statements which attempt, for a given union movement facing certain kinds of challenges, to specify the broad range of likely options from which the union movement might choose. Beyond this we feel unsafe in venturing. If we insist upon viewing unions as actors in a structured but evolving environment, we must grant them a degree of autonomy as choice-makers. This means that the actual outlooks—ideas, conscious and unconscious goals, maps of the social world—of leaders become critical. They constitute the relatively historically specific and only partially predictable filter between environmental challenges specifying the need for change and indicating the broad range of plausible options for change and subsequent union responses.

What we have in mind will become clearer as we turn to a comparative reexamination of the French and Italian cases using our actor-centric focus. Before we do so, however, we must introduce a further element of analytical complexity, particularly, but not only, relevant to cases, like the French and Italian, where multiple unionism exists. At the core of our understanding of unions and their interests is the maintenance of mediational capacity, and thus the ability to attain goals. Moreover, it is the union leadership which is charged with the task of pursuing these interests and goals and initiating response to change. What this suggests is that two further factors influencing the strategic or policy change will be, first, the degree to which the union, as an organization, enjoys a 'monopoly of representation' and, second, the degree to which the leadership of the union is subject to challenge from others within the organization promoting an alternative strategy or policy which, they claim, could better advance the union's interest.

The 'monopoly of representation' of the union may have both formal and informal aspects. In formal terms, it will be a function of the extent to which workers can work without belonging to any specific union. The 'closed shop' is a classic case of formal monopoly, and multiple unionism —as in the French and Italian cases where workers doing a job can, in many sectors, belong to one of three unions or no union at all—is a clear example of the absence of monopoly. A related formal aspect is the degree to which 'exit' from a union and entrance into another is either costly or procedurally difficult. Both these aspects, built into the formal structure of trade unionism in any specific country and into the rules governing membership and the like, will affect the formal degree of potential competition among the unions for support. Where competitive potential is higher, one would expect the unions to be more sensitive to changes which might affect support.

These formal aspects of 'monopoly' and competition are supplemented by informal ones as well. The most important of these is the extent to which other organizations (unions and others) can offer the same incentives offered by the union. This might appear simply another way of stating the preceding point, but this is not the case. What this latter formulation stresses is that since, as we have seen, unions can offer different types of incentives, it is not always the case that even two unions in the same sector base their support on the same types of incentives or incentives built on the same content. A Catholic and a Communist union, for instance, both operating in a specific industry, may base an important part of their support on the identity (and not just material) incentives which they offer. To the extent this is the case, these unions are not really competitive, at least for those of their supporters who are committed because of the different identity incentives. To leave one's traditional union, much less to join the 'opposition's union,' is likely, from an individual's perspective, to involve considerable psychic costs even when there might be material advantages to doing so. In this sense, when unions rely heavily on identity incentives, there is likely, even in cases of multiple unionism, to be considerable segmentation of the 'market' of potential supporters and thus the probability of union change in strategy or policy to environmental change can be expected to be less or to require a greater challenge.

The degree to which the leadership of the union is susceptible to challenge is also likely to affect responsiveness of union strategy and policy to the change conditions we have outlined. All union leaderships have, we argue, an interest in maintaining and, when possible and attractive, strengthening the mediational capacity of their organizations. Yet, the threshold at which the leadership is likely to respond to dangers or opportunities will vary from union to union. If the possibilities for challenges by insurgent leaders are greater, one would expect this threshold to be lower than when the leadership of the union can control, coopt or suppress challengers. It is worth noting that to the degree that the leadership of the union is linked to or determined by a sympathetic political party, the prospect that challenges, by themselves, will be sufficient to induce change in strategy or policy will be further reduced.

We turn now to the application of the approach we have outlined to the analysis of the French and Italian cases and thus to a 'test' of its utility. In doing so, we are largely following what Przeworski and Teune have designated the 'most similar systems' design for research. Our starting point is the mid-1950s when, we would argue, the French and Italian systems, at least with regard to those variables important to our concerns, were quite similar, as were the features of the union movements and their relationships to those systems. By the mid-1970s, however, the two union movements had developed the sharply divergent approaches to the crisis —maximalism in France and interventionism in Italy—which we have described. We turn now to explaining why and how this came to be the case.

Part 3

Critical Junctures, Incentives, and Strategic Change

The process of strategic development which led the French and Italian labor movements from similar Cold War postures to dramatically different responses to the political-economic challenges of the 1970s was cumulative, marked by a series of phases.[43] Both movements periodically confronted critical conjunctures when changes in their political and economic environments threatened the effectiveness of their incentive systems and/or offered opportunities to maintain and extend support on new bases. In response the various unions were obliged to reevaluate their theoretical perspectives, strategies, policies, and organizational practices. As one examines this process, what is striking is the degree to which the challenges faced by the unions in the different countries often occurred at about the same time and often had some of the same general characteristics. The relatively integrated character of the postwar advanced industrial political economies is clearly reflected in this fact.[44]

If, however, there were such similar critical junctures in the French and Italian (and other) national settings, the outcomes in the two cases were different. Responding to the challenges through the prisms created by their own histories, partisan linkages, strategic perspectives, existing organizational patterns, and resultant sense of priorities, the unions revised their analyses, strategies, and behaviors in markedly different ways. In turn, the institutionalization of change created new points of departure from which each individual union and national union movement confronted the subsequent conjuncture. In time these crescive revisions led to ever-larger divergences in analysis, strategy, and policy. By the crisis of the 1970s, these divergent paths of development had set the stage for the responses which we have earlier discussed. Thus, the 'maximalism' of the French and 'interventionism' of the Italians in recent years must be seen as the outcomes of successive phases of adaptation to challenging conjunctures. What by the mid-1970s looked like major differences had their roots in much smaller shifts in strategy and policy in earlier years, shifts which, almost unnoticeably at the time, began in the mid-1950s.

The Mid-Fifties

The first critical conjuncture developed in the mid-1950s. It was bracketed at one end by the death of Stalin and consolidation of the postwar political-economic settlements and at the other by the international and domestic aftermath of the traumatic events in the world Communist movement of

1956. In this period, changes in the international political and economic environment, in the domestic economic structures and in the contours of domestic politics made it imperative for both the French and Italian labor movements to reconsider important aspects of the incentive and resource generating systems and strategic postures which they had forged in the Resistance–Liberation and Cold War years. These had functioned relatively well,[45] especially for the predominant Communist-led unions in both countries, during the most intense period of the Cold War. They had also been remarkably similar in France and Italy. Now their continuation threatened to become a source of weakness.

Stalin's death in 1953 led to a retreat from the extreme international polarization of the deepest Cold War years. Both Stalin's successors and the Eisenhower administration began gradually to move away from extreme confrontation. The notion of peaceful coexistence, openly expressed by Kruschev in 1956, began to take hold among Communists and non-Communists alike. At the same time, the Soviet Union's international reputation began to suffer sharp reverses even among the most loyal Communists, and this while the Soviet Communist party was acknowledging the possibility of greater differentiation in the strategies of national Communist parties.

The effects of such changes on French and Italian domestic politics were significant. International polarization and confrontation had contributed to the isolation of those parts of the political left in both countries which had not accepted anti-Communism. This, in turn, had contributed to the ineffectiveness of the forces of the Center and Center-Left and had assured the predominance of those opposed to social reform and willing to back wholeheartedly employer authority in the workplace. Even the partial relaxation of the political climate began to change this. New, more 'populist' leaderships assumed control in some political parties. New, more reform-minded political coalitions became feasible. New discussions of and proposals for economic and social reform were initiated. The Communist parties and their social allies were, of course, to remain excluded. Efforts were undertaken, however, to draw the non-Communist Left into—or at least toward—the political mainstream; and several currents of this Left were responsive to such overtures.

Changes in the economic arena also signaled the presence of new opportunities for altered political and policy alignments. The years from Liberation to the early 1950s had been a period of major renegotiation of political, economic, and social arrangements in each country, years in which the foundation stones of the 'postwar settlements' were being laid. Each major political and social actor in these negotiations had had specific strategies and goals, and all saw the process as open-ended. The shape of the outcomes which would result had, in fact, been at first quite uncertain. By the early 1950s, however, these outcomes, if not their potential for success, had become clear. In both France and Italy a mixed economy, whose motor was private sector capital accumulation functioning in a progressively more open and integrated international market regulated by US hegemony, looked permanent. Furthermore, there was spreading awareness that private consumption would be an important component of the growth process. In this broad context, the first signs of economic takeoff were beginning to appear. Substantial growth, based initially on exports, took hold. Productivity shot up. Technological innovation moved forward. Private sector profits expanded, especially among those firms which were best adapting to the change in markets and technology. Moreover, growing optimism about economic progress provided reform-inclined politicians and social and economic actors the rationale to consider new policy departures. Even employers were in some cases caught up in the spirit of change, willing to try to pay higher wages—usually without effective union intermediation—in order to stabilize their work forces, improve productivity, and more generally contribute to a favorable economic atmosphere.

To understand the impact of these changes on the unions and their relationships to their supporters and potential supporters, a brief look at these relationships in the preceding years is necessary. The situation of polarization, confrontation, and conservatism had led all unions to rely heavily on identity incentives rooted in political ideology and association with the national and international political forces which were the bearers of those ideologies. Communists in the unions had stressed those identity incentives—linkages to their respective national Communist parties, to the international Communist movement, to the USSR, to Stalin, to socialism and revolutionary rupture, and denunciation of the catastrophe of capitalism—which could help them retain their support in the face of relentless attack. They had little choice but to stress these, both because of the nature of the general context in which they moved and because of their close relationship to the Communist parties.[46] Non-Communist unions had also entered into this logic. They had little capacity to win gains through market action because of the overall weakness of the unions. Their championing of reforms had little credibility despite the Parliamentary presence of some of their leaders. Thus, they too had to rely heavily on identity incentives —anti-Communism, Catholicism, Christian social values, a non-Marxist vision of society and a different 'type' of unionism—to retain their existing backing and to try to draw support away from the Communist-dominated unions. As long as the ideologically polarized and strongly conservative climate of the intense Cold War prevailed, every component of society was drawn into the ideological game, whatever its desire (noteworthy on the part of some non-Communist unions) to use other types of appeals. Once this atmosphere began to relax, however, a new situation confronted the unions. Those who persisted in the ideological game faced increased difficulties in making their identity incentives effective. Those willing and able to break—even in part—with intense ideological politics were offered new opportunities.

The reasons for the growing difficulties which the unions encountered in relying on identity incentives embodied in ideological and political appeals are evident. Such incentives had been particularly potent when part and parcel of open, continual, and across-the-board confrontation in which both sides interpreted all questions as matters of principle. The decline of international and domestic polarization tended, however, to sap the appeal of such incentives, whether they be rooted in religion, class, or simple anticommunism. This problem was particularly acute for the Communist-dominated unions, for they were faced with a sudden, unanticipated 'devaluation' of the key symbols to which their identity incentives had been tied: the Soviet Union, the persona of Stalin, the notion of the USSR as the bulwark of a besieged socialism. The key event in this regard was, of course, the XXth Congress of the CPSU in 1956 and Krushchev's 'secret speech'; but the doctrine of 'peaceful coexistence' also announced at that time contributed to the change. The Communist-dominated unions found themselves faced with a crisis of the identities around which they had rallied their supporters for a decade.

The events of the period also afforded the unions, including the Communist-dominated ones, opportunities for strategic departures linked to the building of different structures of incentives. The decline of polarization itself created chances for seeking alliances and pursuing goals which had been unrealistic when the lines between camps at all levels of social and political relations had been rigidly drawn. In addition, the changing economic and labor market conditions made available, at least potentially, a pool of purposive and/or material incentives on which the unions might draw through effective action in the market or political arenas. Some employers were, in fact, already offering workers higher wages, while some political parties and leaders were openly calling for significant initiatives of economic and social reform. The unions might gain from adjusting their strategies to exploit more effectively the expanding economic pie through action in the market and political arenas; and they might well lose strength if they failed to do so.

Here a distinction between the Communist-dominated and other unions ought to be drawn. For the latter, there was little reason not to embark on a new strategic course which would balance the earlier emphasis on ideological identity with policies which would appeal to the material and/or purposive interests of supporters. To some extent, the groundwork for such a departure had already been laid in these unions' call for a different type of unionism from that of the Communists. No wholesale abandonment of identity incentives and the policies tied to them was likely, however: existing expectations of supporters, uncertainties about the prospects of effectively generating resources on new bases and the political, ideological, and practical linkages between these unions, and their leaders, and the anti-Communist and denominational parties prompted prudence.

Major change was even less likely for the Communist-dominated unions. They remained pariahs within the union movement, and therefore had much less hope of winning market or political arena gains for their supporters, at least in the short run. To abandon the identity incentives on which they had relied would, despite the growing difficulties they were having in maintaining and mobilizing support with such incentives, be a highly risky course to undertake. The other unions were still unlikely to cooperate with them (even if such cooperation were sought) and without cooperation effective market action was improbable. The non-Communist unions might nonetheless—because of employer strategies intended to weaken the CGT and CGIL—make some gains, but certainly not the Communist-dominated unions which, instead, would have to denounce such gains as the product of 'yellow' unionism. Furthermore, these unions, much more than the others, were closely tied to political parties which saw the unions as instruments of *their* strategies, strategies which, of necessity, had to be built around the long-term prospect of continued political exclusion, and thus on a continued major role for the kind of rhetoric which had characterized the preceding years. The Communist-dominated unions might try to adjust their identities, adapting them to the changing conditions in the domestic and international environments, but marked departures from past practices were unlikely. Nonetheless, for these unions reliance on the tried and true presented distinct dangers. The traditional identities were losing their effectiveness—a fact which was evident even before the traumatic events of 1956. Perhaps more important, any failure to exploit the new possibilities for material gains would create strategic openings for their non-Communist competitors. Thus, the Communist-dominated unions would, at a minimum, have to revise their rhetoric and policies to try to restore the attraction of their identities while at the same time competing with the other unions on the market terrain.

The central drama for each of the French and Italian unions in the mid-1950s was how to adapt its strategies and policies, and thus also its organization and incentive system, to the changing environment in which it operated and which presented both dangers and opportunities in terms of its interests and values. What is important to underline, however, is that the shifting context prompted adjustment and constrained options but did not determine the course each union could take. As will become evident, different strategic and policy responses remained possible and factors other than economic and political change were at work in influencing the one selected by any union. Chief among these other factors were three: the competitive dynamic among unions, the nature of the linkages of each union to a political party or parties, and the analyses which each union made of the changes underway and their implications for the values and interests which it wished to promote. To understand how these factors interacted to produce the specific outcomes, we need to look more closely at each national case.

FRANCE

If we open our discussion of France by referring to political events, it is because they, rather than economic and labor-market factors, were the major shaping variables of the changing context French unions faced in the mid-1950s. And if we concentrate our attention on the CGT and its relationship with the PCF, it is because the Communist-dominated union and its actions and reactions were predominant in determining the direction taken by the union movement as a whole. This, as we shall see, is a pattern which will be repeated subsequently.

PCF–CGT relationships during the Cold War had involved a highly politicized 'transmission belt' subordination of union to party, the former deriving considerable identity incentives and concrete resources (money, militants) from its ties to the latter. Both had been well-served by this relationship in the period of fiercest attacks and deepest isolation. With the rise of Mendès-France in 1953–4, however, new prospects for a reformist Center–Left alliance appeared. The PCF read this situation as contradictory. Given proper Communist action, it might open the way towards the full United Front alliance which the party desired. It might also, however, risk producing a 'Third Force' reformist alliance between Mendès' radicals and the Socialists, excluding the Communists while also undertaking significant social change. The PCF thus rapidly concluded that its essential immediate task was to discredit Mendèsism and the prospect for Keynesian reformism tapping the postwar boom on which this reform image was built. The Communists therefore adopted an extremely sectarian analysis, intended to dispel any hopes among party or CGT supporters for an improved economic future. This convoluted logic produced the PCF's 'pauperization' thesis of French economic development, according to which not only was the French economy not growing, but it was actually promoting the relative and absolute immiseration of French workers.

These rather strange PCF elucubrations had important implications for the CGT. While the union had behaved as a transmission belt throughout the Cold War, using its mobilizational capacities to promote party positions on both domestic and international issues, it had also been committed to a 'reformist' economic program. This program which, on paper, resembled the CGIL's *Piano del lavoro*, had sought to sensitize workers to the economic potential which was allegedly being wasted by French governmental subservience to American Cold War policies. When political circumstances changed in 1954–5, however, the PCF leadership decided that this earlier CGT program was dangerous—it might 'mislead' workers to perceive Mendèsist reformism as a plausible political option. In effect, the older CGT program contained measures which were very similar to those advocated by Mendès. The PCF's fear was not only electoral—that parts of its working-class base might shift its voting allegiance—but also trade unionist—that a more reformist union strategy might emerge and that the CGT might slide towards greater autonomy from the party. In effect, in the face of real prospects for reform, the PCF got the CGT to abandon all goals of reform and any analyses which might suggest that reform (without political 'revolution') was possible. In doing so it was also seeking to reformulate the identity incentives of the union rather than allowing a more general restructuring of the incentive system. A more strident rhetoric of doom and confrontation was adopted to counteract potentially corrosive effects of gradual political change and the hopes it might otherwise inspire.

The revived alignment of PCF and CGT economic outlooks, however, was not only rhetorical and symbolic; it also had strategic and tactical consequences. The pauperization thesis pinpointed the primary stress points in French society in new ways. In earlier years, party and union had both focused upon international political questions. In the new setting, if French capital was 'pauperizing' French workers, then the 'primary contradiction' of French society, the nodal conflict area where popular mobilization was most likely to emerge and be effective, was *economic*, as workers organized to resist pauperization. The paradoxical effect of what was basically an inappropriate analysis of economic dynamics was, then, to shift the CGT away from high political strategy back towards labor-market agitation. Struggle to increase popular consumption, if successful, would precipitate political and economic crisis in France, and thereby enhance the coming of maximalist change; and even if unsuccessful, it would at least immunize the CGT base against the reformist contagion. In either case, furthermore, it would avoid any abandonment of the market arena to other unions.

The CGT's general outlook changed at this critical juncture, then, largely because of the PCF's desire to use the CGT for new types of labor mobilization. It is important to stress, however, that the CGT's 'return to the labor market' did not involve any substantial modification of traditional CGT oppositional labor market strategies and tactics. The post-1955 CGT program focused uniquely upon mobilization to win bread-and-butter union demands; the new line was completely economistic. The strategy behind the program was, furthermore, motivated by continuing CGT refusal to assume any positive, much less 'class collaborationist,' responsibility in French economic development. Union action was conceived of as confrontational warfare with capital. The CGT expressed little or no interest in using labor-market power to create new industrial relations institutions and thus a more institutionalized role for labor in the political economy. Moving back to the labor market for the CGT did not imply a new willingness to behave in a 'reformist' way, indeed the contrary.

The CGT's attitudes towards the CFTC, *Force Ouvrière*, the FEN (the teachers' union) and the CGC (the *cadres* union) reflected a similar posture. The Confederation persisted in portraying the other unions as 'yellow' organizations whose purposes were to betray working-class interests. Unified action in the labor market with such unions was not ruled out, but it was conceived of in ways which made actual cooperation extremely unlikely: more as a way of getting access to the rank and file of other groups to seduce them away from the leaderships, than as a way for making significant material gains through cooperation.

As this suggests, the CGT's shift in 1954–6 was essentially from one form of maximalist unionism to another. Economic change, the beginning of the postwar boom, technological change, and rising productivity could have promoted a different type of change, but the CGT's historically defined inclinations and its continuing relationship to the PCF were least disrupted by the response adopted. Furthermore, the balance of power between the CGT and the other unions did not militate towards a sharper break with the posture of the preceding years. The dramatic split of French labor in 1947–8 had left the bulk of rank and file support, especially in industry, with the CGT. *Force Ouvrière*, despite the high hopes of its organizers and outside supporters, had emerged as something of a rump organization, based primarily among civil servants and public sector workers. The CFTC, wedded to earlier class harmony notions of Catholic unionism, persisted in its distinctly nonaggressive behavior. By the mid-1950s the results of the reemergence of trade union pluralism in France had been consolidated: all French unions had lost considerable mobilizing power as a result of the Cold War, but the relative balance between them still strongly favored the CGT. None of the CGT's organizational rivals had the power or the ideological heritage necessary to develop strategic departures which might threaten the CGT's relative predominance by promoting new types of appeals, actions, and incentives (material and/or purposive). Furthermore, neither the French *patronat* nor the French state and political parties were able or willing to aid the non-Communist unions by giving them the ability *credibly* to develop such appeals, policies, and incentives. This would have required a responsiveness to new types of union demands which for both historical and structural reasons neither employers nor the state were likely to show, and which continued Communist sectarian maximalism only discouraged. As a result, the CGT had no particular incentive, other than that which came to it from politics through the PCF, to change its approaches to labor-market action.

The persistence of the traditional CGT class war/confrontation strategic posture was evident in tactics as well. Local union action, where it could be developed, was to be shaped in ways which would enhance 'class' identity among workers as a whole. Such a 'class' orientation tended to deemphasize shopfloor issues in favor of broader mobilization goals. Making a national 'splash' through very large movements which would either force negotiations at high levels between unions and the *patronat* or state or demonstrate dramatically their intransigence, was the CGT's central objective. Strengthening the union locally or on the shopfloor, or decentralizing mobilizational initiatives, were low on the CGT's priority list.

Thus, the essence of the CGT (and PCF) response to the changes of the mid-1950s was to recreate an atmosphere of confrontation in the face of developments which might give credibility to reformist political or effective labor-market initiatives. Through its analysis (borrowed from the Party) and its strategic and tactical adjustments, the CGT shifted the terrain of battle toward the market but without altering the basic goals it was pursuing or structure of alliances through which these were to be advanced. Rather than respond to the new conditions to restructure its incentive system toward greater reliance on material and/or purposive incentives, a policy which would also have required greater cooperation with other unions and far greater autonomy from the Party, the CGT chose to continue to rely on a policy of confrontation, isolation, and ideological drama. This policy allowed it to maintain its support through identity incentives leavened by whatever material gains might be made through its aggressive market actions. The weakness of the other unions and their inability to develop and prosecute alternative strategies *allowed* the CGT to pursue this course; but it was the union's (and Party's) goals and perception of institutional interests which promoted the specific response undertaken. Even in the changed conditions of the mid-1950s, the French situation was such that the CGT did not have to undertake a significant strategic revision unless it wished to, and it did not. That this posture entirely paralleled that of the PCF need not be underlined. As we turn to Italy, however, it will be clear that other options were possible.

ITALY

The Italian unions dealt with the changes of the mid-1950s in markedly different ways than their French counterparts. The contrast is particularly noteworthy in the case of the CGIL. During the height of the Cold War, it had been tied to the PCI much as the CGT had been linked to the PCF: both unions accepted the 'transmission belt' relationship. By the end of the period under examination, however, the CGIL had formally abandoned this tie to the Party and had begun—but no more than this—to develop a new approach to its role and goals in the labor market. In addition, the union's analysis of the economic and political changes under way was more realistic (although it took the union a number of years fully to grasp the changes under way) and adaptive. It had also distanced itself—again only in initial, tentative, ways—from the international linkages and policies of the party. The CGIL, in other words, had begun what with hindsight can be called its (still not completed) transformation from transmission belt to fully autonomous, interventionist unionism.

Part of the explanation for this shift lies in the different characters of the French and Italian Communist parties. In a number of ways, and for a variety of historical and other reasons, the PCI has shown itself to be the more open, flexible, and adaptive party since the war. This had been less apparent during the height of the Cold War but became more so after 1953 and especially in 1956, when the PCI's doctrinal and strategic 'revisions' had even prompted a public polemic on the part of the PCF. From the standpoint of the CGIL, the most important aspect of this flexibility and doctrinal revisionism was the Party's willingness to reconsider its relations with its mass organizations, above all the union. In 1956, the PCI proved willing to abandon the notion of the 'transmission belt' relationship, so much a part of Third International doctrine, as a major feature of its elaboration of the 'Italian road to socialism.' No such reevaluation of Party–union relations, we have seen, was undertaken by the PCF.[47]

It would be incorrect, however, to understand the CGIL's change as simply an expression of Party will. Instead, what we see is a distinct effort of the union, in response to developments both in the labor market and in the political arena, to develop a more autonomous stance. In fact, to a surprising degree we often see the union leading, or at least prompting, Party shifts from the sectarian posture of the preceding years. The limits of this process in these years is shown by the alignment of both Party and union (the latter with some public reluctance) to support the Soviet invasion of Hungary. Nonetheless, changes were clearly underway which demonstrate an effort by the union to adapt to the changing environment by readjusting strategy, policy, and consequently incentive system toward a new mix which, while not abandoning features of the old identity, would combine it with a greater concentration on material and purposive incentives. These latter, again in contrast to the CGT, began to be treated as valuable (and attainable) for themselves and not just as means to other, more global and political, ends. In presenting them this way, the CGIL was, knowingly or not, both restructuring its traditional identity and telling its supporters that the pursuit of material gains and social reform was legitimate even if it did not promote revolutionary change, and even for loyal Communists. This new posture, while embryonic in these years, would have major consequences in the future. Like the PCI's own 1956 'Programmatic Declaration' calling for gradual structural reform in a democratic context, the CGIL's position created the bases for later member pressure and union policies aimed at winning incremental gains in the market and political arenas.

The response of the CGIL is important from a comparative perspective. The dilemmas and tensions caused by changes in the political and economic environment were similar for the French and Italian Communist-dominated unions; yet the responses in the two cases were not. This difference indicates clearly that the task of reevaluating strategies and restructuring bases of support through the development of new policies in the market and political arenas, and the striking of a new balance between them, admitted of different responses.

The general concerns which preoccupied the CGIL and PCI were similar to those of the CGT and PCF. On the one hand, the easing of Cold War tensions seemed to open the possibility of more reform-oriented national political coalitions from which the Communist party would be excluded. In the Italian case, the critical developments in this regard were the emergence of a new, more 'populist' and integralist leadership group in the Christian Democratic Party (DC), and the gradual shift of the Socialist Party (PSI) away from the Communist Party. The latter trend, although gradual, was accelerated by the events of 1956 in the Communist movement. On the other hand, the Italian economy began to 'take off' in these years, with productivity rising, employment expanding, and some employers beginning to pay higher wages. Whereas the French Communist response had been the 'pauperization' theory, however, the CGIL did not abandon its reformist *Piano del lavoro* of earlier years. The *Piano* had been a document in the Resistance–national unity coalition tradition, designed to underline the costs to workers and to the society as a whole of the eviction of the Left from national government. While it was 'catastrophic' in its predictions about what would happen should Italy continue with the policies adopted after the exclusion of the Left, it was reformist in its counterproposals. With the changes of the mid-1950s, the CGIL did not abandon these basic proposals, but instead sought to recast them in the framework of the economic and political changes underway. Rather than restructuring its analysis and rhetoric to reanimate confrontationist stances in the face of hopes for reform as had the CGT, the CGIL began to accept the reality of the economic changes and to seek, within reformist lines, but with a continued overlay of denunciatory rhetoric toward its opponents, to develop a policy which would avoid its exclusion and allow it to exploit the new conditions to bring rewards to its supporters.

The contrasts should not, of course, be overdrawn. The CGIL did not become an openly 'reformist' union, and it did seek to retain its distinctive identity as the only 'class' union linked to a 'revolutionary' tradition. Nonetheless, when we compare the CGIL and the CGT, their different responses at the level of analysis and policy point to an irony which, in turn, highlights the difference between them. The CGT–PCF did reconsider its overall economic vision in the mid-1950s, but this process resulted in the rejection of reformist formulas of the past and the redefinition and reassertion of economic and political maximalism. The CGIL (and, to a lesser extent, the PCI) remained essentially within the lines of analysis and policy formulated in earlier years, but, under the new conditions, this created pressures to begin to act in a manner consistent with the more reform-based orientation. Whereas the CGT restructured its economic vision and rhetoric to rebuild its garrison, the CGIL began to seek to counterattack through the breaches in its analytical and ideological fortifications which the economic and political changes were opening.

Patterns of Party–union relationships reflected this contrast and at the same time, help to explain it. The PCF remained resolutely silent about giving a more autonomous role to the CGT; and the latter did not appear, after its 1955 Congress, to seek such a role. The 'transmission belt,' with its subordination of union to Party and its consequent dependence of the union on the party for identity incentives and for direct transfer of monetary resources and militance, was retained. The CGIL, by contrast, increasingly allowed differences between it (especially Secretary-General Giuseppe Di Vittorio) and the party to emerge into the open. The PCI responded ambivalently. On the one hand, it sought to bring the union back into line. On the other hand, it began a process of reexamination of its relationship with the union and in 1956 utilized the doctrinal ferment surrounding the denunciation of Stalinism to abandon the 'transmission belt' formula. We need not here dwell on why the PCI proved so much more flexible than the PCF. Suffice it to say that latent but real differences between the parties of long standing came to the surface in the context of the shocks of the mid-1950s. It should also not be suggested that the CGIL became wholly autonomous from the PCI: there were still significant transfers of resources, both financial and of militants; the link to the Party remained important for the union in terms of its ability to use identity incentives to maintain support (witness its willingness, after some hesitation to go along with the Soviet invasion of Hungary), and there is little question that the union continued to give special attention to the Party's counsel. Still, the symbolism of the abandonment of the 'transmission belt' formula should not be underestimated, for it created the basis for a policy which would allow the union more autonomously to look out for its own interests through new policies in the market and (to a lesser extent) the political arenas. That the union was doing so was evident already at the time of the formation of the EEC in 1958 when the CGIL took a much more 'possibilist' position than did the PCI.

If the growing differentiation of autonomy of the union from the Party made more possible new departures in other areas of policy, the CGIL's problems in the labor market virtually compelled such innovations. In Italy, as in France, unionism in the 1950s was being progressively weakened by the corrosive effects of union pluralism and politicization, aggressive antiunion policies by employers and the state, something which can only be described as ideological 'fatigue' on the part of many workers, and the hopes which the new economic and political situations fed. The French case clearly shows that one possible response was to try to reinforce the existing basic orientations, an approach made easier for the CGT because of the weakness of its competitors. The CGIL moved in a different direction, and in no small part because its position relative to its union rivals gave signs of rapid deterioration. The symbolic turning point was in 1954–5 when the Communist-dominated union suffered a series of major defeats in factory commission elections, most importantly at Fiat. Moreover, the CGIL's membership had declined by almost 50 percent, while CISL's held. The other unions, pursuing what were at least rhetorically different strategies, appeared to be making major inroads into the CGIL's bases of support.

This message was received with alarm by CGIL. In 1955 it began a serious strategic and tactical self-criticism. Confederal structures were too centralized; some decentralization and democratization were necessary. Moreover, the Confederation's traditional approach to structuring union campaigns had been too general, too national, and too remote from the concerns of rank-and-file workers. The concentration on 'class' objectives (e.g., a 'national' wage structure designed to protect employment even in weak firms) and on the promotion of general national and international political goals had handicapped the unions in adapting to the economic and labor-market changes under way and in responding to the new demands of their constituents. What was needed was organizational and tactical change to rejoin these demands. The union had to rebuild its support at the base. A revised strategy—which would found national action for political-economic reform on solid mobilization at the rank-and-file level built on responsiveness to a diversity of market situations—began, slowly, to take form. In essence, the CGIL began gradually initiating a shift from the Confederation-centered, national, 'revolutionary' and 'class' strategy and mobilizational practices, which had been its hallmark for a decade, toward a more mixed strategy; in this local and sectoral demands would be given a place alongside national goals attainable only through centralized bargaining and mediation with parties and employers, or even 'revolutionary' change. In undertaking this shift, the union was also restructuring its incentive system, giving less importance to its traditional identity and more legitimacy to the immediate material demands of workers and to gradual, piecemeal reforms which would also respond to the day-to-day needs of workers.

The development of CISL in Italy was a crucial factor in the CGIL's reevaluations at this point. In essence, the challenge of CISL to the CGIL was, for various reasons, much more threatening than that of FO to the CGT. Catholic unionism in Italy, as contrasted to France, was dominant among the non-Communist unions and had, by the early 1950s, presented itself as the chief challenger to the CGIL. At first this appeal had been almost as rooted in identity incentives as that of the CGIL. The content of this identity was, of course, different: Catholicism and Catholic solidarism, anti-Communism, a stress on the value of the individual worker and his place in the community. These differences are important because they make clear that from the beginning the CISL's ideology was more easily adaptable to a strategy emphasizing individual values and/or social reform. Nonetheless, in its early years the CISL's weakness and the general climate of political and ideological confrontation meant that the Catholic and anti-Communist identity—embodied in close and highly visible links to the Church, to the Christian Democrats, to the government and to government–employer policy—prevailed. By the mid-1950s, however, these facets of the CISL's identity began to be alloyed with more aggressive strategy and tactical principles concerning collective bargaining and the appropriate autonomous and conflictual, but pluralist, role of trade unionism in a democratic society. The efforts of American trade unions were important in promoting this development. The CISL proved much more receptive than the French FO to American notions of decentralized and institutionalized collective bargaining and many of its young cadres were trained in the Florence union school set up in cooperation with the Americans. These cadres were to assume roles of major importance in the years to come.

While the CISL's rhetoric and strategy began in this period to reflect the changes outlined, it still remained heavily entangled in its past practices and doctrines, a fact which reflected internal divisions about the appropriate union goals. It was concerned with disentangling itself from official ties to the DC, judging such ties to be a serious liability to trade union autonomy and to its ability to extend its support on new bases. At the same time it continued to be prone to manipulation as a 'company union' by Italian employers seeking a vehicle with which to negotiate deals to keep wages down and/or to isolate the CGIL. The ties with the DC also remained close: one faction of the party was rooted in the CISL and a number of unionists were DC members of Parliament. Important currents within the Confederation, however, increasingly advocated a more genuinely pluralist and conflictual unionism directed towards establishing American-style collective bargaining, a system which was predicated upon the acquisition by unions of a legitimate place at plant level and on the aggressive pursuit of wage increases in accordance with the growth of productivity and profits on a firm-by-firm level. To the degree to which the CISL moved towards this focus, it began to represent a strategic threat to CGIL, for it promised material gains to workers in prospering industries whereas the CGIL's strategic orientation tended to underexploit their potential market strength in the name of class solidarity. With its own strength visibly declining in part due to the erosion of the effectiveness of its identity incentives, the CGIL, therefore, also had to face a CISL which, although still in transition, was threatening to exploit new possibilities for market gains by the pursuit of a strategic orientation which would rest far more heavily on building support through the provision of material incentives. To fail to adapt to this challenge might lead to a severe weakening of the CGIL's position in the labor movement, a fear enhanced by the losses at Fiat and elsewhere in union elections. For the CGIL, then, the option of responding through a reaffirmation of a confrontationist stance and thus of identity incentives was much less viable. At the same time, however, it is also evident that the greater willingness of the PCI to accept a reorientation on the part of the union, a willingness based on the Party's own strategic and ideological inclinations, was important in encouraging the process.

At the time—1954–7—the emerging differences between French and Italian union responses to changing environments must have seemed subtle indeed. The Communist-dominated union actors in both countries, CGT and CGIL, often used much the same rhetoric in discussing their new concerns. As we have already remarked, both union movements approached roughly similar new problems in these years from roughly similar points of departure. Nonetheless, their responses to these new problems established the beginnings of divergent trajectories. What lay behind such beginnings? One possible source, different policies of French and Italian employers with different consequences for the types of exchange between unions and employers and consequently, between unions and their supporters, must be excluded. French employers may have been somewhat more intransigent in dealing with unions than their Italian counterparts, but we are dealing here with differences at the margin. Diverse state policies might also be a potential source of differentiation, but again such an hypothesis is implausible. The Communist-dominated unions and the Communist parties were potentially threatened by the hopes for reform which political change fed, not by actual policies of reform and support for the trade unions by government. These years, in fact, did not produce significant reform at the level of the state, nor did a closer relationship between non-Communist unions and government develop. Still another possible source of divergence, major structural differences in economic development patterns, must also be ruled out. Both union movements faced roughly the same kinds of economic change— technological innovation, the beginnings of rapid growth, the debut of the postwar boom.

Two sets of factors—the relationships between the unions and the political parties with which they had close ties, and the relationships of the confederations to one another—do account for much of the divergence in response. The differing strategic postures and styles (and no other word seems better to capture what we intend) of the PCF and PCI played a significant role. These differences were rooted in different party and national histories, in different postwar national political structures and in differing types of national leaderships and organizations. When translated to the trade union level, they meant that the Italian Communist Party proved more receptive, or less resistant, to pressures for greater union autonomy which the changing economic situation and the weakening of the attraction of traditional incentives were exerting on the unions. The PCF was inclined to remain in its bunker and to make sure the CGT remained there with it; rhetoric and analysis were adjusted to this purpose and so too were labor-market tactics. The PCI, by contrast, did not encourage strategic departures on the part of the CGIL, but with sometimes greater and sometimes lesser reluctance it let them go forward. It was also willing to legitimate them by formally abandoning that hoary Leninist formula of the 'transmission belt.' In pointing to this difference, we do not mean to suggest that the Italian Communists did not have good reasons for allowing change to occur. These reasons, however, can only be understood in the larger context of the Party's history of ideological, strategic, and organizational development. Furthermore, whatever its explanation, allowing the process of differentiation between Party and union was to have an important, independent significance in the future.

The relative strengths of the CGT and CGIL *vis-à-vis* their respective organizational rivals also played an important part in explaining the divergent outcomes. The CGT was never effectively challenged in these years; both the FO and the CFTC were very weak and were entrapped in ideological and strategic stances which made it impossible for them to exploit the new opportunities for strategic advantage which had opened up. The CGIL, in contrast, suffered sharp organizational losses and severe symbolic defeats; and it was faced with a CISL which, while still undergoing a transition, was beginning to articulate positions which might well make the CGIL's losses just the first step in an accelerating trend. It is important once again to stress, however, that the CGIL's response cannot only be understood as the 'objectively necessary' outcome of the pressures it faced. These pressures had to be interpreted and filtered through the bases for judgment of the union's (and the PCI's) leaders.

From the standpoint of the incentives systems of the unions, what were the most important consequences of the changes we have observed? The changes of the period tended to weaken the attraction of the identity incentives on which all the unions had relied, incentives which were already losing their hold after so many years of intensely politicized conflict.At the same time, the beginnings of the boom made strategies better geared to winning material gains through aggressive, and decentralized, bargaining in the labor market more attractive, at least potentially. The Italian labor movement, to a significantly greater extent than the French, undertook the initial steps necessary to exploit this potential. None of the Italian unions—and above all not the CGIL—shifted immediately to a reliance on material incentives, abandoning the rhetoric, symbols, and linkages which had been so important to their identities and to the support which they had enjoyed. Yet all the Italian confederations, through the measures they undertook in these years, set in train processes which would lead to important remixing of their incentive systems in the period to come. Furthermore, in doing so, they also legitimated for workers new ways of thinking about their individual interests, the relationship of these interests to those of others in the society, and about at what level (factory, sector, the society), in what arena (market, political) and through what kinds of actions interests could and ought to be advanced. This initial and partial restructuring of consciousness was as important as the changes in union rhetoric, strategies, and policies and partially a result of them. By the early 1960s, when the conjunctures in both Italy and France once more created major new pressures and opportunities for strategic and policy change, the union movements of the two countries faced the new conditions with rather different postures.

The Early 1960s: The Gap Widens

In the early to mid-1960s significantly new political and economic conjunctures developed both in France and Italy. Political changes were again important, but unlike the 1950s they took rather different forms in the two countries. In France, the final resolution of the Algerian problem led to a consolidation of new, and seemingly stable, coalitional patterns for the Gaullist Fifth Republic. From the standpoint of the unions and the Left more generally, the chief characteristics of these patterns were the exclusion of the parties of the Left, Socialists included, from government and, at the same time, the renewal of an aggressive *étatiste* approach toward economic and social affairs. Consistent with this thrust, the Gaullist regime revived economic planning which had receded in importance in the 1950s. The governments seemed determined to give a new expansionist thrust to the economy, allowing workers to participate fully in consumer society, while also promising to undertake social policies intended to improve the economic lot and security of the individual worker and to integrate him better into the tissue of French society. Such improvements, however, would come individually or through new economic and political structures; they would bypass the trade unions and parties. The new vision projected by Gaullism, therefore, tended more towards a statist paternalism designed to weaken the allegiance of workers to their traditional (especially Left) organizations than towards a pluralist politics which might seek to win the allegiance of workers to the Fifth Republic through those organizations. Allegiance to the regime was, primarily, to be direct, not indirect, through an immediate relationship rather than through one mediated by organizational loyalties. The other side of this coin was that unions (and the Left parties) could expect to gain little from the new policies in terms of legitimacy, an expanded economic role and incentives; they would be no more included in the flow of benefits from the state in the new arrangements than they had been in the old.

Such was not the case in Italy. There the early 1960s ushered out the Center–Right and brought in the Center-Left, with the Socialist Party gradually becoming a full government participant. At the same time, the Christian Democratic Party leadership sought to expand the role of the state in economic and social affairs, a policy which, in principle (the practice proved rather different) was consistent with that of the Socialists. The political design associated with these developments was markedly in contrast with that in France. It was not paternalistic and exclusionist of workers' organizations, but rather was intended to split the Left and weaken the PCI by integrating the Socialist party and the organizations associated with it, as well as the organizations associated with Catholicism and social democracy, while freezing out the Communists and their organizations. Rather than denying access to the Left as a whole, the Center–Left hoped to incorporate those parts of the working class and its organizations willing to disavow links, direct or indirect, to the PCI, intending thereby to undercut the appeal of the Communist organizations. Political changes in Italy, therefore, held out (initially) the hope that the non-Communist labor organizations might gain increased resources and legitimacy.

If the political features of the new conjuncture had rather divergent profiles in the two countries, the economic features were more similar. In both France and Italy, economic growth began to produce conditions in the labor markets of some industrial sectors and regions approximating full employment. This tended to increase the militancy of the workers and union strength in the labor market, especially if different unions could cooperate in pressing their demands. It also provoked government concern about keeping the wage bargaining process under control which, in turn, potentially gave the unions greater leverage with government. Accompanying these developments were changes in industrial investment and structure towards greater capital intensity and international trade and, of even more immediate relevance, in the composition of the union rank and file. New groups entered the labor force (particularly as semi-skilled operatives) and seemed to give new impetus to workers in general to push for improvement in their material conditions. Unions were thereby called upon to 'deliver' in money terms, especially as the aspiration to become full-fledged participants in the consumer society became widespread. Thus, at the level of the economy and the labor market, there were both new and more intense pressures on unions to satisfy the demands of their supporters and new potentialities for the unions to do so.

The new conjuncture strained the existing strategies and incentive systems of the various unions while it also offered them distinct opportunities for change and adaptation. The traditional identity incentives on which the unions had relied not only lost even more of their past attraction (the progress of détente augmented this trend), but now, to the extent that they were perceived as an obstacle to the union cooperation necessary for effective action in the market arena, might prove a real weakness for unions which insisted on continuing to depend upon them. This problem was likely to be particularly acute in Italy where the earlier changes in union policy had begun to legitimate market actions for material gains and greater depoliticization and autonomy for unions. At the same time, the chances to produce material gains for workers through action in the market were greatly improved. Finally, in both cases but especially in Italy, the new concern of the governments for social reform might enable the unions more credibly to build support and alliances by pressing for such reforms, thereby building a stock of purposive incentives. Yet, as we shall see in a moment, this period, which, not surprisingly, most closely resembles the conditions discussed by the liberal optimists, did not produce similar responses from the unions in the two countries. Instead, the divergent trajectories which had begun to emerge in the 1950s conditioned the unions' responses, and these responses, in turn, further accentuated the different patterns of development in the two countries.

FRANCE

The effects of the 1958 change in Republics on the structure of French political conflict were delayed by the winding down of the Algerian War, but they began to emerge decisively after 1962. As the Gaullist regime constructed a workable Center–Right electoral majority, prospects for Center–Left governments of the type which had been frequent in the Fourth Republic disappeared. Strong tendencies towards Left–Right polarization emerged, encouraged by changes in the electoral system. The Socialists were obliged to reconsider the question of alliances with the Communists for the first time since 1947. And the Communists, sensing the changing environment, moved towards the promotion of a new Left United Front. In the process the PCF also felt obliged to reconsider its views of the dynamics of the French economy. 'Pauperization' was quietly abandoned, replaced by a suitably Gallicized version of 'State Monopoly Capitalism' theory. According to the PCF's new perspective the likely course of the French economy was no longer immiseration, collapse, and terminal crisis. The 'contradictions' specified in the new theory were, instead, social and political. The misuse of power and resources by the 'monopoly caste' controlling the state created circumstances in which a broad, cross-class social alliance in favor of change was likely. Translated into political support for a United Left pledged to implement a global program of nationalizations, planning, and power and income redistribution, this alliance would move to dispossess the monopolies. In the process, the back of private-sector-controlled capital accumulation would be broken, moving France towards a transition to socialism.

Such strategic and theoretical changes were very important, both for what they changed and for what they did not change in the PCF's outlook. By abandoning 'pauperization' (plus, in the course of the 1960s, a number of other cherished economic and political doctrines), the PCF began to move towards a more plausible view of economic processes in France. On the other hand, such doctrinal changes were not connected with any major retreat from the PCF's 'maximalist' views of social, economic and political change. The package of reforms promoted by the PCF was just that, a single package, which could only be delivered as a whole and only by a government of the Left led by the Communist party. Thus, while the Party adjusted its program to meet the new demands for reforms among its supporters and to counteract the reformist pretensions of the Gaullist regime, this was as much an adaptation of identity as a new commitment to a reformist, purposive, gradualist politics. Specific reform proposals took on greater weight, but they were embedded in an analysis of the French political economy and society and in a political prospect which continued to hearken back to the 'revolutionary' themes of the past.

All of this was of considerable importance for the CGT and, through the CGT, for French unionism more generally. The PCF desired to tap what it saw to be a vast reservoir of potential opposition to the Gaullist regime and turn it towards support for a new Left United Front. In this political strategy trade union mobilization, stirring up the widest possible opposition to the regime's economic policies (connected, in agitational campaigns, to the 'monopoly caste') had a high priority. Perhaps the most important implication for the CGT involved changed attitudes towards 'unity in action' with other French union groups. Prior to the mid-1960s, the CGT had eagerly proclaimed its desire for unified action with other groups while, in fact, insisting upon concessions from them on essential political and trade union questions in ways which rendered unity inconceivable. From 1963 onwards, and paralleling the PCF's search for allies in the political sphere, the CGT sought unity on much less stringent grounds, signalling its willingness to collaborate with other unions on whatever points of common concern could be uncovered.

Much to the CGT's surprise, it found a new union partner willing to negotiate unity of action, the CFDT (formerly the Catholic CFTC). In effect, a decade after the Italian Catholic CISL had begun to reformulate its union objectives in the direction of greater and decentralized militancy, the French CFTC now began to move in similar directions. As the CFTC 'deconfessionalized,' becoming the CFDT in 1964, it started to seek out local factory grievances which it could prod and promote, intending thereby to extend support through an image and practice of decentralized wage and working condition militancy. It rapidly, however, ran up against a completely intransigent *patronat*, backed by a Gaullist government concerned about inflation and intent on maintaining its autonomy in the economic and social sphere. CFDT and CGT thus both saw an interest in union coordination as a way to break through the dam of governmental and employer intransigence which had developed. The meeting ground for such coordination would be the one which would least dilute the unions' respective identities: aggressive market action for material gain; and both unions had a keen sense that workers were ready to follow.

CGT–CFDT unity-in-action—the first formal agreement between the two confederations, was signed in January 1966—marked a decisive turning point in the fortunes of French unionism. It provided the premises for the intensified militancy of the later 1960s. Unity greatly facilitated a major 'resurgence of class conflict' in France.|For our purposes, however, it is important to underline what this change did *not* involve. The CGT shifted its position on unity, consistent with the orientation and strategic aims of the PCF and its own immediate interests. It thereby encouraged more extensive and decentralized rank and file mobilization, a departure from its centralized and highly controlled orientation of the past. It was able to do so, however, almost entirely on its own terms. The changes in the labor market, in the workers' perceptions of their interests and the emergence of the newly energized and reoriented CFDT were factors with which the Communist union had to reckon, and its new policies were partially intended to do so. Nevertheless, it was able once again to adjust without having to abandon the basic identity, strategic orientation and policy which it had cultivated for so many years. Once more, continuity rather than change were the hallmarks of the CGT's adaptations.

The reasons why the CGT both desired and was able to adapt in this way were basically the same as those we saw at work in the 1950s. First, the union's linkages to the Party remained strong and the leaderships of both union and Party wished them to remain so. This meant that the union would seek to retain as much of its political identity as the changed conditions in the environment, and its own and party's strategic and tactical goals, would allow. Second, the CFDT, despite its new image and strategic outlook, did not represent a major challenge to the CGT's predominance within the French union movement, much less a likely drain of CGT support. This was not solely because of the balance of strength between the two unions, although this certainly played a role. We have seen in the Italian case, after all, that a weaker union can, under certain circumstances, present an effective challenge to its larger counterpart. The other factor which contributed to the relative weakness of the CFDT was that its focus on the use of local, shopfloor and plant-level campaigns (in many ways similar to the CISL's 'articulated bargaining' policy) was unlikely actually to reap benefits for most workers or credibly appear able to do so. The intransigence of employers, reinforced by the posture assumed by the government, lent credence to the maximalism of the CGT and of the PCF. Finally, the CGT's identity was peculiarly well adapted to the changed circumstances. While the union (and Party) stressed the ultimate necessity of global political change, they also underlined the fact that the road to such change led through market militance. Of course, this militance was different than that proposed by the CFDT. It was deemed important not so much for the immediate gains which might be won by some workers but rather for the contribution it could make to exposing the 'contradictions' of the Gaullist political economy and to the development of a unified (but Communist-led) opposition to Gaullism. Nonetheless, in practice this meant that the CGT could retain its basic identity while at the same time attaching itself to the new demands of the workers. It could, thereby, impose its larger strategic goals on the movement while at the same time depriving the CFDT of much of the strategic 'space' into which it was seeking to project itself. Taken together, all the preceding factors enabled the CGT once again to change its strategy and incentive system as little as possible while nevertheless effectively adapting to the new conjuncture.

The stress which we have given to continuity should not obscure some important, if relatively less salient, changes which occurred in this period and were to have a considerable bearing on subsequent developments. The first of these was the emergence of an autonomous and aggressive CFDT. While its policies in the mid-1960s did not meet with immense success, they still marked a sharp departure from the union's past. The CFDT was partly able to make such a change because it was weak and had little to lose and because it no longer had any domestic or international points to which to anchor its traditional identity. Cast loose, it first sought to exploit the immediate market conditions in which it found itself. Slowly, however, it came to embed its decentralist and militant stance in a broader ideological stance ('*autogestion*') which was to make it a potentially more effective challenger to the CGT. The second significant change was the growth of unity of action in the labor movement. As we have seen, the CGT was decidedly instrumental in its approach to working with the other unions: unity was never conceived as an end in itself but only as a means to promote the broader political goals of the union (and the party). Nonetheless, the combination of unity of action and the growing material orientation of workers began to take on a significance of its own; for some workers unity came to be seen as indispensable to any other economic or political goals. With hindsight, it is clear that the possibility of the development of powerful tensions between the CGT's continued political subordination and reliance on a politicized and ideological identity, and the material and reformist aspirations of even Communist workers began to take shape. The final change of importance was the tempered polarization of French politics, that is, the split of the French political community into two camps but without the intense ideological confrontation of the Cold War years. The effect of this change was to make more credible the possibility of major political change if the Left could unite and could develop a program and front of action which would, at one and the same time, cover over some of its internal rifts and have a broader appeal to those disaffected with Gaullism. In combination with the other two changes, this last was to have a major impact on how the unions would respond to the new conjuncture which presented itself in the early 1970s.

ITALY

Coalition patterns changed as well in Italian politics in the early 1960s with the emergence of the Center–Left, Christian Democratic–Socialist alliance. The central thrust of the Center–Left was reformist: to adjust government policy to the changed character of the Italian political economy and society which had resulted from the 'miraculous' growth of the preceding decade. The North–South imbalance, the seeming growing tendency towards bursts of cost-push inflation, potential balance-of-payments difficulties, increasingly inadequate public and social services were the chief policy targets. The Center–Left's major remedy for such problems was to increase the state's role in economic and social life. The rigorous liberalism of the 1950s was to give way to a more fully Keynesian policy of macroeconomic management, to a commitment to use government policy to address social ills and to a larger, more politically constrained state sector. Underlying this new approach to policy was a broader strategic design: full integration and incorporation of the working strata of the population and their organizations through a fuller participation in a mixed capitalist, consumer society, increased government concern for the public welfare and full legitimation and institutionalization of workers' organizations. The only ones to be excluded were the Communist Party and its affiliated associations; they were to be isolated and their strength sapped by the success of the new policies.

The other major element of the changed conjuncture of the period was economic: for the first time since the war (in fact, in modern Italian history) the industrial labor market became taut. The effects were dramatic. After years of weakness in which all unions and especially the CGIL had focused on employment as a goal, the union movement found itself in a position of strength. The contracts of 1961–2 brought major wage gains, often on the heels of militance and mobilization on the part of workers which had completely outstripped the expectations of the union leaders. Power within unions tended to flow away from the central confederations toward the shop floor, and workers experienced a new sense of their own power. The altered economic situation brought other changes as well. The government became increasingly concerned with the dangers of wage-push, leading to important internal splits within the new Center–Left about how it should be dealt with. A contradictory combination of policy initiatives, including both classical tight monetary policy and proposals for national indicative planning and incomes policy emerged. All the features of the Italian postwar settlement were strained and the unions too were called upon to adjust their policies, strategies, and bases of support. In terms of the latter, it was evident that there were strong demands, and even spontaneous initiatives, from the workers for more aggressive union action to secure material gains and to promote political reform. It also appeared that there were real opportunities to secure these through action both in the market and political arenas. Yet, for each of the unions the new situation also posed problems about how to adjust their strategies consistent both with their organizational interests and their broader goals.

All the Italian unions were somewhere reserved and skeptical about the Center–Left and its promised changes. The reasons for these reservations, however, differed markedly among the confederations. The differences, and how the unions responded, illustrate well the growing divergence between the Italian and French movement and its causes.

The reservations of the CGIL were not difficult to understand. Despite the increasing autonomy of the Confederation from the PCI, its identity and interests were still bound up with those of the Party. The union was still headed by leaders who for the most part had come to the union through the Party; much the same was true for most of the union cadres and factory-level activists, and for many of them commitment to the Party and what it stood for was still the underlying force behind their union militance. Thus, the anti-Communist thrust of the Center–Left could not leave them indifferent. Yet the response of the CGIL was sharply different from that of the CGT in France. Whereas the latter sought to direct a campaign to discredit the regime through a combination of ideological attacks and market militancy which was itself interpreted in politicized terms, the CGIL's response was more tempered; rather than engage in a head-on confrontation with the government, it sought to challenge the government to undertake the policies it had promised—while expressing skepticism that it would be able to do so. It also endeavored to strengthen its role in the market by promoting the material interests of the workers. Much more than the CGT, the CGIL cast itself as an autonomous organization championing both the particular demands of workers in the factories and the broader reform interests of the working class. The slow shift from reliance on identity incentives growing out of linkages to the PCI, Communist and 'revolutionary' traditions and 'pure' class unionism, toward a mixed incentive system in which material and purposive incentives played a major role had begun in the 1950s; it now sharply accelerated. Why the CGIL's response was of this character will be examined in a moment. Before doing so, however, it is necessary to look at the reaction of the CISL, for it was assuming greater importance and strongly conditioned the policy of the CGIL and the posture adopted by the union movement as a whole.

The CISL was sympathetic to the declared aims of the Center–Left but at the same time extremely wary of overidentification with the government and its policies. The reasons for this flowed directly out of the changes which had begun in the mid-1950s and which had been accentuated as the original Resistance and reconstruction period leadership passed from the scene to be replaced by leaders grounded in the new CISL strategy. On the one hand, this new leadership, especially prominent in the powerful federations (e.g., metalwork), was unwilling to allow the union to appear yet again as an appendage of the Christian Democratic party, and sought to underline CISL autonomy from the government no matter how reformist its policies might appear. On the other hand, the 'refoundation' of the CISL had been premised on effective decentralized and articulated action in the labor market as part of a general posture stressing the autonomous role of unionism in promoting economic growth in a pluralist society. The new conditions which developed in this period promised to make this strategy more successful. To the extent that the CISL was competitive with the CGIL, continuing this emphasis on aggressive, decentralized bargaining in the market arena promised to pay further dividends, especially if the CISL could preempt any CGIL efforts to accuse it of collaborationism with the government.

From this discussion, we have an initial indication of why the CGIL could not simply adopt a politicized opposition to the new political situation: such a response would have made the union less able to compete with the CISL. Other factors were important as well. First, the CGIL's leadership as well had been changing in response to the tentative changes of the preceding decade. The new conditions in the labor market encouraged such changes. Yet, this cannot explain why, unlike the CGT, the

CGIL did not seek confrontation with the government. Here two further factors need to be cited. On the one hand, the internal composition of the CGIL was different from that of the CGT. Although the Communists were dominant, there was also an important Socialist component in the union, and this component was unwilling to allow the union to become an instrument against a reform-oriented government in which the Socialist Party was a major partner. While the Socialists in the CGIL might be unable to force their union to adopt an accommodationist stance, they could keep it from seeking directly to discredit the Center–Left. They could do so, furthermore, not only because of their influence within the union but also because their position could be bolstered by an implicit (sometimes explicit) threat to leave the CGIL and join the social democratic UIL.

Such a split was not only a potential disaster for the CGIL itself, but it also threatened more general PCI goals. The Communist Party (this is a second factor) saw the maintenance of unity within the CGIL as indispensable to prevent its isolation by the Center–Left. Having openly embarked on the gradualist, reformist, alliance-oriented and democratic 'Italian road to socialism' in 1956, the Party assumed a highly critical, but modulated, stance toward the Center–Left. Its strategy was premised on extending the Party's 'presence' at all levels of society. It was, therefore, determined to avoid contributing in any way to its ghettoization. In the Italian setting of the early and mid-1960s, this meant sharply criticizing the Center–Left on practical policy grounds while maintaining communication and organizational ties (where they existed) with all 'potentially reformist' political and social forces even if they were part of the Center–Left's coalition. Such a policy would make more difficult efforts to isolate the party; it would place the PCI in a better position were the Center-Left to fail (as most of the PCI leadership expected it would); and, it would also tend to increase tensions within the Center–Left coalition between those elements more or less committed to thoroughgoing reform.

Third, the government's promised reforms not only were consistent with the demands of workers and the platforms of the PCI and the CGIL, they were also, in contrast to France, part of a design to incorporate, rather than to circumvent and weaken, the union movement. The presence of the Socialists and a union-oriented faction of the DC in the government assured this. Thus, a confrontationist posture was unlikely to be popular and might even undermine the CGIL's determination to present itself as an agent for 'class' interests, to be achieved politically, as well as of 'particularist' interests secured through action in the labor market. A position which stressed the union's commitment to reforms and its ability to pressure the government to live up to its promises, conversely, would be better adapted to the emerging demands of union supporters (demands which had been fed by the CGIL's, and PCI's, own policies since the mid-1950s) and to the union's and Party's broader strategic goals. In promoting such a position, however, the CGIL would be further altering its incentive system toward a greater emphasis on purposive and material incentives.

Finally, the dynamics of response and adaptation just described had the effect of further reducing the differences between the CISL and the CGIL. The former was still more oriented toward the market arena and autonomy from politics than the latter, but both union confederations (as well as the

UIL, which tended to try to define a position between the two) were becoming more similar in the incentives they used to generate and capture support. Identity incentives based on historical traditions, continuing differences in rhetoric and inescapable identifications with different political parties still separated the confederations, but less so than in the past.

The growing similarity between the CGIL and CISL, and their increasing interest in and ability to cooperate, was evident in the period in the unity-in-action of their respective federations in labor market and contractual activity. To a considerable extent, particularly in the early 1960s, this unity also bore substantive fruits. Contracts were good, wages rose and there were new hopes for building effective union organization in the factories. By the mid-1960s, however, the continuing weakness of the unions was once again revealed. The Center–Left proved unable to deliver on its reform promises and even engaged in classical Italian restrictive economic policies to bring wage pressure under control. The unions' militancy declined as the labor market slackened, and by 1965–6 they were unable to exercise effective pressure either in the market or the political arenas. It is important to underline, however, that this changed environment—the downside of the earlier positive conjuncture—did not halt the developments toward unity and a growing similarity between the unions which we have noted. Quite the opposite: in response to this new adversity both the CISL and the CGIL started a process of discussion of general principles which eventually further diminished the differences between them. For the CISL, the evident union weakness in the labor market, and its linkage to the inability of the unions to exercise effective influence over government, fed a growing awareness that strategy could not be entirely focused on the market arena. For the CGIL, these same developments, and the related failure of the design to isolate the PCI and split the union, led to a renewed willingness to search for a more stable ground for union unity, even if this entailed further steps away from past traditions and policies. Why this should have been the response of the two confederations to their perception of weakness cannot be understood, however, except in the context of two more subtle but lasting changes of the period: growing disinterest among workers in the ideological differences between the unions if these interfered with the ability to win material gains and reforms, and the related awareness among workers and lower-level union militants that unity was an indispensable condition of union strength, the necessary prerequisite of major victories. Both these changes were to have dramatic effects on the evolution of the strategies and policies of the Italian unions only a short time later.

The conjunctures of the early to mid-1960s in France and Italy accelerated the divergent trajectories of their respective union movements which had begun a decade before. What then had been subtle differences now emerged as distinctly different features. First, while the French unions clung to their sharply distinct identities and sought to interpret all developments in terms of these, the Italian unions closed the ground which still divided them. Distinctiveness was retained, but increasingly in ways which would expand the scope of issues on which the unions could cooperate. Second, whereas in France the CGT continued to allow its strategic and tactical line to be largely dictated by the immediate strategic interests of the PCF, the CGIL enlarged the autonomy which it had begun to fashion in the 1950s. This should not suggest that the CGIL became entirely autonomous. But the PCI's interests (which were themselves interpreted in ways which would have been inconceivable in the PCF) came to condition the union's policies in a more subtle fashion, a development which could only enhance possibilities for even greater autonomy in the future.

Third, while the Italian union movement as a whole came to be characterized by strategies which recognized—although in different ways and to different degrees—the need to combine strong market-arena, factory-level activity and effective pressure on the government, whatever its composition, for reforms, this was not the case in France. There, the CFDT stressed labor-market action almost exclusively and began to develop an ideology to support such a stance, while the CGT promoted its maximalist political strategy in which the role of labor-market action was instrumental to wholesale political change.

Finally, when viewed from the incentive/resource approach we have proposed, Italian unions were all moving markedly towards mixed incentive systems in which material and purposive incentives were taking on an increasingly large role and identity incentives, while retaining importance, were being restructured in order to make them compatible with the other two types. In France, in contrast, purposive incentives played a relatively minor role as compared to that of material, and importantly, identity incentives. The latter were being adapted to the changing demands of workers, but, especially in the CGT, always with an eye to ensuring that struggle for material gains would be viewed in terms of its contribution to broader ideological goals. The CFDT, after briefly trying to build a strategy around an almost exclusive reliance on aggressive factory-level struggle, began also to develop an ideological context for that approach.

1968–73: The Great Mobilization

As we have seen, earlier critical junctures were accompanied by changes in the strategic and organizational perspectives of both union movements. In the French case, however, changes had come within a broader framework of continuity. The critically important CGT had persisted in structuring its internal life and its relationships to the rank and file around an incentive system which, while using material incentives to the extent possible, stressed identity incentives and, relatedly, an ideology, strategy, and tactics which subordinated labor-market to political goals and piecemeal gains to global change. Although the CGT reformulated its goals and tasks in response to environmental changes, it did so in ways which were designed, ultimately, to enhance prospects for PCF political success. Since the PCF itself defined its longer-term goals in 'maximalist' terms, the CGT remained tinged with such maximalism. And since the balance of power within the divided French union movement was such that no other union actor pursuing different goals was sufficiently powerful or potentially successful to challenge the CGT's relative advantage, the CGT's definition of union tasks continued to carry great weight in the overall cast of French unionism. One further result of the maximalist, politicized, and partisan-ized union posture was the perpetuation of traditional 'class-oriented,' centralized labor-market strategies and tactics.

In Italy, adjustments to similar challenges prodded the unions in very different directions from similar points of departure. Material and purpos-ive incentives became increasingly prominent and labor-market goals and actions sometimes overshadowed political and partisan ones. Furthermore, the market-arena mobilization tended to become more decentralized ('ar-ticulated bargaining') and there was greater room for and toleration of 'spontaneous' labor-market struggle. The view that unionism ought pri-marily to serve the end of promoting political change through support of partisan political options, which had governed CGIL perspectives in the immediate postwar period, was receding. The belief that union action should be connected to broader social change did not disappear in all this, however. Rather it came to be redefined. The unions, to different extents and in different ways, promoted programs of social and economic reform which were in many respects similar to those of the political parties, especially of the Left. Increasingly, however, the unions acted on their own to press the government for reforms, responding to their perception of the demands of union constituencies, to their own conceptions of their institu-tional interests and to their own strategies for building social and political coalitions for change.

As of the mid-1960s, however, these differences between the French and Italian movements were visible mainly as tendencies, and there were still important divergences among the confederations in both countries. Events after 1968 were to lead to a consolidation of the national tendencies into distinctly different types of unionism in France and Italy and were also to promote further convergence in the perspectives of the Italian unions.

The major challenges to, and opportunities for, both union movements after 1968 came from the labor market. In France, the most spectacular manifestation of new labor-market ebullition was, of course, May–June 1968, but substantial levels of labor discontent continued into the early 1970s. In Italy the mobilization was just as fierce but more protracted, extending from the initial 'hot autumn' of 1969 through the mid-1970s. In both countries the explosion of labor mobilization was the culmination of long processes of change in the labor market.

Acute labor tension emerged again in France and Italy because the circumstances of economic growth had begun to change. Tightening labor markets had increased union strength, leading to increased working-class pressure on the wage bill. In both countries the state and private-sector capital attempted to resist such pressure. All major actors at the time, however, failed to perceive that such tension was growing at a moment of dramatic change in the composition of the labor force. New entrants into industry provided new sources of mobilizing energy at the rank-and-file level. 'New workers' from new social backgrounds (agrarian, or from the first cohorts of the 'baby boom') moved to the factory floor, often informed by a rebellious 'youth culture' or the contagion of student radicalism, or 'misinformed' by formal schoolings and its effects on aspirations about what to expect from factory work life, or 'radicalized' when realizing that the factory, rather than a return to the farm and rural life, was their future.

Weakly integrated into traditional union and industrial relations procedures and issues (in part due to the unions' weakness on the shop floor),
ill at ease with industrial work itself, the 'new workers' began to raise new
issues on the shop floor. More often than not they were willing to raise such
issues in unconventional ways, forgoing the protocol and delicacies of past
industrial relations practices. Lest we exaggerate the role of such new
elements, it is essential to note that this 'new worker' phenomenon
emerged simultaneously with renewed efforts by official unions to develop
labor-market struggle and, in Italy, to promote reforms (e.g., the pension
struggle of 1968). The 'old working class,' the backbone of the union
movement, was prepared to act as well, its historic militant zeal revived
behind both the demands of the 'new workers' and those which the unions
had increasingly espoused over more than a decade. The result of this
confluence of unions, 'old' and 'new' workers, and of militant new and newer
demands, was explosive: a massive increase in labor unrest in both countries—strikes, sit-downs and other forms of protest.

The 'resurgence of class conflict' of the late 1960s and early 1970s
presented a tremendous challenge and opportunity for the official
unions.[48] The new mobilization brought with it something which both the
French and Italian labor movements had lacked and which both had long
claimed to desire—the possibility of developing a powerful union presence
on the shop floor and, indirectly, in society as well. As a powerful and
institutionalized market actor, the unions' ability to exert political leverage
would also be greatly enhanced. At the same time the new militancy of the
workers was embodied in a vast array of new, as well as traditional,
demands. These ranged from pressure for higher wages and greater control
over working conditions to the call for greater egalitarianism in the wage
structure, to the demand for more democracy within the unions themselves,
to the desire for major political change and reform. As this suggests, the
new mobilization was multifaceted. The unions could strongly influence
which of these facets would become prominent in the longer run: would the
militancy be translated into efforts to develop new strategies and forms of
organization or would it be used simply to enhance the effectiveness of
traditional policies and perspectives, its 'new' features fading as spontaneity at the base became converted into institutionalized union activity? In
essence, what happened was that the French union movement, still dominated by the CGT, responded by attempting to direct new rank-and-file
energies towards politics, reconfirming its older strategies and organizational practices in the process. In contrast, the Italian movement used the
new energies to complete and enrich its transformation to a new form of
unionism.

FRANCE

The key to the French union response to the new mobilization turned out
once again to be the CGT. As we have seen, the CGT had revised its goals
in the early 1960s in accordance with the PCF's reevaluation of the political
situation. New openness to unity with other unions was developed, but
preexisting notions of union strategy and of union–politics relations were
perpetuated. In May–June 1968 and thereafter, the CGT insisted upon

shaping the new mobilization along lines dictated by this perspective. At the core of CGT strategy was the goal of using union action in the labor market to provide mobilizational support for the emergence of, and then the success of, a new United Front of the political Left. This vision implied the resolute application of traditional union tactics designed to focus emerging labor-market energy upwards towards industry-wide, national level negotiations for the purpose of underlining the interconnections between the Gaullist regime, state economic policies, and the 'monopolies.' Strictly speaking, this did not involve the direct politicization of union actions, but it did involve CGT efforts to divert labor-market mobilization away from decentralized local struggle towards spectacular, highly publicizable, concessions from peak employer associations and the state. From the outset of the new mobilization, then, the CGT placed a very low priority on specific local demands or on using new rank-and-file energies to construct a new organizational infrastructure at shopfloor and branch level.

The CFDT, the CGT's ally and rival, rather rapidly reached very different strategic conclusions, deciding that the promotion of militant local struggles directed towards the construction of a newly solid union stronghold within the firm was one of its major objectives. This was done in the context of the union's emerging '*autogestionnaire*' ideology. It provided the CFDT with a distinct identity and autonomous set of strategic principles, both of which it had lacked since abandoning its earlier identity. At the same time, it threatened to make the CFDT a more effective rival to the CGT by providing it with an alternative set of identity incentives (so important in the French context) to those of the Communist-dominated confederation. Not surprisingly, then, despite the formal agreement of unity of action between the two confederations, the CFDT and CGT came to disagree strongly over how to respond to the new militancy. The disagreement was both over tactics and strategy, over how the unions should react and over what significance for union goals, principles, and strategy should be ascribed to this reaction. These contrasts, of course, had important implications as well for what relationship the unions should have with the parties and political system. Beginning in May–June 1968, and continuing into the 1970s, the CFDT sought to become the representative of the 'new demands' which the mobilization embodied, an effort consecrated in the CFDT's official commitment to *autogestion* as theory, strategy, and societal vision.

In France, therefore, the rank-and-file mobilization of the late 1960s exploded in the context of profound differences in appreciation of its meaning between France's two major union confederations. In effect, what occurred, beginning in 1968, was a struggle between the CGT and CFDT over the definition and channeling of new rank-and-file energies. The CGT stood by its earlier notions of trade union strategy. The CFDT, in contrast, attempted to reconstruct its own identity and bases of support around the new demands and new foci of the mobilization. The CGT ultimately won this struggle, for three basic reasons. To begin with, the CGT was much stronger and more effective organizationally than the CFDT. The CFDT, still engaged in internal changes in 1968, was divided about objectives and tactics and quite unclear about how to proceed on a number of important matters. In contrast, the CGT (especially with its continued close ties to the PCF) could not have been more unified and clear. Secondly, the specific shape of France's rank-and-file mobilization favored the CGT. The 'resurgence of class conflict' in France did not come, like Italy's 'hot autumn,' as an extensive and extended brush-fire of industrial conflict. If new labor conflict in France did stretch into the early 1970s, the vast bulk of it was concentrated in the events of May–June 1968. As a labor uprising, May–June 1968 was a rapid explosion of rank-and-file protest which became an undeclared general strike reaching the totality of the French labor force within a few days. The rapidity and generalization of the conflict, when combined with the momentary teetering of the Gaullist regime, placed great weight on the organizational shaping power of unions—coordination between different local movements had to be achieved while the whole movement had to be pointed in some direction. Moreover, the May–June strike was only part of a larger knot of social crisis which included the student movement and the near collapse of the political regime. In such a context, whether they desired to or not, both the CGT and the CFDT had to be concerned with 'class' issues, national bargaining strategies, and with the role of union action in the unfolding of political events. That the PCF itself was determined above all to assure that the movement did not slip from political control only reinforced the CGT's resolve in this direction. Thus the situation of May–June 1968 was stacked in favor of the CGT's positions. Finally, the subsequent development of mobilization in France after May–June 1968 occurred constantly in the shadow of progress towards, and the eventual consummation of, political *Union de la Gauche*. In a context in which the French Left was moving towards a plausible alliance and claim for power for the first time in decades, and in which the CGT remained an instrument of the PCF's general strategy, the Communists' strategic perspective, which foresaw the use of the union power to enhance the Left's progress, had a decisive advantage.

Thus the 'resurgence of class conflict' in France was ultimately turned towards traditional union goals and towards indirect political support for the French Left, as the CGT desired. Confronted by a challenge to its notions of desirable trade union action coming both from the working-class rank and file and the CFDT, the CGT stood its ground and used its considerable resources to blunt the challenge and refocus it on different goals. The most significant consequence of this was that the vast energies of new rank-and-file action were *not* ultimately translated into the construction of new beachheads of union power at shopfloor and firm levels nor focused on 'new' demands. Such a translation would have involved decentralizing and depoliticizing unionism in ways which the CGT opposed. The CGT's goal in responding to the new mobilization was, in large part, to reaffirm its own version of 'maximalism.' In this view of French society and change, the route to the kinds of policies which would genuinely change the situation of workers passed through a global program of nationalizations, planning, and income redistribution designed to dispossess the monopolies. Such a program had to be enacted by political parties through the state. Union strategies, therefore, had to be designed to point shorter-term rank-and-file labor-market energies towards longer-term political outcomes. Not that labor-market struggle *per se* was to be neglected, of course. Instead, the CGT saw its task as carrying on such labor struggle in ways which would ultimately contribute to Left success in the political sphere. In the last analysis, this strategic picture had an *either/or* character: either unions directed the mobilizational energies which they could promote or channel towards obtaining changes at the political level, or they would obtain little of worth at all. In this vision there existed little or no space for union efforts to strengthen their positions in the labor market *per se*.

ITALY

The new mobilization in Italy, if it flowed from sources similar to those in France, took a substantially different shape. In Italy there was no total social crisis of the May–June 1968 kind to force union actions towards national-level bargaining and political concerns. Instead, the new rank-and-file energy was decentralized and continuous over a long period of time. In Italy, likewise, there was no dramatically new Left political alternative to drain rank-and-file union energies towards politics. In France, partly because of the nature of May–June 1968 and partly because of the power and astuteness of the regime, many of the gains of the mobilization were undercut in one gesture through devaluation in summer 1969. In Italy, no such central event occured to alter the course and effectiveness of the mobilization. Instead Italy, in contrast to France, possessed a more institutionalized collective bargaining system which dictated that regular contractual negotiations had to be carried on periodically, no matter what. Furthermore, the presence of the Socialist Party in the government meant that the state was unable to bring its power to bear against the workers' mobilization and that pressure for reforms could credibly be brought against the government. (In fact, for the first time since immediately after the war the Minister of Labor appeared to be siding with the unions.) Finally, the changes in union strategy, structure, and incentives in the preceding years legitimated militant demands for higher wages, dramatically altered working conditions, greater worker and union control at the workplace and major economic and social reforms. Taken together, these conditions ensured the existence of intense struggle at all levels of society and enduring targets of worker and union fervor.[49]

The new mobilization in Italy nonetheless presented a major new challenge to Italian unions. It emerged at precisely the location where the unions were weakest and had the least direct control over events, the shop floor. Thus the unions had to decide how best to capture and structure this mobilization. For the movement as a whole this presented an enormous opportunity; for the individual unions, however, there were also present the dangers inherent in a loss of control over their constituencies and in the possibility that other confederations would better respond to the workers' demands; or that the fervor of the hot autumn would be succeeded by failure and disillusionment even worse than that in the mid-1960s. The choices before the unions were even further complicated by the fact that the massive increase in strikes and other protests during and after the 'hot autumn' carried a host of new demands. Old issues of remuneration, job security, and hours persisted, to be sure, but profound new questions about equality, democracy, and control over work on the shop floor were posed. Organizational innovations accompanied new demands as well, involving workers assemblies within firms, the direct election of shopfloor delegates by all workers, embryonic factory councils and, accompanying and in some ways implicit in all of these, the demand for a deepening of the process of unification of the three confederations.[50]

In the abstract, at least, the structures of the new mobilization created a situation of stark choice for official Italian unions. On the one hand, the events challenged trade union 'business as usual' in dramatic ways. On the other, they promised the beginnings of a working-class, potentially union-ist, beachhead in that part of the economy—the shopfloor/firm level—where unions had been traditionally weakest and where the same unions had long claimed a desire to construct new positions. The choice was therefore between regarding the rank-and-file movement as a threat to preexisting positions and strategies and acting to channel movement ener-gies towards more traditional patterns of behavior, and thus toward the reinforcement of the existing system of incentives; or riding with the movement in an attempt to capitalize upon its energies to strengthen union positions, an option which involved reconsidering preexisting positions and strategies, and the incentives on which they had been built.

Italian unions rejected the conservative option and, in light of the preceding discussion, this should come as no surprise. It is important, however, to pay close attention to why this was the case and to how the decision to ride with and seek to channel the wave of mobilization affected the strategic, organizational, and incentive features of the union move-ment. As will be evident, the reinforcing interaction between earlier union changes and the specific conditions of the conjuncture of the early 1970s in Italy assumed great importance.

The first reason why the conservative option was not adopted was that the Italian rank-and-file movement was extremely strong, widespread, and enduring and that it rapidly captured the enthusiasm of the unions' lower-level cadres and militants. The risk of loss of control or deep disillusion-ment, were the unions to oppose the movement, were great, whereas an effort to join and gradually steer the movement toward coordinated goals which would help restore coherence and a measure of control for the confederations seemed to have greater promise of success.

Pushing in much the same direction were the changes which had taken place in the leaderships of the confederations. The responses to the critical junctures of the 1950s and 1960s, and the passage of time itself, had produced new leadership personnel with rather different outlooks than those of their predecessors who had been products of the Resistance and early postwar years. The 'founding fathers' of postwar unionism had been first and foremost political and partisan figures, no matter how great their commitment to unionism. They had viewed unionism in the context of the political and partisan struggle for control of the postwar Italian state along ideological lines of cleavage and had had a (related) bias toward control of union activity from the center and in coordination with partisan and political goals. The labor-market and political situations of the first postwar decade had only tended to reinforce this orientation. The new generation of leaders which had begun to emerge in the 1950s and which was now acceding to peak leadership in the most important federations and in the confederations was both the product of and agent for the changes in strategic orientations and organizational and incentive characteristics we have discussed. These leaders were almost all, although to different degrees and in different ways, more sympathetic to tactical and strategic decentralization, to a greater focus on the labor market as an autonomous arena for the achievement of union goals, to a greater autonomy of the unions from partisan politics, to the importance of strengthening union organization at the shopfloor and branch levels and to the goal of greater unity among the confederations. They had, furthermore, risen to leadership during years in which the unions had been adapting their strategies and incentives in response to changing political and economic conjunctures; and they were attuned and inclined to the necessity to do so.

These factors encouraged a more 'cooperative' than competitive response of the Italian unions to the developments of the late 1960s. This was further reinforced by clear manifestations at the rank-and-file level of discontent with the traditional bickering among the confederations. Especially in the metalworking sector, but in other sectors as well, the workers were behaving as if their confederal ties did not, and should not, impede their working together to attain both their old and new demands. Again here the patterns of responses which the unions had developed since the mid-1950s encouraged such an orientation, which in fact went further than the confederal leaderships appeared prepared to go. The growing emphasis on material and purposive incentives, and the declining and reinterpreted role of identity incentives, made the workers particularly inclined to see the new conjuncture as an opportunity to work together to achieve goals which they all shared. That the confederal leaderships should be more concerned with maintaining distinct identities and should have greater differences about long-term policy for the union movement, including its relationship to partisan politics, should come as no surprise. That they should also have to be responsive to the unitary pressures from the base, however, is also not surprising in the context of the developments we have described. Given the orientations and demands of the workers and lower-level union militants, and the potentially competitive logic of union pluralism, no union could afford to appear too conservative, too anxious to bring the militancy under control, too out of step with the workers' movement.

The willingness of the confederations to try to ride with and at the same time channel the mobilization and to do so in ways which would be more cooperative than competitive, then, grew out of both the specific features of the Italian conjuncture and the heritage of preceding responses to other conjunctures. It was inevitably different from the response of the French unions. To understand the specific features of the 'new' Italian unionism which emerged, however, it is also necessary to recognize that in the process of responding, the Italian confederations were propelled strategically along lines of policy which they had previously discussed only in highly abstract, theoretical, terms and that how this occurred continued to be influenced by the structure of the Italian political system and state.

A critical example of the internal dynamics of the process of adaptation had to do with the development of new factory-level structures of worker representation. Prior to the 'hot autumn,' the unions had been unable, despite their expressed desire to do so, to develop effective factory-level units of bargaining and representation. The mobilization of the 'hot autumn' spontaneously generated such institutions—the shop delegates and factory councils—and the unions gradually accepted and sought to generalize them, a process which was politically sanctioned with the 1970s *Statuto dei lavoratori* passed by the Parliament and granting a wide range of organizational and jurisdictional rights to the unions in the workplaces and new protections and rights to individual workers.

The new factory-level organizations embodied the emerging interaction between longstanding union goals and orientations and the particular characteristics of the conjuncture. Whereas earlier union reflections and efforts to build such base-level organizations had foreseen union domination, the new organizational forms contained marked features of direct democracy. Workers elected their own representatives, with only partial union mediation and regardless of union affiliation. Thus, if the new delegates and council members were affiliated with official unions, it was often a matter of rank-and-file choice rather than a consequence of union hierarchical determination. To the extent that the official unions hoped to establish their presences in the new institutions, they were obliged to be responsive to rank-and-file desires.

This, in turn, encouraged a qualitatively new type of unity between the different official union organizations, one which would go well beyond the unity-in-action in the market arena of the 1960s to include unity in the political arena and even some peak-level unification as well. To attain such unity, however, further 'depoliticization' of the Italian unions was a prerequisite. A new quality of unity between the confederations could be effective and lasting only if each one could be assured that its energies would not be turned, through unity, towards the achievement of a political agenda which was that of another confederation. Several developments in preceding years prepared the ground for the attainment of greater and more principled unity: the PCI's abandonment of 'transmission beltism'; its subsequent practice of focusing its organizational energies more on territorial jurisdictions than on the factory, leaving the latter more to the union; the CISL's movement away from the Christian Democratic Party; and finally, both the initial optimism and subsequent disillusionment with the Center–Left which had brought the confederations closer together and had encouraged debate over their philosophical differences in a spirit of compromise. Under the pressure of the new mobilization, these earlier developments made it possible for the confederal leaderships to come to agreement on the critically important issue of the incompatibility between union leadership at all levels and official positions in the parties or in Parliament.

Incompatibility was of enormous symbolic and practical significance. On the one hand, it announced both to the rank and file and the parties (all of which were decidedly ambivalent) that unity was of such importance that decades-long ties should be broken and political positions of importance abandoned in order to advance its prospects. In a similar vein, it formally embodied the full autonomy of the union movement from the political system. On the other hand, it meant that the unions had much greater freedom and legitimacy to perceive the new situation, and develop strategies and tactics, as independent actors, no longer 'relays' for the parties. In fact, the symbolic breaking of links with the parties necessitated this: no longer instruments for and expressions of the parties, the unions had to develop their autonomous identities if they were to establish and maintain their authority with an already mobilized and potentially restive rank and file, and if they were effectively to resist any attempts by the parties to reassert control. Taken together, these effects of the incompatibility decision and others taken at the same time had the effect of making unity something quite different from what it had been before: no longer an instrumental stepping stone to the achievement of other ends, but an important end in itself and a critical aspect of the fundamental identity of the union movement and its component unions. In the decade to follow, this new characteristic of unity—its incorporation into the identity component of the incentive systems of each of the confederations—was repeatedly to encourage compromise when division might otherwise have resulted.

The development of factory-level organization and more autonomous and unified confederations which occurred in the early 1970s institutionalized the shift from highly centralized and partisan unionism which had been proceeding by fits and starts for the preceding fifteen years. As the values of union democracy, workplace bargaining and power, and union autonomy became integral parts of the unions' identities, embedded in organizational structures and rules, they had consequences as well for the strategies which the unions pursued and how they intended to pursue them. Yet, once again the specific content of these cannot be understood except in the light of the conjuncture in which they were formulated and the enduring, if adapted, traditions of the different confederations.

The strategy which the Italian unions adopted in the early 1970s has been described in detail in the essay devoted to that country. What needs to be underlined here is that it did not entail a radical shift to market-arena and 'corporative' or particularistic goals, as might be anticipated in light of either the liberal optimist theory or simply an analysis of the organizational changes which had taken place. Rather, the unions developed their own broad-based strategy. It comprised both political and market objectives: social reforms which would affect not only union constituents but broader strata of the working populace as well, and changes at the level of the workplace which included not just advances in wages and working conditions but issues of greater worker and union control over management prerogatives in view of concerns which extended beyond the workplace and not just within it. It also comprised a view of the appropriate role of union action and pressure which meant that the union should use its power in the labor market to advance its objectives not just through pressure on and bargaining with other labor-market actors but also with government. Ironically, the reduction of union partisanship and growth of autonomy did not lead to depoliticization in *strictu sensu* but to a new kind of politicization which, especially in this period, projected the union as almost an alternative structure of political initiative and consensus to the parties and party system, which were judged to be inefficient, unrepresentative and out of touch with the nation.

In this new strategic vision, 'maximalism' was little in evidence. The unions accepted the necessity of a genuine 'mixed' economy for Italy far into the future. The problems which they perceived were not stark dichotomies between a capitalism which didn't work and a socialism whose outlines were unknown. The real issue which they began to address was the actual structure of the Italian 'model of development.' The liberal model of the postwar settlement pursued after 1947 had bought successes at the cost of economic and social distortions which, besides leading to injustice and inefficiency, had created longer-term problems. Were this liberal model to be pursued into the future, Italy was likely to face ever-growing economic difficulties. What was needed was a different 'mix,' which would follow from different decisions about basic economic choices. Italian capital was incapable of making these decisions. The unions, using their new resources and deploying their new vision, might be able to weigh in the balance for more rational and just political-economic decision. The first objectives of the new unionism involved, to be sure, direct redress of grievances on the shopfloor and firm level—wages, hours, working conditions, employment security, lessening inequalities between categories of workers, legitimation and legalization of new working-class and union representative structures. In this area there was a kind of union economic maximalism, but very different from the French. The Italian unions refused to recognize almost any constraints which the broader 'needs' of the economy might put on their wage and workplace behavior, an attitude which became embodied in the expressed belief that wages were an 'independent variable' and in the slogan, 'the escalator cannot be touched.' Both these economic 'maximalism' doctrines were gradually to be eroded at the end of the decade.

Why such attitudes became part and parcel of Italian union behavior at this time is not hard to discern. On the one hand, to do otherwise and therefore seek to repress worker wage demands, threatened to rupture the still tenuous ties which the unions were developing with the intensely mobilized workers and factory and lower union militants. It might, furthermore, have reopened rifts between the confederations and within them, both because all the confederations had internal currents which were wholly wedded to wage militancy and because, given the attitudes of workers, a policy of greater wage control would have opened a terrain for union competition. On the other hand, the leaders of the confederations saw wage and shopfloor militancy as the major resource which they could employ in advancing the second prong of their strategy: pressuring for social and economic reforms by the government. In fact, a peculiar aspect of Italian union behavior in this period was its quasi-neosyndicalist attempt to enter into direct negotiations with the government, going around the parties, for reforms. The unions made the 'struggle for reforms' a centerpiece of their strategy and this responded to a 'representational' logic—the workers wanted reforms which would deal with the chaos that twenty years of development had created; it responded to an 'alliance' logic—reforms were a terrain where worker interests coincided, at least in part, with other strata of the population; and it responded to an organizational logic—the struggle for reforms, with its focus on government, tended to recentralize authority and decision-making, to embody the autonomy of the unions from individual parties and to provide a meeting place for the confederations, which did not, at least in the short run, raise the issues of a more ideological character that still divided them. It should also be obvious, however, that the combination of the struggle for reforms with wage militancy pursued through unified union action tended strongly to place material and purposive incentives at the core of the unions' incentive systems while submerging the traditional identity incentives which each individual confederation had utilized. To the extent that identity incentives continued to play a role—and they did—these were more incentives based on unity and on the critical role of unions as the prime source of initiatives for change in Italian society through the pressure they could bring to bear on the political system.

The mobilizations of the late 1960s and early 1970s were critical events for all European union movements. For the French and Italian they proved decisive in crystallizing the pattern of divergence which had emerged from earlier critical junctures. In France, as we have seen, the mobilization was greeted by the CGT (and PCF) as a challenge to be turned towards reaffirming longstanding structures of union identity which articulated in obvious ways with quite specific partisan and political goals. For the CGT the task was to divert the energies of mobilization towards a trade union-ism which posited that the kinds of change which counted could only occur in the political arena through the change in the partisan composition of government necessary to implement a 'maximalist' program of reforms to dispossess the monopolists. Other French unions, in particular the CFDT, did not share this vision, to be sure. The post-1968 period therefore became a struggle between the CGT and its ally-rival the CFDT over the disposition of the new resources revealed by the mobilization. The CFDT did what it could, embracing the decentralizing tendencies of the rank-and-file explosion, converting them into a theory and an identity and espousing a number of the mobilization's new demands and approaches. But it was never able to accumulate sufficient organizational power either to outflank the CGT or to deter the CGT from its chosen path. The CGT was, of course, tremendously aided by parallel dynamics in the political realm. Promoting a perspective which foresaw the salvation of trade unions through maximalist political change was much easier as the French Left coalesced into unity around the 1972 Common Program. Thus the new mobilization in France was gradually turned away from the labor market towards more partisan political concerns. Whether or not the immense reinforcement of union power at shopfloor level which occurred in Italy would have occurred in France had union policies and goals been different, is difficult to determine. There was a brief moment after 1969—the Cha-ban Delmas-Jacques Delors *Nouvelle Société* episode—when it seemed as if the French state might be willing to facilitate the construction of a genuine decentralized collective bargaining system implying recognition of unions as *interlocuteurs valables* in the firm. The moment passed, however (aided by CGT and patronal opposition), without a great deal of change. Thus when economic crisis began in 1973–4, French unionism faced it with much the same organizational perspectives which it had held prior to the later 1960s.

In Italy, even prior to the new mobilization, unions had reacted to earlier conjunctures by beginning to reconsider important aspects of their identities. 'Transmission belt'-type connections with political parties had been considerably attenuated. Unions had started to perceive themselves as strategic actors of their own, whatever the goals of political forces. They had begun to explore new possibilities of increasing their resources by militant, unified action around a wide range of 'material' questions about shopfloor life and power. Moreover, for a series of reasons, connected both to union life and to the logic of Italian politics, political and economic 'maximalism' of the kind which persisted for so long in France receded in importance. Visions of global and rapid transformation of the political economy to be achieved through partisan change in the political arena gave way to visions of piecemeal reform to redirect Italy's faltering liberal postwar economic trajectory towards a more economically promising and equitable 'model of development.' The rank-and-file explosion of the 'hot autumn' and afterwards pushed these tendencies forward rapidly, to the point where Italian unions were transformed. Decentralized labor-market militancy connected with widespread rank-and-file participation and broad union unity recast union incentive structures. Changing the world of the workplace—not only 'materially,' in terms of wages, hours, and security, but also in terms of authority and power—became a central concern of exchanges between unions and their supporters. In the process notions of the articulation between workplace union action and broader social change were redefined. Unions, *qua* unions, could, by using bargaining and mobilizational power, intervene to shape the nature of investments and public policy in ways which would, at one and the same time, promote a more effective economy and a more just society. Italian unions would therefore greet the crisis of the 1970s immensely strengthened at shopfloor and branch level (which was to prove both a great asset and a problem) and prepared to think in terms of a trade union-centered 'interventionism' in political-economic decision-making.

Part 4

A Summing Up

From the preceding analysis it should be evident why the French and Italian union movements responded so differently—maximalism and interventionism respectively—to the crisis of the mid-1970s. These responses were deeply ingrained in the strategic and policy postures and related systems of incentives which had emerged over the preceding twenty years in response to several challenging conjunctures of economic and political change. Yet, as in the case of these earlier conjunctures, the implications for union strategy and bases of support of the crisis were not unequivocal, understandable in the abstract. Rather, they could only be understood in light of how the national movements themselves had evolved and of the strategies and goals of the unions themselves. We do not intend here to examine this recent period in detail, but some general analysis is necessary in order to raise some broader issues.

At its simplest, the crisis of the mid-1970s embodied a multifaceted threat to the material condition and security of workers. The slackening of the economies threatened widespread unemployment; inflation menaced workers' real purchasing power; the transfer of national income to the oil-producing countries threatened to lead governments to reduce their expenditures for social programs and to be less supportive (to the degree they had been) of worker wage demands. No union could ignore these dangers or fail to seek to develop policies which would protect the interests of their constituents; at the same time, as we indicated at the outset of this chapter, the crisis also created opportunities for the unions and their political and social allies.

If there were these very general similarities between the French and Italian situations, however, the specific characteristics of the conjunctures faced by the two union movements were markedly different, in part because of earlier union policies. These differences can be briefly outlined following the scheme of analysis we have earlier used.

The first major difference was in the market strength of the two union movements. The Italian unions were much stronger than the French both in terms of the extent of unionization and of the workplace presence and efficacy of union and worker organization. This was an important heritage of the different ways the two union movements had responded to the surge of militance at the end of the 1960s, if obviously not solely due to those responses. Its significance at the moment of crisis was that the Italian unions had both greater capacities to resist the threats to workers' income and job security, and, through such resistance, to maintain significant market pressure on the larger political economy. Some Italian union strength in the overall economy began to be sapped by the growth of the 'hidden economy' (itself an expression of the inability to force workers in the unionized economy to bear the costs of economic downturn) and there was a major increase in unemployment, although this too tended to be concentrated outside the most unionized sectors of the industrial work force. Nonetheless, the Italian unions retained the ability to defend their supporters and to transfer many of the costs of crisis onto other social sectors or into inflation. This was much less the case for the French unions.

A second major difference in the two conjunctures was to be found in the political arena and had two features. On the one hand, while the crisis in both countries was accompanied by a seeming decay of the political strength of the governing coalitions and new possibilities for the parties of the Left, in France this prospect resided in an electoral victory of the parties of the Common Program, whereas in Italy it rested in the possibility of the gradual entrance of the PCI into a government which would still include the DC and PSI. This had several implications. It meant that in Italy electoral outcomes would be less important than in France, while the 'legitimacy' of the PCI and its ability to present itself as a guarantor of union cooperation would assume significant weight. It also meant that the probability of sweeping change emanating from government was far less in Italy than in France. More generally, maneuver and political bargaining between the government, the Communists and the unions would take on greater importance in Italy, while in France the relationship between the parties of the Left would be pivotal. The political relevance of union positions and actions was thus different in the two cases.

On the other hand, the differences in the coalitional situations also had a significant bearing on the unions even were little political change to occur. In France, the government remained hostile and inaccessible to the unions. Without political change, there was little prospect of winning concessions in the political arena. In Italy, in contrast, the decaying Center–Left, and the attempts of the parties of government to shore up their positions led them often to seek to curry favor with the unions. Even in the absence of political change, the Italian unions could hope to bargain with and win gains in the political arena.

The third major difference between the French and Italian situations was in relations among the unions themselves. In France, as we have seen, there was a considerable latent and sometimes open conflict between the union confederations, each bearer of a different strategy, policy program, and identity. The unions were cooperating in the market arena, but such cooperation and the terms on which joint actions would proceed was a continual source of tension. This was only aggravated by the potential that the Left parties might win power, a prospect which augmented the struggle between the PS and the PCF for dominance within the coalition. The CGT still maintained its tight linkage with the PCF and, in this spirit, still treated its relationship with the CFDT primarily as instrumental to PCF goals. The CFDT, in contrast, attempted to maintain its distance from the *Parti Socialiste* and remained weaker than the CGT in the labor market. As a result, it was a relatively ineffective counterweight to the Communist union. Thus the likelihood in France was that overall union policy would reflect the CGT's and PCF's policy priorities.

In Italy, relations among the confederations were of quite a different character. Union unity and partisan autonomy had proceeded much further, becoming values in and of themselves for many unionists. Furthermore, the unions had developed their own broadscale programmatic platform which served, among other functions, to allow them to promote political goals without openly siding with any particular party or coalitional arrangement. This was the case both because they sought to advance this program not just in the political, but also in the market, arena and because, as suggested above, the political situation made credible a direct political role for the union movement. Each confederation did, however, retain some loyalties to specific parties, a fact which assumed greater importance after 1975 when the possibilities grew of major changes in the composition of national government, including the incorporation of the PCI. There remained, therefore, latent tensions among the confederations both about what priority to give to the market and political components of the movement's strategy and about what stance to assume toward the government and its makeup. Nonetheless, the confederations cooperated more than they competed and they retained considerable autonomy.

A fourth difference between the French and Italian movements can be summarized very briefly. While the French union movement remained highly centralized, the Italian one had a significant diffusion and distribution of power and independent competency among the confederations, federations and factory-level structures. This was, of course, once again a heritage of earlier union developments and strategic choices. Its importance in the present context is that it meant that the confederations in Italy, even should they wish to do so, could not impose a centralized economic or political bargaining strategy on the movement. To do so threatened to foster both interlevel conflict (some of which existed in any case) and to create space for interconfederal competition. In France, in contrast, central control was the rule, despite the CFDT's attempts to work toward a decentralized '*autogestionnaire*' policy.

The final important difference between the two union movements lay in their incentive systems and the expectations these fostered among workers. The Italian unions operated with a mixed system of incentives, in which material and purposive incentives had increasingly assumed independent importance and in which identity incentives had become progressively a product less of the unions' linkages with political parties and ideologies and more of the values which the unions themselves espoused, including unity and autonomy. The Italian unions were expected to 'deliver' both material gains and social reforms and to do so through their own actions and policy initiatives. Italian workers, conditioned by union rhetoric and policy, and by the successes of the preceding years, came to some considerable extent to want 'everything, and now,' and to expect the unions to use both the market and political arenas to meet these expectations. There were still some restraining factors: the continuing loyalties of some workers to the political parties, including the PCI, which were openly counseling restraint; the broad commitment, fostered by the unions, to democracy and to the necessity to assure that union demands did not undermine the commitment of nonunion sectors to democratic institutions; the legitimacy and authority which the union leaderships had attained by their policies in the preceding years; the awareness, once again fostered by the unions (and parties) that success in the market and political arenas was to some extent contingent on the unions' ability to maintain a broad set of social alliances for which they would act as a reformist spearhead. Nonetheless, neither deference to the confederal centers nor deferral of desired gains could be easily achieved. In a situation of growing economic and political crisis and shrinking national resources, this was to create profound internal tensions and problems for the union movement.

The incentive system in the French union movement was profoundly different. It too had gradually become more mixed over the two preceding decades as the role of traditional ideologies as sources of mobilization had declined. There were, however, several important ways in which the incentives used, and the expectations fostered, differed with the Italian. First, purposive incentives played a smaller and different role than in Italy. Reforms were an important part of the unions' rhetoric, but they were presented as being achievable primarily as a single package which would be secured through the conquest of government by the parties of the Left. This way of viewing reforms had several implications for the unions' incentive system. It meant that the unions themselves were no more than an indirect contributor to the reform effort. It would not be union action itself which would (or could) lead to social change. Relatedly, it also meant that no significant change was possible without a Left victory; piecemeal reform was an illusion and union pressure for it no more than part of the effort to create the conditions for a party victory. To the extent, therefore, that the unions fostered hope for reforms, they were to a considerable extent focusing that hope on the parties.

Second, material incentives also played a less important role than in Italy. This was to a considerable extent due to the market weakness of French unionism and to the absence of industrial relations institutions which would have given the unions a legitimate and widespread role in wage determination. In fact, in France significant features of the wage structure remained the product of state intervention. A further factor contributing to the relatively lower importance of material incentives, however, were the ideologies of the unions themselves. In different ways both the CGT and the CFDT argued that significant gains were impossible without a major transformation of society and that, furthermore, the struggle for wages was illegitimate if not seen in the context of more global goals of societal transformation. It is evident that such ideologies served to rationalize the unions' actual inability to produce widespread wage gains, but it is also the case that they tended to reduce the importance of material gains themselves in the appeals of the unions.

As the two preceding points suggest, identity incentives were of much greater importance in France than in Italy. The specific content of these incentives varied between the CGT and the CFDT. In the former, the association with the Communist Party and with its traditions and revolutionary rhetoric was of critical importance. In the CFDT, in contrast, the emphasis was on the image of a 'self-managed' society which would be built from the bottom up, with the union movement taking an important initiating role in the transformation. Yet, in addition to these identity incentives, specific to each confederation, it is important to note that increasingly the two unions also shared a common identity: their association with the Common Program and its goals. The program, of course, had two valences in the incentive structures of the confederations. As societal ideal, it represented a part of their identity; as package of reforms, it was the embodiment of the reform goals to which the unions claimed to contribute. In both its valences, however, the Common Program could become a source of tension within the union movement and within each confederation. Such tension would arise if the confederation were faced with the choice of promoting the interests and goals of one of the parties of the Left coalition at the expense of the prospects of success of the coalition as a whole. A further consequence of the growing importance of the Common Program to the unions was that they could expect to lose support if the program's victory became less likely.

From the preceding discussion it should be clear how conditions in the market and political arenas and in the union movements themselves in the mid-1970s fostered the maximalism of the French union movement and interventionism of the Italian. These strategic responses were, of course, also consistent with the strategic orientations which the two movements had been pursuing since the late 1960s and, especially in the French case, for much longer. That there should be such consistency between the strategies of the unions and a number of these external and internal conditions should not be surprising. The unions, through their earlier policies, had to a considerable extent contributed to their character. There was, furthermore, nothing about the nature of the crisis which was likely, in the short run, to stimulate major strategic departures. Neither movement had obvious and attractive options in seeking to defend the acquired positions of their supporters, nor did the opportunities for political change which the crisis at the outset seemed to offer suggest the need or desirability of strategic changes, particularly when we take into consideration the relationships which the unions in each movement had with each other and with specific political parties. Thus, the maximalist response of the French movement and the interventionism of the Italian were entirely predictable responses to the onset of the crisis in the mid-1970s, consistent with both the opportunity structure of the environment in which they were operating and the unions' own strategic inclinations. Ironically, at the beginning of the most profound political-economic crisis of the postwar period, there was little reason to expect that the union movements in the two countries would alter how they pursued their goals and interests.

This argument for the 'rationality' of strategic continuity, however, cannot be left unqualified for it begs two critical questions. First, whatever sense it may have made at the outset of the crisis, did such continuity create longer-term problems for the unions as the effects of the prolonged crisis made themselves felt? Second, under what conditions does our analysis of the entire postwar period suggest that strategic change in the movements might become more likely? We will address these two issues in closing this essay, intending thereby to give a future cast to what has otherwise been a retrospective analysis.

We look first at the issue of the critical factors which appear in the past consistently to have conditioned the strategies, policies, and incentive systems of the unions and which have repeatedly played an important role in explaining the differences between the French and Italian cases. In doing so, we have two purposes. On the one hand, this will enable us to briefly underline once again the variables which our approach indicates are critical to understanding the constraints under which unions in these, and we would argue any, democratic systems formulate their strategy. On the other hand, it will make possible a brief examination of how the effects of the crisis might be expected to influence the strategies of the unions.

The variables which have been most important in our analysis can be divided into three basic categories: those which describe features of the political arena, those which describe features of the market arena and those which describe features of the individual unions and union movements as institutions. The first two of these, we have argued, are important because they constrain the types of incentives which the unions can draw on in attempting to build, maintain, extend, and intensify support. The third is important because it enables one better to understand the strategic choices made within those constraints. Taken together, the variables in these three categories allow one to narrow quite far the range of strategic choices which one would expect.

Three features of the political arena have proven of greatest importance. The first is the *partisan composition of government* and more specifically the extent to which parties sympathetic to and supportive of the trade unions are in control of government or at least play a significant role in its policy-making. The exclusion of the Left from government in France as contrasted with its partial inclusion in Italy meant that French unions were much less able and inclined to seek to develop purposive incentives through specific, but piecemeal, economic and social reforms which they would press government to enact. It is important to underline here that it was not the declared or actual willingness of government to undertake reforms which proved of importance. We saw, for instance, that Gaullism's *étatiste*/paternalistic approach to social reform, with its intention to circumvent the unions, did not draw the unions into the reformist process, nor, in our view, could it be expected to, for such an approach did not promise to allow the unions to use reforms as a source of incentives. An additional impact of the partisan composition of government was felt in the labor market. To the extent that parties sympathetic to the unions played a governmental role, the governments tended to be more supportive of the unions' demands in the labor market, thus enabling them more effectively to pursue material gains for their supporters.

The second feature of the political arena which proved of importance was more structural: the *structure of the state and the degree to which it fulfilled functions—such as wage setting—which might otherwise have been undertaken by collective bargaining institutions*. The highly centralized, self-consciously impermeable French state which also played a major formal role in setting the terms between capital and labor created far fewer opportunities for labor to develop either purposive or material incentives than did the 'available' Italian state[51] which generally stayed out of capital–labor relations and which, even when it did intervene (increasingly in the 1970s), did so to mediate issues rather than to remove them from determination through bargaining between unions and employers.

The third feature of the political arena which was influential was the *competitive dynamic* between the parties with linkages to the unions or seeking their direct support. How this variable worked itself out in each national case was extremely complex, in part because of the strategies and goals of each of the parties, and because of the ways these parties were represented within different unions. As a general rule, however, it was clear that to the extent there was strong and open competition between the union-oriented parties, it tended as well to foster competition among the party-related factions within the unions and union movement. The consequences of this intra-union competition for union strategies and incentives depended to a considerable extent on the specific kinds of incentives each union or faction of a union could derive from its association with the party.

Turning now to features of the market arena, three have appeared most important. The first is the *strength* of the unions as measured by the extent of unionization, the degree of implantation of union organization in the factories, and the cohesion among the unions. Together these aspects of strength have enabled the unions to improve the situation of their supporters and to defend them even in conditions of economic downturn. To the extent that the unions have been strong, as, for example, became the case in Italy after the 'hot autumn,' this has encouraged the development of material incentives and, to a lesser but important extent, of purposive incentives as well. The reasons for this have been amply demonstrated in the country chapters and in this conclusion. Two points, however, need to be underlined. Strength has not necessarily meant that the unions would concentrate their attention on making material gains through action in the market arena; market strength can be and has been turned toward the political arena and applying pressure for social and economic reform. Furthermore, great market strength can, as it did in Italy in the later 1970s, become a danger, threatening the unions' ability to win sustained material gains or further extensions of social expenditures through action in either arena and even putting in peril gains already won. This paradoxical situation arises when great strength is combined with sharp and sustained economic difficulties for firms and for the national economy as a whole.[52]

The second feature of the market arena which has been shown to play a major role has been the degree of *institutionalization* of collective bargaining between employers and unions. The existence of collective bargaining institutions has at least two important consequences. On the one hand, it promotes the development of material incentives on the part of the unions, although not necessarily—and this should be stressed—to the exclusion of purposive incentives (witness the Italian unions' use of collective bargaining to try to get firms to invest in the Italian south while at the same time pursuing the strategy of reforms with the government). On the other hand, established structures for union–employer bargaining increase the importance of action in the market arena in the overall strategic profile of the unions. The relative weakness of such institutions in France worked to inhibit any of the unions from trying to use the market to advance its interests, even when, as in the case of the CFDT, there was an ideological and strategic inclination to do so and when such an approach might have improved the CFDT's competitive position relative to the CGT.

The third feature of the market arena which has proven of major significance is, of course, the overall *condition of the economy*, especially the tautness of the labor market and the prosperity of employers or at least some of them. The tautness of the labor market has been important because it has been an underlying structural constraint on the strength of the unions. Institutional characteristics of the unions have been able, particularly in the 1970s and in Italy, to counteract the effects of higher unemployment on worker militancy and the ability of the unions to win wage gains. Nonetheless, to the extent that the market has been slack, unions have tended to rely more on purposive and especially identity incentives (e.g., the 1950s in both France and Italy), and to focus more on the political arena. Paradoxically, as noted earlier, great union strength can also promote conditions which lead the unions to focus on the political arena. The prosperity of employers, especially their ability to pay higher wages due to growth in profits and productivity, has been important in creating the conditions in which unions have been drawn toward the market and toward its use in ways which fostered the development of material incentives. This was most noticeable in the 1960s when both the French and Italian union movements, despite the significant strategic differences between them, directed greater attention to winning material gains through aggressive activity in the market arena.

Four features of the unions and union movements as institutions have assumed a prominent part in our analysis. The first of these is the *degree of centralization* of the unions. Greater centralization has been associated with a predominance of identity incentives in the unions and, to a lesser extent, with an important role for purposive incentives.[53] Decentralization, in contrast, has been associated with a major focus by the unions on material incentives. These associations, or at least that between decentralization and material incentives, however, may be peculiar to the French and Italian cases, a product of the complex of variables we have been highlighting and their particular form in the two countries. That this may be the case is suggested by the Swedish unions which, although highly centralized, nonetheless give great importance to material incentives and have been quite strong in the labor market throughout the postwar period.

The second major institutional feature was the *relationship between specific unions and parties*, in particular the extent to which the party played an important part in the development of union incentives and/or in supplying the union with militants or money. To the extent the latter was the case—the 'classic' case is the tie between the PCF and the CGT—the union remained very much an instrument of the party and its strategic interests and goals. The PCI–CGIL case showed, however, that even where there were such ties, if the union wished, and the Party was willing to allow, greater autonomy, this was possible. Direct party–union linkages, however, were not the only way that party interests could affect union policy. It was also the case that, depending on the types of incentives which the unions were employing or wished to rely upon, they would be more or less concerned with the ability of the party to play an influential role in government. As an example, as the unions in Italy relied more heavily on purposive incentives in the form of economic and social reforms initiated by government, they also became more concerned to try to help the parties sympathetic to them to retain or gain a governmental role. The Scandinavian unions' relationships to the Social-Democratic parties in those countries clearly offer further examples of this type of indirect (and sometimes direct) linkage.[54] It should also be noted, however, that in cases of union pluralism, with different unions having ties with different parties, even the indirect party–union linkages can become a source of major tension within the union movement.

The third institutional factor of major importance is a feature of the union movement as a whole: the *degree of competitiveness between unions*. This factor was not shown to have a direct bearing on what types of incentives unions employed or whether and to what extent they sought to use the political or market arenas (except that an inability to cooperate in the market made it difficult for the unions to develop material or purposive incentives and fostered weakness which, in turn, promoted a focus on the political arena). It was, however, critically important in explaining change in the strategic orientations and incentive systems of different unions. Repeatedly, the threat that another union would derive a competitive advantage from policy innovation led to change. And weaker unions, seeking such an advantage, would undertake policy innovations which a stronger union with an established position would be averse to making. Thus, the contrast between the French movement—where the competitive balance was such that the dominant CGT could impose its desired policies on the movement as a whole—and the Italian movement—where the CGIL, although it was stronger, was repeatedly threatened by the CISL —is instructive. In the Italian case, the competition between the unions, and their later efforts to reduce the room for competition while each maintained its autonomous identity, led to significant strategic innovations. No similar observation could be made for the French case.

The final institutional feature of importance was the *strategic and incentive heritage* of each union. It was clear in our analysis that history mattered: unions, as institutions, tended to want to do in the present what they had done in the past and to assume that support was best maintained by continuing to provide the incentives on which that support had been built. Often, this proved to be the case, as the relative success of the CGT demonstrated. It was also evident at a number of points, however, that under certain conditions this inertial tendency was not best in keeping with the individual union's or union movement's interest in building or maintaining support. We do not wish here to recapitulate these conditions, some of which have been discussed not only in the country chapters and earlier sections of this concluding chapter but in the immediately preceding pages as well. Two important issues about the conditions for change, however, should be briefly addressed. The first is under what conditions was change 'from below,' due to changes in the expectations and demands of workers, most likely. Here our analysis has suggested two. On the one hand, such change has seemed most likely when there were major infusions of new workers into the work force. Under these conditions changed demands could appear rather suddenly as the 'new workers' made new demands which fell outside of the established practices of the unions, those demands interacted with the longstanding but perhaps dormant demands and grievances of 'old workers' (especially when they had been reared in a 'revolutionary' tradition) and an insurgency within the unions would develop. On the other hand, change 'from below' could also be the product of gradual shifts in the incentive systems of the unions interacting with the effect on workers' attitudes and desires promoted by secular socioeconomic and political change (e.g., the slow increase in the use of material incentives in the 1960s). For this process to produce substantial revision of union strategy and organization, however, there also had to be major changes (usually of a relatively discontinuous nature) in the environment in which the unions operated such that they could actually deliver the types of incentives their supporters were increasingly seeking. If both the preceding points indicate the conditions under which change from below is most probable, however, the French case has made clear that such a drive for change need not be responded to by the unions. Here again the competitiveness factor or, more generally, the threat that the union or unions will lose support if they do not respond by taking up the new demands seems critical. Where this threat is weak or absent—perhaps because 'exit' from the union is made difficult by rules or because identity incentives are sufficiently strong to retain even discontented workers' loyalty—the unions have a very strong ability to resist pressures for change which come from below.

On the basis of the preceding discussion, it seems appropriate and worthwhile to close this essay with some hazardous observations and hypotheses about recent and future developments in the French and Italian labor movements. We will focus on two changes in the environments in which the unions in each country operate, one in the market arena and the other in the political.

Looking first at France, there have been two developments of major interest for our concerns. The first has been the worsening of the economic situation since 1974–5; the second is the 1981 accession to governmental power of a new coalition dominated by the Socialists. The degeneration of the economic situation in France in the last few years was in no ways worse and in some ways less bad than in most other European countries. Nonetheless, it still was marked by a major increase in unemployment, severe job loss in some large employment sectors of industry, significant rates of inflation, and attempts to cut back or at least stop the growth of some social service programs.

What is striking, although it should at this point come as no surprise, is that the French union movement made very few changes in its maximalist strategy in response to these developments. The economic decline did little to affect the incentive system on which the unions built their support and, to the extent it did, the weakness of the unions in the market made it difficult for them to defend the workers' positions. On the other hand, the damage to workers' interests and the policies and general hostility of the government to the unions tended to render more effective the unions' rhetoric, especially their appeals to partisan support for the parties of the Left, to the Common Program and to the need for a complete replacement of the governmental coalition if anything was to be done to defend the working class. The identity incentives with which the unions had been, in different ways, working for a number of years, therefore, remained effective, and the unions continued their intense focus on the political arena.

This situation, however, changed in late 1977–early 1978 with the defeat of the parties of the Common Program on the heels of the PCF's initiatives which broke up the coalition. What is interesting about this turn of events is that it posed a severe strain for Communist union supporters between loyalty to and identification with the Party, on the one hand, and with the Common Program and thus the need for alliance, on the other. At the same time, this strain also embodied two conceptions of unionism, one stressing union autonomy and the need to pursue a strategy geared to union interests, and the other stressing the union's tight linkages to the PCF and need to gear its strategy to the Party's conception of *its* strategic interests. Neither of these conceptions—as the Italian comparison makes clear—implied an apolitical unionism, but the former certainly meant a much less narrowly partisan one and therefore also one in which the union would rely far less on the incentives it derived from its close association with the party in developing support.

The political crisis of the French Left and French Communist unionism had three impacts, all showing the extent to which expectations among workers about the Common Program had become a critical part of the unions' appeals. First, the unity of the union movement was shattered, as the CGT, following the line of the PCF, began to attack the CFDT for 'reformism' and even as potentially available to sell out the working class. This was a predictable response, the CGT trying to reinforce its traditional identity incentives. The CFDT, not surprisingly, geared up some of its traditional anti-Communism and sought to present itself as the only union determined to defend and advance the concrete interests of the workers. Second, despite their efforts, both unions lost support and were faced with significant disillusionment among members and cadres. This was manifested in a decreased ability to mobilize workers for any types of demonstrations, be they workplace or nationally oriented. This was perhaps the clearest sign that the Common Program, and the identity and purposive incentives it generated, had become a very important component of the structure of incentives through which the French unions built and maintained support. Finally, within both the CGT and the CFDT different factions sought to undertake a thoroughgoing reexamination of union strategies and policies. These are amply described in Chapter 1. What should be underlined is the form these took. In the CFDT, the *recentrage* position sought to find a strategy which would allow the union to break out of the oft-repeated pattern—autonomous policy innovation followed by subordination to the CGT—which had characterized its position for the last fifteen years. To do so, it argued that the union had to come to terms with the concrete problems faced by the workers in the market and had to develop a strategy and tactics designed to engage these problems. In the CGT 'proposition force' unionism had as its underlying premise the need for the CGT to develop a strategy and policy platform which would make it far more autonomous from the PCF, a need which could only be met, and would be embodied in, a strategic line which engaged what the union saw as the major difficulties faced by the workers and the French economy and sought to propose and bargain for its own solutions to those problems. Thus, in both unions but with different concrete proposals, factions argued that the union movement, if it was to recover and develop its strength, had to become less partisan, more autonomous and more willing to pursue partial solutions using its scope for initiative in not only the political but also the market arena. Especially for the CGT, a strategy operating on the basis of such principles would develop an incentive system very different from any which it had used in the postwar period.

Until the surprising Presidential election campaign of 1981, however, neither majorities nor minorities in either major French union were able to resolve the problems which the unions faced. 'Proposition force' groups in the CGT faded as the Confederation was dragged by the PCF towards new service as an auxiliary to the Party's attempts to persuade French workers that the Socialists and the CFDT were class collaborationist allies of the Giscard regime. For the CGT, of course, this involved an intensification of 'revolutionary' identity incentives at the expense of material incentives (which crisis and trade union division rendered rather more scarce) and purposive incentives (which the blocked political situation removed). The CFDT, in contrast, sought to regenerate its position through much greater labor-market moderation—the 'radical recenterers' lost out—and willingness to negotiate. Identity incentives declined in importance as the CFDT's early-1970s radicalism vanished from sight. However, the CFDT's new posture depended for success upon the accumulation of new material incentives through successful labor-market dealing and such an accumulation proved impossible, again given the crisis and the political situation. Thus the CFDT's reoriented mix of incentives worked little better than the CGT's. Up through springtime 1981, then, the results of CGT and CFDT post-1978 shifts in incentive mixes were competitive union disunity, growing union impotence in the market, and declining union membership and support.

François Mitterrand's election to the Presidency in May 1981, the subsequent success of the Socialists in the 1981 legislative elections and the inclusion of Communists in the French government soon thereafter promised to change the situation of French unionism in dramatic ways. These events, first of all, confirmed the total failure of the PCF's (and CGT's) sectarian post-1978 strategy. They also demonstrated the existence of a powerful cross-class political desire among the French people to proceed differently in the context of crisis, a stinging repudiation of the Giscard–Barre politics. While it would be hazardous to predict too much at the time of writing (summer 1981), these momentous political changes are almost certain to break the union *impasse* which has prevailed, in different ways, since the onset of the crisis. The new French government will be very eager to gain union cooperation in its reformist economic policies. For such cooperation, and for reasons of principle from a Left-of-center regime, unions may well receive much in exchange: a great deal more real negotiation between unions and the state (and, undoubtedly, because of state prodding, between unions and the *patronat*) about wages, hours, and working conditions, very real concessions on the length of the work week, employment security, income distribution, union power at firm level and union influence over government policy, and perhaps greater industrial democracy in the public sector brought with new nationalizations.

The regime change will almost certainly weigh heavily on preexisting union incentive systems. Oppositional identity incentives will decline in efficacy relative to new purposive and material incentives. Perhaps more significant, this dramatic change in environment will fall upon the two major French union confederations in different ways. The CFDT is, of course, much closer in sympathy to the Socialists, to begin with (as the rapid inclusion of many top CFDT officials in the entourage of the new regime indicated). Moreover, the CFDT's earlier shift away from identity to material incentives makes it more likely to be receptive to governmental initiatives for more extensive bargaining more easily than the CGT. The CGT, in contrast, was deeply mired in a posture of sectarianism when the 1981 political breakthrough occurred, denouncing both the Socialist Presidential candidate and the CFDT as class traitors. The abrupt shift of the PCF away from its own sectarian posture back to United Frontism after Mitterrand's victory plus the new situation itself may well push the CGT towards policies better geared to promote its interests (i.e. a shift in strategic perspective and incentive system not unlike that of the CFDT). On the other hand, it is at least equally likely that the PCF will try to hold the CGT in oppositional reserve as a hedge against the economic failure of the new regime.

What is most important to note is, of course, that the change is likely to favor the CFDT. It is virtually certain that the Socialist leadership will attempt to use its governmental power to give advantages to the CFDT at the expense of the CGT. In doing so its hope would be to shift the balance in the union world away from the PCF in the same ways that François Mitterrand's political success ultimately shifted the political balance on the Left away from the Communists. Whatever happens then, it is clear that French unionism will change and that the CGT will be obliged to deploy a great deal more strategic intelligence in the near future than it has in the recent past in order to maintain its position.

In the case of Italy too we examine the impact of changes in the market arena—the effects of the crisis—and changes in the political arena—first the inclusion and then the exclusion of the PCI from the 'governmental area.' Not surprisingly, we find a pattern of responses very different from that in France.

The crisis following 1974 was very severe in Italy: unemployment rose sharply; inflation was, with that in Britain, the highest in Europe; the country faced a balance of payments crisis so severe that it was forced to negotiate terms with the IMF in order to secure loans necessary to restore its reserves; the public debt became enormous; and a number of very large, heavy industrial sectors were sharply in deficit.

The Italian unions' interventionist strategy was severely affected by these developments and the unions gradually sought to develop new responses. At the most general level, the problems posed for the unions were two: how to translate their continuing power to inflict enormous damage on the economy into policies which would both satisfy their supporters and create the conditions for effective responses to the worst features of the economic crisis; and what policy priorities to set now that economic conditions were such that only a few demands, if they were economically costly, could be immediately met. As should be evident, both these problems were themselves products of the unions' interventionist perspective combined with their continuing ability to mobilize their support. As should also be clear, these problems raised questions about what relationship should be established between union demands and actions in the market arena and in the political arena, and about what types of incentives the unions had to and should try to emphasize as they pared down their issue agenda. Finally, they also carried important implications for the degree of centralization in the union movement and the relationship it should have with political parties and the government.

As is detailed in Chapter 2, the response which the Italian unions eventually formulated, and after much debate and internal paralysis, was the EUR line. From the standpoint of the problems and questions just indicated, the EUR line, at least as articulated, offered the following 'solution': The union movement would be willing to undertake to ease somewhat the marketplace, union-induced pressures on the economy and on the political expenditures of the state, but only on two conditions. First, the workers' gains in the market, on the shop floor and in the social policy of the last decade would have to be respected. There could be no rollback, except in those areas where the union itself decided it would be appropriate. Second, the easing of economic and political pressure could only occur as part of a bargain (never explicitly called such) in which, in exchange for the unions' moderation, the government and employers would, with the unions' full participation, develop and implement policies designed to: restructure the economy and public spending in order to remove the structural defects which had fed the crisis; benefit the poorest strata and economically most impacted regions of the country. The reduction of union pressure and formulation and implementation of structural policies had to be relatively simultaneous. There could be no notion of 'trickle-down' nor of 'austerity now, reform later.' Furthermore, the unions would not enter into formally binding institutional arrangements but wished instead to reserve their autonomy and ability to operate in the market.

It is immediately evident that this was a hard bargain, both in the sense that the unions intended to operate from strength and in the difficulties entailed in putting such a bargain into effect. At the same time, it represented the attempt of the unions to confront some of the issues which the unfolding of the crisis had posed. The unions' market power would, in the future, be employed less to make further material advances and more as a lever to try to promote structurally transformative political-economic policies; but this would be done while defending, where it was deemed reasonable, the gains already made (e.g., greater mobility could be restored at the workplace but only as negotiated with the union). Union supporters, therefore, would have to be willing to dampen their expectations about individual wage gains and about social policy reforms of direct benefit to them; material improvements would primarily be directed toward the poor, especially in the South. Most of these were not part of the unions' core constituencies but were argued to be part of the social and political alliances necessary if the unions were to achieve their broader goals. The core working class was being promised greater security about the medium- and long-term economic future, guaranteed by forms of workers' and union participation and control at all levels of economic decision-making, and defense of the gains they had already made. The implications of this approach were clearly to focus more union attention in the political arena and to increase the coordinative and decisional role of the federal and confederal leaderships. Whatever the degree of putative control and autonomy assigned to the shopfloor level, the EUR line could not help but have, to the degree it was implemented, a centralizing and politicizing role. As should also be evident, it represented a significant shift in the balance among the types of incentives which made up the unions' incentive systems. Material incentives would decline in importance, although they would certainly remain important. Purposive incentives embodied in redistributive social welfare policy would also be reduced in weight, at least with respect to those policies which most directly affected the core working-class constituency in the unions. In contrast, purposive and identity incentives growing out of notions of the right of workers and their organizations to exercise control would increase in importance, as would identity incentives linked to the unions' vision of a transformed political economy. Finally, identity incentives which grew out of different unions' remaining linkages to specific political parties would retain their importance, for it was in fact the case that all the major parties were rhetorically favorable to the EUR line, although each one with its own interpretation of what the line meant.

The initial implementation of the EUR line was, even when put in the best light, only a partial success: wage pressure was somewhat reduced and in general the market behavior of the unions became less militant; there were also some attempts made (unsuccessfully) to formulate plans for political-economic restructuring. When viewed with a little more distance and hindsight, however, the EUR line must (to date) be judged more a failed than an effective response to the problems faced by the unions in the late 1970s. To understand why this was the case brings us back to the environmental context in which the unions operated, and to the constraints this context imposed, especially in the political arena. It also points to the possible limits of interventionism in a situation of political-economic crisis, at least in the Italian case and perhaps more generally.

The EUR line was an expression of changes in both the economic and political contexts in which the unions operated. On the one hand, as already suggested, the deepening of the economic crisis made it ever harder for the unions to deliver through action in the market arena, at least in terms of material gains, and if the union leaders were concerned, as they had to be, with more than the shortest-run interests of their members. In effect, in the market arena the unions faced a strategic stalemate: they had great power, but to translate it into material gains was to put the economy and thus the longer-term employment and wage situation of their constituency at risk. This stalemate was aggravated by the danger that further economic decay might endanger what the unions deemed as crucial social and political alliances and even, they and the parties of the Left were arguing, Italian democracy itself. Terrorism was only the most dramatic signal for them of this danger.

On the other hand, changes in the political arena after 1976 made the purposive and identity incentives embodied in the nonmonetary goals of the EUR line far more credible than they had been in the past. The entrance of the PCI into the 'governmental area' and possibly eventually into the government itself, seemed to make the structural transformation goals of the unions much more realistic. It also promised to provide governmental support for the unions' attempts to exercise greater influence at the firm level over investment and other decisions. Further, to the extent that leaders and supporters of the CGIL were still loyal to the PCI and willing to give primacy to its goals, there was little question that union moderation would strengthen the Party's claim that its participation in government was essential to a general improvement of the political-economic situation. Finally, the new line was sufficiently consistent with the principles on which the unions, as a relatively unified entity, had been operating since the early 1970s to maintain confederal cooperation and autonomy. Ironically, just as had been the case when the Communists were clearly out of government, their inclusion tended to reduce political tensions between the confederations. This is not to suggest that EUR did not cause major tensions within the unions and between them. These were primarily, however, rooted in the longstanding differences between them about what emphasis to give to the market, decentralized action, and material gains over the political arena, centralization, and reforms. In the new context, the latter gradually got the upper hand.

Yet, as this suggests, the success of the EUR line was critically dependent on a favorable response from the government. The unions were asking their supporters to make what were, in the light of the expectations built up over the preceding decade, major sacrifices and to do so in order to promote goals which, while they too had been an important part of the unions' appeals, were of less direct and tangible significance for the individual worker. In order for these to be an effective source of incentives (and therefore to override the Olsonian stricture), the unions had to get visible results at the governmental level, especially since their ability to 'impose' the policy was weak. Failing to get such results ran the risk of a loss of support or even a factory-level resistance to making the sacrifices which the program required.

The unions were unable, however, to get such results. Interparty competition, the basic weakness of the PCI's status as governmental partner and the unions' own hesitancy to make any but the most limited sacrifices prior to the implementation of the governmental measures deemed necessary led first to a failure by the government to formulate and undertake measures the unions deemed indispensable and then to the withdrawal of the Communists from the governmental area, significant Communist electoral losses and eventually to a sharp decline in the prospect that the Party would soon return to a position of direct governmental influence. Furthermore, all this occurred in a situation in which the most visible features of economic crisis disappeared, especially in the northern unionized economy, in which the Italian balance of trade improved and in which, in general, appeals for the need to sacrifice to meet a dramatic political-economic crisis lost much of their effectiveness. Thus, most of the conditions which had given a positive impetus to the EUR line and to the type of interventionist approach to union strategy which it embodied, disappeared.

The subsequent effects of this on the union movement have been much as one would expect. First, the EUR line itself has fallen into disarray. Second, internal tensions within the union movement have dramatically increased, both between the unified Federation and individual confederation centers and the periphery, and between the confederations themselves. Third, there has been a partial but significant 'repartinization' of the unions. The CGIL has tied its policy positions more closely to the openly oppositionist stance of the PCI; some of the Socialist elements within the CGIL, the UIL and, gradually, the CISL have sought to support certain aspects of government policy. Fourth, the unions have suffered a significant decline of support and militance, measured both in terms of membership and, more important, in terms of the workers' willingness to follow the unions' lead. None of these problems has reached crisis proportions, in part because of the confederations' determination to try to maintain some degree of unity even in the face of their increased internal bickering. Nonetheless, as the 'solidarity fund' incident discussed at the close of Chapter 2 makes clear, all of these problems have become of major significance.

At a more general level, the present problems indicate the limits and perils of interventionism in a situation of economic crisis and inability to exercise effective influence over government by the union movement. The Italian union movement is today in considerably worse shape than it was at the time the EUR line was formulated. Not only are its unity strained and its strategy confused and undirected, but its system of incentives is weakened. There is no way to say whether this might not also have been the case if the EUR line had not been adopted, but the failure of EUR to date has left its mark. The shift embodied in that line was a 'natural' outgrowth—in the economic, political, and institutional conditions of the late 1970s—of the general interventionist posture which the movement had adopted throughout the 1970s. It was also a viable strategy because of the type and content of the incentives which the unions had developed over even a longer period of time. Yet, the absence of the necessary sustained political support to implement the line proved an insurmountable obstacle. Thus, the unions are faced with the problem of trying to reconstitute their strategic and institutional unity and to rebuild their support.

It might appear that the first step in such a process would be what could be called a 'return to the market,' that is, a return to the aggressive pursuit of material advantage for the workers in the marketplace, perhaps combined with calls for social and economic reform. There are, in fact, some signs that this is what significant elements of the movement want to attempt. Some have proposed, for instance, that the unions give up their resistance to any changes in the wage escalator, arguing that the escalator deprives the unions of a significant function (and thus source of incentives) in defending their supporters in the marketplace. Precisely this proposal, however, indicates the limits on a 'return to the market': the function to be restored would be that of defending the real wages of their supporters, not necessarily of increasing them. The underlying crisis of the economy still constrains union market actions severely and still presents them with the strategic dilemma indicated earlier. This does not suggest that Italian unionism is likely to collapse, but only that its options remain severely constrained. Without effective appeal in the political arena, it does not have a wide range of policies open to it. Its interventionism has brought it far, certainly farther than the maximalism of the French movement, but as in France, political conditions seem critical to what form future developments are likely to take.

'Maximalism' and 'interventionism,' as we have found them in France and Italy, obviously do not exhaust the range of conceivable union responses to the crisis of the 1970s. Volume Two of this study, which will review three Northern European Social Democratic union experiences (Sweden, West Germany, and the United Kingdom) will undoubtedly uncover others. In fact, there may well be a wide variety of possible union responses caused by different national combinations of union-employer-state-party relationships, union structural variables and the differential incidence of economic crisis itself. Two further types of general union strategic response ought to be noted here, however. They are the 'defensive-particularistic' and the 'corporatist.'

Economic crisis is likely to increase tendencies towards defensive-particularistic responses at rank-and-file level for almost all union movements. In the face of rising income and employment insecurity, groups of workers will seek to protect themselves above all, no matter what the fate of other groups may be. Depending upon other factors union organizations may be able to counteract and limit such tendencies in the interests of mounting a coherent general response to crisis. In cases where both the unions' organizations and the industrial relations system are strongly decentralized, however, defensive particularism may well become a union response to crisis in itself constructed from rank-and-file level upwards as groups of workers deploy their local organizational power to block threatening economic events insofar as possible. As strategy, defensive particularism may have varying effects. To the degree that base-level unions possess the requisite resources, defensive-particularistic reactions may veto efforts at structural change by employers and the state. These veto attempts—which are, in effect, attempts by local unions to promote 'interventionalism' in their own parochial interests—may work to block change and thereby indirectly play an important role in economic evolution. They may also contribute to the political underpinnings of the movements whose desire is to 'do something about the unions.' Although defensive particularism as strategy may correlate with a number of different high theoretical union understandings of the economy and union policy proposals there does seem to be an affinity between it and simple Keynesianism (reflate the economy without structural change) and protectionism.

Corporatism as strategy, of which we are likely to see a great deal in Volume Two, involves open or de facto union collaboration with the state and employers to maintain certain basic economic equilibria, its most common form being union cooperation in schemes of an incomes policy type to control wage evolution and wage drift. Since entering into corporatist arrangements involves public sacrifice for unions, such arrangement are often sealed by certain trade-offs granted in exchange for union cooperation, often having to do with the shape of general economic policy. Corporatism tends therefore to draw union movements towards greater concern with such policy, even though corporatist arrangements are compatible with a broad range of union positions on the economy, ranging from simple Keynesianism to full-fledged interventionism.

It is worth noting, finally, that national union movements may present us with a combination of different types of response at any given moment, and may in time shift from one dominant response predilection to another. The French movement which we have already reviewed was, in fact, constituted of a predominant maximalism coupled with a degree of defensive particularism in labor-market behavior. Moreover, after 1978, under the impetus of the failures of the 1970s, strong advocacy for interventionism emerged. The Italian movement was, in the 1940s and 1950s, predominantly maximalist before turning towards the interventionism which we describe, while the 1978 EUR program had overtones of a willingness to undertake corporatist arrangements, should the proper structure of trade-offs be made available. A much greater sense of the varieties of response and their change over time is to be gleaned from reading Volume Two, however.

Notes and References

1 In proceeding in this fashion, we are loosely following what Adam Przeworski and Henry Teune have designated the 'most similar systems' design for comparative research in their *The Logic of Comparative Inquiry* (New York: Wiley, 1970), pp. 31–4, and therefore potentially fall prey to the limits of this design which they indicate. Nonetheless, we think in this case the design is both appropriate and fruitful, especially in light of other studies which have also compared the French and Italian systems. In this regard, see particularly Donald Blackmer and Sidney Tarrow, eds., *Communism in Italy and France* (Princeton, NJ: Princeton University Press, 1975).

2 Much of the following discussion draws on John Goldthorpe, 'Theories of industrial society: reflections on the recrudescence of historicism and the future of futurology,' *Archives Européenes de Sociologie*, vol. 12 (1971), pp. 263–288. See also Peter Lange, Peter Gourevitch, and Andrew Martin, 'Industrial relations, some reflections,' in Peter Doeringer *et. al.*, *International Industrial Relations Perspectives* (London: Macmillan, 1981).

3 Clark Kerr, John T. Dunlop, Frederick Harbison, and Charles A. Myers use the concept of the 'logic of industrialism' as the core of their analysis of union and industrial relations development in advanced industrial societies. See *Industrialism and Industrial Man* (Cambridge, Mass.: Harvard University Press, 1960).

4 S. M. Lipset, 'The changing class structure and contemporary European politics,' in Stephen R. Graubard, ed., *A New Europe?* (Boston, Mass.: Beacon Press, 1967), pp. 337–8. The volume of 'liberal optimist' literature is enormous, including prominently the works cited in this essay. For some critical evaluations, see Chaim Waxman, ed., *The End of Ideology Debate* (New York: Funk and Wagnalls, 1968).

5 Suzanne Berger, 'Discontinuity in the Politics of Industrial Society,' in Berger and Michael Piore, *Dualism and Discontinuity in Industrial Societies* (New York: Cambridge University Press, 1980), p. 134.

6 Goldthorpe, op. cit., p. 267.

7 Kerr, *et al.*, op. cit., p. 283.

8 Kerr and his colleagues, op. cit., seek to temper this inference, referring often to the role of human will and choice and to the important (but, it seems to us, intervening and eventually relatively unimportant) role of industrial elites. Ralf Dahrendorf, in his *Class and Class Conflict in Industrial Society* (Stanford, Cal.: Stanford University Press, 1959), to which we make reference below, also notes the possibility of 'countertrends' (pp. 276–9) to those developments which he argues are the expression of the development of advanced industrial 'postcapitalist' society. Nonetheless, it is difficult not to agree more generally with Goldthorpe's comment on Kerr, *et al.*: the 'view of the logic of industrialism is in fact such as to force him willy-nilly . . . to see hitherto clearly different processes of industrialization as becoming progressively similar in their sociocultural correlates' (Goldthorpe, op. cit., p. 268).

9 Karl Marx, *Wage Labor and Capital* (Moscow: Progress Publishers, 1952).

10 Dahrendorf, op. cit., p. 244.

11 ibid., p. 257. See also, chapters 2 and 10 of Kerr, *et al.*, op. cit., especially pp. 289–296.

12 Kerr, *et al.*, op. cit., pp. 6–7 and Dahrendorf, op. cit., pp. 269–272.

13 Kerr, *et al.*, op. cit., pp. 292–4 and Dahrendorf, op. cit., pp. 267–279.

14 Dahrendorf, op. cit., p. 268.

15 ibid., p. 269.

16 ibid., p. 275.

17 ibid., p. 297.

18 Dahrendorf, op. cit., p. 271.
19 Kerr, *et al.*, op. cit., p. 293.
20 For a broad comparative study, see Jack Barbash, *Trade Unions and National Economic Policy* (Baltimore, Md: The Johns Hopkins Press, 1972), and Everett M. Kassalow, *Trade Unions and Industrial Relations: An International Comparison* (New York: Random House, 1969).
21 For an examination of this period including both national studies and comparative essays, see Colin Crouch and Alessandro Pizzorno, eds., *The Resurgence of Class Conflict in Western Europe since 1968* (London: Macmillan, 1978), Vols. 1 and 2, which is the most sophisticated and theoretically stimulating collection. See also, Solomon Barkin, ed., *Worker Militancy and Its Consequences, 1965–1975* (New York: Praeger, 1975). The discussion which follows draws heavily on the studies in these collections and on our own research.
22 For an extremely stimulating rationality-based discussion of why unions under capitalism have a strong interest in moving in the direction of increased investment control, see Adam Przeworski and Michael Wallerstein, 'The Structure of Class Conflict in Advanced Capitalist Societies,' paper presented at the Annual Meeting of the American Political Science Association, Washington, DC, August 1980; and Przeworski, 'Material Bases of Consent: Economics and Politics in a Hegemonic System,' Maurice Zeitlin, ed., *Political Power and Social Theory*, Vol. 1 (Greenwich, Conn.: Jai Press, 1979).
23 There is now an ample literature on these developments, although much of it is contradictory and there is, as yet, no agreement on central concepts. For an ample survey of viewpoints, see Philippe Schmitter and Gerhard Lehmbruch, eds., *Trends toward Corporatist Intermediation* (Beverley Hills, Cal.: Sage, 1979). See, as well, Leo Panitch, 'Recent Theorizations of Corporatism: Reflections on a Growth Industry,' *British Journal of Sociology*, vol. XXXI, no. 2 (June 1980); Claus Offe, 'The Attribution of Public Status to Interest Groups: Observations on the West German Case,' in Suzanne Berger, ed., *Organizing Interests in Western Europe* (New York: Cambridge University Press, 1981); Alessandro Pizzorno, 'Political Exchange and Collective Identity in Industrial Conflict,' in Crouch and Pizzorno, op. cit., vol. 2; and Peter Lange, 'Sindacati, partiti, stato e liberal corporativismo,' *Il Mulino* no. 226 (November–December 1979).
24 Kerr and his colleagues, op. cit., are noteworthy for having taken a different stance on this point, arguing that the societal complexity of advanced industrialism might well lead the state not just to set the 'rules of the game' but also 'to set the rules relating members to their organizations' (p. 290). Even in their discussion, however, the state is treated very much as an apolitical arbiter in the public interest and there is little examination of how this role of the state is to be reconciled with the notion of greater subsystem autonomy for industrial relations.
25 See Andrew Martin, 'Distributive conflict, inflation and investment: the Swedish case,' paper prepared for the Brookings Project on the Politics and Sociology of Global Inflation, 1980, forthcoming in a Brookings publication edited by Charles Maier and Leon Lindberg.
26 ibid., p. 277. As he points out: 'We are given no clear indication of the nature of the *connection* between the immediate historical world, in which individuals and groups pursue their interests, uphold their beliefs, exercise their power, etc., and the emergence of the theoretically intelligible regularities that are postulated' (p. 277).
27 The concept of institutionalization as we are using it here is close to that developed by Philip Selznick in his *Leadership in Administration: A Sociological Interpretation* (New York: Harper and Row, 1957), pp. 1–21. He writes: 'There is a close relation between "infusion with value" and "self-maintenance." As an organization acquires a self, a distinctive identity, it becomes an institution. This involves the taking on of values, ways of acting and believing that are deemed important for their own sake. From then on self-maintenance becomes more than bare organizational survival; it becomes a struggle to preserve the uniqueness of the group in the face of new problems and altered circumstances' (p. 21).
28 Richard B. Freeman and James I. Medoff, 'The two faces of unionism,' *The Public Interest* (Fall 1979), especially pp. 70–4.
29 The issue of the boundaries of union jurisdictions or desired jurisdictions and how these boundaries are defined and maintained is obviously of importance here. Alessandro Pizzorno has addressed this problem in his discussion of 'associative' and 'class' unionism. The former seeks to represent only its members and to control both access to union

membership and the ability of employers to draw workers from other than union members. The latter seeks a much broader representation and to coordinate the demands of specific subgroups with those of workers more generally, whether they be union members or not. For our present purposes a lengthier discussion of these issues is not important, but note should be taken of them. See Pizzorno, 'Azione di classe e sistemi corporativi,' chapter 6 of his *I soggetti del pluralismo* (Bologna: Il Mulino, 1980).

30 ibid.

31 On the application of a theory of incentives to the analysis of organizational behavior see, among others, James Q. Wilson, *Political Organizations* (New York: Basic Books, 1973). In his 'Le due logiche dell'azione di classe' in *I soggetti*, op. cit., Pizzorno makes a fundamental contribution to the analysis of unions as institutions of exchange which can use a variety of types of appeals to win the consent of supporters and which, relatedly, can function in different ways with respect to their environment. He does not, however, develop a general and systematic typology of appeals or incentives. For another analysis somewhat similar to that offered here, see Mario Regini, 'La crisi di rappresentanza dei sindacati di classe,' paper presented to the Conference of the Instituto Gramsci on 'Democratic Governability and the Crisis of Representation,' Turin, June 1980.

32 This scheme is a variant on that developed in Peter Lange, 'La teoria degli incentivi e l'analisi dei partiti politici,' *Rassegna Italiana di sociologia* vol. 18, no. 4 (October–December 1977), and is developed on the basis of a critical reading primarily of Wilson, op. cit., and of the earlier Peter B. Clark and James Q. Wilson, 'Incentive systems: A theory of organizations,' *Administrative Science Quarterly*, vol. VI (1961).

33 Wilson, op. cit., p. 33.

34 See Wilson, op. cit., chapters 2 and 3, and Lange, op. cit.

35 The following discussion is indebted to the analyses of Alessandro Pizzorno; see especially, 'Sull'azione politica dei sindacati e la "militanza" come risorsa,' 'Azione di classe e sistemi corporativi,' and 'Le due logiche dell'azione di classe,' chapters 5–7 of his *I soggetti*, op. cit., and 'Political exchange and collective identity in industrial conflict,' in Crouch and Pizzorno, op. cit., chapter 11 of Vol. 2.

36 On this point, see Pizzorno, 'Political Exchange,' op. cit., which focused attention on the union's role in what he calls the 'political market' and in which he underlined that 'in the political market the resource given in exchange may be called consensus or support. An actor (generally the government) which has goods to give is ready to trade them in exchange for social consensus. . . . In a situation of pure collective bargaining, industrial action means threat to withdraw continuity of work. The exchange becomes political when the threat is withdrawal of the wider social consensus or social order' (p. 279).

37 In this sense, so-called neo- or liberal-corporatist bargaining with the state (see Note 23) may be an advantage, for it clarifies responsibility and 'empowers' the union. Of course, the extent to which this actually is an advantage for the union will depend in considerable part on how its supporters judge the quality of the bargain which has been struck. Panitch, for instance, has pointed out in several of his articles that this kind of empowerment may simply produce dissidence within the union. See, for instance, his 'Trade Unions and the Capitalist State,' *New Left Review* 125 (January–February 1981). For a dissenting view, see Przeworski and Wallerstein, op. cit., esp. pp. 36–42.

38 Mancur Olson, *The Logic of Collective Action* (Cambridge, Mass.: Harvard University Press, 1965).

39 S. M. Lipset and Stein Rokkan, 'Cleavage structures, party systems and voter alignments: an introduction,' in Lipset and Rokkan, eds., *Party Systems and Voter Alignments* (New York: The Free Press, 1967), esp. pp. 26–30.

40 See, in this regard, Pizzorno's discussion of how unions which are weak in the market rely on ideology to stimulate militancy, using as his prime example the CGIL in the 1950s, 'I sindicati nel sistema politico italiano: aspetti storici' and the other essays already cited from *I soggetti*, op. cit. The first of these essays is a provocative analytical sketching of developments in the Italian movement from the war to 1970 and has provided much stimulus for our analysis.

41 Pizzorno shows this clearly for the CGIL in the 1950s in 'I sindicati,' op. cit., esp. pp. 99–110.

42 It would, of course, be dangerous to push this point too hard. Both gradual socioeconomic and political change and relatively sudden breakdowns of prevailing social norms can lead to a loss of efficacy of precisely the union policies which previously successfully garnered support. What union supporters want from the union may change faster or in ways that the

organizational leaders fail to grasp, leading to a weakening or even crisis of support. Furthermore, union policies themselves may unwittingly encourage such change, as supporters respond to different facets of policy and for different reasons than the leaders think. A number of such instances appear in the case studies in this volume and will be discussed again below. The country analyses in Crouch and Pizzorno, op. cit., shows this to have been the case in many countries in the late 1960s. Pizzorno's essay, 'Political Exchange,' op. cit., gives a theoretical interpretation of some types of these disjunctions between supporter demands and leader perceptions of them. In this connection, see also Henry Phelps Brown, 'A Non-Monetarist interpretation of the pay explosion,' *The Three Banks Review* 105 (1974), pp. 3–24.

43 The pages which follow will be only occasionally annotated. The reader is referred back to the chapters on individual countries for relevant union and nonunion sources.

44 There is always some distortion involved in any periodization, for it tends to diminish the amount of change which occurs between change points and to magnify the amount that occurs at them. Nonetheless, we believe the periodization embodied in the suggestion that major strategic challenges for the unions occurred at a few critical conjunctures effectively captures the reality of the processes we are examining. Furthermore, the stress we have given to institutionalization and the argument we have made for how change occurs would suggest that change in union strategy and organization is less likely to occur steadily and smoothly and more likely to occur in spurts. On the parallelism in the economic cycles and development of the postwar European economies, see Angus Maddison, 'Economic policy and performance in Europe, 1913–1970,' in Carlo M. Cipolla, ed., *The Fontana Economic History of Europe: The Twentieth Century* (London: Fontana, 1976), Part 2, pp. 442–509.

45 By this we mean simply that the unions had, despite the attacks upon them and their inability to play much of a role in wage bargaining, been able to retain most of their support and even to mobilize it around a number of domestic and international issues.

46 In 'Azione di classe,' op. cit., Pizzorno writes: 'The difficulty of obtaining immediate gains brings with it not only a general weakness of the union, but also a tendency to nurture the hopes of supporters in long-term goals which can be pursued through means other than day-to-day contractual struggle. Weakness . . . leads the unions to link themselves to and depend upon political parties. From this, as from the ideological propensity to be oriented towards long-term ends, the predominance of political action or of political aspirations over narrowly union ones is born' (p. 198).

47 For a discussion of PCI policy in this period, see Donald L. M. Blackmer, 'Continuity and change in postwar Italian Communism,' in Blacker and Tarrow, op. cit., esp. pp. 45–52. For comparisons of the PCI and PCF, see Sidney Tarrow, 'Communism in Italy and France: Adaptation and Change,' in the same book; and Peter Lange, 'The French and Italian Communist parties: postwar strategy and domestic society,' in *Radicalism and the Contemporary Age, Vol. 3: Strategies and Impact of Contemporary Radicalism* (Boulder, Col.: Westview Press, 1977).

48 The most important and comprehensive work on the 'resurgence of class conflict' is that edited by Crouch and Pizzorno, op. cit. For a detailed study of the Italian case, see the six volumes of the ISSOCO studies directed by Alessandro Pizzorno and especially the last of these, authoried by Pizzorno, Emilio Reyneri, Marino Regini, and Ida Regalia, *Lotte operaie e sindaco: il ciclo 1968–1972 in Italia* (Bologna: Il mulino, 1978).

49 For a fascinating comparative study of the reactions of the French and Italian ruling classes to the events of the late 1960s, see Michele Salvati, 'May 1968 and the hot autumn of 1969: The responses of two ruling classes,' in Suzanne Berger, ed., *Organizing interests*, op. cit. See also Salvati and Alfredo Gigliobianco, *Il maggio francese e l'autunno caldo italiano: la risposta di due borghesie* (Bologna: Il mulino, 1980), which presents more detailed presentation of the arguments made in the Salvati article.

50 The changing structure of demands is discussed in detail in Ida Regalia, Marino Regini, and Emilio Reyneri, 'Labour conflicts and industrial relations in Italy,' chapter 4 of Crouch and Pizzorno, op. cit. See also Pizzorno's 'I sindacati,' esp. pp. 126–130, and 'Le due logiche,' both op. cit.

51 The term is that of Giuseppe DiPalma in his 'The available state: problems of reform,' in Peter Lange and Sidney Tarrow, eds., *Italy in Transition: Conflict and Consensus* (London: Frank Cass, 1980), pp. 149–165.

52 See Peter Lange, 'Sindacati, partiti,' op. cit.

53 See Pizzorno, 'Azione di classe,' op. cit., esp. the chart on p. 197 and accompanying discussion.
54 For a discussion of this point, see the concluding pages of Andrew Martin and George Ross, 'European trade unions and their economic perceptions and strategies,' *West European Politics* Vol. 3, no. 1 (January 1980). This paper represents an initial attempt to bring together the findings of the larger project of which this volume is a part.

Index